Governing Insecurity

About the Series

Democratic Transition in Conflict-Torn Societies

Series editors

Anne Marie Goetz and Robin Luckham

This three-book series explores the politics of democratic transition in conflict-torn countries in the developing South and post-communist East, focusing upon the interplay between democratic institutions and democratic politics. The different volumes in the series identify the institutional arrangements and political compromises, which can assure democratic control of military and security establishments, facilitate the peaceful management of conflict, and enhance the participation of excluded groups, particularly women.

VOLUME 1

Governing Insecurity: Democratic Control of Military and Secnrity Establishments in Transitional Democracies

edited by

GAVIN CAWTHRA AND ROBIN LUCKHAM

VOLUME 2

Can Democracy be Designed? The Politics of Institutional Choice in Conflict-Torn Societies

edited by

SUNIL BASTIAN AND ROBIN LUCKHAM

VOLUME 3

No Shortcuts to Power: African Women in Politics and Policy Making Uganda and South Africa

edited by

ANNE MARIE GOETZ AND SHIREEN HASSIM

Governing Insecurity

Democratic Control of Military and Security Establishments in Transitional Democracies

Edited by

GAVIN CAWTHRA and ROBIN LUCKHAM

Zed Books
LONDON & NEW YORK

Governing Insecurity was first published in 2003 by
Zed Books Ltd, 7 Cynthia Street, London N1 9JF, UK and
Room 400, 175 Fifth Avenue, New York, NY 10010
www.zedbooks.demon.co.uk

Cover designed by Andrew Corbett
Interior designed and set in 9½/12 pt Photina
by Long House, Cumbria, UK
Printed and bound in Malaysia

Distributed in the USA exclusively by Palgrave, a division of
St Martin's Press, LLC,175 Fifth Avenue, New York, NY 10010

A catalogue record for this book
is available from the British Library

US Cataloging-in-Publication Data
is available from the Library of Congress

ISBN Hb 1 84277 148 5
Pb 1 84277 149 3

Contents

Abbreviations

ADF Allied Democratic Front
AEPC Association of European Police Colleges
AFCDRs Armed Forces Committees for the Defence of the Revolution
AFDL Alliance of Democratic Forces for the Liberation of Congo–Zaïre
AFRC Armed Forces Revolutionary Council
AID Agency for Intelligence and Documentation
AIS Armé Islamique du Salut
ALC Armé de Libération Congolaise
ANC African National Congress
ANC Congolese National Army
APC All People's Congress Party
APLA Azanian People's Liberation Army
ARD Alliance pour la Résistance Démocratique
ARENA Aliança Renovadora Nacional
AUC Autodefensas Unidas de Colombia
BiH Bosnia and Herzegovina
BNI Bureau of National Investigation
CDCC Constitutional Debate Coordinating Committee
CDF Civil defence force
CDRs Committees for the Defence of the Revolution
CDSM Centre for Defence and Security Management
CEH Comisión de Esclarecimiento Histórico
CID Criminal Investigation Department
CNES Conseil National Économique et Social
CNS La Conférance Nationale Souveraine
CONADEP Comisión Nacional de Desaparecidos
CP Communist Party
CPDTF Commonwealth Police Department Task Force
CWC Ceylon Workers' Congress
DDRR Demobilisation, disarmament, repatriation and reintegration
DFA Department of Foreign Affairs
DFI Directorate of Foreign Intelligence
DII Directorate of Internal Intelligence
DINA National Intelligence Bureau
DMI Directorate of Military Intelligence
DoD Department of Defence
DRC Democratic Republic of Congo
DSP Presidential Special Division (Zaïre)
ECOMOG Economic Community of West African States' Monitoring Group
ECOWAS Economic Community of West African States
ELN Ejército de Liberación Nacional
EMP Estado Mayor Presidencial
EPRLF Eelam People's Revolutionary Liberation Front
EROS Eelam Revolutionary Organisation of Students
ESCOR Economic and Social Committee on Overseas Research
ESTNA Centro de Estudios Estratégicas para la Estabilidad Nacional
EU European Union
EZLN Ejército Zapatista de Liberación Nacional
FAC Forces Armées Congolaises
FALA Armed Forces for the Liberation of Angola
FAR Forces Armées Rwandaises
FARC Fuerzas Armadas Revolucionarias de Colombia
FAZ Forces Armés Zaïroises
FDD Forces pour la Défence de la Démocratie
FFS Front des Forces Socialistes
FIS Front Islamique du Salut
FLACSO Latin American Faculty of Social Sciences
FLEC Front for the Liberation of Cabinda Enclave
FLN Front de Libération Nationale
FLN Front Rebel de Libération Nationale
FLNK/C Front de Libération Nationale du Katanga/Congo
FLOT Front de Libération Contre l'Occupation du Territoire
FRF Forces Républiques et Fédéralistes
GDP Gross domestic product
GEAR Growth, Employment and Redistribution programme
GIA Groupements Islamiques Armés
GNU Government of National Unity
HDI Human Development Index
HDZ Croatian Democratic Union
HIS Croatian Intelligence Services
HR High Representative (UN)
HVIDRA Croatian Association of Veterans and Invalids of the Homeland War
ICITAP International Criminal Investigative Training Assitance Program (US)
ICTY International Criminal Tribunal on Former Yugoslavia
IDP Internally displaced person
IEBL Inter-Entity Boundary Line
IFIs International financial institutions
IFOR Implementation Force
IFP Inkatha Freedom Party
IISS International Institute for Strategic Studies
ILEA International Law Enforcement Academy
IMF International Monetary Fund
IPS Institute of Policy Studies
IPTF International Police Task Force
IRC International Rescue Committee
ISS Institute for Security Studies
ISU Internal Security Unit
ITAK Illanki Tamil Arasu Kadchi (Lanka Tamil State Party)
JMC Joint Military Commission

JMCC Joint Military Coordinating Committee
JNA Jugoslovenska Narodna Armija
JVP Janatha Vimukthi Peramuna
KLA Kosovo Liberation Army
LPA Lusaka Peace Accord
LSSP Lanka Sama Samaja Party
LTTE Liberation Tigers of Tamil Eelam
MAP Membership Accession Plan
MAPE Multinational Advisory Police Element
MINUGUA Misión de las Naciones Unidas de Verificación en Guatemala
MK Mkhonto we Sizwe
MLC Mouvement de Libération du Congo
MoD Ministry of Defence
MOS Moslem Intelligence Service
MSP Movement for a Peaceful Society
MST Movimento Sem Terra
MSU Multinational Specialised Unit
MONUC Mission de l'Organisation des Nations Unies au Congo
MPRI Military Professionals Resources Incorporated
MUP Ministarstvo Unutrašhje Poslove
NALU National Army for the Liberation of Uganda
NATO North Atlantic Treaty Organisation
NCD National Commission for Democracy
NCPS National Crime Prevention Strategy
NDC National Democratic Congress
NGO Non-governmental organisation
NIB National Intelligence Bureau
NMS National Management System
NPKF National Peacekeeping Force
NPP National Patriotic Party
NPRC National Provisional Ruling Council
OAU Organisation of African Unity
OHR Office of the High Representative
ONUC Organisation des Nations Unies au Congo
OSCE Organisation of Security and Cooperation in Europe
PA People's Alliance
PfP Partnership for Peace
PIC Peace Implementation Council
PLOTE People's Liberation Organisation of Tamil Eelam
PNDC Provisional National Defence Council
PSD Presidential Security Division
PTA Prevention of Terrorism Act
RACVIAC Regional Arms Control Verification and Implementation Assistance Centre
RCD Rassemblement Congolais pour la Democratie (Congolese Rally for Democracy)
RCD Rally for Culture and Democracy
RDP Reconstruction and Development Programme
REMHI Recuperación de la Memoria Histórica
RENAMO Resistência Nacional Moçambicana (Mozambique National Resistance)
RND Rassemblement National pour la Démocratie (National Rally for Democracy)
RPF Front Patriotique Rwandai
RS Republika Srpska
RUF Revolutionary United Front
SAA Stabilisation and Association Agreement
SADC Southern African Development Community
SADF South African Defence Force
SANDF South African National Defence Force
SAP South African Police
SAPS South African Police Service
SCMM Standing Committee on Military Matters
SDA Party of Democratic Action
SDS Serb Democratic Party
SECI South-east European Cooperation Initiative
SEECAP South-east European Common Assessment Paper on Regional Security Challenges
SEEGROUP South-east Europe Security Cooperation Steering Group
SEEI South-east Europe Initiative
SFOR Stabilisation Force
SIN Sistema de Inteligencia Nacional (Peru)
SIPRI Stockholm International Peace Research Institute
SIS Secret Intelligence Service
SLA Sierra Leone Army
SLFP Sri Lanka Freedom Party
SLMC Sri Lanka Muslim Congress
SLP Sierra Leone Police
SLPP Sierra Leone People's Party
SNS Service for National Security
SPD Social Democratic Party
SPS Serb Socialist Party
SRS Serb Radical Party
SRT Serb Radio and Television Station
SSD Special Security Division
STF Special Task Force
TBVC Transkei–Bophuta-tswana–Venda–Ciskei
TC Tamil Congress
TEC Transitional Executive Committee
TID Terrorist Investigation Department
TELO Tamil Eelam Liberation Organisation
TULF Tamil United Liberation Front
UN United Nations
UNAMSIL United Nations Mission in Sierra Leone
UNAREL Union des Nationalistes Républicains pour la Libération
UNCIVPOL United Nations Civilian Police
UNDP United Nations Development Programme
UNHCR United Nations High Commissioner for Refugees
UNICEF United Nations Children's Fund
UNITA Union for the Total Liberation of Angola
UNMIBH United Nations Mission to Bosnia-Herzegovina
UNP United National Party
UNTAES United Nations Transitional Administration in Eastern Slavonia
UPR Union pour la République
URNG Unidad Revolucionaria Nacional Guatemalteca
USA United States of America
USSR Union of Soviet Socialist Republics
VF Vojska Federacije
VRS Vojska Republike Srpske
WEU West European Union

About the Contributors

Gavin Cawthra is Professor of Defence and Security Management at the Graduate School of Public and Development Management at the University of Witwatersrand, South Africa. He has published extensively, including *Policing South Africa* (1994) and *Securing South Africa's Democracy* (1997).

Comfort Ero is director of the West African Project of the International Crisis Group based in Sierra Leone, and prior to that, a Research Fellow at the Centre for Defence Studies, King's College, London.

Eboe Hutchful is Professor in African Studies at Wayne State University, Detroit, USA, and executive director of African Security Dialogue and Research (ASDR) in Accra, Ghana. He has published extensively, including *Ghana's Adjustment Experience: The Paradox of Reform* (2002).

Mary Kaldor is currently a Professor at the Centre for the Study of Global Governance, London School of Economics, and Co-Chair of the Helsinki Citizens Assembly. Her many publications include *New and Old Wars: Organised Violence in a Global Era* (1999).

J. 'Kayode Fayemi is the Director of the Centre for Democracy and Development in London and Lagos. He is an adviser to the Nigerian Human Rights Violations Investigations Commission.

Roger Kibasomba is a Senior Lecturer at the University of Witwatersrand, South Africa, specialising in economic management of security structures, civil–military relations, peacebuilding and military expenditures in Africa.

Kees Koonings is Associate Professor of Development Studies in the Faculty of Social Sciences at Utrecht University. His recent publications include the co-edited volume *Political Armies: The Military and Nation-Building in the Age of Democracy* (2001).

Robin Luckham is a Research Associate at the Institute of Development Studies, University of Sussex. His publications include *The Nigerian Military: a Sociological Analysis of Authority and Revolt 1960–67* (1971).

Jagath Senaratne is a researcher in Sri Lanka studies. He is the author of *Political Violence in Sri Lanka, 1977–1990* (1997).

Patricio Silva is Professor of Contemporary History of Latin America at the Department of Latin American Studies, Leiden University, The Netherlands.

Frédéric Volpi is a lecturer in international politics at Bristol University.

Susan Woodward is Professor of Political Science at the Graduate Center of the City University of New York. She is the author of *Balkan Tragedy: Chaos and Dissolution after the Cold War* (1995).

Preface

This book brings together the work of leading scholars on military and security issues in the developing South and post-communist East. It forms part of a wider research programme on strengthening democratic governance in conflict-torn societies. This programme was coordinated by the Institute of Development Studies (IDS) at the University of Sussex, in partnership with research institutions in Bosnia, South Africa, Sri Lanka and Uganda. It was funded by ESCOR, the research wing of the British government's Department for International Development.

The present volume is the product of close collaboration between IDS and the Centre for Defence and Security Management (CDSM) at the Graduate School of Public and Development Management, University of Witwatersrand, South Africa, and is based on the proceedings of a workshop held in Johannesburg in September 2000.

The book focuses on the challenges of establishing democratic accountability and control of military and security establishments where they have been problematised by authoritarian government, by violent conflict or by both. Democratic control is not analysed in isolation, but is linked to the broader issues of good governance and of security sector transformation. The book considers both successful democratic transitions and failed ones.

We cannot claim to have been comprehensive. Key parts of the developing and former communist world (the Middle East and large areas of Asia) and important countries that have undertaken democratic transitions have not been considered. It might be argued that some of our choices have been eccentric; they were influenced in part by the availability of expertise. Nevertheless, we have covered countries as divergent as Sri Lanka and South Africa, or Chile and Bosnia-Herzegovina. Half of our chosen countries are African. Perhaps this is appropriate, given that the challenges of governing insecurity are probably starkest in Africa.

The book is divided into four sections. An introductory chapter considers the global context in which debates about the governance of insecurity have occurred. It places democratisation in the context of post-Cold War transformations in global and regional security arrangements. It focuses on the emergence of new forms of military politics and new sources of conflict and insecurity – and spells out the implications for democratic transition, peace building and security sector transformation.

Part II of the book is devoted to case studies of transitional democracies, including South Africa, Nigeria, Ghana and Chile, together with a regional survey of Latin American transitions. South Africa is the only one of these cases where there was simultaneously a transition from armed conflict (although Guatemala, Colombia and other conflict-torn countries are considered in the Latin American chapter). The section examines their efforts to overcome the legacies of authoritarianism, to increase democratic control over military, police, paramilitary and intelligence structures, to assure their accountability for human rights abuses, and to develop appropriate security roles for them in a democratic setting. It singles out South Africa as providing especially comprehensive blueprints for security sector transformation. Yet it emphasises that in none of the other countries has it been possible to take progress toward democracy for granted. They have all faced difficult decisions concerning military and security questions. In some (notably Chile) democratic control has been delayed by authoritarian residues. In others (notably Nigeria) it is potentially challenged by the weakness of democratic institutions and their inability to handle new sources of conflict and insecurity. The final chapter of this section considers the lessons of democratic consolidation in Latin America, where the seeming retreat of the armed forces from political power has not necessarily increased democratic participation in governance, nor made the armed forces more accountable, nor ended political and military violence. Despite real democratic gains in some countries, the overall record has been uneven.

Part III considers the peculiarly complex problems of democratic control in countries caught up in political violence and armed conflict, including Algeria, Sri Lanka, Sierra Leone, the Democratic Republic of the Congo, Bosnia-Herzegovina and the countries of the Balkan region in general. In Algeria, at one extreme, political violence has been associated with re-transition to authoritarianism within a military-dominated state. In Sri Lanka, a long-established democracy has been weakened by protracted armed conflicts with both ethnic and class dimensions. Efforts to make the armed forces and police more accountable have been frustrated, in a context in which a ruthless armed opposition has also operated in conditions of impunity. In contrast, the violence in Sierra Leone, in the Democratic Republic of the Congo and in Bosnia-Herzegovina has been linked to the fracturing of the state and its formal military and security establishments, which have been supplanted by dissident armies, paramilitary bodies, mercenaries and armed mafias. The conflicts in all three countries have spread across national boundaries and have been sustained through a wide variety of regional and global interconnections. At the same time much of the pressure for democratisation and security sector reform has come from the international community; this has sometimes proved counterproductive in the absence of strong domestic support for reforms. The last chapter in this section considers the many paradoxes of donor-promoted security sector reform in the Balkans, which has been impeded by the weakness of democratic institutions, acute national and regional insecurity and the proliferation of military and paramilitary bodies, all with their own international as well as domestic sources of support.

A concluding chapter compares these different efforts to reform military and security structures and to assure their democratic accountability, and tries to draw appropriate conclusions for policy. The approach is inductive. In what circumstances have reforms succeeded, and when have they failed? On the one hand, the chapter focuses on the historical and contextual factors, which have facilitated or limited reform. On the other it considers the political and policy choices made by governments, donors and international agencies, civil society groups and military and security establishments themselves.

We wish to thank the Department for International Development (ESCOR) for its generous support in funding our research, although of course it takes no responsibility for the findings of individual case studies, or for our conclusions, which are very much our own. At the IDS, Sussex, Aaron Griffiths coordinated the research, co-organised the Johannesburg workshop and helped edit this volume. At CDSM Shirley Magano organised the workshop and provided other support. We have also greatly benefited from administrative, secretarial and research support from Julie McWilliam, Kim Collins and Andie Helman-Smith. We give them our heartfelt thanks: without their hard work neither our research nor this book would have been possible.

I
Introduction

1

Democratic Strategies for Security in Transition and Conflict

ROBIN LUCKHAM

This chapter explores five central issues. First, it considers how the quest for security and the quest for democracy have become interlinked in the present liberal world order. Such an order is founded on two presumptions: (a) that global security is best assured through a legitimate international order based on shared democratic values; (b) that national security and public order depend upon a democratic (and thus legitimate) framework of public authority.

Yet, second, this quest has come up against a series of paradoxes and contradictions. Democratisation, as the case studies in this volume show, has often coincided with new forms of militarism, violent conflict and insecurity. The end of the Cold War has introduced new insecurities and globalised violence. Indeed democratisation and insecurity have coincided often enough to make one ask whether they might be different aspects of some deeper hegemonic pattern.

The particular aspect of these paradoxes, which this chapter deals with as its third issue, is the demise of the forms of militarism – coups and military governance – which were the traditional preoccupation of civil–military relations, and their replacement by new forms of military politics, privatised violence and armed conflict.

Fourth, the chapter will consider the governance of these new forms of insecurity. Hence the apparent oxymoron, which forms the title of this book. It is argued that the policy choices made about the management and control of military and security forces at moments of crisis or transition – 'democratic strategies' toward them – are decisive for the consolidation of democracy, the prevention of conflict and the building of a sustainable peace.

Finally, these policy choices, and the constraints they face, are shaped by varying national histories and relationships to common global transformations. The chapter explores some of the different historical trajectories which may be followed both by countries in transition from authoritarianism, and by those in transition from violent conflict.

Governing security or governing insecurity? Two global narratives

The manufacture of global order has become intimately connected to the manufacture of global disorder, as poignantly illustrated by the tragedy of 11 September 2001. Both have been shaped by growing international inequalities – in military capabilities, in political power, in communications and in trade and production. Deep contradictions have been exposed between two global narratives.

The first narrative (see Figure 1.1) has celebrated the triumphal advance of Western liberal democracy. This started in Latin America and parts of Asia well before the end of the Cold War and continued in the 1990s, with the rout of state socialism in the USSR and Eastern Europe and the wholesale dismantling of 'developmental dictatorships' or 'bureaucratic-authoritarian regimes' in the South. By the 1980s neoliberal (free market) economics was already installed as the development orthodoxy of international financial institutions (IFIs) and donors. Political pluralism and 'good governance' followed not far behind, added to the donor agenda, to clear the path for market-oriented economic reforms in failing states. However, in the South and East themselves democratisation was driven forward by genuine mass-based demands for political freedoms, human rights and political participation.

New liberal paradigms of international security and global governance have (in this narrative) displaced the ideological competition of the Cold War. These have built on international norms of cooperation, democracy, human rights, human security and development. Where insecurity and conflict have still not been banished, there has been a range of ready-made policy solutions at hand: conflict management, 'humanitarian' military intervention, emergency relief, peace building, democratisation and development, etcetera. These have mostly implied a multilateral approach, where possible through the United Nations, its agencies and regional organisations.

The second narrative (see Figure 1.2) gives a far gloomier account of the 'same' historical transformations (Kaldor and Luckham 2001). It questions whether the demise of authoritarian regimes in the South and the upheavals unleashed by the collapse of communism have secured

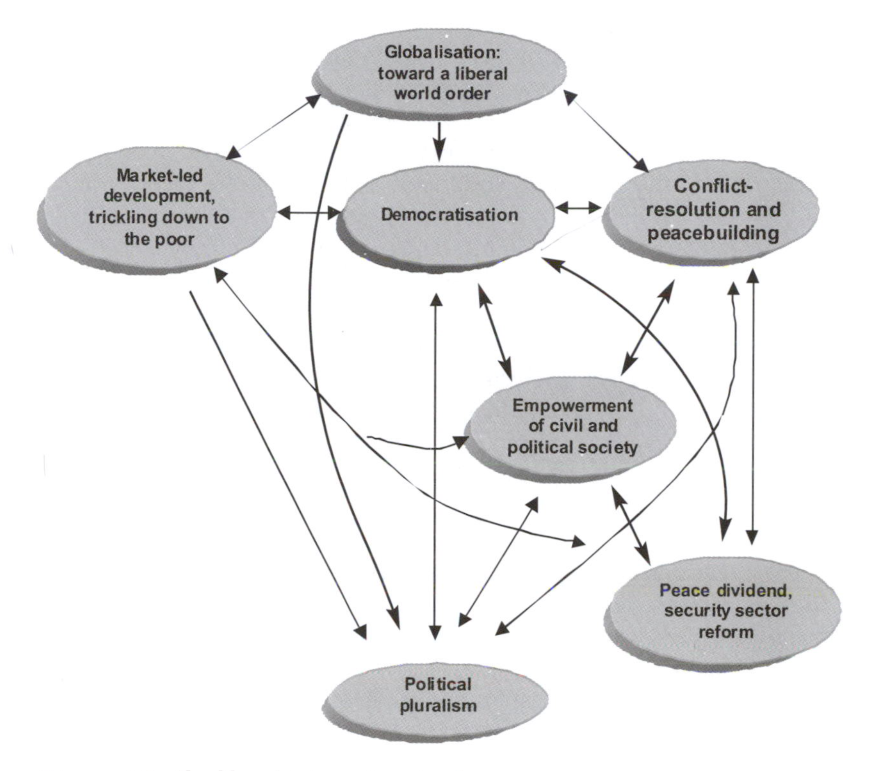

Figure 1.1 The liberal international order

genuine democratic transitions – rather than new forms of élite domination, misrule, or (in the worst cases) state failure, behind the forms of constitutional and democratic governance. Rather than enjoying healthy political pluralism, many new democracies have been torn apart by ever more violent 'new' conflicts, often on the basis of ethnic or religious identities.

These political crises are partly attributed to the contradictions of the new orthodoxies of democracy and the market, and their failure to address international inequalities and rising world-wide poverty, arguably aggravated by economic stabilisation and adjustment policies imposed by IFIs and donors (Kaplinsky 2001; Willett 2001). The armed conflicts sweeping across the developing and post-communist worlds are seen as a response to poverty and injustice, transforming 'structural' into violent conflict. The latter has also spread by new forms of insertion into the global economy: for example, by international flows of natural resources, drugs, small arms, etcetera.[1] Added to these have been the growth of spidery global networks among non-state organisers of violence, including 'terrorists'.

The events of 11 September 2001 arguably re-imported these global insecurities to the developed world itself. But even before then, cynicism had become widespread about the post-Cold War liberal agenda, including international humanitarianism and the entire enterprise of 'development'. The liberal order's noble aspirations were contrasted with its meagre achievements and reinterpreted as new forms of global hegemony. Such a critique has acquired additional force because of the unilateral character of Western military interventions, and the apparent incoherence of international institutions and collective security mechanisms in the face of worsening global security problems.

Though seemingly opposed, the two narratives are also complementary: the relationships in Figure 1.1 are in many respects the reversed Janus face of those in Figure 1.2. Neither of them, moreover, is without internal tensions and contradictions. Economic liberalisation can conflict with as well as reinforce political liberalisation. And, as we shall see, there have often been tensions between democratisation and the prevention and management of conflict.

The fact that democratisation has so often been associated with rising political violence is probably no accident. One reason is that democratisation raises political expectations, but at the same time tends to be actively resisted, often forcibly, by those whose power and privileges it threatens. Democratisation is also undermined by global contradictions, including its relations with free market capitalism, whose economic dislocations arrive along with political freedoms.

The liberal world order, moreover, is far from consistent, and global inequalities and conflict are increased by the prevailing double standards. All too often, the free market trade and investment regime under institutions such as the World Trade Organisation has been tailored to suit the interests of large firms and powerful states. Multilateral institutions, including the UN, have been neglected, underfunded, manipulated or simply treated with contempt, only to be called upon when a fig-leaf of international legitimacy has been needed. Democracy has been promoted, but rather selectively, and in ways that have sometimes served the cause of democracy badly, or weakened the sovereignty of fragile states.

None of this, of course, is an adequate reason for rejecting democracy, or even its promotion by international donors. But it does compel some serious rethinking about how democracy in the South and East

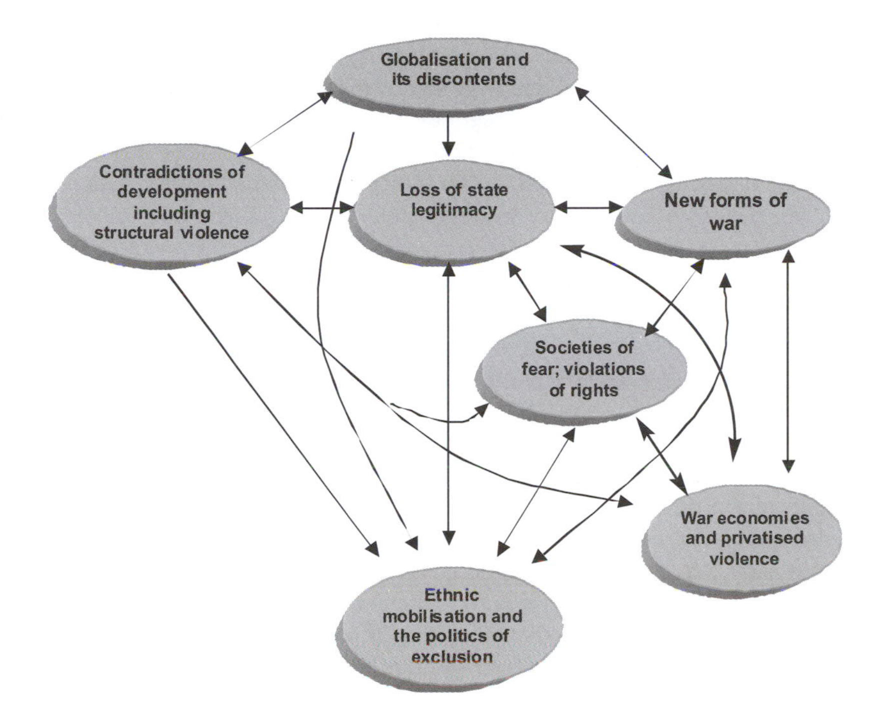

Figure 1.2 The globalisation of insecurity

can be weaned from self-interested democracy promotion by the West and develop sustainable domestic roots. It requires equally serious rethinking about the sources of insecurity – global, regional and national – and how new democracies can best be protected from them.

The decline of coups and military governance – and the rise of new forms of military politics

The past two or three decades have seen an apparent dramatic shrinkage in the political role of military and security establishments. The facts would appear to speak for themselves. Elections have replaced military coups (though these still occur) as the mechanisms for regime succession and élite circulation. Full-blown military regimes, like those in Burma or Pakistan, have become something of a dying breed.

In Latin America no military governments *per se* remain – in stark contrast to the 1960s and 1970s, when they were the regional norm. In Asia the military's political role has also diminished. In 1980 more than half the region's sixteen regimes were military or military-backed, but by 2000 only three were military-controlled (Alagappa 2001: 433–5). Many African governments still originate from previous military regimes, or are headed by ex-military heads of state. But few if any are 'military' governments in the previously accepted sense of the term. Much the same is true in the Middle East, although political liberalisation has passed it by, and the region is dominated by variegated non-democratic regimes. Democratisation in former communist countries has mostly been traumatic, and often violent. But although some post-communist regimes are authoritarian, there are no military regimes as such.

Of course, the whole issue of who governed under military governments – and whether it was actually the military – was always a conundrum (Finer 1982: 281). But the point is that it is now no longer internationally acceptable for soldiers to claim the mantle of political authority. But has this really reduced the political role of military and security establishments? And is the extensive literature on civil–military relations now of no more than historical interest?

Traditionally the key concern of civil–military relations was how to assure 'civilian control' of military establishments (Huntington 1957; Luckham 1971a). Linked to this was a cluster of other issues: the reasons for military coups and intervention in politics (Finer 1988); the nature of military government (Janowitz 1977; Rouquié 1987) and its class basis (emphasised by radical analysts like First 1970 and Alavi 1972); together with transition from military to democratic government, focused on by the Latin American literature (Rouquié 1986; Stepan 1988).

The limitations of these approaches had become evident even before the end of the Cold War. In particular, the concept of civilian control obscured important questions about the nature of regimes. Civilian autocracies have often depended just as much as military dictatorships upon military and police repression and surveillance by intelligence agencies. Nor has military professionalism necessarily been the antidote to military intervention it was made out to be in Huntington's (1957) influential analysis of 'objective' civilian control.[2] In Latin America, indeed, it was often the more professional officers who took power, inspired by the 'new professionalism' of internal security and counter-insurgency promoted under US military aid programmes (Stepan 1973; Koonings in Chapter 13 below).

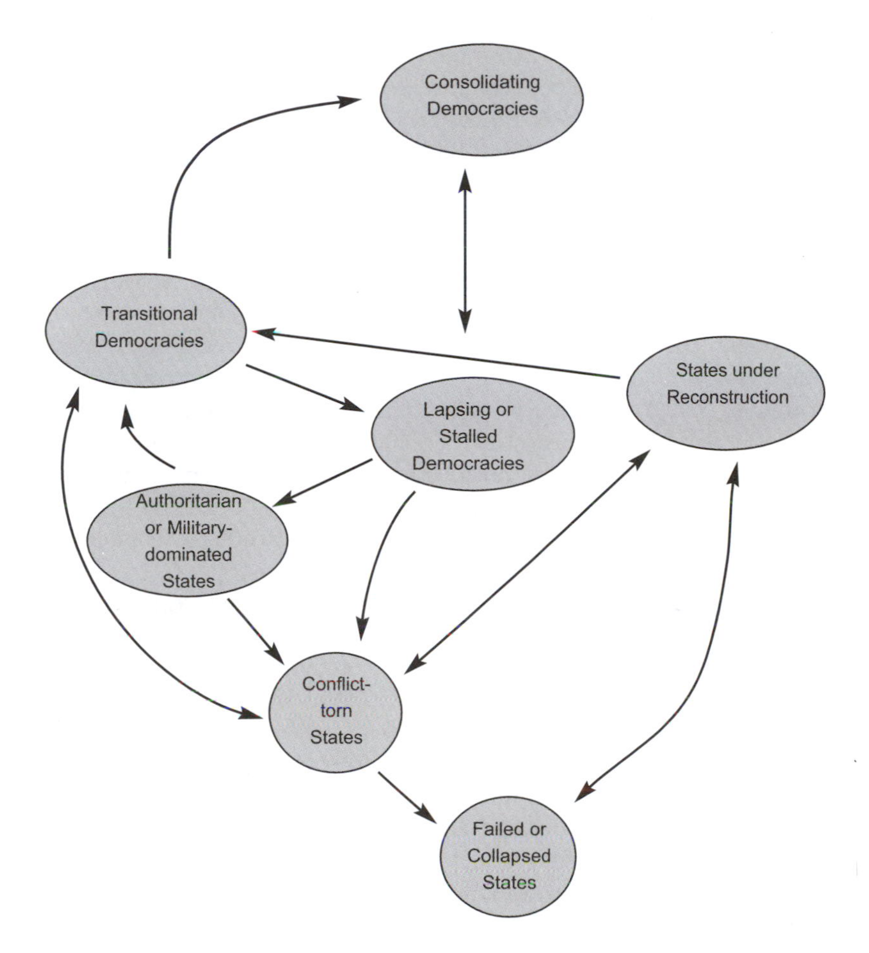

Figure 1.3 Transitions from authoritarian governance and from conflict: varying historical trajectories

The cutting edge of political analysis shifted for a time from military governance *per se* to the broader question of the state in its various guises ('bureaucratic-authoritarian', 'postcolonial', 'neo-patrimonial', 'developmental'). This enabled a more sophisticated analysis of state power and its broad relationships to development – but led to some neglect of the military, whose political projects and organisational interests went under-analysed (Stepan 1988: 9–12).

It was not until the Third Wave of democratisation was initiated that interest in the military revived, mainly because it was seen as a major potential stumbling block (Huntington 1991, Chapter 5). There followed many detailed studies of political armies, most confined to specific regions (on Latin America, see Rouquié 1987, Stepan 1988; on Africa see Luckham 1994, Hutchful and Bathily 1998; on Asia see Alagappa 2001; Koonings and Kruijt 2001 include case studies of political armies from all these regions, the Middle East and Eastern Europe).

As we shall see, the reduced political visibility of the military has by no means curtailed its political influence or its impact on development. But a different *kind* of analysis is required from that found in the more traditional civil–military relations literature. This would focus on a range of new issues, including the diverse and often subterranean forms of military political influence under civilian or democratic regimes; the role of other security apparatuses, including the police and intelligence services; the privatisation of violence and emergence of non-state armed formations; the spread of armed conflict and its impact on security, including human security; and the complex and troubled relationships of all of these with democratic governance.

One way of conceptualising these new forms of militarism emerging alongside the old, and diverting the Third Wave from its democratising course, is in terms of the series of interacting historical trajectories depicted in Figure 1.3. The trajectories on the left of Figure 1.3 show the stereotypical cycle of transition dealt with in the civil–military relations literature. Crises in lapsing civilian political dispensations generate coups and military or authoritarian rule. When military governments in turn crumble, 'transitions to democracy' occur. Either democracy is consolidated or it fails to take root, in which case further cycles of military intervention continue. This was, very broadly speaking, the pattern which used to prevail in some of the countries studied in this book: Algeria, Ghana, Nigeria and Sierra Leone, together with the Latin American cases considered by Koonings (Chapter 13).

What has changed, however, in the post-Cold War era is that open military governance has been delegitimised. Democracy is the sole internationally acceptable form of government, and elections are the main criterion for its presence. But, as argued in the companion volume to this book (Bastian and Luckham, *Can Democracy be Designed?*, forthcoming), the quality and extent of democracy varies enormously. Many supposedly democratic governments still depend partly upon repressive and surveillance apparatuses of state for their political survival. New forms of military politics, of state repression and of political violence have emerged behind the façade of political and economic liberalisation disguising the problems and contradictions they express.

This creates new problems for analysis, including how to decipher underlying shifts in military power relations when these are no longer flagged by open military intervention. It also generates new policy problems: how to counter the subtler manifestations of military role expansion; how to assure democratic accountability of military and security bureaucracies; how to manage incipient violent conflict; and how to do so whilst preventing human rights abuses and ensuring respect for the rule of law by military and security forces services. We will return to these issues later.

Thus a second series of cycles (toward the right of Figure 1.3) has become increasingly prominent, especially since the end of the Cold War, revolving around the growth of political violence and armed conflict. Like cycles of military intervention, they stem from crises in fragile and delegitimised states. Unlike them they challenge not just democratic governance, but also the state itself.

The state starts losing its monopoly of public power and of public coercion to armed groups challenging it. In the more extreme cases (like the Democratic Republic of Congo, Sierra Leone and Bosnia) the state itself has decomposed. Other states, however, have proved more robust. In countries like Sri Lanka or Colombia, major political violence has continued, often for decades, within the framework of a functioning and even democratic state. Some conflicts have been resolved through military victory. In others there have been protracted military and/or political stalemates, or alternating periods of war and peace. And in others the state has fallen apart, only for war to continue among various non-state military formations, as well as a variety of external military actors, as in Somalia.

The terms 'state failure' and 'state collapse' are often used to characterise the state's loss of its monopoly of public power and public coercion during conflicts. Both have to be used with a certain amount of care, since the problem is not always so much the state's loss of its coercive powers, as its abuse of them. 'State failure' is the more usual situation, and implies a normative conception of the state's failure to meet its responsibilities toward its citizens. What this book focuses on is the state's non-delivery of basic physical security and human rights, although these are linked to other dimensions of state failure, like corruption or inability to deliver development. 'State collapse', the complete disappearance of state structures and public authority, as in Somalia, has been relatively rare – although the retreat of state authority from significant parts of national territory is more common, and tends to be associated with spreading political and criminal violence.

Both conceptions have been questioned for offering an excessively normative and Eurocentric view of the state, 'closely linked to the praxis of the postcolonial state as a "well-policed state" (*policeystaat*), supreme architect of modernity' (Bayart 1993: 11) – rather than analysing states as they emerge, innovate, produce the effects of power and become vehicles for political (and military) entrepreneurs in particular national and regional contexts. Disorder is a political instrument, so Chabal and Daloz (1999) argue, that can serve the interests of political élites and indeed of states. Even state collapse is not quite what it seems, since behind it there are usually struggles to create new forms of political domination.

These critiques provide a useful antidote to the more simplistic accounts of state failure and collapse. They also reinforce a methodological point: that the real politics of democratic transition and of state reconstruction are ignored at one's peril. Nevertheless it is impossible, as well as undesirable to dispense with a normative conception of the state. The bottom line is that states are indeed supposed to be 'well-policed states', able to deliver security to their citizens. This is what both their own citizens and the international community of states expect of them. States not meeting this responsibility are not only failing their citizens, they are less likely to be legitimate and less likely to survive.

Civil wars and 'internal' conflicts have global and regional as well as national ramifications. A distinctive feature of the post-Cold War period has been the altered character of international interventions. During the Cold War, the major powers often supported belligerents, whilst IFIs and donor agencies mostly pretended (with a few honourable exceptions like UNICEF) that conflicts did not exist, or were an issue they could safely ignore. But from the 1990s a wider range of international actors has become involved, including IFIs, UN agencies, NGOs and peacekeeping bodies. The nature of their interventions has also altered. Military interventions by the major powers and alliances, and the arming and funding of belligerents, still continue. But 'humanitarian' interventions including emergency assistance, peacekeeping, conflict resolution, post-conflict reconstruction and support for democracy have assumed increasing importance.

However, this new international humanitarianism has paid disappointingly meagre dividends. Despite the decline of military coups, there is little sign of conflicts abating. Even where formal peace agreements have been signed, the conflicts have often not 'ended', tending to go under the surface, re-ignite and trigger further cycles of war and violence. Clearly analysts and policy makers still have an enormous amount to learn about the most basic issues: how to prevent and 'resolve' conflicts; how to contain the spread of violence within and across national boundaries; how to demobilise combatants (politically, as well as militarily); and how to build a sustainable democratic peace.

Indeed, there has been a distressing tendency for international humanitarian interventions to misdiagnose conflicts, or even to make them worse (De Waal 1997; Duffield 2001, Chapter 4). The disarray has been increased when great power politics has entered by the back door, and reshaped humanitarian intervention around its own imperatives, as in the current 'war on terrorism'.

Below we consider each of these two major historical trajectories in turn. Both are reshaped continually by global changes, and each interacts with the other in complex ways. Most of the transitional democracies considered in Part II have at one stage or another been imperilled by actual or potential violent conflict. And most of the countries we classify as conflict-torn states in Part III have been trying to establish democratic political institutions as part of building peace.

Toward democratic governance of military and security establishments in contested democracies

Transitional democracies, where democracy is in varying states of construction (or in some cases deconstruction) have been a fast-growing category, due to the delegitimisation of authoritarian governance and the break-up of the communist bloc. However, classifying them as 'democracies' can be somewhat misleading. Democracy itself is an unresolved and contested process, rather than a fully achieved end state (Bastian and Luckham, forthcoming). And not all countries claiming democracy's mantle are in fact in transition towards it. Some have stuck in one state or another of semi-democracy. Others may even have regressed toward some form of authoritarianism. Four main categories can be distinguished:

- countries, which are genuinely in transit to or consolidating democracy, like South Africa, Chile, or (more uncertainly) Ghana;
- those where democratisation remains highly contested and its outcome uncertain, as in Nigeria, Peru or Guatemala;
- those where the dominant political élites have stabilised some kind of managed democracy over long periods of time, as in Malaysia or Botswana;[3]

- those regressing toward authoritarian governance behind a shell of formal democracy, like Algeria or Zimbabwe.

It should be emphasised, however, that in all these cases democracy is in different degrees and in varying ways an object of political contest. Also, it tends to be characterised by gaping 'democracy deficits'. These tend to be widest when democratic institutions are undermined by the absence of democratic politics. Contests for the control of democracy have major implications for military and security establishments: both because they can influence the outcomes of these contests; and because they have to deal with the consequent political instability and conflict.

The transitions literature has often emphasised that the armed forces are the neuralgic point of democratisation (Rouquie 1986 and Luckham 1996). Their control of coercion gives them a unique capacity to obstruct or even to reverse political changes, as shown in the chapters on Chile and Algeria below. Whilst the military's direct veto powers have declined since the end of the Cold War, they still cannot be entirely discounted. Indeed, the recent rehabilitation of unilateralism and *realpolitik* seen under the Bush administration in the USA could conceivably revive Western support for strategically placed military regimes like that of Pakistan.

But for the present what is of more concern is the manifold ways authoritarianism and military politics may continue behind the formalities of civilian and democratic governance. This is often reinforced by the unresolved legacies of military and authoritarian rule (Stepan 1988; Luckham 1996). These include the perpetuation of military, police and security service privileges and prerogatives; the continued assertion of military 'guardianship' of the national interest; the entrenchment of military and ex-military men in politics, administration and business; military and security impunity for past and present human rights abuses; protected military and security budgets; secrecy and the insulation of military and security issues from public debate.

However, this is not necessarily a temporary or transitional problem which will be overcome as democracy is slowly consolidated. As Koonings shows in Chapter 6, formal democratisation in Latin America has opened the way to new forms of violence and insecurity. Much the same is true, our case studies show, in Africa, Asia and Eastern Europe. Struggles still continue over how national security is defined and by whom. Moreover, they are complicated by the proliferation of new security actors like paramilitaries, police rapid reaction units, militias and even criminal mafias.

This is closely connected to another observation, that there are 'political armies', together with diverse forms of military and security influence, under civilian governments, even those which have never fallen under military rule. Colombia, Sri Lanka, South Africa (in the apartheid era) and the Ivory Coast are among the more obvious examples (the first three are considered in this volume; see N'Diaye 2000 on the Ivory Coast). Zimbabwe is a salient recent example of the politicisation of a previously professional force (or of powerful elements within it) as the *de facto* political and business partner and electoral enforcer of a contested 'democratic' regime – all within the formal parameters of democracy and the constitution, but not without strong misgivings on the part of some of the more professional officers.

Of course such forms of military politics are by no means unprecedented: the many diverse and subtle forms of military influence were documented many years ago in Finer's classic *Man on Horseback* (1988). Nor have they been confined to developing countries alone. The political reliance of post-communist regimes on their military and security apparatuses has become a major issue in post-communist Russia and Eastern Europe, reflecting the general weakness of democratic institutions. Even in Western democracies, professional military establishments and military–industrial complexes wield considerable behind-doors influence upon security policy. Despite trends toward more open government, the military, police and security agencies remain by far the least publicly accountable of all the state's public bureaucracies.

The concept of 'civilian control', which used to be the dominant concern of civil–military relations theory and practice, is rendered irrelevant by the widespread continuation of authoritarian politics by 'democratic' means. The idea of 'democratic control' (Luckham 1996) is more useful, since it recognises that civilian governments are not necessarily democratic. However, one should see democratic control as a contested process, not as a fixed attribute of existing democracies – first, because of the contested nature of democracy itself; and second, because some of the largest democracy deficits are to be found in the security sector. Even democratic governments tend to halt democracy at the barracks door and the inner corridors of the secret state.

The concept of 'democratic control' thus requires a more nuanced political understanding of governance, including the fact that even 'democratic' governments may abuse their national security powers and misuse their military and security forces. It should also be based on a realistic appraisal of democracy deficits in the security sector – pervasive secrecy, lack of accountability, corruption, human rights abuses, over-reliance on coercion, etcetera – and the difficulties they pose for policy.

Further constraints upon democratisation are imposed by the limits of national development and relationships to the global economy. The past two decades have seen certain important shifts. On one hand the myth that military or authoritarian regimes had any unique capacity to promote capital accumulation or national development no longer carries much conviction.[4] On the other hand the global trend toward economic and political liberalisation, together with unstable world markets, have had certain important impacts on military and security spending, and thus on military and security institutions themselves.

Since the end of the Cold War military and security budgets have come under closer scrutiny by international financial institutions and donors than ever before, both in developing and in post-communist states. Budgets have been tied to economic stabilisation programmes and 'structurally adjusted', above all in poor, aid-dependent countries. Cuts introduced to resolve fiscal crises and satisfy donors have aggravated the crises of fragile regimes and of their military and security establishments, all the more where military spending has already fallen due to economic decline, resulting in 'demilitarisation by default' (Luckham 1995). In the worst cases, like the Democratic Republic of Congo or Sierra Leone, the authorities simply ceased paying their own armed forces and police, wrecking their discipline and capacity to ensure basic security and public order.

Donors and IFIs have now become more sensitive to the dangers of insisting on military cuts in fragile states. Instead they are fostering a new discourse of 'security sector reform' and 'democratic governance of the security sector' (Hendrickson 1999; Ball 2001; Smith 2001; DFID 2000;[5] OECD/DAC 2001). The emphasis has thus shifted from military spending to the *processes* through which resources are allocated to and within the security sector. More generally, donors have sought to promote the same standards of 'good governance' and public sector management in the security sector as in all other areas of government activity.

Although the terminology is new, one should recognise that security sector reform has been on the international agenda for far longer. The links between disarmament, security and development were spelt out by the Brandt and Palme Commissions in the early 1980s (Report of the Independent Commission on Development Issues 1980; Report of the Independent Commission on Disarmament and Security Issues 1982).

Moreover, the present donor discourse simply codifies military and security transformations already in progress in certain developing and post-communist countries. They, rather than the donors, are the true progenitors of security sector reform. The most outstanding example has been South Africa, where a unique transition has fostered a broad range of groups in the state and outside it with a shared interest in reform. What is important for our purposes is the creation of genuine domestic constituencies for democratic governance of the security sector. Without such local 'ownership', reforms promoted by donors are far less likely to succeed.

Most discussion of security sector reform so far has focused on the broad goals of reform and on policy prescriptions to make them operational. There has been much less consideration of the political and economic conditions which facilitate reform, the obstacles which confront it, and the conditions which determine when it is sustainable – and when it is not. The chapters in this volume are meant to fill this gap, and we return to the policy issues surrounding security sector reform in the conclusion.

Above all, reform requires an adequate understanding of the security sector itself. Military and security establishments should be deconstructed, and their micro-politics understood. Research shows that they are often far from the stereotype of hierarchical, unified bodies acting in a politically coherent manner (Luckham 1971b and 1994; Rouquié 1987). They differ considerably from one to another. They are almost invariably differentiated internally, containing divergent organisational interests and competing factions. Formal organisational blueprints are usually a poor guide to the real distribution of power. This can have a crucial impact on how military and security bureaucracies relate to government, and how they respond to reforms.

Moreover, besides the armed forces there are other security actors to be taken into account. Some belong within the formal structures of government, like intelligence agencies, presidential guards, gendarmeries, paramilitaries, police, including rapid response units, and parts of the judicial and criminal justice system. Added to these are the armed formations operating outside and sometimes against the state, especially in conflict-torn societies: mercenaries (Musah and Fayemi 2000), security firms, guerrillas, warlord followings, criminal mafias and so on.

Hence instead of conceiving of the security sector as a coherent and unified 'sector', it may be more fruitful to see it as a shifting terrain of security coalitions, which are assembled and reassembled as crises occur, or reforms take place. One advantage of such an approach is that it challenges the conventional assumption that the state should necessarily be at the centre of transformation. Our case studies of Chile, South Africa and Ghana demonstrate that groups in political and civil society have played a crucial role in reforms. Most current definitions of the security sector indeed factor in government agencies, legislative committees, judicial bodies, media and civil society groups seen as responsible for ensuring that the armed forces, police and other security services are accountable to government, parliaments and the public (OECD/DAC 2001).

Moreover, military and security bureaucracies should not be unduly stereotyped as obstacles to transformation, which have to be 'controlled' by civilian structures. Sometimes the relationship may be the other way around. Elected civilian governments with a faltering or non-existent commitment to democracy may co-opt the armed forces and police as instruments of political control, having little serious interest in security sector reform, even if they pay lip service to satisfy the donors. In contrast, the more professional elements in military and security establishments may have a real stake in good government, and be open to arguments for greater accountability – believing their professional interests to be compromised by partisan politics, corruption or human rights abuses. The danger in the past was that military professional discontents simply triggered military intervention against unpopular civilian governments. But some professional soldiers seem to be on a learning curve concerning the dangers of coups and may be more willing to engage with civilian reform coalitions instead – as certain of our case studies suggest.

In the final analysis of course, democratic control of the armed forces, police and security services depends upon the health and quality of democracy itself, as shaped by the interplay of democratic institutions and democratic politics in each specific national context. It cannot be isolated from struggles to democratise democracy, where the latter remains stalled or contested. However, it can certainly make an important difference to these struggles if the armed forces, police and security services are professional, are able to resist partisan political influence, respect human rights and operate within the rule of law.

One may draw considerable encouragement from the growing number of examples of good practice in the non-Western world, some considered in this volume. There is arguably greater democratic accountability within the security sector in new democracies like South Africa than obtains in many established democracies like India, France or the United Kingdom.

Governing insecurity in contexts of political exclusion and violent conflict

Although this book is structured around the distinction between countries making 'normal' transitions to democracy, and those democratising (or not) under conditions of violent conflict, in reality both experience many of the same insecurities. Even countries that can be said to be consolidating democracy, like Chile, South Africa and Ghana, still grapple with problems of social exclusion, rising crime, privatised violence and potential military unrest. Such problems are all the more severe where, as in Nigeria, democratic governance and indeed the very nature of the state are contested and fragile.

Democratisation itself (it has been argued) has been among the principal causes of insecurity and violent conflict. Comparative studies (Regan and Henderson 2002) suggest that violent conflict occurs more often where democratisation is incomplete (semi-democracies, or 'democracies with adjectives' to use the terminology of our companion volume: Bastian and Luckham, forthcoming), than in authoritarian systems or in consolidated democracies. Our case studies include a number of countries (Algeria, Bosnia, Congo, Sierra Leone) where the transition process – or its mismanagement – has worsened political violence, and one could provide several further examples, the most traumatic of all being Rwanda (Uvin 1998).

One should avoid drawing unwarranted conclusions, however, about the responsibility of democratisation itself for such conflicts. Often the latter may be traced back to efforts by departing political élites, members of the security forces or paramilitary groupings to subvert or co-opt the transition through state-orchestrated violence. Democratisation itself is not the problem, so much as those who subvert or oppose it, together with the enduring legacies of undemocratic politics.

We return now to the paradox identified in the title of this volume. Is it possible to govern the security sector, let alone democratically, in polities where many citizens feel excluded from politics and from the benefits of development, and where political violence and armed conflict have become endemic? As Woodward (Chapter 12) argues in relation to the Balkans, security sector reform in situations of great regional and national insecurity, where entire systems of government, economy and society are being contested, is at best a quixotic enterprise. One certainly cannot assume that institutions, policies and practices which work in more stable polities can be adopted unmodified in conflict-torn societies. For the room for political agency and policy choice is heavily constrained where insecurity prevails, and powerful political, economic and social forces propel conflict.

Yet conflicts can sometimes sweep away vested interests, weaken structures and institutions which previously resisted change, and transform whole societies and economies. They are undeniably traumatic and damaging for development. But they may also open spaces in which certain kinds of change may be more feasible than they were under more 'stable' conditions. Our task is to make a clear-headed evaluation of these openings, as well as the risks and damage conflict causes.

Of course, all conflicts are not the same. They demand different analyses and varying policy approaches. Four main historical patterns may be distinguished (although each could be subdivided further):

- First, there is the prototypical situation (shown on the lower right of Figure 1.3) where transitions from military or authoritarian governance in failing states go badly wrong. The state is delegitimised, or never had legitimacy in the first place. The official armed forces and police fracture, are unable to assure law and order, and start to lose their monopoly of violence. Instead of transition to democracy, there is transition to violent conflict or, in a few cases, state collapse.

- A second, contrasting case is where, during armed resistance to authoritarian regimes, parallel structures of power and legitimacy emerge that are able to remove the regime (Nicaragua in 1979, for example, or Ethiopia and Eritrea in 1991), or to force a negotiated retreat from power (the case of South Africa in 1989–94).

- A third situation is one in which the political institutions of democratic or semi-democratic states exclude significant minorities or subaltern classes, as well as reinforcing their social and economic marginalisation, encouraging them to mobilise militarily as well as politically against the state (as in Sri Lanka, India and Colombia).

- Finally, there have been the conflicts of the post-communist world, where triple transitions from command to market economies, from socialist to non-socialist ideologies and from totalitarianism to liberal democracy have generated vast upheavals, spawned virulent nationalisms and produced violent struggles over the very identity of the state.

One may view these trajectories as varying responses to common processes of globalisation. It has been argued that global changes have shaped and in certain respects homogenised 'new wars' or 'postmodern conflicts' (Kaldor 1999; Duffield 1998). Of course the wars themselves are not necessarily new. Most current conflicts (except in post-communist countries) were initiated well before the end of the Cold War. But there have been significant transformations in the way they are organised, funded and fought.

One marker of these changes is the decline of the ideologically driven popular struggles of the Cold War period (the second category distinguished above). Conflicts, which used to have strong ideological dimensions (Angola, for example), or which expressed deep popular or minority discontents (Sierra Leone, Sudan), have tended over the years to degenerate into naked struggles for power, to appropriate natural resources or to control the ethnic and national identity of the state.

This is not the place for an extended discussion of the roots and dynamics of contemporary conflicts (discussed in Kaldor and Luckham 2001, a companion essay to this volume). The focus here is upon their legacies (as identified in Figure 1.2 above), together with the democratic strategies that might be deployed to overcome them (considered in more detail in the Conclusion).

Loss of state (and military) legitimacy

Major political violence, as we have already argued, typically stems from profound crises in state legitimacy and state capacity. These crises tend also to manifest themselves in deep institutional crises in military, police and security establishments, reinforcing the erosion of the state's monopoly of public order and of public violence. Hence reconstitution of legitimate public authority and reconstruction of the instruments of public order are interdependent and need to be coordinated (Cliffe and Luckham 2001). But it does not follow that the state should be restored and its military, police and security apparatuses should be rebuilt in their problematic pre-conflict form. Both must be reconstructed on more legitimate foundations. Democratic accountability and the rule of law are not luxuries that can safely be postponed until order and security are restored; they are inseparable from the latter.

Contradictions of development, including structural violence

Violent conflicts are often rooted in conditions of poverty and social exclusion. They cannot be considered separately from the problems of development, as well as the failings of national and international development policy. In this book we place ourselves firmly in the camp of those who believe social and economic grievances, or structural violence, are crucial factors in many conflicts (Luckham *et al.* 2001; see Uvin 1998 for an especially eloquent analysis of the roots of the Rwandan genocide in failed development policy).

What converts structural into physical violence is the belief that economic and social conditions have worsened (relative deprivation), along with the perception that governments (and international donors) are indifferent. That is, it is not separate from the problems of governance. The sense of grievance is made all the greater, when the contending government and rebel forces in conflicts destroy civilian livelihoods or even profit from the hostilities. Thus one cannot really separate the need to rebuild structures of public security from the need to restore livelihoods and human security. The latter in its turn requires the restoration of public order. Indeed the World Bank's study of the *Voices of the Poor* (World Bank 2001) makes it very clear that basic physical security is a major priority for the poor themselves.

Ethnic mobilisation, the politics of exclusion and the 'tribalisation' of security

A major feature of many recent conflicts has been the mobilisation of ethnic, religious, linguistic or regional identities. Stewart (2000) terms these horizontal inequalities, arguing that they play a major role in causing violence. But it is not these identities themselves that are problematic. It is the way they are used as markers of economic, social and political exclusion – and how they are mobilised for political purposes and ultimately for war.

There is an important military and security dimension, which has received relatively little attention since Enloe's pioneering book on *Ethnic Soldiers* (1980). Governments and their military and security forces often use markers of ethnic or religious identity to recruit, to define potential security threats and to maintain political control. All the more during violent conflicts, when such identities are mobilised to control both people and territory. Ethnic cleansing is the most extreme manifestation, creating legacies of fear and hate that are enormously difficult to eradicate.

When ethnic patronage is built into military, police and security bureaucracies, it corrupts them, weakens discipline, reinforces a sense of impunity and fosters public (and especially minority) distrust of the state itself. Bosnia (see Chapter 9) is an extreme example, where the reorganisation of military and security forces on largely ethnic lines, without an integrated command system, has perpetuated insecurity and made democratic control impossible.

Societies of fear and the violations of rights

Conflicts invariably sow deep seeds of hatred, often greatly sharpened by ethnic mobilisation, specially so in the many wars in which civilians and social capital have been deliberately targeted to gain control over territory and resources. Human rights have been violated almost as a matter of routine, not just by state military and security forces, but also by rebel groups. In relatively few recent conflicts have protagonists sought to win the hearts and minds of the civilian population, as in the former guerrilla and liberation struggles.[6] Instead, violence is socially and culturally embedded within what Koonings and Kruijt (1999) term *Societies of Fear*.

A democratic strategy for security thus can only be built through dialogue and national reconciliation. There needs to be peace building from below, as well as negotiation of peace from above. At the same time explicit policies are required to end impunity for violence as well as violence itself – the aim of the Truth and Reconciliation Commissions discussed in the chapters on Chile and South Africa.

New forms of war – and the proliferation of armed groups

Conflicts have increasingly diverged from the old stereotype of symmetric wars between the organised military forces of nation states.[7] This does not mean that the state is not also a significant protagonist. In many conflicts, indeed, it has been a major perpetrator of 'politicide' against civilians (Holsti 2000). Sometimes this has involved direct military or police action by the state itself, as in Sri Lanka; sometimes the subcontracting of repression to paramilitaries and militias, as in Bosnia, Algeria or Guatemala; and sometimes the orchestration of civilian violence, as in Bosnia or the Rwandan genocide.

Yet in many cases states have lost their monopolies of public coercion. Sometimes the demise of state authority follows the fracturing of government military and security apparatuses into competing fragments which eventually become the nuclei of warlord or criminal bands, as in Somalia. At other times competing groups emerge outside the framework of the state – party militias, guerrillas, warlords or mafias with their own commercial and political interests in fighting. More often the process displays some combination of the above, as in Afghanistan, Sierra Leone or the Congo.

As will be seen in the case studies, this fragmentation of military powers poses particularly severe difficulties for security sector transformation, since democratic control of official military establishments, though necessary, is far from sufficient. Combatants have to be demobilised, politically as well as militarily; without such a demobilisation, peace agreements tend to be worthless. Yet sometimes the cleavages entrenched by competing armed groups are so deep that the very framework of the state and its security structures has to be re-thought, as argued in the chapters in this volume on Sri Lanka and Bosnia.

War economies and the privatisation of violence and security

In a world where the state is in retreat, and public goods are being converted to private gain, it is no surprise that the means of public coercion too are being privatised. Such a privatisation has been hastened by the end of the Cold War, which deprived both government and anti-state forces of the superpower funding that financed their wars. Instead they have often turned to other sources of finance: exploitation of natural resources (diamonds, timber, oil); the drug trade; 'attack trade', profiting from war-induced scarcities; criminal and mafia activity; smuggling and gun-running; 'taxation' of foreign firms and humanitarian agencies, etcetera. All these in turn have created incentive systems that entrench violence and those who profit from it.

In the long run the most obvious counters to the privatisation of violence are sustainable development, together with restored public (and democratic) control of security provision. In the short run, security sector reform needs to be coordinated with a variety of measures to normalise the economy and day-to-day security: adequate livelihoods for demobilised combatants; rebuilding taxation systems; anti-smuggling and anti-corruption measures; reconstruction of police and judicial systems; and the regulation of private security bodies.

All these things require more decisive action by the international community, both to cut off 'non-legitimate' conduits for trade, weapons, mercenaries and other destabilising factors, and to pressure governments, like that of Liberia, which extract profit from the conflicts of their neighbours.

The globalisation and regionalisation of insecurity and security

'Internal' conflicts, 'civil' wars and national insecurity have almost without exception been rooted in international as well as internal processes. Globalisation has shaped conflicts in five major respects. First, conflicts are sustained by global flows of resources and weapons. Second, global geopolitics and the interests of major powers and international corporations continue to have a shaping influence. Third, the theory and practice of international humanitarianism, and 'humanitarian intervention' in peripheral conflicts, are a defining feature of globalisation. Fourth, the regionalisation of conflicts causes them to spill across national boundaries and create expanding regional conflict complexes, as in the African Great Lakes or the Middle East and West Asia. Finally, there are the dense and complex informal global networks that sustain conflicts: diasporas, 'terrorists', holy warriors, mafias, illicit arms suppliers, etcetera.[8]

Security sector transformation must be set within this broader international picture. Since conflict and insecurity themselves have been regionalised and globalised, regional and global collective security mechanisms should be strengthened to counteract them. At the same time transformations in the security sectors of the developing and post-communist worlds should not become hostage to the donors' international humanitarian agenda, still less to the 'war against terrorism'. Transformation will only work if there is local ownership, and if it is appropriate in each national and regional context.

References

Alagappa, M. (ed.) (2001) *Coercion and Governance. The Declining Political Role of the Military in Asia*, Stanford: Stanford University Press.

Alavi, H. (1972) 'The state in postcolonial societies: Pakistan and Bangladesh', *New Left Review*, 74: 59–81.

Ball, N. (2001) 'Transforming security sectors: the IMF and World Bank approaches', *Journal of Conflict Security and Development*, 1 (1): 45–66.

Bastian, S. and R. Luckham (eds.) (forthcoming) *Can Democracy be Designed?* London: Zed Books.

Bayart, J-F. (1993) *The State in Africa. The Politics of the Belly*, London: Longman.

Berdal, M. and D. M. Malone (eds.) (2000), *Greed and Grievance. Economic Agendas in Civil Wars*, Boulder: Lynne Rienner.

Chabal, P. and J-P. Daloz (1999) *Africa Works. Disorder as a Political Instrument*, Oxford: James Currey.

Cliffe, L. and R. Luckham (2001) 'What happens to the state in conflict? Political analysis as a tool for planning humanitarian assistance', *Disasters*, 24 (4): 291–313.

De Waal, A. (1997) *Famine Crimes: Politics and the Disaster Relief Industry in Africa*, Oxford: James Currey.

DFID (2000) *Security Sector Reform and the Management of Military Expenditure: High Risks for Donors, High Returns for Development*, Report on an International Symposium Sponsored by the UK Department for International Development, London.

Duffield, M. (1998) 'Postmodern conflict, warlords, post-adjustment states and private protection', *Civil Wars*, 1 (1): 66–102.

—— (2001) *Global Governance and the New Wars. The Merging of Development and Security*, London: Zed Books.

Enloe, C. (1980) *Ethnic Soldiers: State Security in Divided Societies*, Harmondsworth: Penguin.

Finer, S. E. (1982) 'The morphology of military regimes', in Kolkowicz, R. and A. Korbonski (eds.), *Soldiers, Peasants and Bureaucrats; Civil–Military Relations in Communist and Modernizing Societies*, London: Allen and Unwin.

—— (1988) *The Man on Horseback – The Role of the Military in Politics*, second enlarged edition, London: Pinter.

First, R. (1970) *The Barrel of a Gun. Political Power in Africa and the Coup d'Etat*, London: Penguin.
Hendrickson, D. (1999) 'A review of security sector reform', Working Paper No. 1, Centre for Defence Studies, King's College, University of London.
Holm, J. (1989) 'Botswana : a paternalistic democracy', in Diamond, L., J. J. Linz and S. M. Lipset (eds.) (1988–1989), *Democracy in developing countries. Vol. 2. Africa*, Boulder: Lynne Rienner: 179–215.
Holsti, K. J. (2000) 'Political Causes of Humanitarian Emergencies', in Nafziger *et al.* (eds.) 2000.
Huntington, S. P. (1957) *The Soldier and the State. The Theory and Politics of Civil–Military Relations*, New York: Vintage Press.
—— (1991) *The Third Wave. Democratisation in the Late Twentieth Century*, Norman: University of Oklahoma Press.
Hutchful, E. and A. Bathily (eds.) (1998) *The Military and Militarism in Africa*, Dakar: CODESRIA.
Janowitz, M. (1977) *Military Institutions and Power in the Developing Nations*, Chicago: University of Chicago Press.
Kaldor, M. (1999) *New and Old Wars. Organised Violence in a Global Era*, Cambridge: Polity Press.
Kaldor, M. and R. Luckham (2001) 'Global transformations and new conflicts', *IDS Bulletin*, 32 (2): 48–67.
Kaplinsky, R. (2001) 'Globalisation and Economic Insecurity', *IDS Bulletin*, 32 (2): 13–24.
Koonings, K. and D. Kruijt (eds.) (1999) *Societies of Fear. The Legacy of Civil War, Violence and Terror in Latin America*, London: Zed Books.
Koonings, K. and D. Kruijt (eds.) (2002) *Political Armies. The Military and Nation Building in the Age of Democracy*, London: Zed Books.
Luckham, R. (1971a) 'A comparative typology of civil–military relations', *Government and Opposition*, 6 (1): 15–35.
Luckham, R. (1971b) *The Nigerian Military. A Sociological Analysis of Authority and Revolt 1960–67*, Cambridge: Cambridge University Press.
—— (1994) 'The military, militarization and democratization in Africa', *African Studies Review*, 37 (2): 13–75.
—— (1995) 'Dilemmas of military disengagement in Africa', *IDS Bulletin*, 26 (2): 49–61.
—— (1996) 'Faustian bargains: democratic control over military and security establishments', in Luckham, R. and G. White (eds.), *Democratization in the South. The Jagged Wave*, Manchester: Manchester University Press: 119–77.
Luckham, R. *et al.* (2001) 'Conflict and poverty in Sub-Saharan Africa: an assessment of the issues and evidence', IDS Working Paper No. 128.
Musah, A-F. and J.'K Fayemi (eds.) (2000) *Mercenaries. An African Security Dilemma*, London: Pluto Press.
Nafziger, W., F. Stewart and R. Väyrynen (eds.) (2000) *War, Hunger and Displacement: the Origins of Humanitarian Emergencies*, Volume 1, Oxford: Oxford University Press.
N'Diaye, B. (2000) 'Ivory Coast's civilian control strategies 1961–1998: a

critical assessment', *Journal of Political and Military Sociology*, 28 (2): 246–70.

OECD/DAC (2001) 'Security issues and development cooperation: a conceptual framework for enhancing policy coherence', *The DAC Journal*, 2 (3).

Regan, P. M. and E. A. Henderson (2002) 'Democracy, threats and political repression in developing countries: are democracies internally less violent?', *Third World Quarterly*, 23 (1): 119–36.

Report of the Independent Commission on Disarmament and Security Issues (the Palme Report) (1982) *Common Security: a Programme for Disarmament*, London: Pan Books.

Report of the Independent Commission on International Development Issues (the Brandt Report) (1980) *North–South: a Programme for Survival*, London: Pan Books.

Rouquié, A. (1986) 'Demilitarization and the institutionalization of military-dominated politics in Latin America', in O'Donnell, G. and P. Schmitter (eds.), *Transitions from Authoritarian Rule. Comparative Perspectives*, Baltimore: Johns Hopkins University Press: 108–136.

—— (1987) *The Military and the State in Latin America*, Berkeley: University of California Press.

Sklar, R. (1987) 'Developmental democracy', *Comparative Studies in Society and History*, 29 (4): 686–714.

Smith, C. (2001) 'Security-sector reform: development breakthrough or institutional engineering?', *Journal of Conflict, Security and Development*, 1 (1): 5–19.

Stepan, A. K. (1973) 'The new professionalism of internal warfare and role expansion', in Stepan, A. K. (ed.), *Authoritarian Brazil. Origins, Policies and Future*, Princeton: Princeton University Press.

—— (1988) *Rethinking Military Politics: Brazil and the Southern Cone*, Princeton: Princeton University Press.

Stewart, F. (2000) 'The root causes of humanitarian emergencies', in E. W. Nafziger, *et al.* (eds.), *War, Hunger and Displacement: the Origins of Humanitarian Emergencies*, Volume 1, Oxford: Oxford University Press.

Uvin, P. (1998) *Aiding Violence. The Development Enterprise in Rwanda*, West Hartford: Kumarian Press

White, G. (1998) 'Constructing a democratic developmental state', in Robinson, M. and G. White (eds.), *The Democratic Developmental State: Political and Institutional Design*, Oxford: Oxford University Press: 17–51.

Willett, S. (2001) 'Insecurity, Conflict and the New Global Disorder', *IDS Bulletin*, 32 (2): 35–47.

World Bank (2001) *Poverty Trends and Voices of the Poor*, Washington DC: World Bank.

Notes

1 See the current debate between those who argue that conflicts are sustained by 'grievances', including poverty, underdevelopment and development policy failures, and those who contend that 'greed' is more important (Berdal and Malone 2000). As argued elsewhere (Luckham *et al.* 2001), however,

'grievance' and 'greed' interact: the latter is a more powerful explanation of why conflicts continue than of why they begin in the first place.

2 Huntington contrasts 'objective control', based on a balance between strong civilian political institutions and an autonomous, professional military establishment, with 'subjective control' exercised through civilian political penetration of the armed forces (via patronage networks, corruption, or political party penetration in socialist regimes).

3 In both countries there has been a debate about whether and how far they are democratic. Botswana's political process is perhaps the most open despite those who have argued that it is or was a 'paternalistic' democracy: see Holm (1989).

4 The arguments for and against the hypothesis of 'developmental dictatorship' are discussed in relation to South Korea, Chile and Ghana in Luckham 1996. However, these were special cases and many authoritarian governments have been more corrupt and patrimonial than developmental. On the case for 'developmental democracy' see Sklar (1987) and White (1998).

5 See also speeches by the Rt Hon. Clare Short MP, Secretary of State for International Development: (1) at the Security Sector Reform and Military Expenditure Symposium, 17 February 2000; and (2) on 'Developing the Security Sector Reform Agenda', at the International Institute for Strategic Studies, 4 February 2002. Both at www.dfid.gov.uk

6 The establishment of parallel civilian structures by the Liberation Tigers of Tamil Eelam (LTTE) to secure the allegiance of Sri Lanka Tamils (see Chapter 8) is an important exception, although the LTTE has also shown a very ruthless disregard for human rights.

7 Whether or not such war is 'new' is beside the point for our purposes. Already before the end of the Cold War, many of the wars fought in the developing South were internal rather than inter-state wars, were asymmetric between conventional and non-conventional forces, and involved the proliferation of military formations of many types – all said to be among the characteristics of new wars.

8 Some analysts argue that this creates a new category of 'network wars' (Duffield 2001) – though such networks have become a major factor in many other kinds of war.

II

Democratic Control and Security Sector Transformation in Transitional Democracies

2

Security Transformation in Post-Apartheid South Africa

GAVIN CAWTHRA

South Africa, although regarded as an international outcast until 1994, was not immune to the global processes that coincided and were interrelated with the end of apartheid and the transition to democracy. Apartheid was a highly evolved form of settler colonial rule with many features that, by the 1980s, had become anachronistic. South Africa's democratic transition had many unusual or unique features. Because of the conjuncture with global transformation, however, South Africa's experience may disclose features that are more widely applicable. It is from this perspective that I shall analyse security transformation in the wake of apartheid.

In retrospect, it was evident by 1987 that the end of apartheid would come through negotiation and not through revolution, although this would almost certainly be accompanied by ongoing violence and conflict. The main conditions facilitating this included the exhaustion of the apartheid state, which had run out of political options as it fought to suppress sustained mass struggle from the black population and to deal with mounting international political and economic pressure. The end of the Cold War had undermined the ideological justification for much of the apartheid regime's war effort, while the African National Congress (ANC) could no longer rely on ongoing support from the Soviet Union and its allies or on the continued use of Southern African states as bases for its military–political campaign against the apartheid state. Furthermore, the independence of Namibia had demonstrated the possibility of a peaceful transition to democracy while stripping South Africa of its last bastion against the north; and in Mozambique and Angola, too, peace beckoned.

All these factors, combined with a fortuitous leadership change, led to the announcement on 2 February 1990 by the new State President,

F. W. de Klerk, that the ANC and other liberation organisations would be unbanned, political prisoners would be freed and negotiations initiated. For both the National Party (NP) and the ANC, negotiations appeared to be the only remaining option (Lawrence 1994: 8).

This set in train the period known as the 'talks about talks' (1990–3), during which the ANC reestablished itself as an open political organisation inside the country and the ground rules for a new constitutional and electoral process were laid. Negotiation – a messy, stop-start process – was accompanied by ongoing mass struggle. The transition has often been characterised as an élite pact but this ignores the prominent role played by popular organisations, especially trade unions. The transition was also accompanied by an upsurge in political violence. This was partly stoked by 'third force' elements in the security forces intent on scuppering the negotiations, was partly a result of rolling mass action by the ANC and its allies, and was partly fomented by parties championing ethnically based vested interests, notably the Inkatha Freedom Party (IFP) and the parties of the Afrikaner right (Atkinson 1994: 14–43).

In terms of the National Peace Accord signed by the major parties to the negotiations in September 1991, various steps were taken to reform the police and to establish multi-party mechanisms for the control of political demonstrations. Military formations, however, including the South African Defence Force (SADF), were left largely untouched. By the last quarter of 1993, the ANC and the NP had reached agreement on the road to national elections. Although this was presented as an all-party deal, in reality it was up to the other parties to find their place within it, and some forces continued to resist, although the 'independent homeland' administrations rapidly collapsed. A Transitional Executive Committee (TEC) was established. Through a Joint Military Coordinating Committee (JMCC), the TEC laid the basis for the integration of the various armed forces in the country – the 'homeland' armies, the SADF and the armed wings of the liberation movements – and also supervised the national elections that were held, chaotically but peacefully, on 27 April 1994.

Although the ANC won the elections it was obliged, as a result of deals struck during the negotiations, to enter into a Government of National Unity (GNU) with the NP. The ANC adopted a conciliatory stance, promoting the national unity of a 'rainbow nation' and – especially in the first five years, under Nelson Mandela's presidency – the ruling party sought to allay the fears of whites and other minorities. The ANC, once committed to partial nationalisation, aimed systematically to redress racial inequalities and promote socio-economic development through the umbrella policy of the Reconstruction and Development Programme (RDP), but its economic policy shifted progressively to the right as it sought to position South Africa competitively in the global economy through neoliberal policies.

Given the high levels of racial and political polarisation, political violence and fragmentation in South Africa, the relatively peaceful transition to democracy and the subsequent period of stability are testament, in the first instance, to effective political leadership, in particular from the ANC. Political change has been effective, transformation of the public service has been achieved quite rapidly, and in policy terms the ANC is firmly in the driving seat. Throughout the transition period (from 1990 onwards) a decisive shift of political power away from the NP – which effectively disbanded in July 2000 – and towards the ANC has been evident. This has made it possible for the ANC to compromise without losing face or popular support. Indeed, after the 1999 elections, the ANC was in a position to discard the agreements it had made during the negotiations and rewrite the constitution had it deemed such action necessary. That it did not even consider this is evidence of how effectively it had established itself in power during the transition.

However, many features of the South African political economy remain much the same as they were under apartheid and some economic inequalities have been exacerbated by South Africa's re-inclusion into the global economy. Inequality has probably increased, although a minority of blacks have joined the economic élite; formal unemployment has risen and *per capita* gross domestic product (GDP) has declined; the economy is still dominated by 'white capital', and the vast majority of blacks continue to live in segregated townships or impoverished rural or peri-urban settlements.

Background

Security during the apartheid era

During the apartheid era, particularly in the period of P. W. Botha's leadership – as Prime Minister (1979–84) and as State President (1984–89) – the policy-making process in South Africa was significantly militarised. This occurred mainly through the mechanism of the National Security Management System, which had at its apex the State Security Council, and which provided military, intelligence and defence officers and officials (securocrats) with considerable leverage over the policy process. A militaristic 'Total Strategy' became the organising principle of state policy – essentially arguing that all activities of state and society had to be orchestrated through a counter-revolutionary security agenda aimed at preventing a communist takeover of the country. As might have been expected, the military came to dominate policy making on national security and defence during the Botha era. Without a functioning Ministry of Defence, defence policy was largely the preserve of the defence general staff and was carried out in a closed, secretive environment in which little public or political consultation took place (Cawthra 1986: 26–38; Grundy 1988: 34–57).

From 1985, while the ANC and its allies were engaged in making South Africa 'ungovernable' through mass protest action and attacks on administration in black areas, the apartheid regime ruled largely through successive states of emergency. Several thousand people were killed and tens of thousands detained without trial. Many of the administrative structures in black areas were destroyed, the schooling system was severely disrupted and communities became politically polarised and fractured. In parts of the country virtual civil war ensued. Sections of the police and the SADF – notably the so-called Civil Cooperation Bureau (CCB) – operated outside of the rule of law and engaged in various actions including assassinations, poisoning and chemical and biological warfare. The military was extensively deployed in internal security operations, and was involved in warfare outside the country's borders. In other Southern African countries, too, civil conflict and struggles against South African hegemony had profoundly destabilising effects (Cawthra 1986).

At the end of the 1980s, and for the reasons explored above, the apartheid regime changed tack and the Total Strategy framework was largely discarded, resulting in a reduction in the political influence of the military, although it remained a powerful institutional force within the state. The more politicised sections of the defence force, such as the CCB, continued to play a (freelance) destabilising role, fuelling counter-revolutionary violence.

Countering violence during the transition

Predictions of a so-called Yugoslavian scenario unfolding in South Africa, as apartheid collapsed, proved unfounded. The reasons for this included:

- The approach of the ANC, which adopted a strongly inclusivist approach to nationalism – that of the 'rainbow nation' – and managed to build a strong coalition.
- A supportive international environment. At crucial moments pressure

on the protagonists from various international sources was decisive in making peace.

- A strong civil society.
- Relatively strong, intact central state institutions, including a (mostly) disciplined military that obeyed orders.

Nevertheless, ethno-national tensions during the transition remained high. Armed groups mobilising on ethnic grounds at times threatened to plunge the country into uncontrolled violence. Various parties promoting right-wing white Afrikaner interests mobilised and armed tens of thousands of men and women, though they proved not to have the stomach for a fight. Key groups on the right were keener to maintain their economic self-interests than their national identity. Unity proved elusive, the psychology of white domination proved fragile in the face of a few deaths, and – perhaps above all – the ANC and the NP comprehensively outmanoeuvred the extreme right wing.

Ethno-nationalism in the bantustans was always weak. In most cases, the majority of the people in these areas opposed the concept of fragmentation as a divide-and-rule strategy by the apartheid state, and the bantustan regimes rapidly collapsed. A far greater threat was posed by the IFP, which mobilised and armed thousands of people against the ANC. Again, however, there were powerful political forces countering ethnic politics and, at the last moment, the IFP was persuaded to contest the national elections peacefully, although not before some 15,000 people had lost their lives in local-level ANC–IFP power struggles (Cawthra 1986: 66–83).

One of the key elements in the effective staunching of violence during the transition was the political hegemony of the ANC. It occupied the moral high ground as a result of its opposition to apartheid; it enjoyed international support from a wide range of countries that was unprecedented for a liberation movement; and it was led by the hugely popular Nelson Mandela. The ANC was able to bring to the negotiations (although not without tension) a mass democratic movement in the form of an alliance of churches, civil society groups, trade unions, community organisations and non-governmental organisations (NGOs). Such was the ANC's credibility that it was able to rally this diverse range of groups into a non-violent resistance front after formally suspending its armed struggle in August 1990.

Another key element in the relatively peaceful transition was the existence of hundreds of organisations dedicated to resolving conflict, making peace and monitoring violence. These played a critical role in bringing together former adversaries to agree on the ground rules, to monitor the activities of the security forces and political parties, and to address the causes and symptoms of conflicts.

Policing the transition

Issues of policing and political violence were a major focus of the negotiations, since this directly affected the ability of political parties to mobilise their supporters. After the first formal talks between the ANC and the apartheid government in May 1990, the government undertook to review security legislation, to work towards lifting the state of emergency, to release political prisoners, to allow the return of exiles, and to set up channels of communication with the ANC in order to curb political violence.

Relations between the South African Police (SAP) and the ANC remained tense, however, especially as violent conflict between the ANC and the IFP escalated, mostly in Natal and in the greater Johannesburg area. Some of the IFP-initiated violence was fanned by the police or sections of the SADF, and the ANC made repeated demands for government to rein in the security forces. The National Peace Accord, as mentioned above, established transitional structures for investigating police misconduct, drew up a code of conduct for the police, set up systems for monitoring political violence and established local dispute resolution structures and channels of communication between the police and communities. This was the beginning of community policing, where communities themselves were drawn into policing activities and given a monitoring role over the SAP. As a result, steps were taken to demilitarise the police and to adopt less forceful approaches to dealing with public demonstrations (Rauch 1993).

The military in transition

Both the South African government and the ANC kept their respective armed forces out of the negotiation process for a variety of reasons. The first was a deliberate strategy pursued by both parties to use their security forces as a 'security fallback' in the event of the negotiation process collapsing. The second was the initially firm resistance – from both the armed forces and the white public – to any suggestion that the liberation movements' armed forces would eventually be integrated into a national defence force.

Initial contacts between the commanders of the SADF and Mkhonto we Sizwe (MK, the 'Spear of the Nation') were made during the political negotiations, however, when the commanders often represented their political heads in a non-military capacity. Informal ('track two') discussions were also initiated.

The main features of the emerging policy framework promoted by the ANC were:

- The establishment of joint operational control over the security forces (the police, the military and intelligence) through the TEC and the development of a neutral multi-party paramilitary force to police the transition – the National Peacekeeping Force (NPKF).
- The integration of the armed forces or military formations of the parties participating in the negotiated settlement and the establishment of a new South African National Defence Force (SANDF).
- The demilitarisation of government by dismantling the National Security Management System, by strengthening parliamentary supervision, by establishing a civilian defence secretariat and by reorganising the Department of Defence (DoD).
- The reallocation of resources from defence to human security and development objectives, which entailed disarmament and reassessing procurement requirements.
- The reorientation of defence policy towards a defensive doctrine, collaborative security in Southern Africa, external rather than internal operational orientation, and cooperation with the international collective security system and in terms of international humanitarian law.

In 1992 a series of off-the-record meetings were held between SADF and MK commanders, with the agreement of their respective political principals, in an attempt to initiate a discreet dialogue. In April 1993, SADF and MK commanders met in Simonstown and issues relating to the force levels, equipment and training of their respective forces were discussed. This meeting laid the basis for the subsequent collaboration that was to emerge in the JMCC (Shaw 1994b: 228–56).

After its establishment, the TEC instructed that the JMCC be established, consisting of commanders of all the armed forces of the political parties participating in the negotiations. This included the SADF, MK and the forces of the TBVC 'homelands' (Transkei–Bophutatswana–Venda–Ciskei). The Azanian People's Liberation Army (APLA), the armed wing of the Pan-Africanist Congress (PAC), was excluded as the PAC was not formally represented in the TEC and was not participating in the negotiations.

Certified personnel registers were established which listed the SADF strength as 90,000 civilian and military members; MK 28,000 members; APLA 6,000 members; and the TVBC homeland forces approximately 11,000 members. Not all of the 135,000 registered members reported for attestation in the SANDF and, at its height, it numbered no more than 101,000 (JMCC 1994 a/b). The plans produced by the JMCC were eventually approved by the TEC and became the basis on which the restructuring of the integrated SANDF was to proceed.

Establishing democratic control over security

Acutely aware of the anti-democratic role played by the SADF, and the relative lack of civil supervision of the security organisations during the apartheid period, the incoming ANC-led government went to considerable lengths to ensure not only that civilians had a security policy role, but also that control and supervision was strongly vested in democratic structures.

The constitution

Key to the transformation process in South Africa was agreement on a new constitutional framework. An interim constitution was drawn up during the negotiation process. This formed the basis for the elections and the establishment of the GNU, and also provided for the establishment of a constitutional assembly to agree a post-apartheid constitution, which was finalised by October 1996.

The interim constitution paid careful attention to issues of democratic control of the security forces, as well as their roles and functions. These provisions were reiterated in the final document. Key aspects included specifying the role of the President as Commander-in-Chief of the armed forces, clarification of the respective roles of the military and the police, and the entrenchment of civilian secretariats for both the military and the police. The constitution also specifies that 'national security must be pursued in compliance with the law, including international law', and that 'no member of the security forces may obey a manifestly illegal order' (sections 198 (c) and 199 (6) of the constitution).

The role of Parliament

As well as providing for civilian secretariats, the constitution specifies that 'to give effect to the principles of transparency and accountability, multi-party parliamentary committees must have oversight of all security services' (section 199 (8) of the constitution). The interim constitution specified the nature of these committees in some detail, in particular establishing the Joint Standing Committee on Defence (JSCD) – a multi-party joint committee of the two houses of Parliament constituted from the largest parties within Parliament. Its responsibilities were to ensure supervision of the activities of the Department of Defence (DoD), including its budget, and to make policy recommendations on defence management.

The JSCD has continued to exist, along with the Portfolio Committee on Defence in the National Assembly and the Select Committee on Safety and Security in the National Council of Provinces. These two committees are mostly concerned with legislation. A Joint Standing Committee on Intelligence was also established to oversee the intelligence agencies and their expenditure, to deal with intelligence legislation and to make policy recommendations. Unlike the other committees, this committee meets in secret (Cawthra 1996: 60–5).

The parliamentary committees, especially the JSCD, were very active in the first years of the new Parliament, notably in drawing up the White Paper on Defence (see below). While their level of activity diminished somewhat after 1996 – perhaps a reflection of a shift in the policy locus towards the executive and the civil service – they nevertheless continued to actively oversee the security services. The work of the committees has been marked by a high level of multi-party cooperation and by extensive public consultations. Public hearings have been held on a wide range of policy issues and have canvassed the views of academics, NGOs and the ordinary public (Mapisa-Nqakula 2000; Ngculu 2000).

The Defence Secretariat

The establishment of the Ministry of Defence Workgroup as part of the JMCC process in February 1994 and the subsequent appointment of a new Minister of Defence in May 1994 saw detailed plans being devised for the transfer of certain key functions from the SANDF to the newly established Defence Secretariat. The first Secretary for Defence was appointed in August 1994.

After much deliberation, a model known as the balanced model was chosen as appropriate for South Africa's defence needs. The balanced model was essentially a creature of political compromise that saw both the Secretary for Defence and the Chief of the SANDF remaining at the same level with specific roles and responsibilities (although later the Secretary was made the accounting officer for the Department). The Minister of Defence, the political head of the DoD, is responsible for political supervision of the Department, communicating its needs to the political authorities, and approving defence policy, budgets and programmes.

The Secretary for Defence is responsible for the formulation of defence policy, acting as the chief accounting officer to Parliament, managing the acquisition process and liaising with the legislature. The Chief of the SANDF commands the defence force; translates defence policy into military strategies, plans, budgets and programmes; and directs the activities of the defence staff.

While this division of labour was clear in theory, in practice it proved difficult to implement. For a start, civilians had been excluded from most aspects of the defence policy process since the mid-1960s, and civilian expertise was lacking. There was also concern as to whether military officers, particularly those from the old SADF, would accept civilian supervision. Within a few years, despite the provisions of the constitution, the concepts of a civilian secretariat and of civilian control had been modified. Although the Secretariat continued to exist in theory, in practice an integrated civilian–military head office had become functional.

Operating along similar lines to the British Ministry of Defence, the South African Defence Headquarters now consists of some 18 functional divisions. Some of these fall primarily under the Secretary (notably policy, planning, finance, liaison and communication); some under the Chief of the SANDF (notably the employment of forces and the command of the arms of service) and some are the responsibility of both (including training, defence intelligence, command and management systems and logistics). Civilians and military officers work side by side in these various divisions.

The Secretariat for Safety and Security

As with the military, the ANC was eager to establish civilian supervision of the police, and a decision was taken to establish a secretariat to achieve this. The Police Service Act of 1995, which established the Secretariat for Safety and Security, defined its functions as advising the Minister for Safety and Security and promoting democratic accountability and transparency in the police service, monitoring the implementation of policy, conducting research and providing legal services, advice, communication and other support to the Minister. It was later also charged with coordinating the National Crime Prevention Strategy (NCPS).

It took some time for the Secretariat to get up to speed with regard to its policy and advisory functions, and its success in monitoring the South African Police Service (SAPS) for its adherence to policy and for promoting accountability and transparency has been limited. Tensions between the uniformed service and the Secretariat became obvious, and while the Secretariat generated considerable policy outputs, implementation remained a problem. The division between policy and operations was never entirely clear. Many police officers resisted the Secretariat, regarding its role as political interference. To deal with these problems, collaborative arrangements were made within the department between the SAPS, the Minister and the Secretariat. However, these served to further weaken the Secretariat which was subsequently downgraded (Pelser 1997).

Civil society

While civil society had been able to contribute little to defence and security debates during the apartheid era, research-oriented groups became important players in policy debates during the 1990s. These NGOs continued to play a vital role during the development of the White Paper on Defence. While they were less involved in the Defence Review, the highly consultative nature of this process brought into play a wider range of NGOs, many of whom had no specific interest in security issues but who were nevertheless consulted by the DoD as representatives of civil society. Furthermore, a few research-oriented NGOs – notably the Institute for Security Studies (ISS) – were by then generating important policy-directed research.

Institutional transformation

Defence

The integration of the various armed formations active in South Africa during the negotiation period – the homeland armies of the TBVC, the SADF, MK, APLA, and later elements of the IFP's self-protection units – resulted from decisions taken in the JMCC. The existing infrastructure of the SADF was used for this process. While there may have been little alternative, this decision ensured that SADF doctrine, personnel procedures, training, structures and equipment formed the basis of the new SANDF. Many would argue that absorption, not integration, best characterised the process. This was compounded by the fact that far fewer MK and APLA personnel participated in the integration exercise than had been expected, while many of them left after a short period. By 1998, of the uniformed component of the SANDF (then totalling 73,500 personnel), only 16 per cent were formerly from MK and less than 7 per cent from APLA (Department of Defence 1998: 70).

The integration process required former non-statutory force (MK and APLA) personnel to report to SANDF military bases where they were accredited if their names appeared on the certified personnel register provided by the liberation movement, and they were assessed for rank. This process was fraught with difficulty, given that the guerrilla armies did not operate on a rank structure. However, integration at officer level proceeded fairly smoothly, and the presence of a neutral adjudicator in the form of the British Military Assistance Training Team was of some assistance.

Significant problems occurred in some assembly areas, partly caused by inadequate administration and facilities. By the end of 1994, a number of protests, walk-outs and near-mutinies by groups up to 6,000 strong had taken place. However, the demonstrations stopped short of violence and by 1996 the integration process was firmly back on track, and in due course was completed (Taole 1997; Motumi 2000). Problems also occurred in relation to individuals who could not be integrated through age or infirmity, but these individuals were eventually given cash hand-outs. Cash hand-outs were also given to former SADF personnel, many of whom took generous severance packages.

As a result of these measures and natural attrition, the size of the SANDF was reduced by about 20,000 between 1996 and 2000 (Motumi 2000). The SANDF is still deemed to be too large, however, and a rationalisation process has been agreed to reduce the personnel complement to between 65,000 and 70,000. The reduction is a result of recommendations in the Defence Review requiring expenditure to be reallocated to capital and operating costs rather than personnel costs. How this will be managed is unclear, and it is likely to lead to tensions within the force. It is also politically sensitive, as it will increase unemployment. There has been a noticeable reluctance by any of the key role players to lead the process.

Even without the threat of rationalisation, it is evident that integration has been only partially successful and that tensions exist between former non-statutory force members and former members of the SADF in particular. Often these are expressed in racial terms. Simmering discontent is manifested in a number of ways, most obviously by at least two shootings of white former SADF officers by disgruntled black former MK members. The growth of trade unionism in the military is another manifestation of dissatisfaction. Initially this was illegal, but it continued anyway. In 1999, the Constitutional Court overturned military regulations prohibiting unions (but stopped short of granting military personnel the right to strike). Discipline and professionalism within the SANDF is questionable, and this has been exacerbated by the departure of many experienced officers, leading to questions about its operational effectiveness (*Business Day*, 20 July 2000).

Efforts to deal with racial, cultural and political divisions within the SANDF have included an equal opportunity and affirmative action process and the establishment of a Civic Education Task Group. The latter was tasked with developing training curricula on the constitution, democratic civil–military relations, international humanitarian law, civil rights and cultural and gender sensitisation throughout the DoD, at all levels from private to general, along the lines of the German *innere fuhring* (internal leadership) programme. Principles of leadership, command and management were also re-examined and management and doctrinal practices introduced which are intended to be consistent with the practice of defence in a democracy. It is unclear what effect these measures have had. It is a truism that it is easier to change policies and structures than values and practices. Transformation in the SANDF is an ongoing concern that has caused many institutional stresses, and is still incomplete.

Safety and security

Integration challenges with regard to safety and security were somewhat different to those for defence, as there were virtually no liberation movement personnel to be integrated. Nevertheless, eleven separate agencies had to be merged (the SAP, the police forces of the TBVC 'independent states' and the six 'self-governing homelands' or 'bantustans', including KwaZulu). While many of these forces were offshoots of the SAP, they nevertheless brought with them different organisational cultures and histories, and varied levels of training, expertise and resources.

To accommodate this merger, a new organisational structure had to be created and a unified command established. New structures had to be set up at provincial level as eight new provinces were carved out of the previous four provinces and the various bantustans and 'independent states'. To complicate matters further, some 80 district commands were abolished in favour of 43 new area offices. Reforms relating to public order policing, and ongoing efforts to centralise command of this function to prevent abuses, resulted in the establishment of a specialised Public Order Police Service under national command in 1996. Further restructuring took place in November 1999, with the creation of five new national divisions. That this difficult restructuring task was accomplished without an overall breakdown in service is a considerable achievement, although there were understandable disruptions and confusion relating to command structures and political authority (Department of Safety and Security 1998: 20–1).

Integration of the former bantustan forces improved the demographic representation of the SAPS. By the end of 1999, about 70 per cent of the approximately 125,000 strong force was black, although less than 30 per cent were female. However, half of the middle managers in the service were white and white men constituted 70 per cent of senior management. Racial and political tensions have been evident in the service, as in the defence force, with many white employees feeling threatened and many blacks frustrated at the pace of change. Labour relations have been very strained, with three unions, each with different political backgrounds, vying with each other and with management and the government: the South African Police Union, the militant Police and Prisons Civil Rights Union (POPCRU) and the Public Service Staff Association (which organises across the public service).

By the end of 1999, the initial preoccupation with securing political control and ensuring accountability and legitimacy had given way to institutional reforms aimed at combating crime. Some of these reforms involved the Department of Justice, in recognition of the need to align policing work more closely with the criminal justice process. A National Director of Public Prosecutions was appointed, a three-year plan was drawn up to review station-level policing, the detective service was streamlined and an FBI-type crime-fighting agency known as the Scorpions was established. This showed a new determination by government to tackle crime but, as will be discussed below, it could be taken as an indication of 'securitisation'.

Constructing new policy frameworks[1]

The White Paper on Defence, 1994–6

The inauguration of South Africa's GNU on 15 May 1994 radically changed the policy environment. A flurry of white papers resulted as the new ministers moved, with varying degrees of urgency, to establish policy frameworks and justify their departmental budgetary demands. The latter was an important factor in the decision by the Minister of Defence, Joe Modise, to initiate the White Paper on Defence.

The drafters of the White Paper worked closely with the JSCD and the first draft was published for public comment on 21 June 1995. A second draft (which incorporated public submissions) then went to the JSCD, which scrutinised it paragraph by paragraph with the aim of achieving multi-party support for the document. A final version was presented to Cabinet on 8 May 1996, and was subsequently approved by Parliament with multi-party support (Minister of Defence 1996: 1).

The White Paper represented a remarkable compromise, essentially between those promoting demilitarisation and disarmament, on one side, and the institutional interests that naturally supported a strong defence force – the SANDF and the defence industry – on the other. The White Paper took as its point of departure the 'widened' agenda of the 'new' security studies, and the 'human security' concept of the United Nations Development Programme (UNDP):

> In the new South Africa national security is no longer viewed as a predominantly military and police problem. It has been broadened to incorporate political, economic, social and environmental matters. At the heart of this new approach is a paramount concern with the security of people.
>
> Security is an all-encompassing condition in which the individual citizens live in freedom, peace and safety; participate fully in the process of governance; enjoy the protection of fundamental rights; have access to resources and the basic necessities of life; and inhabit an environment which is not detrimental to their health and well-being. (Minister of Defence 1996: 5–6).

However, while the White Paper adopted a broad definition of security, it reverted to the classical realist formula when it came to defining the primary role of the Defence Force:

> The SANDF may be employed in a range of secondary roles as prescribed by law, but its primary and essential function is service in defence of South Africa, for the protection of its sovereignty and territorial integrity. (Minister of Defence 1996: 6)

This formulation was motivated by a desire to delimit as narrowly as possible the role of the military. The solution adopted by the White Paper to this conceptual conundrum was unsatisfactory and led to inherently contradictory policies. On one hand, the White Paper talked of 'a compelling need to reallocate state resources to the RDP ... [and to] rationalise the SANDF and contain military spending', while on the other it called for a defence force which was balanced, modern and technologically advanced in order to carry out its primary task of conventional defence (Minister of Defence 1996: 6). The White Paper dealt extensively with the principles of civil–military relations and the organisational architecture of defence management, but it was incomplete as a policy document. It was strongly normative in content and in some places open to various interpretations. It avoided dealing with some key issues such as force design. It was therefore necessary for the DoD to institute another phase in the policy process.

The Defence Review

The Defence Review was a remarkably transparent and consultative process and the Defence Secretariat, which drove the process, went to considerable lengths to ensure public participation. One reason for this was undoubtedly the fact that some of the key activist intellectuals who had taken part in the first two policy processes remained actively involved in the third phase, and some of them had by this stage moved into strategic positions in the Department of Defence.

The Defence Review working groups maintained close links with the JSCD but by this stage some key members of the Committee had left Parliament and it took a less detailed interest in this process than it had in the White Paper. In part this was the result of increasing work pressure; but another reason was that the Executive was becoming a more important locus of policy making than the various parliamentary committees.

In some working groups (notably that on human resources), NGOs were strongly represented and argued their case vigorously, sometimes with better information and analytic skills at their disposal than the government officials or military officers present. There is certainly a case to be made that this had a direct influence on the policy outcome (Department of Defence 1998: Chapter 10). Nevertheless, many anti-militarist groups became disillusioned. Despite their minor victories, they felt that the Review had been presented in a triumphalist way by the DoD as a national consensus on the value of defence, and that they were in danger of being co-opted.

In other working groups, NGOs were largely absent, and in the more technical groups SANDF officers and defence officials clearly had the advantage of information. This is particularly true of the working group dealing with force design. The SANDF had developed a sophisticated computer modelling programme, Project Optimum, to assist in force design, and this formed the basis for the four options which were presented to the JSCD and then to Parliament and the Minister for a decision.

The Review sets out frameworks for implementing the policies of the White Paper, as well as identifying budgetary, human resource and equipment targets and requirements. It reiterates South Africa's commitment to building a common security regime in Southern Africa, based on confidence- and security-building measures including multilateral treaties on disarmament. It also commits the SANDF to regional and international peace support operations of various types, including peace making, peace building, peacekeeping, humanitarian relief operations and peace enforcement operations (Department of Defence 1998: Chapter 4).

The Review also spells out the conditions under which the SANDF will carry out secondary tasks, including support to the police and essential services and various maritime tasks. It argues that such operations may be 'economically inefficient and politically unwise' but are nevertheless necessary in 'extreme situations' (Department of Defence 1998: Chapter 7).

The organisation and structure of the DoD is also set out and detailed attention is given to the transformation of the DoD to make it more representative. At present around 30 per cent of the Department is white, and whites predominate overwhelmingly at senior officer level (Department of Defence 1998: Chapters 10 and 11).

Foreign policy frameworks

Defence policy is classically regarded as a subset of foreign policy. South African foreign policy has been outlined mainly through presidential speeches, national visions (notably that presented by President Thabo Mbeki in his New Partnership for Africa's Development), and foreign policy guidelines that have emerged in concept documents of the Department of Foreign Affairs (DFA). These have been used as broad indicators of South Africa's intentions within the sub-region, the continent and the international arena.

The key principles of South Africa's foreign policy are officially summarised in commitments to promote human rights and democracy, to uphold the principles of justice and international law in the conduct of relations between nations, to support international peace and internationally agreed-upon mechanisms for conflict resolution, to promote the interests of Africa in world affairs, and to pursue economic development through international cooperation (Department of Foreign Affairs 1999: 22.)

While these principles arise from South Africa's constitutional and political evolution, they are very idealistic and hardly provide a guide to action in the world of *realpolitik*. Indeed, it is difficult to see how these commitments are manifested in key foreign policy decisions where, unsurprisingly, South Africa's trade and political interests appear to be the key factors in decision making.

An important dimension of foreign policy is South Africa's expected role in international peacekeeping operations, especially in Africa. This was identified as a 'secondary function' for the SANDF in the White Paper, and political responsibility was apportioned to the DFA. South Africa adopted an extremely cautious approach, however, and it was only in 2000 that it committed itself to significant participation in UN peacekeeping operations in the Democratic Republic of Congo (DRC) and later in Burundi.

Policy frameworks for safety and security

As was the case with defence, much of the policy introduced by the new government in 1994 in relation to safety and security was a result of policy work by activist academics, in this case a small group clustered in the Policing Policy Group that drew up the principles contained in the ANC's election manifesto.

The ANC was even less prepared to deal with the police than with the military, however. In part this was because while it had a large body of military practitioners in MK, many of whom had been trained in various parts of the world at officer level, it had no comparable expertise when it came to the police. Some analysts have also argued that because of its emphasis on the armed struggle, the ANC overestimated the importance of military issues (Shaw 1994a).

As with defence, the main aim of the ANC's initial policy thrusts was to tame the police, to ensure that they were placed under democratic supervision and control and would not become a 'wild card' during the transition. Other agendas included demilitarisation, transformation to ensure a more representative force, and improvements in organisational effectiveness. Many of these agendas were encapsulated in the concept of community policing, an effort to build relations with communities that previously had been antagonistic towards the police. These changes were symbolised by the change of name from a police force to a police service.

In September 1998, the long-awaited White Paper on Safety and Security was published. Drafted by the Secretariat and ministerial advisers, it followed an extensive consultation process similar to that of the Defence Review. Five committees with wide representation worked on drafts for over a year. Provincial public hearings and a national hearing in Parliament were organised, and consultation was carried out with local government, political parties and government departments involved in the NCPS (Department of Safety and Security 1998: 4–5). The White Paper focused on four issues: law enforcement, social crime prevention, institutional reform at national level, and policing at provincial and local level.

The White Paper tacitly acknowledged the criticism often levelled at policing policy: that the concern with establishing democratic control and civilian supervision had led to a neglect of the social policies and institutional changes needed to tackle crime. While it did not abandon community policing, it sought to move beyond that concept, arguing that criminal investigation, victim support and visible policing needed to be radically improved. At the same time, crime prevention strategies would focus on social, political and developmental aspects that would be integrated at all three levels of government. Accepting that the need for political supervision and monitoring was diminishing, the White Paper argued that the focus of accountability should be on ensuring effective service delivery (Department of Safety and Security 1998: 13–27).

Assessment

This section assesses the implementation of the policy frameworks and the efficacy of institutional reform in relation to security governance. There are many dimensions to this issue, and what follows is, of necessity, quite schematic.

Controlling political violence

On the political level, the ANC government has moved effectively to stabilise and entrench democratic processes, and has largely succeeded in eliminating the political violence that characterised the last years of apartheid. It has succeeded in creating conditions that have ensured that all but a few political factions are participants in the democratic process and seek their objectives through non-violent strategies. The South African state functions fairly effectively, in many cases far better than under the apartheid regime. Transformation of the public service has been achieved without a breakdown in services, fiscal discipline has been imposed, policy making is effective (although implementation often remains a problem), budgets are fairly efficiently managed and a wide range of measures have been introduced to make the state more transparent and responsive.

Political violence has not been entirely eliminated, however. Criminals or extremists continue to wage a violent campaign in the Western Cape, and in Kwazulu–Natal pockets of political warlordism persist. The politics of identity are still dominant in South Africa, although they are often disguised in various ways, but the ANC has – at least for the time being – successfully prevented this from degenerating into serious widespread conflict. It has done this by pursuing a broad, inclusivist nationalism, by making real and symbolic concessions to minorities while introducing affirmative action and other measures to ensure the advancement of the previously disadvantaged black majority. By combining radical rhetoric with conservative neoliberal economic policies, it has managed to keep both militant trade unions and business interests reasonably satisfied.

All South Africans have a new democratic freedom and a new dignity. Some would question whether this means very much without concomitant improvements in the standard of living and in human security, but the South African struggle has been as much about dignity and freedom as it has been about social and economic rights.

Combating crime

Crime remains one of the greatest threats to individual security and to the security of communities, and it also challenges state security, although criminal mafias have not fatally penetrated the South African state. The causes of crime in South Africa are not easily addressed, however, because they are wide-ranging. According to the NCPS documents, these include the delegitimisation of the legal system and the social order as a result of apartheid; inequalities; backlogs in housing and education; unemployment; poor social planning; the break-up of families through the migrant labour system; the ready availability of firearms; the sudden opening up of South Africa to the world, allowing for the penetration of international crime syndicates; and even the lack of public transport (which leads to taxi violence). Many more factors could be added to this list (Departments of Correctional Services, Defence, Intelligence, Justice, Safety and Security and Welfare, 1996).

Crime levels are amongst the highest in the world, and certain types of reported crime have increased since 1994, notably rape, but it is quite likely that some of these increases are attributable to an improved reporting climate and greater public awareness. Murder rates have declined since 1994, although this in large part reflects the decline in political violence. Conviction rates are low and have remained stable (Africa Monitor: Southern Africa, September 2000: 5) It was expected that crime would increase during the transition, as authoritarian methods proved inappropriate in a democratic environment and new instruments took time to develop (Department of Safety and Security 1998: 9).

None of these arguments assuage the fear and anger of citizens of course. They have responded by resorting to vigilantism, which has a long tradition in South Africa, to scapegoating and sometimes attacking foreigners, and – for those who can afford it – to contracting private security. The commercial security industry has many more employees than the Department of Safety and Security. There are increasing signs of authoritarian, even militaristic, approaches to crime, not only from citizens but also from the private sector and the state. This may be understandable, but in the long term it could erode the gains made in establishing a culture of human rights and respect for the rule of law.

Building human security

If human security can be measured by the UNDP's Human Development Index (HDI), then there has been no progress in South Africa since the onset of democracy. HDI, as measured by the UNDP, declined slightly over this period and South Africa also slipped in relative ranking. In part this decline is due to the spread of HIV–AIDS. Estimates of infection rates vary widely, usually between 12 and 20 per cent, and this is likely to have a devastating effect on all aspects of human security, as well as on economic growth.

On some fronts progress has been made, notably in the delivery of housing, electricity and water and in the provision of healthcare facilities. Economic growth has been disappointing, however. In 1996, the government adopted the Growth, Employment and Redistribution (GEAR) framework which, through essentially neoliberal means, aimed to reshape the process of socio-economic reconstruction and development, as set out in the RDP. GEAR aimed at 6 per cent annual growth by 2000. Instead, largely as a result of global instability, growth rates have been marginal. GEAR aimed to create 400,000 jobs by 2000 – instead, roughly the same number were shed from the formal sector. Unemployment, according to some calculations, stands at 37.6 per cent (South African National NGO Coalition (SANGOCO) 2000). As a result, many South Africans – especially trade unionists – are questioning whether adherence to a neoliberal policy framework can deliver on human security, but there is little agreement on alternatives.

An obvious policy implication of prioritising human security over state security would be a reallocation of resources away from narrow security institutions such as the police and the military towards socio-economic development. As mentioned earlier, defence expenditure in real terms has been cut by around 60 per cent since 1990. However, the peace dividend has been somewhat compromised by increases in the safety and security budget (mainly in the early 1990s). When this is taken into account, the peace dividend is in the region of 20 per cent.

While military expenditure as a proportion of GDP is now less than 1.5 per cent, the downward trend appears to be being reversed, mostly as a result of a 1998 Cabinet decision to purchase major weapons systems, valued at approximately US$5 billion, including naval corvettes and submarines, helicopters and fighter aircraft. This procurement was rationalised on the basis of expected inward investment in the form of both military and non-military offsets attached to the deal, although it is by no means certain that this will happen as planned (Batchelor and Dunne 2000).

Building regional security

South Africa has had great difficulty building a foreign policy around a commitment to human rights and democracy, and there are growing signs that it is adopting a far more pragmatic approach. It has also largely failed to institutionalise these commitments in Southern Africa. It has proved difficult to construct a common security regime through the Southern African Development Community (SADC). Initially, government was very cautious about asserting a leadership role, given South Africa's history of aggression and hegemonic ambitions in the region. When it did so, in a military intervention to prevent a coup in Lesotho on 22 September 1998, the operation was initially disastrous, and was largely outside the framework of SADC (Winkates 2000: 459).

Although arrangements were made in 1996 for a SADC Organ on Politics, Defence and Security, this has still not been implemented, with disagreements amongst member states about its relationship to the SADC Summit delaying implementation. In the meantime, member states have continued to act in their own interests, using SADC as little more than a smokescreen. The crisis in the DRC has demonstrated both the fragility and the impotence of SADC's security functions: three SADC member states (Angola, Namibia and Zimbabwe) intervened militarily, and South Africa's call for a political solution initially appeared hopeless.

While some progress has been made in moving towards economic integration within SADC, it is clear that on a political and security level little has been achieved, except on the military-to-military level where technical cooperation through the Interstate Defence and Security Committee has been effective.

Conclusions

At the beginning of the 1990s, the prospects for the violent dissolution or dismemberment of South Africa appeared strong. Many pundits were predicting a decline into ethnic civil war, military praetorianism, secession or even state collapse. That these now seem remote is a tribute to the political will and skill of the leading parties, especially the ANC.

Security transformation in South Africa stands out in three ways: first, for the conscious incorporation of the new, widened security discourse and the concept of human security; second, for the consultative and transparent way in which policy reviews and organisational transformation were conducted; and third, for the close attention to civil control and supervision.

The consultative and transparent approach has certainly paid dividends for the military and for the health of civil–military relations. It is indeed a remarkable achievement that virtually all South African political parties, and the vast majority of civil society organisations, have endorsed the White Paper on Defence and the Defence Review. The DoD, once seen as a bastion of apartheid and militarism, has undoubtedly managed to legitimise itself, although it has done so by playing a much smaller role in the state ensemble, being given a much smaller share of the budget, and giving up much of its land and other resources.

The attention to civil–military relations, both in principle and in practice, has also been beneficial. It is today unthinkable that the military would play the praetorian roles of the past. Parliamentary supervision is effective and the integrated civilian–military defence headquarters functions reasonably well, even if it still suffers from a lack of appropriate civilian expertise.

South Africans in government, in NGOs and in the academic field, have striven to find appropriate policy and organisational responses to a new approach to security. Major challenges in this regard remain. Despite the commitment to redirect resources to human security, militaristic approaches are often taken in response to political and social crises provoked by human security deficits, both in South Africa and regionally.

Considerable resources have also been devoted to a conventional military rearmament drive. It is questionable whether the core assumptions that underpin this are appropriate. The insistence that the SANDF be primarily orientated towards external defence and conventional warfare, for fear of remilitarising society, has meant that it has not been configured, trained or equipped for what it actually does – rendering assistance to the police, border protection and peacekeeping.

Domestically there is a growing 'securitisation' of public policy discourse around crime and the policy and institutional frameworks for policing have been found wanting. In its sub-region South Africa has largely failed to secure the collaborative and common security it desires, as witnessed by continuing wars and gross human rights violations, especially in the DRC and Zimbabwe. South Africa has been unable to export its democratic governance, its conflict resolution models and its core democratic values, and the ground rules for the behaviour of states in the region have not been institutionalised.

Despite these continuing challenges, however, the South African experiment with security sector transformation has been successful in institutional and policy terms given the dire scenarios predicted. In many ways, particularly in regard to policy processes and establishing democratic controls, South Africa's approach to security management in its transition to democracy has been innovative and effective – all the more so for being largely self-directed and having anticipated the international debate on security sector reform.

Chronology

1948	National Party comes to power and begins to implement its apartheid policy.
1960–61	African National Congress and Pan-Africanist Congress banned and launch armed struggles.
1975–88	South African war in Namibia and Angola and destabilisation of other Southern African states.
1976	National uprisings centred on Soweto countered by police repression.
1984	Nationwide uprisings lead to a State of Emergency.
1986–89	Successive States of Emergency lead to greater military involvement in policing and emergency governance.
1989	President P.W. Botha replaced by F.W. de Klerk; independence of Namibia.
1990	Liberation movements unbanned; process of negotiations begins.
1994	First national democratic elections bring ANC to power with Nelson Mandela as President.
1996	White Paper on Defence establishes policy framework for defence transformation, followed by Defence Review.
1999	ANC wins second post-apartheid elections with Thabo Mbeki as President.

References

Atkinson, D. (1994) 'Brokering a Miracle? The Multiparty Negotiating Forum', in Friedman, S. and D Atkinson, *South African Review 7: The Small Miracle*, Johannesburg: Ravan.

Batchelor P. and P Dunne (2000) 'Industrial Participation, Investment and Growth: The Case of South Africa's Defence Related Industry', Cape Town: Centre for Conflict Resolution, unpublished paper.

Cawthra, G. (1986) *Brutal Force: The Apartheid War Machine*, London: International Defence and Aid Fund.

—— (1996) *Securing South Africa's Democracy: Defence, Development and Security in Transition*, Basingstoke, Hampshire: Macmillan.

—— (1998) 'From "total strategy" to "human security": the making of South Africa's defence policy 1990–98', in Copenhagen Peace Research Institute, *Working Papers*, April.

Department of Defence (1998) *South African Defence Review*, Pretoria: Department of Defence.

Department of Foreign Affairs (DFA) (1999) *White Paper on South African Participation in International Peace Missions*, Pretoria: DFA.

Department of Safety and Security (1998) *White Paper on Safety and Security: In Service of Safety 1999–2004*, Pretoria: Department of Safety and Security.

Departments of Correctional Services, Defence, Intelligence, Justice, Safety and Security and Welfare (1996) *National Crime Prevention Strategy*, Pretoria: Government Printer.

Grundy, K. W. (1988) *The Militarization of South African Politics*, Oxford: Oxford University Press.

Joint Military Co-ordinating Committee (JMCC) (1994a) 'Post Election Control and Ministry of Defence Structure', Pretoria: JMCC, Transitional Executive Council (TEC).

—— (1994b) 'Strategic Planning: Situation Analysis', Pretoria: JMCC, TEC.

Lawrence, P. (1994) 'Introduction: From Soweto to Codesa', in Friedman, S. and D Atkinson, *South African Review 7: The Small Miracle*, Johannesburg: Ravan.

Mapisa-Nqakula, N. (2000) 'Oversight of Intelligence in South Africa', *Roundtable on Security Sector Reform and Democratisation: Ghana and South Africa*, Accra.

Minister of Defence (1996) *Defence in a Democracy: White Paper on National Defence for the Republic of South Africa*, Pretoria: Ministry of Defence.

Motumi, T. E. (2000) *Defence Demobilisation and Rationalisation in Southern Africa*, unpublished masters thesis, Johannesburg: University of the Witwatersrand.

Ngculu, J. (2000) 'Policy and Oversight Role of the South African Parliament', *Roundtable on Security Sector Reform and Democratisation: Ghana and South Africa*, Accra.

Pelser, E. (1997) *The Accountability and Control Functions of the National Secretariat for Safety and Security*, unpublished masters thesis, Johannesburg: University of the Witwatersrand.

Rauch, J. (1993) 'State, Civil Society and Police Reform in South Africa', Johannesburg: Centre for the Study of Violence and Reconciliation, working paper.

Shaw, M. (1994a) 'Point of Order: Policing the Compromise', in Friedman, S. and D. Atkinson, *South African Review 7: The Small Miracle*, Johannesburg: Ravan.

—— (1994b) 'Biting the Bullet: Negotiating Democracy's Defence', in Friedman, S. and D Atkinson, *South African Review 7: The Small Miracle*, Johannesburg: Ravan.

South African National NGO Coalition (SANGOCO) (2000) 'Advancing Socio-Economic Transformation'. Discussion paper, August. Johannesburg: SANGOCO.

Taole, E. K. (1997) 'Management Practice in Military Integration of the National Defence Force between 27 April 1994–27 April 1996', unpublished masters thesis, Johannesburg: University of the Witwatersrand.

Winkates, J. (2000) 'The Transformation of the South African National Defence Force: A Good Beginning', *Armed Forces and Society* 26 (3).

Note

1 Parts of this section have been published previously in Cawthra 1998.

3

Governing the Security Sector in a Democratising Polity *Nigeria*

J. 'KAYODE FAYEMI

After fifteen years of military and authoritarian rule, great expectations accompanied the resumption of civilian rule in Nigeria in May 1999. For a country that had suffered severe deterioration in its economy and politics over the thirty years of military rule, the assumption that civilian rule would herald a dawn of peace and a deepening of democratic values and norms in society was understandable. However, this assumption did not take into account the deep-seated divisions inherent in Nigeria's body politic. These were not the products of military rule even if it had exacerbated them.

The scale, scope and intensity of conflict in Nigeria since the end of military rule challenges the assumed link between military disengagement from politics and the demilitarisation of Nigerian society. Societal violence has increased since the start of civilian rule. Although there are several reasons for this (not least the expanded political space provided by democratic governance) the fact that the public still casts doubt on the state's capacity to manage domestic crises and to protect the security of life and property underscores the importance of governance in the security sector (Okunmadewa and Williams 2000: 5).

As Nigeria drifts down the path of increasing violent conflict (even with its record of relative success in managing its post-civil war reconciliation and reconstruction agenda) the democratising polity faces two key security challenges. These are the establishment of effective and accountable security agencies 'in pursuit of individual and community security in tandem with state security' (Obasanjo 2001: 1) and the establishment of effective governance of the security sector through the empowerment of civilian supervision mechanisms.

However, these structural challenges can only be addressed within an historical context: to understand the nature of the challenges, and to be able to offer solutions to them, an assessment of Nigeria's political environment is critical.

The legacies of Nigeria's military and authoritarian past

When the Nigerian military first intervened in politics in January 1966, their action was acclaimed as a nation-building and transformational project aimed at eradicating corruption and reordering the state. Six months later, the Nigerian army had become the catalyst for national disintegration as it divided into ethnic and regional factions and exacerbated pre-existing divisions that had earlier undermined its professionalism and eventually led to civil war. The 1967–70 civil war was important in helping the military to regain a level of legitimacy after the war ended. In the aftermath, the head of state, General Yakubu Gowon, projected the military as the vanguard of Nigeria's nation-building project.

The post-civil war agenda of rehabilitation, reconstruction and reconciliation that was to culminate in military–political disengagement in 1976, elicited a high level of consensus both within the military and political society, although the agenda signified more the continuity of the old order than change.

While state power was enhanced by the civil war, the improvement in the country's economy as a result of its newly discovered oil wealth sharpened the predatory instincts of the military ruling élite and its allies in the civilian bureaucracy and business sector. This greatly undermined the institutional capacity for proper governance and, in turn, the nation-building project.

Furthermore, while state military power was potentially enhanced by the post-civil war reconciliation policy of 'no victor, no vanquished', the Gowon administration failed to concentrate on reorganising the military institution. Although military planners sought to improve service coordination and put forward proposals for demobilising and mechanising the military – which was, at the time, spending 90 per cent of its budget on salaries for the 250,000-strong force (up from a pre-war strength of 10,000) – there were no doctrinal principles that guided defence management. Indeed, the failure to seize the opportunity to reorganise the military laid the foundation for the progressive decline of the entire security structure in later years.

During thirty years of military involvement in politics the extent of sectional loyalties that existed within the military hierarchy became evident. On the one hand, it was possible for successive military regimes to retain power with some measure of authority in areas where the personal projects of the military ruling élite coincided with the military institution's corporate interests. On the other hand, and especially in areas where the rulers made no attempt to respect military institutional interest, military rulers clung to power on the strength of their coercive capabilities and co-option strategies that depended on alternative power centres outside the military – in the civilian bureaucracy, in intelligence units, the business sector and intellectual circles – all of which helped in the rupturing and de-institutionalisation of the military. To varying degrees, successive military regimes adopted this strategy – from General Gowon to General Abdulsalami Abubakar. However, the regimes of generals Ibrahim Babangida and Sani Abacha represented two extremes.

The legacy of a politicised and de-institutionalised military

Most observers of the Nigerian military agree that the military institution was divided by a variety of corporate, ethnic and personal grievances that developed over time during the military's prolonged years in government (Adejumobi 2000: 1; Ihonvbere 1996). Factions of service interests, service needs and service power continued to dominate the Nigerian military structure, frustrating all efforts to establish a rational system of strategic planning, force development, resource allocation and collective military coordination throughout the period of military rule. A limited attempt was made to implement central coordination during the period of civilian rule (1979–84) but this was hobbled by the combination of civilian inexperience and the military's continued inter-service rivalry.

The implications of military involvement in politics, however, went beyond defective defence organisation and management. One aspect that deserves particular examination is the impact of military coups on corporate professionalism in the defence force. By their very nature, coups are high-risk ventures. Success or failure will almost always result in the loss of the perpetrators or their targets, or both. The persistence of coups in Nigeria and the resultant decimation of the officer corps had a negative impact on the armed forces and national security. No fewer than 400 officers lost their lives in or as a result of coups. In addition to the losses occasioned by executions there were high levels of premature retirement, unexpected dismissals and rank inflation that resulted from both failed and successful coups.

On another level, the political careerism resulting from successful coups also engendered resentment, rivalry and disunity amongst military officers. In this sense, organisational dysfunction in the Nigerian military apparatus resulted primarily from political involvement.

The personalisation of power and the quest for a military party

In the early days of military rule, extensive consultation and regular feedback within the military constituency was the norm. The institutions established for decision making did not function as mere rubber stamps for the whims and caprices of the head of the military junta. Although the sheer force of the personality and charisma of the leader influenced the interface between his personal agenda and the institutional project, the institutional agenda prevailed for much of the period preceding the Babangida regime that took power in 1985.

The subsequent breakdown in institutional cohesion and *esprit de corps* in the context of the personalised nature of leadership (especially under generals Babangida and Abacha) also owed something to another ingrained strategy. Unlike in the past, when it was anathema for serving officers to stake a claim to permanent political participation, many began to raise the stakes for including military involvement in politics in the institutional sense in the country's constitution. Various institutional designs were discussed, implemented and discarded.

One of the proposed designs was that of establishing a military party. Military officers and civilian intellectuals were assigned the task of studying a variety of institutionalised military–political party projects. Prominent models that attracted the regime's attention included the Nasserist/Baathist models in Egypt, Syria and Iraq as well as the foundational regimes in Latin America and South-east Asia. Although it was General Babangida who put the idea of establishing a military party in motion, it was his successor, General Abacha, who implemented the blueprint through the brazen creation of artificial political parties. At the time of his death in June 1998, all five of the parties in his democratic transition project had 'unanimously' nominated him as the presidential candidate. Although there was strong opposition to this phoney democratisation project in Nigerian civil society, it was apparent that General Abacha had the presidency within sight.

While it can be argued that these personal political projects did not succeed in the manner envisaged, the legacy of constitutional and institutional engineering from above that was bequeathed by the military is partly responsible for the stunted growth of the Nigerian political party structure. Indeed, the limited success achieved by generals Babangida and Abacha in the creation of political parties by military fiat with imposed but quite pedestrian ideological identities ('a little to the left and a little to the right', as General Babangida described the two-party arrangement he created) underscores the reasons why the present political parties are still controlled by the praetorian guard of an erstwhile military era. The fact that very little differentiates these political parties explains the popular disillusionment with mainstream politics and the popularity of ethnic and religious constituencies as a means of providing safety and security for the people of Nigeria.

The weakening of accountability and the growth of the intelligence agencies

One of the most harmful consequences of the de-institutionalisation of the military was its loss of the monopoly over the means of coercion and the management of violence in the Nigerian state. This loss could be traced to one critical factor: the gradual and quite surreptitious disengagement of other security agencies that were previously subsumed within the military hierarchy, especially as the military moved towards a more personalised type of rule. For example, the rise in influence of military intelligence and associated bodies became directly proportional to the loss of influence by the 'constitutional' military as a corporate institution and the Ministry of Defence as the bureaucratic institution responsible for accountability. This led to the development of an alternative power centred on the security and intelligence networks that was used by successive rulers to undermine the military institution to prevent it threatening the ruler.

This developed a non-institutional side especially under the Babangida and Abacha regimes. With the ascendancy of the security and intelligence units, the associational and corporatist character of the regimes at inception assumed an authoritarian cast as power was consolidated and the leader's dependence on the security and intelligence network grew. Whilst this practice had started with the creation of the Nigerian Security Organisation in 1976, it was institutionalised under General Babangida when he set up a number of security networks culminating in the creation of the alternative paramilitary service – the National Guard. By this time, the role of private military companies in the activities of the intelligence services and in the overall management of the regime's security had become a source of concern within the military as an institution.

This took on more insidious dimensions under the late General Abacha with the formation of the Libyan- and Korean-trained Special Bodyguard Services (for the personal protection of the head of state) and the Strike Force and K Squad (responsible for carrying out state-sponsored assassinations of political enemies). That this alternative power bloc clustered around General Abacha made a mockery of the military institution, and destroyed the hierarchy that is so central to it, is evident from recent revelations made at the Human Rights Violations Investigations Commission's hearings and in the trials of the junior officers who ran these alternative security structures.

Business élite–military links and corruption-fuelled institutional designs

The origin of what has been referred to as Nigeria's 'bureaucratic-economic militariat' (Fayemi 2000) can indeed be traced back to the central role of the military in the control and management of Nigeria's post-civil war oil wealth, especially after the promulgation of the Indigenisation Decrees of 1972 and 1977. If one traces the personal, political and financial links of business individuals associated with the military prior to their exit from government and in the immediate aftermath of civilian politics in 1979, the emerging trend of a network comprising the military, the civilian bureaucracy and the business élite becomes immediately apparent. At this stage, however, it appears that predatory acquisition by the military personnel involved was largely in pursuit of personal wealth. In no time at all, however, this pursuit of individual wealth set the tone for a conscious institutional programme for the wielding of political influence (Adekanye 1999).

It was not just the economy that suffered in the 'private good, public bad' legacy of the era. The prospects for democratisation and meaningful politics also dimmed. Given the diffused level of autonomy exercised by the military institution that resulted from the parcelling out of the state to private military interests, the class and group project engendered by previous military rule was replaced by the rule of the 'benevolent dictator', since many officers close to power had become beholden to the personal ruler as direct beneficiaries of the financial incentives he distributed.

In the larger society, privatisation exacerbated prebendal politics with its attendant pressure on ethnic relations, as many who had lost out concluded that the overwhelming power of the centre was responsible for their fate. By institutionalising favouritism and corruption as legitimate instruments of governance, Babangida's military regime succeeded in breeding a myriad of anti-democratic practices that were reproduced regularly, either in the form of a common belief that everyone had a price, or in the disappearance of loyalty to the state as militarism became embedded in the psyche of the average person.

The restructuring of the economy along monetarist lines can be said to have represented an ambitious attempt by the 'techno-military' authoritarian state under General Babangida to generate a new hegemonic bloc. First, as a result of the government's privatisation agenda, several of the state-owned industrial and commercial ventures were sold directly to ex-military generals or to conglomerates linked to them. In addition, the new merchant banks that emerged to take advantage of the liberalisation of the financial sector featured several retired military officers on their boards. Indeed, many military generals were prominent beneficiaries of the bad loans allocated by these failed banks.

Second, General Babangida went beyond the personal pecuniary motives of erstwhile military rulers by ensuring that the stratification of the military from the rest of society extended the level of personal arrangements to the institutional level. Hence, by adopting a practice common to Latin American and some South-east Asian military institutions, he announced the formation of an Army Bank (which never took off), an industrial armaments city (which also did not happen) and the Nigerian Army Welfare Insurance Scheme.

Under General Abacha the Nigerian economy became a personal fiefdom. The stripping away of any official pretence at the collegial façade military rulers had projected in the past was complete by the time Abacha died in June 1997. Unlike Babangida, who parcelled out the state to friends and mentors within the military and political society with a view to consolidating his political base, General Abacha kept the spoils of office for himself, his family and a coterie drawn from his security apparatus, and mostly from his ethnic base.

The emergence of the ethnic–regional factor in the armed forces

In discussing the emergence of the ethnic–regional factor in the Nigerian security structure, it is important to start by underscoring the fact that representativity was not emphasised in the establishment and recruitment process of the colonial army. A division of labour emerged in the colonial army in which the bulk of the rank and file soldiers came from the so-called 'martial races', mostly from northern minority ethnic groups, whilst southern ethnic groups dominated the officer corps.[1] This early pattern of recruitment was replicated in the post-independence armed forces.

The end of the civil war in 1970 offered the opportunity to redress perceived imbalances. The subsequent introduction of a 'federal character' in recruitment that guaranteed equality of opportunity in military institutions helped in this regard. However, the involvement of the military in politics continued to strengthen the unitary characteristics of Nigeria's federal structure and seriously weakened the basis of Nigeria's federalism.

This failure to resolve issues of nationality in an inclusive manner is evident in the varied responses across the country to conflicts over identity, nationality, self-determination and autonomy. The introduction of Sharia law in many of the northern states, the rising tide of ethnonationalism (the Odua People's Congress and Egbesu Boys uprisings), and arguments over the control of state and federal resources (particularly in the Niger Delta) are all examples of demands for 'genuine federalism'. The increasing privatisation of violence in the country represents one of the main challenges to the reform of the military institution and the eventual transformation of the security structure. While most Nigerians still favour a federal nation, it is clear that the nation state as it is constituted is a source of violent conflict. The failure of the various institutional mechanisms adopted to manage diversity and difference – including the federal character principle, the quota system, the rotational presidency and political zoning – is an indication of the lack of a social contract between governors and governed with a view to devising politically legitimate and inclusive mechanisms that are consensus-driven.

Yet it is important to draw a distinction between the character of the military in government and the military as an institution. While the military in government clearly looked 'regional' and 'ethnic', the military institution continued to show even-handedness in its recruitment. However, there is a perception that the national military is not there to serve the interests of all Nigerians, and it is this that underscores the prevalence of private armies and militias, mostly formed along ethnic and regional lines in defence of particular interests. It is to this last legacy of military rule, which is perhaps the most worrying given the growth in societal and structural violence, that we now turn.

The legacy of societal militarisation and violence

Perhaps the most enduring of all the legacies bequeathed to Nigeria by the years of military rule is the level of militarism and societal violence.

Despite various steps taken by the civilian government since it assumed power in May 1999, the intensity of conflict under civilian rule underscores the reasons why military restructuring can only take its proper place within the context of institutionalised national restructuring.

Formal military disengagement from politics has widened the space within which concrete democratic reform is possible and sustainable. However, it has also exposed various central divisions, reopened old wounds and generated new forms of conflict in the country (Agozino and Idem 2000). While the immediate causes of increased violence and crime reside in a perception of inequality in society, the loss of a culture of compromise and accommodation in the resolution and management of conflicts appears to lie at the heart of the issue. This point cannot be overemphasised: Nigerians lost their culture of dialogue in a period when militarisation and the primacy of force had become state policy and it will require a return to consensus-based politics, rather than the current adversarial model, to regain that culture.

A critical task in consolidating Nigeria's fragile democracy and rebuilding stable civil–military relations is that of reclaiming the militarised mind, which has been entrenched by a deep-seated experience of social exclusion under military rule. Given the prevailing political culture – bred by three decades of militarism and authoritarian control – the current political transition only represents a reconfiguration of the political, economic and military élite, rather than an opening up of the political system and the broadening of participation

The greatest challenge, therefore, lies in addressing the psychology of militarism that has become reified in the context of Nigeria's politics of exclusion. Herein lies the paradox of democratisation and demilitarisation, not just in Nigeria but also in the rest of post-Cold War Africa. How attainable is a complete overhaul of politics from its military roots, especially in an atomised body politic in which the symbols, values and ethos of the military are replicated in large sections of society?

Political reform, governance and democratisation

The nature of General Abacha's exit and the ascension to power of General Abubakar arguably determined the outcome of the democratisation project in 1999. However one may view the eventual outcome of the rushed transition programme, the fact that the military élite was not responding to a full defeat by the population can hardly be discounted in understanding the *pacted* nature of the transition and the push for a graceful exit for the military through a political machine that remained deeply sympathetic to its hierarchy. The dominance of the political party hierarchy by retired military officers and civilians closely connected to the military élite has set the tone for a party formation that pays little attention to ideology.

This compromised political settlement was therefore perceived in several sectors (especially in the civilian polity) as a reason why military disengagement ought to be viewed with a great deal of scepticism and not as a panacea for demilitarisation. Indeed, many were deeply concerned by the secretive nature of the transition, which saw a government elected with no public access to the constitution. At a time when the constitution is no longer seen merely as a set of rules and laws regulating the state and society, but rather as a social contract and an expression of the general will, many objected to an imposed constitution and predicted it was bound to ensnare the new democracy.

In spite of the vociferous campaign for an open debate on the constitution, the idea of popular participation in deciding the new form of governance was largely ignored by the military. Instead, the Abubakar government established a Constitutional Debate Coordinating Committee (CDCC) to collate public comments on the draft 1995 constitution produced by General Abacha. However, the CDCC had only two months to undertake this exercise and, in spite of its members' determination to do a good job, it was already hobbled by some of the central principles that guided its work, including a lack of transparency, openness and credibility. More importantly, even when the Committee's members managed to produce a draft of the views gathered, they discovered that the ruling military élite, intent on its own agenda and seeking to avoid any issue that might return to haunt them after their exit from power, had ignored many CDCC recommendations.

This led to the eventual marginalisation of civil society voices that cautioned against a rushed transition programme and an exclusive focus on electoralism. It also paved the way for the low quality of the elected representatives, the majority of whom emerged from the shadows of the military parties created during General Abacha's rule. Since many of the protagonists of those parties controlled resources through various rent-seeking activities undertaken while they were still in office, they were able to transfer these resources to the newly registered parties.

The security sector under Obasanjo's administration

Given the above context of the military hangover, the election of an ex-military general with significant support from the military constituency was seen (in civil society) as an extension of military rule. His initial moves, however, surprised many and he was able to turn the limited expectation of change and the perceived lack of room in which to manoeuvre to his advantage. His first move – the appointment of new service chiefs on the day he came into office – gave the impression of a government committed to military professionalism and determined to ensure civilian supremacy. It was also a careful balancing act to ensure that all the senior service chiefs came from minority ethnic groups in the north and south.

The administration's agenda for military professionalisation has followed the traditional pattern embraced in countries moving from prolonged military and authoritarian state structures to civilian, democratic structures. The focus has therefore been on the depoliticisation and subordination of the military to civil authority; the constitutionalising of security sector reform; a policy of reorientation and re-professionalisation; the demilitarisation of public order and the increasing relevance of civil policing; and balancing the demands of defence with the need for development.

As indicated above, the incoming administration gained the confidence of sceptics by tackling the immediate challenge of choosing military chiefs to lead the restructuring and re-professionalisation project in the armed forces. The next move by the administration was even more popular. 'Politicised' military officers were retired on 10 June 1999 – two weeks after the government was sworn in. The retirement exercise saw the exit of 93 officers (53 from the army, 20 from the navy, 16 from the air force and 4 from the police). The third move, which also elicited the support of Nigerian society, was the government's announcement of an anti-corruption crusade that saw the immediate termination of several contracts awarded by the previous military administration as well as the establishment of a judicial commission to investigate human rights violations under military rule.

Popular as these measures were, the government's attention still appeared to be focused on the dominant model of civil–military relations that assumes a level playing field to facilitate 'autonomous military professionalism' predicated on 'objective civilian control'. This model encourages an 'independent military sphere' that does not 'interfere in political matters'. In reality, however, this perspective treats civilian control as an event, a fact of political life, not a process that has to be negotiated within a continuum, especially in states emerging from prolonged authoritarian rule. Civilian control should not be seen as a set of technical and administrative arrangements that automatically flow from every post-military transition, but rather as part of complex political processes, which must address the root causes of militarism in society, beyond the formal removal of the military from political power or the retirement of politically tainted officers. There is a need to redefine the notion of the apolitical military – a notion that has been central to the discourse of the dominant literature on civil–military relations.

In Nigeria, where the military has become entrenched in all facets of civic and economic life, and where politics has featured a reconfiguration rather than a transformation of power, anchoring the need for objective civilian control to the notion of an apolitical military underestimates the seriousness of the issues at stake. While formal mechanisms for control are not in themselves wrong, the reality underpinning Nigeria's crisis of governance underscores the fact that subordinating the armed forces to civil control can only be achieved when civil control is seen as part of a complex democratic struggle that goes beyond elections and beyond subordination to the presidency and other supervisory institutions. (Williams 1998; Fayemi, 1998). These processes are expressions of institutional relationships that are inherently political, subjective and psychological. Only when the political and psychological issues arising out of military involvement in politics are grasped can we begin to look at objective control mechanisms.

If the objective of creating efficient and effective professional armed forces is to be achieved, particular attention must be paid to the principle of accountability to the people and their elected representatives. The location of the military in terms of its accountability to the executive, the legislature and wider society must be clarified in constitutional terms. This is important for a number of reasons. First, accountability, transparency and openness have become fundamental constitutional tenets and the Obasanjo administration is leading the way in this respect. Second, as a national institution, the military relies on the public for support and sustenance in order to fulfil its constitutional mandate. Third, the idea that security matters reside exclusively in the realm of the military constituency is one that is increasingly challenged by the broadened and more inclusive meaning of security to society.

Unfortunately, previous constitutions have been rather silent on the armed forces and their role in society. Section 217(1) of the 1979 constitution, stipulating the role and broad functions of the armed forces – namely, 'defending Nigeria from external aggression, maintaining its territorial integrity and securing its borders from violations on land, sea or air; acting in aid of civil authorities to help keep public order and internal security as may be prescribed by an Act of the National Assembly; and performing such other functions as may be prescribed by an Act of the National Assembly' – was repeated verbatim in the 1999 constitution. There was no attempt to reflect on the problems that arose from prolonged military rule in the intervening two decades. While it is arguable that this broad depiction of the roles of the security forces gives the political authority enough flexibility to define what it seeks, this lack of clarity can also be a problem – especially in circumstances where civilians frequently lack knowledge and understanding of military affairs, and where the apportioning of civilian and military responsibilities often depends on the military itself, or on a small coterie of elected civilian officials close to the President.

Given the burden of Nigeria's authoritarian past and the military's loss of credibility, it was thought that elected civilians would be allowed to play a key role in military restructuring and in the redefinition of roles and missions. However, there is a conflict between one public view that legislative supervision should be central to democratic control and another holding that the President and his Defence Minister, as ex-military leaders, should have the freedom to restructure the military without checks and balances simply because 'they know what they are doing'.

As a result the legislature has largely functioned as a rubber stamp as far as military matters are concerned. Not only are parliamentarians often unaware of developments, but their role in terms of determining policy on the size and character of the armed forces, overseeing their activities and approving the orders under which they function, has been short-changed by an overbearing executive. It is expected that the current review of the country's constitution will provide an opportunity to re-examine the constitutional dimension of military matters and to clarify the role of the executive, the legislature and the wider society in ensuring stable civil–military relations.

Even on the issue of the need for an anti-coup strategy (an issue that has become extremely contentious with the Nigerian public) the current constitution is muted. For many observers the clause that is most worrying is Section 315(5)c of the 1999 constitution, which states that the National Security Act (a body of principles, policies and procedures on the operation of the security agencies) remains in law and cannot be overridden by the constitution without the support of two-thirds of the legislature in the national and state assemblies. Opponents argue that for an act that came into being via military decree to still have this legitimacy makes a mockery of the democratisation process and exposes the country to the whims and caprices of security agencies which operate largely in the dark.

As if to complicate matters, the 'anti-coup' clause contained in Section 1(2) of the 1999 constitution stipulates that 'The Federal Republic of Nigeria shall not be governed, nor shall any person or group of persons take control of the Government of Nigeria or any part thereof, except in accordance with the provisions of this Constitution'. Yet, as stated above, the National Security Act can override the same constitution, in which case an interpretation of the above clause could be that any person or group that successfully removes a constitutional government in accordance with the provisions of the National Security Act is acting in a constitutional, or at least a legal, manner.

Although the government has strenuously avoided the term 'military restructuring', the thrust of its programme indicates that a reorganisation agenda is on course. Taking his cue from a speech made at the National War College in July 1999, the Vice-President, Atiku Abubakar, promised a 'comprehensive transformation of the Armed Forces into an institution able to prove its worth'.[2] According to Abubakar this transformation would include:

- The continuation of rationalisation, downsizing and right-sizing to allow the military to shed its 'dead wood' and discard obsolete equipment.

- Re-equipping the services and improving the welfare of soldiers, albeit within the limits of budgetary allocation.

- Reversing the harm inflicted on civilian–military relations by years of military rule, using measures to subordinate the military to the democratically constituted authority.

- Building, rehabilitating and strengthening the relationship between the Nigerian military and the rest of the world, especially African countries, following years of diplomatic isolation and sanctions.

Although the word demobilisation was avoided, it was clear that other phrases such as downsizing and right-sizing meant precisely that. Indeed, the Minister of Defence, Lieutenant-General T. Y. Danjuma, indicated in 1999 that the military should be reduced by at least 30,000 men from its current strength of 80,000 men (*Daily Times*, 29 July 1999). The President, however, was more diplomatic, saying that the government had yet to make up its mind on questions of demobilisation. Because the desire for demobilisation and/or rationalisation was not based on informed analysis, the military was able to argue for the maintenance of its current force strength. By December 2000, the Defence Minister had acknowledged that the government had decided against demobilisation because of the 'multifarious commitments of the military ... the Armed Forces even have commitments for the maintenance of law and order in this country' (Pan-African News Agency, 24 December 2000).

It would appear that this shift in the official position has been informed partly by the perennial concerns over recruitment and representativity in the armed forces: hence the government's wariness to confront the issue openly. The perception of the disproportionate recruitment of northerners into the Nigerian military in spite of the rigorous operation of the federal quota system in military recruitment is one that previous regimes have had to deal with. The retirement of 'political' officers by the Obasanjo government was immediately perceived in affected circles as a response to the demand to 'right-size' the ethnoreligious dimension of the military institution. Critical to its programme of re-professionalisation, as far as the military is concerned, is the state's ability to provide efficient and well-functioning institutions and infrastructure, and an enabling environment within which the armed forces can fulfil their constitutional responsibilities.

The need to negotiate a process of reconciliation or restitution between the military and society – one that takes into account the long-term best interests of human rights and fundamental freedoms in consolidating democracy, without generating new conflicts – is more crucial than ever and the government appears to recognise this. Given the military's chequered history of political intervention and the inherent fear that some might use the immense economic power acquired over the years to undermine the gains of the democratic dispensation, the government's careful approach to this issue is understandable.

In a consolidating democracy, the government was correct to recognise that a blanket declaration of amnesty or a refusal to revisit past misdeeds would pose a serious challenge to the strengthening of stable civil–military relations. Indeed, revisiting past misdeeds is an essential cathartic exercise, located within the context of civil–military relations that are already sufficiently stable to be sustainable. In establishing a 'truth commission' to investigate past violations, the right balance must be sought between restitution and reconciliation, between the search for immediate justice and the need for long-term democratic stability. The key, therefore, is to ensure an institutional strategy that will streamline and ensure proper accountability and legislative supervision of security actors. There is no evidence to suggest that such a strategy has been formulated.

Given the threats posed to internal security by the militarised (dis)order since the new government assumed office, the role of policing has been the subject of widespread debate in the country, especially against the backdrop of opposition to the use of military power to enforce civil authority, the rise of ethnic militias, and public perceptions of police inefficiency and collusion with agents of crime and insecurity. Whilst the United Nations suggests a police to citizen ratio of 1:400, the ratio in Nigeria is currently 1:1,000. Added to the severe personnel shortages are inadequate accommodation and transportation, poor communication networks; poorly funded training institutions; and an insufficient crime intelligence-gathering capacity.[3]

The new government has shown its determination to:

- restructure and 'demilitarise' the responsibility for internal security by giving the police the sole responsibility for maintaining internal security and public order;
- strengthen the efficiency of the police force by reforming its doctrines, codifying its procedures, improving training and standards (especially to prevent the recurrence of human rights abuses), increasing the resources available to the police, reducing the 'dead wood' in its ranks, expanding its role in intelligence and security information gathering, and injecting new blood into the force;
- increase the size of the police force and the pay of its members.

In spite of the government's declared commitment to the above, there is evidence to suggest that it still has serious doubts about excluding the military completely from internal security issues. This is especially so given the recurrence of situations where the police have found it difficult to cope with internal dissension.

The question of engaging civil policing for democratic governance is central to the issue of exorcising militarism from the body politic as it is relevant to the issue of returning security to the community, ensuring democratic accountability and revisiting the structure of federalism in the country. The issue of decentralising the police organisation, structure and operations has been central to this discourse, given the problems that have attended the centralised control of the police force and the uses to which it has been put under previous regimes. To create a service culture, and not a regimented force arrangement, accountability must be central to public order and a police force cannot be trusted within the community if it retains a structure that is only accountable to the centre and not to the community it seeks to serve. Concerns have been expressed, however, about the possible negative uses of decentralised policing, especially given the nature of the inter-ethnic squabbles and community clashes that are prevalent in the country today.

Yet, emboldened by their citizen's campaigns for security, many states are responding by employing the services of ethnic militias for internal security duties. For example, in Anambra, Rivers, Enugu, Oyo, Osun and Lagos states, 'Bakassi Boys' and Odua People's Congress operatives have taken full charge of traffic management and are confronting armed robbers with the approval of the state executive and with the tacit endorsement of the federal police authorities.

The problems of policing cannot be seen in isolation from the criminal justice system. Reforms to the judicial system have been much slower than reforms to the military and the police. Until there is a comprehensive approach to access to justice and law enforcement, even the resolution of the resource deficit in this sector will not bring change.

Another effect of military reorientation has been the challenge posed by the management of security expenditure. The debate on how much is enough to maintain defence remains a realistic issue on the agenda. In this regard, it is commendable that the government recognises that strengthening the military professionally without the corresponding provision of adequate resources and political support may lead to frustration and possibly to unfulfilled and exaggerated expectations. On the other hand, it is important for government to realise that downsizing, right-sizing and sectoral reform may lead to an increase in military expenditure, at least in the interim. It is for this reason that planning and building mutual confidence and transparency remain at the heart of organisational effectiveness and security sector transformation. On one hand, adopting a single-minded approach that defence spending must be reduced from the outset may serve as a disincentive to reform. On the other, ignoring concerns about the need to attend to social and developmental spending may threaten the overall goal of stability, security and democratic consolidation.

For this reason, there is a growing clamour to broaden the definition of security in the military reform agenda. This broader conception seeks to articulate security in a manner that the individual, the group and the state may better relate to its fundamental objectives of promoting and ensuring the right to life and livelihood. While the government recognises the need to strike the right balance and to understand the dangers that might accompany too broad a conception of security, altogether dismissing the legitimate need for the military, it is not doing enough to develop a consensus in society around this issue.

The international and regional dimensions of security sector transformation

The Nigerian nation state is caught between the Scylla of ethno-nationalism and the Charybdis of globalisation. That the international community has a role to play in security sector transformation is not contested. The issue, rather, is how to determine the process of engaging the international community in this process.

Although there were various options open to the administration in seeking international assistance, it decided to engage the services of a foreign private concern of retired military officers known to have close connections with the United States government. The organisation, Military Professionals Resources Incorporated (MPRI), describes itself as a 'professional Services Company that provides private sector leader development and training and military-related contracting and consulting in the US and international defense markets'.[4] MPRI has become a permanent fixture in the Ministry of Defence and has an office and full complement of staff. Apart from the undisguised opposition from military officers to MPRI's unrestricted access, MPRI's belief that models of civil–military relations from one social-cultural context can be wholly transferred into another, entirely different, context is seen to be more problematic.

What seems clear is that the involvement of MPRI has been more donor-driven than would ordinarily have been the case. It is important that partnerships between donors and national governments be on an equal footing if these are to produce the desired results. Supporters who assist in military reform should be discouraged from seeking to drive the process, nor should they place a premium on ownership and claiming credit. This relationship will require a determination to seek engagement over the long term, greater transparency and a willingness to engage in a more open and sustained dialogue with government, Parliament, civil society and the broader security sector. It is also important that security sector reform be treated as complementary to, rather than separate from, the broader development and institutional reform process.

Caught between the politics of globalisation and the sub-nationalism of local politics exacerbated by the claims of ethnicity, the Nigerian state seems to have concluded in favour of a regionalist project in its security sector transformation programme. Given the intertwined nature of many of the conflicts in the region, the government takes as its departure point the belief that demilitarisation can only occur as part of a concerted effort by the Economic Community of West African States (ECOWAS). Consequently, the Nigerian government has been pivotal in the re-invigoration of ECOWAS.

To a large extent, the government's continued focus on peacekeeping is also tied to a strategy of using opportunities presented abroad to address some of the problems faced at home. Peacekeeping was the main mechanism for maintaining professionalism in the military during the three decades of military involvement in politics. It now seems that the government is interested in institutionalising this role and carving a niche for the military and other security outfits in preventive diplomacy and peacekeeping.

Prospects for reform and lessons for the future

Overall, the government has shown fidelity and commitment to the issue of security sector reform, but has concentrated largely on military reform in the two years that it has been in office. However, militarism still poses a major problem for the Nigerian state. The need now is to recognise that security sector transformation is part of overall national restructuring. For this reason the single most important need is to develop a consensus-based security sector review that takes into account the roles of all the security actors and supervisory institutions (both public and private) in fashioning an agenda that all stakeholders can identify with and own.

While it is clear that the question of structure is a central issue, the presence of delivery agents is crucial. Based on the above analysis, a number of measures suggest themselves in developing an agent–structure approach to security sector transformation in Nigeria:

- Security sector restructuring can only succeed in the long term within the context of a broader national restructuring.
- There is a need for conceptual clarity in government through a comprehensive approach to security sector reform to produce a rationally ordered, codified security sector review framework and plan of action.
- There is a need to deepen the regional approach to security sector transformation with a view to integrating political, social and economic elements.

- Policy instruments must recognise the need to reconcile economic and social development and enhance the input of non-state actors in policy formulation in order to promote social capital.
- International assistance is only helpful within the context of a clearly felt need.
- Recognition of the legitimate security needs of the communities and constituencies that make up the nation must be factored into the human security approach to poverty reduction.
- Policy instruments must recognise the link between globalisation and conflict, rather than assuming that the effect of introducing global market principles is always going to be positive in the promotion of pro-poor growth.
- Policy instruments must locate the security agenda within the democracy and development framework and reflect the link between politics and economics, and between security and opportunities in the set of values adopted to enhance security sector transformation.
- Democratic, not just civilian, control of the military and security establishments in democratising polities is necessary.
- The human security approach is a process whose results will not necessarily be immediate. Hence there is a need for a long-term view by interested stakeholders.

References

Adejumobi, S. (2000) 'Demilitarisation and democratic reorientation in Nigeria: issues, problems and prospects', unpublished manuscript presented at the round table on Democratic Control of the Military and Security Establishments in Nigeria and South Africa, 20–23 September 2000.

Adekanye, J. B. (1999) *The Retired Military Phenomenon*, Ibadan: Heinemann.

Agozino, B. and U. Idem (2000) *Democratising a Militarised Civil Society in Nigeria*, CDD Occasional Paper 5, London: Centre for Development and Democracy.

Fayemi, J. K. (1998) 'The future of demilitarisation and stable civil–military relations in West Africa: challenges and prospects of democratic consolidation', *African Journal of Political Science*, 3 (1), special issue on security in Africa.

—— (1999) 'Military hegemony and the transition program in Nigeria', *Issue: Journal of Opinion*, African Studies Association, New Jersey, USA.

—— (2000) 'The military in business in Nigeria', in *The Project on the Military as an Economic Actor*, Bonn: Bonn International Conversion Center. Also available at www.bicc.de

Ihonvbere, J. O. (1996) 'Are things falling apart? The military and the crisis of democratisation in Nigeria', *Journal of Modern African Studies*, 34 (2): 200.

Obasanjo, O. (1990) *Not My Will: an Autobiography of a Former Head of State*, Ibadan: Ibadan University Press.

—— (2001) *Grand Strategy for National Security*, Abuja: Government Printer.

Okunmadewa, F. and K. Williams (2000) *Voice of the Poor – Consultation with the Poor*, Nigeria Country Study, Abuja: World Bank.

Williams, R. (1998) 'Towards the creation of an African civil–military relations tradition', *African Journal of Political Science*, 3 (1): 20–41.

Notes

1 Prior to the first military coup in 1966 two-thirds of the middle-ranking officers were Ibo.

2 Atiku Abubakar, inaugural address to Course Eight participants at the National War College in Abuja on 10 September 1999.

3 Interview with the Inspector-General of Police, Musiliu Smith, 11 August 2001.

4 From www.mpri.com

4

Pulling Back from the Brink
Ghana's Experience

EBOE HUTCHFUL

In spite of the fact that studies of conflict have become an academic growth industry, and despite the adoption of conflict prevention policy frameworks by major donors, rather less analytical attention has been paid to African countries that have been able to pull back from the brink of conflict, or have been able to reverse conflict trends and restore some form of social peace. Ghana may well be one such neglected case.

In the 1970s and 1980s, Ghana had many of the attributes that suggested a potential for violent conflict: a collapsing state, characterised by a crisis of legitimacy and shrinking economic and institutional capacity; a severe economic crisis; massive out-migration; and the militarisation of the state and politics along with an increasing loss of control of the institutional instruments of violence. There was a prospect (at least in the eyes of some scholars) of national disintegration. These fears reached their apogee in the violent subaltern coup of 4 June 1979, which was followed – after a brief period of civilian rule – by a second popular coup on 31 December 1981. The events in Ghana also had important implications for overall regional stability. Flight-Lieutenant Rawlings' radical praetorian model inspired similar subaltern coups in the sub-region – Master-Sergeant Doe in Liberia in 1980, Captain Sankara in Burkina Faso in 1983, Captain Strasser in Sierra Leone in 1992, and Lieutenant Jammeh in The Gambia in 1994 – and raised the possibility of destabilising other regimes even further afield.

Yet, barely a decade later, Ghana had shed its image as the 'sick man' of West Africa. Economic viability and political order had been restored. There was an end to the debilitating cycle of military coups; state institutions were reconstructed; and a functioning new democracy was forged and tested through two peaceful elections. These developments allowed the state once again to claim credibility as a regional and international actor. Instead of being seen as a potential threat to regional security, Ghana had emerged as one of the more stable and viable regimes; with its participation in the Economic Community of West African States' Monitoring Group (ECOMOG), it became a bulwark of security in the West African sub-region.

The peaceful change of power that occurred with the elections in December 2000 seems to suggest that Ghana may be well on the way to consolidating its democratic experiment, the increasingly fragile economic circumstances in the country notwithstanding. In the 2000 elections, the New Patriotic Party (NPP) displaced Rawlings' party, the National Democratic Congress (NDC), which had been in power in various guises for almost twenty years. The turnaround in Ghana in the 1980s and 1990s seemed all the more remarkable given that, during the same period, economic decline and conflict persisted, or even deepened, in some states in the region.

How did Ghana pull itself back from the brink? What lessons about conflict transformation may be learned from this experience? Answering these questions requires a more detailed understanding of the character of the Ghanaian crisis. Ghana in the 1970s and 1980s was a classic example of policy-induced decline. Severe structural misalignments emerged in the political economy in the 1960s and 1970s, the outcome of critical policy distortions and external and internal shocks. The state lost almost all capacity to collect taxes, while at the same time radically expanding spending. In 1980, only about 5 per cent of taxable gross domestic product (GDP) was collected in taxes, as against the 15 per cent normal for countries at this stage of development. The real economy also shrank dramatically. The production of cereals and other agricultural staples also dropped sharply and exports fell. One reason for this was the gross misalignment of exchange rates. By 1981, Ghana had the most overvalued currency in Africa (May 1985: 13). Not surprisingly, *per capita* GDP declined by 20 per cent between 1970 and 1980 and by almost 22 per cent between 1980 and 1983 (for further analysis see Hutchful 2002).

This crisis was aggravated by a number of factors including the militarisation of Ghanaian politics, the determined resistance to fiscal correction of powerful social groups (in particular the bureaucracy, the military and the public sector unions), and the growing instability and loss of legitimacy of successive Ghanaian regimes. The state lost control over policy direction. Key government institutions were increasingly unable to perform the basic functions of regulation, taxation and service delivery. Informalisation of the economy and smuggling on a grand scale sapped resources from the state and depleted both its power and its legitimacy.

Decomposition of the security system

A crucial aspect of this crisis was the decomposition of the security network. The causes were both long term (structural and institutional) and more immediate (budgetary and political). Within the armed forces, coups led to a rapid turnover in top command positions and decimated the senior officer corps. Involvement in politics entailed the transfer of some of the most capable officers to civilian administration, leading (particularly under Acheampong's regime) to a sharp deterioration in the standards of professional management within the armed forces.

Politics also opened up avenues for corruption. Officers who were in a position to take advantage of this accumulated considerable property. The result was increasing polarisation and class contradictions in the barracks, the erosion of *esprit de corps*, and a decline in the legitimacy of the entire military hierarchy. Institutional decline was aggravated by a severe contraction in military budgetary allocations in the 1970s and 1980s. According to a commission appointed to inquire into the armed forces, by the mid-1980s the Ghanaian armed forces had almost ceased to exist as a fighting force.[1]

It was not only the armed forces that were affected by this decay. The entire security sector, including the police and the intelligence services, came under pressure. The politicisation of intelligence meant that each change of regime brought with it extensive purges and a reconstitution of the intelligence network. A deliberate ethnicisation of the security organs took place. This meant that different agencies sometimes came to be underpinned by rival ethnic constituencies. There was also distrust and misuse of these organisations by government, perennial conflict between the political authorities and the security services for control over intelligence organisations, and rivalries between the intelligence agencies – the Special Branch and Military Intelligence. All of these took their toll. The police were plagued by atrocious service conditions, poor morale, a reputation for corruption at all levels, severe resource constraints, and (like the armed forces) an erosion of internal cohesion.[2]

The implosion of its security structures not only exposed the state to new levels of vulnerability and threats from within, but also led to escalating and unprecedented levels of violence in Ghanaian society, culminating in the bloody Rawlings coup on 4 June 1979 and the second, less bloody coup of 31 December 1981. These events, followed by the murder of three judges in June 1982, and repeated invasions by dissidents from across Ghana's borders, seemed to bring Ghana to the brink of disintegration.

Pulling back from the brink

What proved unique, however, was the way in which Ghana dealt with the crisis. Many African conflict situations have followed a pattern in which conflict, driven by a number of factors, spirals out of control. This tends to occur because various actors perceive violence to have a certain political, psychological and economic utility. While violent conflict has a variety of root causes, trigger mechanisms and trajectories (Nafziger *et al.* 2000), a frequent scenario involves the tendency of incumbent regimes to respond to political challenges by using intensified repression, because they see violence as the most efficient and economical way of repressing demands for reform and political change. Such violence is usually aimed at political and social groups (often, but not always, ethnic in character) who are identified as supporting the opposition. Such state terrorism (or politicide) has in turn elicited violent resistance, and has thus constituted the trigger for uncontrolled (and potentially catastrophic) conflict (Holsti 2000; Cousens and Kumar 2001). Opposition groups, encouraged by easy access to weaponry, may also turn to (or respond with) violence, either to protect themselves from the state security apparatus (for instance by creating their own militias), or to vent their frustration at their disempowerment and misgovernment. In many cases, however, the rebels are entirely new actors (rather than established opposition groups) with little organisational structure and few political aims discernible.

Most importantly, however, once begun conflict opens up opportunities for new forms of accumulation by both rebels and government officials. A war economy develops involving the illicit extraction of resources, rent seeking, taxation, drug smuggling, gun running, and so on. The longer conflict persists, the more deeply this economy takes hold. Conflict breeds further conflict and corruption saps the moral stature of the incumbent leadership, as well as its motivation for pursuing the war with any conviction or public support. This plays right into the hands of the rebels, whose objective is to undermine the credibility of the state leadership. Rapid disintegration of the security forces means that even a relatively small-scale insurgency may be allowed to fester out of control, or that the war may be lost even before it begins.

Ghana, however, did not follow this all too familiar pattern, departing from it in a number of ways. First, the violence in Ghana was relatively contained, occurring principally among factions of the armed forces. The worst incident, in which nine senior officers, three of them former heads of state, were executed, followed a 'revolution from below' which took place in June 1979. Although the threat was there, the state did not experience a complete loss of control over the instruments of violence, at least not on the scale witnessed in either Liberia or Sierra Leone. To the extent this did occur, it was instigated by the Rawlings regime and took the form of popular forces mobilising in defence of the Provisional National Defence Council (PNDC). (This explains why popular resistance was incorporated into the regime's security system from the start.) However, there were successive waves of violence, as the new regime in turn came under threat of being overthrown by a new set of dissidents.

Second, these dissidents, who attempted several invasions from neighbouring countries, were often themselves former soldiers, some previously allied with Rawlings. Like Rawlings himself, they remained classic *putschists*, not guerrillas pursuing a war of attrition. Rather, their objective was to overthrow the regime by inflicting quick and decisive blows in the capital city and seizing control of key installations. They were fairly easily defeated. However, the beginning of the 1990s saw an ominous development when known Ghanaian dissidents appeared alongside Charles Taylor's Liberian fighting forces. Ghanaian security was increasingly convinced that Taylor and his backers and financiers (most importantly Libya and Burkina Faso) were using a domino strategy, where the fall of Liberia would be followed by the toppling of the regimes in Sierra Leone, Guinea and other West African states, Ghana included. Ghana's active role in ECOMOG, and an increasing tendency to coordinate national and regional security concerns, reflected this anxiety.

There was a third, and critical, respect in which Ghana avoided the familiar conflict trajectories. Paradoxically, the second Rawlings coup of 31 December 1981 (which removed a fragile and ineffectual civilian government and seemingly exposed Ghana to the potential for open and irreversible conflict) proved to be the catalyst that Ghana needed to begin a process of reform. The events of 1979 and 1981 provided the starting point for an extensive reconstructing of the state. This contrasts with the acts of looting and destruction that seemed to characterise many post-coup regimes in the region.

The 1981 coup was, in many respects, a popular revolution, and it provided a basis for new articulations of power and a new strategy of incorporation. It produced a dedicated leadership committed to substantial reform, the suppression of corruption, and the restoration of the confidence of citizens in the probity and accountability of government. Perhaps even more important, however, this revolution came to be characterised by considerable policy and political pragmatism, and provided a basis for the most comprehensive programme of reforms that Ghana had ever known. When the initial 'socialist' programme of nationalisation, rationing, administrative controls and market repression appeared not to be working, the regime abandoned it for a structural adjustment programme negotiated with the IMF and World Bank. These reforms sought to transform Ghanaian governance in almost every respect. They restructured (and disciplined) fiscal practices, liberalised the economy, extensively re-equipped public and development administration, decentralised politics and administration, and eventually permitted some democratisation of political life. In the process, the Rawlings regime showed its willingness to confront the historical legacies – in particular, what Bosumtwi-Sam (1995) calls the 'statist-distributionist mode of governance' – that had undermined the state, refashioning the postcolonial social compact in a manner that better responded to the demands of insurgent neoliberalism and the realities of globalisation.

Economic reform and resource control

The reforms probably had their most important implications at the level of resource control. Recent scholarship (particularly the new 'political economy of violence' school) has emphasised the role of resources in generating violent conflict (Keen 1998; Berdal and Malone 2000; Reno 1997; Le Billon 2000; and Klare 2001). In my view, this literature does not always adequately distinguish between the role of resources in *causing* conflict and in *sustaining* it once it has begun. Specifically, it is suggested that Ghana was able to escape violent conflict similar to that of Liberia, Sierra Leone and Angola because of the absence of 'precious and tradable resources' (Vayrynen 2000). This is of course not entirely correct. Ghana has long been a producer of gold, diamonds, lumber and cocoa. These resources reflected a diversified ownership and exploitation regime.

Issues of resource management and control were central to the crisis, and the recovery, of the Ghanaian state. As earlier analysis suggested, the 1970s and 1980s were characterised by a sharp contraction in the resource base of the state, and were reflected in a deepening fiscal crisis.

These problems were largely self-inflicted, and the Ghanaian state also progressively lost control of this resource base as a result of the increased shifts away from the formal economy towards informal methods of operation and rent seeking by state officials and non-state actors. Organised smuggling of cocoa (mainly through the neighbouring borders in Togo and Ivory Coast), gold and diamond smuggling, and, to a lesser extent, lumber smuggling were common. In the gold industry, the institution of *galahamse* (illicit gold mining) developed, mostly carried out by gangs of unemployed young men.

As stated earlier, the success of the Ghanaian state in reviving as well as recapturing control of resource flows and rents was perhaps the most crucial outcome of stabilisation. As a result of these developments, government revenue rose from 5.3 per cent of GDP in 1983 to 14.4 per cent of GDP in 1986, and averaged 14.5 per cent before declining to 12 per cent in 1992. With external grants and other inflows, revenue rose to over 16 per cent of GDP in 1986 and averaged 15.7 per cent between 1988 and 1992. In turn, this success had major implications for the state's ability to reassert its centrality in political and economic life.

However, there was a further way in which Ghana's resource structure and ownership distribution proved critical to the economic and political impact of reform. First, Ghana's export structure proved relatively responsive (in the short term) to macro-economic reform and changes in relative prices. Second, the peculiar ownership structure in the export sector – a mix of the state and large-scale foreign private capital, and small- and medium-scale indigenous private capital – meant that the distribution of benefits from recovery was relatively broad-based and equitable, benefiting not only the state and private large-scale exporters, but also the rural export sector and the thousands of cocoa farmers on whom the whole rural economy depended.

The political dialectics of the regime as it sought to impose these reforms were equally important. As a regime, the PNDC proved rather elastic, reshaping the ruling bloc – not once but three times – in accordance with changing political imperatives, and becoming more inclusive over time. But even as the original historic bloc underwent reconstitution and expansion (to incorporate the right wing of Ghanaian society), it retained elements of its social and political roots through a brilliant, if precarious, articulation of populist politics (which were popular with the people) and neoliberal economics (favoured by business, donors and the multilateral agencies), mingling the themes of justice and market logic.

Second was the progression from development to democracy that was engineered (however reluctantly) by the regime in the early 1990s. A democratic opening followed the economic 'miracle'. Admittedly this was driven less by the regime than by its opponents, which emphasises the extent to which the Ghanaian process incorporated multiple (and even contradictory) logics and forces. Nevertheless, the *parti militaire* that was cobbled together by the regime in response to the challenge of democratisation (and which succeeded in holding on to power in the 1992 and 1996 elections) was inclusive and representative, in both social and regional terms.

Security sector reform

A significant re-engineering of the security apparatus was a critical dimension of the reform process. In some respects, the security sector was at the centre of Ghana's remarkable transformation, both in terms of ensuring the regime's survival and in providing the stable environment needed for policy reform.

Security sector reform took place in two phases. The first preceded the restructuring of national political institutions, and the second occurred in tandem with it. The collapse of hierarchy and corporate boundaries initially facilitated an alliance of radical soldiers and civilians in the form of the so-called defence committees[3] and brought about control of the armed forces from below. With the 'thermidorisation' of the regime, however, a process of re-engineering support within the armed forces began. This process sought to reassure the officer corps and reintroduce professionalism without compromising Rawlings' pro-ranks image. In addition to measures to restore discipline and command, reforms in the defence committee system in 1984 led to the deradicalisation of the armed forces defence committees, the de-linking of the armed forces from the popular movement, the imposition of greater political control by the government, and a change in name from popular defence committees and workers' defence committees to committees for the defence of the revolution (CDRs). Peacekeeping operations (increasingly a major function of the armed forces) served multiple purposes as training exercises, outdoor relief, cheap labour export (for the government) and a form of official patronage which allowed soldiers to supplement their meagre wages and acquire various goods not available to them in Ghana (Erskine 1989: 156). In these ways, peacekeeping contributed indirectly to the stabilisation of civil–military relations in Ghana.

These measures were combined with the introduction or restoration of key governance institutions within the armed forces. These were the

Armed Forces Council (the highest body regulating the military); the Defence Administrative Committee (the highest policy-making body within the Ministry of Defence and chaired by the minister); and the Defence Staff Committee (a committee of top military commanders responsible for professional advice to the Minister on strategy and military operations).

The intelligence structure was also overhauled. The military intelligence apparatus was abolished (although it would later be re-established with more limited powers). The Special Branch was restructured as the Bureau of National Investigation (BNI). New volunteers were recruited and trained from the regime's own revolutionary organs, to work side by side with the existing officials. The new recruits were better educated, with a minimum education level of secondary school. The BNI remained technically part of the police but fell under the control of the President through the Chief of National Security. The Research Bureau, the intelligence arm of the Ministry of Foreign Affairs, also became a much more significant player in the new dispensation, particularly in terms of monitoring the activities of Ghanaian dissidents in Togo and elsewhere in the sub-region. The more prominent role played by the Research Bureau and its closer integration into the overall intelligence structure was also facilitated by the fact that the Security and Foreign Affairs portfolios were held by one person, Kojo Tsikata.

A new security paradigm

Under the PNDC, a new security paradigm emerged with the following characteristics:

- Security was elevated to a level of priority unknown in any previous regime and was coordinated, for the first time, by the Chief of National Security (Kojo Tsikata).
- Particular emphasis was placed on a viable intelligence system.
- A system of parallel and multiple security organs was established, ensuring that the regime was never entirely reliant on one security source. This was constructed in part by establishing new security and intelligence agencies, and in part by seizing the nerve centres of existing security entities. This system depended on informal networks of control wielded directly by the Chief of National Security. The membership, structure and location of these forces were often secret.
- The formal security system was articulated with popular grassroots

security arrangements located in the so-called revolutionary organs: the defence committees, the civil defence organisation, the 31 December Women's Movement, and so on.

If these are the main characteristics of the new security paradigm, other aspects are also worth mentioning:

- Security and development (macroeconomic) policy were closely articulated, both in terms of the policy process and in terms of an awareness of their mutual implications. Tsikata was also one of the leading economic policy officials in the regime, while P. V. Obeng (functionally the Chief Minister of the regime) was closely involved in defence restructuring.
- As part of a process of fiscal rationalisation, overall defence expenditure was cut.
- In the regime, there was a close relationship between national security and foreign policy, and between regional and national security. This was as a result in part of the regime's earlier experiences when dissidents attacked from across the border, and in part of the insurgencies in Liberia and Sierra Leone. The National Security Council saw sub-regional security and the conflict-management mechanisms coordinated by ECOWAS as essential to national security.
- New ways of articulating, controlling and utilising existing security forces emerged under Tsikata, and were reflected in a more flexible and holistic approach to managing internal security. The essence of this was an integrated approach that viewed security as a sector, thus dispensing with the traditional division of labour between the armed forces, the police, the intelligence services and paramilitary forces (such as customs and immigration). This approach was designed in the emergency circumstances of the early rule of the PNDC, and was a crisis response to the collapse of the state's security structures and widespread resource constraints.[4] However, the proven success of this coordinated approach in suppressing internal and external threats to the state led to the further elaboration of the strategy. Increasingly, other advantages to this holistic approach were recognised in areas such as training and threat assessment. Coordination was initially provided through the office of the Chief of National Security, and later the National Security Council. This holistic approach had several important implications. The positive implications were:

- Its relative success in suppressing threats to the regime. The system scored several notable successes, including the unearthing of a Central Intelligence Agency spy ring in the mid-1980s and the capture, in 1999, of terrorists who attempted to blow up the American embassy in Accra. The system was well adapted to meeting the diffuse threats confronting the regime.
- Its effectiveness as a comprehensive and coordinated approach to security assessment and problem solving.
- Its ability to respond effectively to resource constraints, thus improving resource rationalisation and eliminating duplication.

Its negative aspects, however, were:

- A lack of transparency (particularly regarding the real locus of control of security forces).
- The blurring of distinctions between security institutions and their mandates – particularly in terms of the involvement of special units of the armed forces in domestic crime control and state security, which was the source of many complaints of human rights abuses.
- The potential for the militarisation of civil institutions (such as customs and immigration, the police and the BNI) through joint operations and training with the army.
- A tendency to use this system as an excuse to perpetuate resource shortages, particularly in the case of the police.

The 1992 constitution took some of the positive institutional developments in the security sector a step further. It did so, however, by reviving the basic institutions of civil command established by earlier constitutions. In terms of governance in the security sector, it laid down the following structure:

- The President acts as Commander-in-Chief of the armed forces.
- The Vice-President chairs the service councils – the Armed Forces Council, the Police Council and the Prisons Council.
- Parliament approves security budgets and exercises supervision.
- The National Security Council has overall responsibility for coordinating national security policy and for overseeing the intelligence and security agencies.

- The Service Councils exercise overall policy control for the individual security services, under the control of the President, even though the Vice-President chairs them.

The most significant single development under the new constitutional order was the Security and Intelligence Agencies Act, which for the first time established a legislative basis for the operation and regulation of the intelligence agencies.

This legislation:

- centralised the three intelligence services – the BNI, military intelligence and the Research Bureau – under the control of one body;
- specified the National Security Council as the 'governing body of the intelligence agencies', and provided for the appointment of a National Security Coordinator to coordinate the activities of the intelligence agencies and the national, regional and district security councils, and to collate and evaluate intelligence reports and facilitate their dissemination within government;
- established regional and district security councils which reported to the National Security Council;
- empowered the President to assign responsibility for security to a specific minister – a Minister for National Security was appointed for the first time;
- required the Minister to submit an annual report to Parliament on the operations of the intelligence agencies;
- empowered Parliament to vote funds from the Consolidated Fund for the National Security Council and the intelligence agencies, with accounts to be audited by the Auditor-General each financial year;
- provided for a Complaints Tribunal and a complaints process for abuses by the intelligence and security agencies;
- required warrants to be issued in writing by a judge, the chairman of a tribunal, or a senior police officer with the rank of superintendent or above, authorising investigation by an intelligence agency – warrants authorising the interception of communications have to be issued by a judge of the Superior Court; and
- enjoined the director of an intelligence agency to ensure the 'political party neutrality of his intelligence agency in the performance of its functions'.

Reversing conflict trends

The reversal of conflict trends in the 1980s and 1990s in Ghana was, to a large extent, the result of comprehensive and relatively effective policy reform, the reconstruction of the state and governance, reform of the security sector and public institutions, and restored (although still precarious) economic growth. In particular, it lay in the ability to articulate the objectives of security–development–democracy. Development would have been impossible without security and an end to the cycle of political instability that plagued the country. In addition, liberalisation had real political and security implications. The regime was, for the first time, able to carry out a process of liberalisation without being overthrown. On the other hand, political stability could not have been achieved or sustained without visible improvements in the economy and the lives of people, or without the democratic opening that allowed people some measure of political voice. An important dimension was the key role played by external aid in this process, both directly (in terms of designing and funding many aspects of the reform process), and indirectly, in terms of giving the regime the room to manoeuvre and resources required to reconstruct political alliances. External inflows (official grants and long-term concessional loans) rose from less than 1 per cent of GDP in 1983 to about 10 per cent of GDP by 1990. Nevertheless, reforming the security sector was the critical and essential starting point, since the sector was the primary source of insecurity and political instability. Restoring its professionalism and efficiency also allowed the state to restore its own credibility as the primary source of security for its citizens.

However, one needs to note the limitations of the reform process, particularly with regard to the security sector. While reforms had been successful in suppressing manifestations of orthodox praetorianism and producing what has come to be regarded as one of the better-run armed forces in sub-Saharan Africa (all the more impressive given the reduction in defence expenditure to one of the lowest levels in Africa),[5] there were also some negative aspects to the process.

Reform of the security sector was lopsided. Priority was placed on intelligence, and to a lesser degree, the armed forces. The police force, by contrast, was neglected (Government of Ghana 1997).[6] Reform also lacked transparency as well as any form of public input. The process of developing formal institutions noted above did not displace but rather coexisted with personal and informal controls. The process involved manipulation as well as direct interference in the internal operations of the armed forces by the executive, in addition to a reliance on special units such as the 64 Regiment and the Armed Forces Committees for the Defence of the Revolution (AFCDRS), and, within the police, the paramilitary Panther Unit, which were, in effect, Rawlings' personal praetorian guard. The influence of commanders and the officer corps, many of whom were, at best, lukewarm toward the regime, was contained by the tight grip that Rawlings maintained over the ranks and the NCOs in particular. The military itself was perceived (not altogether correctly) as one of the props of the NDC regime, with the result that the public had little confidence in its political neutrality even under constitutional rule. A survey conducted by a local non-governmental organisation in 2000 showed that 44 per cent of respondents did not regard the armed forces as non-partisan. Because there was little parallel effort to reform the legal and judicial system, particularly in terms of its ability to enforce accountability and curb abuses by the security agencies, a sense of impunity persisted: abuses by the security forces (although substantially curbed) remained an issue.

Governance of the security sector also remained a problem. In spite of the positive developments associated with the 1992 constitution, civil control and supervision have been hindered by limited institutional capacity at all levels. Within Parliament, the Committee on Defence and Interior, which is responsible for overseeing the armed forces and the police, has suffered from inadequate funding, infrastructure and technical expertise, and a general lack of clarity regarding its functions. The National Security Council, the operational apex of the security system, is dominated by the security services (which provide twelve of the twenty members) and has difficulty carrying out its functions of coordination and elaborating a strategic vision. Given its rather large membership, it has rarely met formally as a full council. Within the Ministry of Defence (MoD), there has been a tradition of military autonomy (and even dominance) and weak ministerial control. A report in the mid-1980s noted that the MoD was the only ministry in which there was no ministerial control over the budget (Hutchful 1997a).

While recent measures (in the areas of procurement, budgetary control, etcetera) appear to have had some impact, and while the personnel complement in the civil wing of the MoD has also improved markedly in recent years, the ministry remains marginal in its ability to influence defence issues owing to the lack of a defence policy framework and the specialists required for the analysis of strategic policy and budgetary and procurement processes.

Finally, up until the end of 1996 (when the constitution was changed) there could be legitimate concern as to how far (and how independently) the vice-presidency could execute its onerous constitutional responsibilities in the security sector, overseeing the service councils for the Armed Forces, Police, and Prisons, as well as serving as deputy chair of the National Security Council.[7]

More broadly, there were contradictions in the state's project under Rawlings. In reality, the linkages between security, development and democratisation in the regime were often problematic and, if anything, conflictual and counter-intuitive, in part because these processes were driven by different logics, dynamics and forces. Hence, the process of reform in Ghana, far from being linear, was marked by significant breaks and reconstitutions (Hutchful 2002: 242).

Three overlapping stages could be identified: (1) an initial populist phase (1982–3) driven by a radical alliance of left-wing civilians and junior officers; (2) a stabilisation and adjustment phase (1983–93) dominated by the international financial institutions (IFIs) and external donors; and (3) a democratisation phase (from 1992 onwards) driven by civil society groups of various ideological leanings and persuasions. To the extent that each of these phases forced the PNDC substantially to redesign its social base and ideological thrust, making it more inclusive (even while retaining its previous populist base), this was not necessarily a negative aspect of the reform process. Indeed, this disjunctive process was, if anything, fundamental to the positive outcomes of reform. Each of the forces driving particular phases of the process brought something different to the table, thus facilitating a sense of ownership of various aspects of the process.

Nevertheless, this embedded several contradictions in the process of reform. The first of these was the conflict between security and development – between security sector reform on the one hand and economic restructuring on the other. The two reflected separate trajectories. While economic restructuring involved extensive foreign intervention (by the IFIs and donors), security sector restructuring was local in its management and direction. To the extent that it involved foreign assistance, this came not from Western countries, but from communist and socialist countries (Cuba, Bulgaria and Algeria). The security sector was not articulated to the overall reform process, but was (with the exception of budgetary cuts) insulated from it, and as such reflected few of the principles driving economic and public sector restructuring (such as fiscal transparency and good housekeeping).

Hence, we find friction between the forces and the principles driving the different sectors. On the one hand, revolutionary cadres in the security apparatus were disillusioned by the turn to capitalist solutions, and there was a crisis of loyalty within security organisations like the BNI and the Forces Reserve Battalion (which later became the 64 Regiment). On the other hand, the private sector felt threatened by the lack of transparency in the security services, particularly given the weakness of legal and judicial processes, and by occasional displays of arbitrary power by the regime.

A second area of friction was that between security and democracy. Democratic control of the armed forces and security agencies – as opposed to keeping the armed forces out of politics – was not a priority in the constitution-making process. As a result, institutions of civil and legal supervision remained weak or non-existent. More ominously, pro-democracy forces viewed the lack of control over the security forces and their (perceived) lack of political neutrality as a significant potential threat to democracy in Ghana.

The third was the tension between democracy and economic restructuring. Rawlings may have been a reformer, but he was no democrat. He and the former PNDC complained that democracy had allegedly undermined policy resolve and encouraged a return to patrimonial behaviour (see Hutchful 2002: 218–19).

Finally, this narrative overemphasises the role of the state and political leadership in conflict transformation, and should (at the very least) be supplemented by two other critical levels of explanation. The first of these relates to the strength and resilience of social networks in Ghana and the second to the role of civil society.

Social networks

The quality of social networks is the missing ingredient in much of the analysis of African conflict. Social networks refer to the horizontal ties and transactions between ethnic, community, religious and other voluntary associations, through which individuals and social groups conduct the business of everyday life beyond the purview of the state. It includes the critical elements of trust and reciprocity.

This dimension is important for a number of reasons. It is clear that the decline of the state and the deliberate destruction of its infrastructure are but one aspect of the overall scenario in these new conflicts. Another is the deliberate attack on the structures of everyday collective life, and the equally deliberate promotion of antagonistic micro-identities. A further ingredient is the destruction of gender relationships through the conduct of systematic violence against women: rape, sexual slavery, forced labour, and other forms of abuse. This occurs precisely because these are fundamental to the organisation of collective life in every society.

How does the quality of pre-existing social networks deter or lend itself to this outcome, and thus either inhibit or aggravate conflict?[8] Ghana provides one possible answer. The country has a particularly vibrant village and rural society that functioned, under colonialism, as autonomous and viable development networks. In most cases, this also incorporated strong structures of (relatively democratic) traditional authority centred on the chief and the system of elders, particularly in the Akan areas. In these largely matriarchal societies, women enjoy a prominent role and various degrees of social and economic (and even political) power and autonomy, centred in particular around the marketplace. The most important factor, however, is the strong and elaborate conflict-resolution mechanisms embedded in most traditional Ghanaian societies. Traditional Akan values emphasise dialogue, arbitration and reconciliation – often employing impartial intermediaries and third parties – as methods of settling disputes. Those who refuse to submit to peace making are shunned.

Furthermore, the existence of strong social networks and institutions meant that the progressive weakening of the state was counterbalanced by the emergence of alternative centres of social cohesion. Various social institutions replicated the functions of the state, providing some form of regulation, administration and welfare. Individuals and groups diverted their energies away from cultivating vertical solidarities centring on the state and access to state-controlled resources, and focused instead on developing horizontal solidarities based on professional, ethnic, extended family, and community loyalties. The state itself became increasingly irrelevant to the daily lives and survival of many Ghanaians. Some have suggested that social networks, freed from the yoke of the state, actually flourished (Chazan 1983).

Of equal importance, new survival spaces and strategies were created as the formal economy shrank or collapsed. As imported and manufactured commodities dried up, local and traditional subsistence resources were rediscovered. Ghanaians deployed an extraordinary range of survival strategies, structured around the informal economy, multiple livelihoods, outward migration, dietary changes, self-medication, subsistence farming, and even religion.

On the other hand, the very scenario sketched above has often been conducive to the emergence, not of democracy, but of ethnic and communal competition and conflict. In addition, the promotion of ethnic rivalry is one of the classic strategies by which threatened political élites in Africa have attempted to deflect pressures for democratisation. To understand why this did not happen in Ghana, one has to consider a second factor, which is the rise and relative solidity of civil society in that country.

Civil society

The struggle against militarism and despotism galvanised and strengthened civil society in Ghana (Chazan 1992). In particular, the campaign against military regimes linked students, the professional middle classes, the churches, and some left groups based at the universities and the unions in a broad democratic front demanding an end to military rule and a return to some form of democratic rule. With the formal restrictions on political activity, the civil society institutions became directly politicised and served as the base of mobilisation, using their membership resources and organisational autonomy.

In this context, civil society refers to the space in which social agglomerations of all kinds (including student and professional associations, unions, churches, business groups, etcetera) come together to pursue their organisational interests, and in so doing, act on the state and otherwise try to affect (through various forms of advocacy and pressure) the allocation of social values and the overall conduct of power. In this respect, I follow Harbeson (1994) and others in distinguishing between civil society on the one hand and 'mere associational life' on the other.

The concept of civil society has emerged as the most important variable used by theorists seeking to explain the dynamics of political transition and the process of democratisation. Its potential role in conflict transformation has also been recognised (Poulton and Youssouf 1998) although in some cases it has had an aggravating impact on conflict (Uvin 1998). However, I have argued elsewhere (see Hutchful 1995), against the dichotomous conceptions that pit 'civil society' against the state. Civil society in Ghana spanned elements of *both* society and the state (junior civil servants and military other ranks, for instance) to the extent that the latter (irrespective of physical location) participated in the struggle for democracy and accountability. There are two sound reasons for this more nuanced position. First, in Ghana, as is the case elsewhere in Africa, both unions and members of what are often called the liberal professions or intelligentsia are often located preponderantly in the public sector, and lack that presumed distance from the state. Second, in Rawlings' Ghana it was not the mobilisation of civil society, as conventionally understood, but the fracturing of the state apparatus and its coercive institutions that was to provide the opening for change. The decomposition of the army, and the defection of its subaltern ranks, opened the way to the possibility of a far-reaching reorganisation of state and institutional relationships.

Yet civil society was not the site of unqualified virtue. Dominated by what the World Bank would call an 'urban coalition', it had historically resisted, and continued to resist, fiscal correction and policy reform. Civil society in Ghana was susceptible to ideological cleavage and the allure of revolutionary violence, and both occurred in the aftermath of the two Rawlings coups: with civil society polarised, the focus shifted from democratic to revolutionary contest. Owing to the relative sophistication and solidity of local civil society, conflict in Ghana was characterised as social, 'class' and ideological in nature, not ethnic, regional or communal.

Conclusion

Ghana's example helps to demonstrate that conflict trends are not irreversible. It suggests that it is possible to pull back from the brink through responsive governance, focused (and largely successful) reform, and economic growth. This highlights the central role of the quality of political leadership in reversing conflict trends. In particular, Ghana is a good example of the relationship between security and development, not only in terms of the (oft-acknowledged) fact that they are preconditions for each other, but also in terms of the conduct of the policy process under the PNDC. This process involved ongoing consultation between development policy makers and security practitioners and closely articulated development and security concerns. A new incorporative strategy, based on realignment between the state and the market, emerged. The peaceful and successful transfer of power in the elections in December 2000 suggests that democracy may be well on its way to consolidation in Ghana.

However, Ghana's example also shows that the role of political leadership, critical as it is, may also necessarily be limited as well as contradictory and self-serving. As both a peace maker and a democrat, Rawlings had limitations.[9] Strong social networks and a vibrant civil society are also necessary, both for conflict resolution and democratic accountability. The ability of all social and political actors to learn from historical experience is also important, particularly regarding the dangers of poor governance and unrestrained conflict.

On the other hand, Ghana's case also suggests that the path away from conflict and toward some form of national reconstruction may be far from formulaic or straightforward, and by no means free of new or renewed vulnerabilities. Among other things, the Ghanaian economy has deteriorated significantly in recent years, as has the quality of policy coherence and implementation. Corruption has returned.

The injections of foreign aid that subsidised the reconstruction of the Ghanaian state and its economy have begun to dry up, precipitating a renewed round of deficits. Under Rawlings, continuing impunity and a lack of accountability in the security forces contributed to new forms of insecurity even as old sources of insecurity, rooted in state and economic collapse and unpredictable and violent changes of regime, were ameliorated or allayed.

The unorthodox security system put in place by the Rawlings regime poses an important challenge that the new civilian regime has sought to tackle by replacing commanders in the armed forces, the police and the intelligence service, and by seeking to neutralise the sources of support of the old regime in the security apparatus. Nevertheless, it is apparent that low-level violence is becoming endemic in Ghanaian society. There have been cases of village shoot-outs involving the use of automatic weapons, armed robberies, the serial murders of women in the capital, and occasional but persistent outbreaks of ethnic violence among several communities in the north. Poorly regulated private security companies are flourishing. The consolidation of democracy and social peace in Ghana will depend on how these continuing challenges are handled.

Chronology

24 January 1966: Government of Kwame Nkrumah overthrown in a coup by army and police.

October 1969: New civilian government installed under Prime Minister K. A. Busia.

13 January 1972: Busia's government overthrown in an army coup led by (then) Colonel Acheampong.

4 June 1979: The first coup by Jerry Rawlings takes place against the Supreme Military Council (SMC) II, headed by General Akuffo. (The SMC I, under General Acheampong, had been overthrown by General Akuffo in May 1978.)

27 September 1979: There is a return to civilian rule under President Hilla Limann.

31 December 1981: The second Rawlings coup topples the government of Hilla Limann. The Provisional National Defence Council (PNDC) is formed to rule the country, and is chaired by Rawlings.

June 1982: Three judges and a former army officer (then the personnel officer of Ghana Industrial Holding Corporation) are murdered.

April 1983: The first of a succession of stabilisation budgets is introduced in agreement with the International Monetary Fund (IMF).

25 March 1991: The National Commission for Democracy (NCD) recommends the reintroduction of a democratic system based on the principles of multi-party politics.

December 1992: The National Democratic Congress (the party fostered by the PNDC) wins the presidential and legislative elections (the latter boycotted by the opposition).

7 January 1993: Ghana returns to constitutional rule under President Rawlings.

December 1996: Rawlings and the NDC win the second democratic elections.

December 2000: The National Patriotic Party (NPP) wins the presidential and parliamentary elections, removing the NDC from power

7 January 2001: The new government is inaugurated under the leadership of President J. A. Kuffour and the NPP.

References

Berdal, M. and D. M. Malone (eds.) (2000) *Greed and Grievance: Economic Agendas in Civil Wars*, Boulder, Colorado and London: Lynne Rienner (for the International Peace Academy).

Bosumtwi-Sam, J. (1995) 'Beyond structural adjustment: governance and economic growth in Ghana in the 1990s and beyond', unpublished paper, University of Toronto.

Chazan, N. (1983) *An Anatomy of Ghanaian Politics: Managing Political Recession 1969–1982*, Boulder, Colorado: Westview Press.

—— (1992) 'Liberalisation, governance and political space in Ghana', in Bratton M. and G. Hyden (eds.) *Governance and Politics in Africa*, Boulder, Colorado: Lynne Rienner.

Cilliers, J. and P. Mason (eds.) (1999) *Peace, Profit or Plunder?: The Privatisation of Security in War-Torn African Societies*, Pretoria: Institute for Security Studies.

Cousens, E. M. and C. Kumar (2001) *Peacebuilding as Politics: Cultivating Peace in Fragile Societies*, Boulder, Colorado and London: Lynne Rienner (for the International Peace Academy).

Erskine, E. (1989) *Mission with the UNIFIL: an African Soldier's Reflections*, London: Hurst and Company.

Government of Ghana (1997) 'Report of the Presidential Commission into the

Ghana Police Service' (Archer Commission) (mimeo).

Harbeson, J. (1994) 'Civil society and political renaissance in Africa', in Harbeson J., D. Rothchild and N. Chazan (eds.), *Civil Society and the State in Africa*, Boulder, Colorado: Lynne Rienner.

Harbeson J., D. Rothchild and N. Chazan (eds.) (1994) *Civil Soceity and the State in Africa*, Boulder, Colorado: Lynne Rienner.

Holsti, K. (2001) 'Political causes of humanitarian emergencies', in Nafziger, E., F. S. Wayne and R. Vayrynen (eds.), *The Origins of Humanitarian Emergencies: War and Displacement in Developing Countries*, Oxford: Oxford University Press.

Hutchful, E. (1995) 'The civil society debate in Africa', *International Journal*, 51 (1) (Winter).

—— (1997a) 'Military policy and reform in Ghana', *Journal of Modern African Studies*, 35 (2) (July).

—— (1997b) 'Restructuring civil–military relations and the collapse of democracy in Ghana, 1979–81', *African Affairs*, 96 (Winter).

—— (1999) 'Peacekeeping under conditions of resource-stringency: the Ghana Army in Liberia', in Mills, G. and J. Cilliers (eds.), *From Peacekeeping to Complex Emergencies: Peace Support Missions in Africa*, Johannesburg: South African Institute for International Affairs and Institute for Security Studies.

—— (2002) *Ghana's Adjustment Experience: the Paradox of Reform*, Oxford: James Currey.

Keen, D. (1998) 'The economic functions of violence in civil wars', *Adelphi Paper 320*, Oxford: Oxford University Press (for the International Institute for Strategic Studies).

Klare, M. T. (2000) *Resource Wars: the New Landscape of Global Conflict*, Metropolitan Books.

Leaning, J. and S. Arie (2000) *Human Security: a Framework for Assessment in Conflict and Transition*, Washington: USAID/Complex Emergency Response and Transition Initiative.

Le Billon, P. (2000) *The Political Economy of War: an Annotated Bibliography*, London: Overseas Development Institute.

May, E. (1985) 'Exchange controls and parallel market economies in sub-Saharan Africa: focus on Ghana', Washington: World Bank Staff Working Papers, No. 711.

Nafziger, E., F. S. Wayne and R. Vayrynen (2000) *The Origins of Humanitarian Emergencies: War and Displacement in Developing Countries*, Oxford: Oxford University Press.

Poulton, R. and I. ag Youssouf (1998) *A Peace of Timbuktu: Democratic Governance, Development and African Peacemaking*, New York and Geneva: United Nations Institute for Disarmament Research.

Quantson, K. (1996) *Chapters from a Career*, Accra: New Times Corporation.

Reno, W. (1997) *Warlord Politics and African States*, Boulder, Colorado: Lynne Rienner.

Uvin, P. (1998) *Aiding Violence: the Development Enterprise in Rwanda*, West Hartford, Connecticut: Kumarian Press.

Vayrynen, R. (2000) 'Weak states and humanitarian emergencies: failure, predation and rent-seeking', in Nafziger, E., F. S. Wayne and R. Vayrynen (eds.), *The Origins of Humanitarian Emergencies: War and Displacement in Developing Countries*, Oxford: Oxford University Press.

Notes

1 Report of the Commission of Enquiry, Structure of the Ghana Armed Forces (Erskine Commission), Ministry of Defence, 1988, in 5 volumes. See the discussion of the findings of this Commission in Hutchful 1997a.
2 Note that the subaltern revolution of June 1979 was repeated in the police – although the army suppressed it.
3 These were the Popular Defence Committees, which were community organisations; the Workers' Defence Committees, which were based in the workplace; and the Armed Forces Defence Committees. There were also defence committees in the police. These committees acted as instruments of popular mobilisation as well as providing political support for the regime.
4 Of course, this also allowed for the manipulation of the security services, and ensured that no service became powerful enough to constitute a threat.
5 Military spending as a proportion of total government expenditure fell by over 50 per cent in the 1980s, from 8–9 per cent in the mid-1970s to less than 4 per cent at the end of the 1980s. Between 1986 and 1987, the budgetary allocation to defence declined from 6.5 to 4.1 per cent of the total budget and averaged 3.7 per cent between 1988 and 1990 and 4.7 per cent between 1991 and 1993.
6 For details, see the Archer Commission Report (cited here). The report gave an unflattering view of the police, revealing a multitude of crippling problems and resource constraints. The Commission was severely critical of government neglect, and also of the police leadership for failing to undertake reforms and provide proper leadership.
7 The 1992 constitution originally followed the previous constitution (of 1979) in allocating these functions to the vice-presidency, thus giving the vice-presidency unusual prominence in overseeing the security sector. The conflict between Rawlings and his former Vice-President, Arkaah, showed the weakness of this arrangement, in particular by virtually crippling the Armed Forces Council, which was unable to meet. The conflict led to a change in the constitution, placing the chairmanship of the service councils under an appointee of the President. Despite these changes, the next Vice-President, Atta Mills, served as chairman of the Armed Forces and Police councils.
8 Using a different approach, Leaning and Arie (2000) argue that, in order to understand why conflict breaks out in some societies but not in others, one has to understand the sources of vulnerability or resilience in a society. For a society to be resilient, they argue, it need not be rich: 'Instead, what is required is a core bundle of basic resources – material, psychological and social – which together ensure a minimum level of survival.' At the psychosocial level (which they stress the most), they suggest that 'individuals

and communities have greater resilience when their core attachments to home, community and the future remain intact'. When these attachments are eliminated, individuals may turn to other sources of participation, recognition and empowerment, usually 'identity groups' established around race, religion, geography or age and characterised by an aggressive stance toward established institutions and practices.

9 Throughout, Rawlings seemed uninterested in genuine reconciliation, and in atoning for some of the atrocities earlier in the life of his regime. The extensive reforms attempted in Ghana were thus not concretised by any formal attempts at peace making.

5

Between Autonomy and Subordination

Government–Military Relations in Post-Authoritarian Chile[1]

PATRICIO SILVA

In this chapter I explore the main challenges and obstacles Chilean governments have had to face since democratic restoration in 1990 in their attempts to subordinate the armed forces to civilian rule. During the 1980s countries such as Argentina, Brazil and Uruguay faced similar strong military challenges and the difficult issue of military prerogatives (cf. Remmer 1991). However, in the Chilean case civilian authorities have had to face some additional historical, constitutional and political obstacles that have severely complicated the goal of redesigning government–military relations in order to suit the new democratic reality. Similar obstacles can be found when one compares the Chilean case with the South African situation in the post-apartheid period.

To begin with, the discussion about the factors that led to the destruction of Chilean democracy in 1973 – and particularly the question of responsibility for it – is still very much alive after almost three decades among the Chilean people, who remain divided in two antagonistic blocs.[2] The existence of this division implies that following democratic restoration government–military relations have been conducted within a political scenario in which the military institutions have permanently counted on firm support from a considerable part of the population and right-wing members of parliament. In South Africa, by contrast, the Mandela government and the ANC were able to obtain the support of the overwhelming majority of the population, thus impeding the creation of a strong parliamentary opposition able to check the executive's capacity to transform the legal framework and institutions.

Second, Chilean democracy has inherited from the former authoritarian regime a constitution and a large body of laws that were explicitly intended to guarantee a tutelary role for the armed forces in the country's political development in the future. The 1978 amnesty law, for example, precludes criminal prosecution of military men, while a National Security Council, including representatives of the military, is mandated to 'supervise' the government performance and the President is powerless to change the chiefs of the armed forces. These and other legal and constitutional constructs, which have generated veritable 'authoritarian enclaves' within the Chilean democratic system, have been kept in place by the persistent opposition of right-wing representatives in Parliament to a series of legal amendments proposed by the executive. In South Africa, the breakdown of the apartheid regime led to the adoption of the 1993 constitution and the abolition of the entire authoritarian and racist legal framework of the *ancien régime*. In addition, the new South African constitution has paid careful attention to issues of democratic control of the security forces and fully recognises presidential authority and civilian control over the military institutions (Cawthra 2000: 10–11). As we shall see in this chapter, both the formulation of a new constitution and the complete re-establishment of civilian supremacy over the military are still unthinkable in the Chilean case.

Third, the Chilean transition has been enormously influenced by the figure of General Augusto Pinochet, who became the personification of the former military regime. In this matter, government–military relations in the democratic era have not been solely dominated by strictly institutional matters: the 'Pinochet factor' has been a constant strain, especially after his arrest in London. The South African National Defence Force, in contrast, adopted from the very beginning a cooperative attitude *vis-à-vis* the new democratic authorities and accepted the total restructuring of the armed institutions (Le Roux 2000: 4–5). But perhaps the greatest difference between the two cases has been the openness, transparency and high degree of participation by both civil society organisations and Parliament in the reformulation of South Africa's defence policies and institutions (cf. Cawthra 1996). In Chile, however, defence and security issues have been monopolised by both the government and the armed forces, while the input of the civil society and Parliament have been almost non-existent.

The Chilean case shows the importance of the existence of an efficient government supported by a strong coalition of political parties in dealing with the military during transitional processes. In addition, the strong popular support for democratisation – manifested in Pinochet's electoral defeat – as well as the existence of both a well-established party system and a relatively well-organised civil society, have certainly facilitated the consolidation of democratic rule in the country and the gradual elimination of the authoritarian legacies of the former Pinochet era. This has also been the case in South Africa, where the effective political leadership provided by the ANC, and its ability to agree on the rules of the game with the outgoing white élite, proved to be critical in achieving a relatively peaceful transition to democracy (Cawthra 2000: 5).

Finally, the good performance of Chilean civilian governments (high rates of economic growth, political stability, considerable reduction of poverty levels, etcetera) has helped to change the *de facto* balance of power between the executive and the military in favour of the former. My contention here is that despite the inability of the Chilean democratic governments to eliminate antiquated legal norms, during the last decade gradual but substantial progress has been achieved in reducing the severity of the military challenge and in informally enhancing civilian control of the military institutions.

Military challenges, prerogatives and civilian control

In a seminal contribution, Alfred Stepan discusses the main political and institutional challenges the new South American democracies face in order to regain civilian democratic control over the military institutions. As he points out, this attempt can be frustrated by articulated military hostility to the policies of the new democratic authorities in those areas in which intense disputes exist between the military and the incoming government. He mentions three issues with great potential for conflict: the way the new government deals with the legacy of human rights violations committed by the former military regime; the government's initiatives related to the organisational mission, structure and control of the military; and the government's treatment of matters related to the military budget (1988: 68–9).

Stepan also refers to military prerogatives as another major potential source of conflict between civilian government and the armed forces. As he points out, military institutional prerogatives refer

> to those areas where, whether challenged or not, the military as an institution assumes they have an acquired right or privilege, formal or informal, to exercise effective control over its internal governance, to play a role within extramilitary areas within the state apparatus, or even to structure relationships between the state and political or civil society (1988: 93).

Fuentes (2000: 119–20) identifies three general types of strategy used by civilian governments in South America in their attempts to achieve civilian control over the military: division of spheres; non-cooperation; and engagement. These strategies are mainly related to the question of how much the democratic authorities are intending to include or exclude the armed forces from the government's decision-making process. A strategy based on the principle of 'division of spheres' has historically been the result of a tacit agreement between civilian authorities and the military on the roles each has to fulfil in the country. While civilian authorities regard as inappropriate open intervention in matters considered to be part of the military domain, military officers restrain themselves from involvement in political and institutional matters considered to be part of the civilian sphere. As he points out, Chile seems to have followed this pattern of civil–military relations in the period 1932–73 as politicians and military leaders accepted the existence of a division of spheres. A non-cooperative strategy is based on the objective of maintaining military exclusion from the decision-making process on matters related to defence policies and civil–military relations. By not considering the military's opinion on these matters, the government attempts to reinforce its supremacy over the military institutions: this strategy assumes that subordination implies complete military obedience to civilian policies. In contrast, a strategy of engagement attempts to incorporate the military in decision making. The basic tenet of this strategy is that the best way to obtain the military's subordination is by cooperation and by providing strong civilian leadership in strategic matters, without neglecting the armed forces' contribution to the policy process. In this strategy the government consciously attempts to increase the levels of expertise among civilian officials on strategic issues and defence policies. As we shall see for the case of Chile, since 1990 the democratic governments have been following mixed strategies in which elements of engagement have been applied to certain matters, while in relation to others elements of non-cooperation have dominated the approach.

In the following section I briefly assess the several legal and institutional constraints bequeathed by the military government to safeguard the tutelary role of the armed forces in the new Chilean democracy.

Crafting the military's political guardianship

Following the military takeover on 11 September 1973 a military junta representing all branches of the armed forces and police was established. Although initially the position of Pinochet *vis-à-vis* the chiefs of the other armed institution was one of *primus inter pares*, within a couple of years he managed to concentrate all state executive powers under his command.

In an attempt to legitimise his regime Pinochet ordered the establishment of a commission of legal experts with the task of writing a new constitution according to the authoritarian principles established by his regime (and with the aim of allowing him to remain in power until 1998). He wanted to be sure that the main pillars of the new authoritarian order (what he called 'protected democracy') would remain intact after his departure from power. This constitution was adopted in 1980 after a referendum to which the democratic opposition forces strongly objected. This constitution established a timetable for institutional changes, which included the realisation of a mid-term referendum in 1988, allowing the Chilean people to say 'yes' or 'no' to another eight years of military rule. Against official expectations, a majority of the population (56 against 44 per cent) voted 'no'. Also unexpected was the fact the armed forces recognised their defeat and accepted the consequences of this referendum. As established in the 1980 constitution, in the eventuality that the 'no' option should win the referendum, general elections would take place within fourteen months. The December 1989 elections were won by the democratic forces organized in the *Concertación* coalition (dominated by Christian Democrats and moderate Socialists). For a second time the armed forces recognised the opposition's victory and the way was cleared for the restoration of democratic rule in the country.

Following the defeat of the Pinochet government at the 1988 referendum, a series of laws were introduced by the military in order to limit the options of a future democratic government. These laws were primarily directed at safeguarding military prerogatives in the fields of political autonomy, professional and doctrinal autonomy, and institutional involvement. The prerogatives obtained by the military were mainly established by the 1980 Constitution, and in the Organic Law of the armed forces, adopted in 1989, only a few months before elected President Patricio Aylwin was installed.

The most patent example of the current political autonomy exerted by the military is the fact that the President is not entitled to remove the Commander-in-Chief of the armed forces and heads of services at his discretion, as the 1980 constitution allows the commanders-in-chief to fulfil that position for a period of four years. In addition, the President is not allowed to promote or remove officers of the armed forces without the approval of the Commander-in-Chief (Ensalaco 1994: 422). The military's political autonomy is also guaranteed by the existence of a protected military budget mechanism. A constitutional law established a minimum budget, which cannot be less than the military budget existing in 1989, adjusted yearly according to inflation. In addition, the armed forces obtain 10 per cent of the annual earnings from copper exports.

In the judicial field, the armed forces had passed an amnesty law in 1978 to protect themselves from possible legal or political prosecutions for human rights abuses committed in the period 1973–8, when most of the crimes and disappearances took place. As we shall see later, the existence of this amnesty law has become one of the most formidable obstacles to prosecuting those responsible for human rights violations committed during the authoritarian period. The armed forces also procured for themselves a professional and doctrinal autonomy, as their Organic Law of 1989 does not allow civilian involvement in the military training programmes, or changes in logistical structures and military acquisition policies.

Finally, the 1980 constitution consecrates the institutional involvement of the armed forces in matters that previous to the coup were reserved for the executive and legislative powers. In this manner, a series of new legal provisions and institutions were created to guarantee a permanent tutelary role for the armed forces in Chile's political system. The 1980 constitution gave the armed forces an open-ended mandate as 'guarantors of the institutional order'[3] and created a National Security Council (NSC) which was originally charged with the task of acting against any public initiative or expression of concern that 'in its judgement gravely threatens the institutional order or compromises national security'. But following Pinochet's unexpected defeat in the 1988 referendum the military government negotiated with a group of opposition leaders a series of constitutional reforms, by which the NSC integrated another civilian member[4] and changed its mission to advising the President, Congress, and the Constitutional Tribunal on issues related to national security (Loveman 1991).

Another major incursion of the armed forces in the political domain has been the creation by the 1980 constitution of nine non-elected institutional senators (the so-called *senadores designados*), who were selected by the outgoing Pinochet government on the eve of the democratic restoration. In addition, ex-presidents of the Republic (starting with Pinochet) could become 'senators for life' (*senadores vitalicios*) after their presidential terms. This provision permitted Pinochet to obtain a senatorial seat when his position of armed forces Commander-in-Chief expired in March 1998, allowing him to enjoy parliamentary immunity.[5] As we shall see in the following section, after the restoration of democratic rule, the institution of non-elected senators tipped the balance of power in the Senate in favour of the right-wing opposition, effectively preventing constitutional reforms and modifications of organic laws without the consent of the right-wing parties and the military.

The Aylwin government: searching for civilian supremacy

During the presidential campaign in 1989, the democratic *Concertación* coalition led by Patricio Aylwin had already pinpointed the elimination of the military's political prerogatives as one of its main objectives in fully restoring democracy to the country. The *Concertación* programme called for restoration of the traditional civilian authority over the armed forces, the derogation of the 1978 amnesty law, and the investigation of human rights abuses committed during the military regime.

Following his installation in March 1990, Aylwin placed the democratisation of Chile's political and legal structures, together with the aim of national reconciliation, at the top of his agenda. However, the strong representation obtained by right-wing parties in Parliament (partly the result of the binominal electoral system – favouring the right-wing parties – introduced by Pinochet, and his appointment of the nine constitutional senators) made it clear from the very beginning that the government would meet strong resistance from the legislative power to any attempt to eliminate the 'authoritarian enclaves' left by the former regime within Chile's constitutional system. Moreover, the Aylwin government would have to face the strong figure of General Pinochet who, according to the 1980 Constitution, would remain as Commander-in-Chief of the armed forces until March 1998.

According to Fuentes (2000) Aylwin followed a strategy of 'non-cooperation' *vis-à-vis* the military establishment. It can be argued, however, that both Pinochet and the armed forces immediately adopted a marked uncooperative stance towards the new democratic authorities. In this situation, Aylwin had little alternative but to assert civilian supremacy as best he could, particularly in the face of the military's efforts to assert not just extreme autonomy but also its political prerogatives (cf. Luckham 1996).

Despite the evident lack of sufficient legal and political means to force the military to subordinate itself to civilian supremacy, Aylwin showed his firm determination to make use of any symbolic representation of presidential power to enhance civilian control. The military, however, also responded with special gestures to demonstrate their institutional autonomy from civilian rule.

The question of the military budget also generated tensions during the time of the Aylwin government. As noted before, previous to the restoration of democratic rule the armed forces established that the military budget for the coming years would not be inferior to the 1989 budget (adjusted to inflation). As the economy and the national budget rapidly expanded after 1990, the share of the defence budget as a percentage of the national budget decreased from 17.2 per cent in 1989 to 8.9 per cent in 1997 (representing 2.96 and 1.56 per cent of the GDP, respectively). Although the existing legislation established only a minimum amount, the Aylwin government in practice treated it also as a maximum. In contrast, social expenditure increased in the same period from 64.7 to 67.1 per cent of the national budget. As Fuentes correctly concludes, 'what originally was considered a powerful institutional tool of military autonomy that inhibited any legal transformation in the military budget was transformed during the Aylwin administration into a political tool to show some civilian control over the military' (2000: 125).

The Aylwin government combined decisiveness with caution when addressing the most delicate issue in Chile's democratic transition: the question of human rights. Although the 1978 amnesty law protected the military from legal prosecution, Aylwin decided to establish the truth about the magnitude of human rights violations committed during the former regime. He argued that national reconciliation could not be accomplished before the truth about the recent past was completely established. For this purpose, and only a month after his installation, he created the Commission for Truth and Reconciliation (the so-called Rettig Commission, named after its chairman) with the task of conducting a full investigation into the subject and preparing an official report. Right-wing parties and the military strongly criticised this initiative, arguing that this investigation went against the 1978 amnesty law. The government rejected this criticism, stressing the fact that this Commission had no penal powers, and that amnesty can only be granted after crimes have been established. But left-wing parties and human rights organisations criticised the government, as, in their view, this initiative did not go far enough. This situation, in which the *Concertación* government was criticized for its human rights policies simultaneously from both wings, has become the norm ever since. This shows that the *Concertación* governments have been active in the field of human rights but without openly trespassing over the limits of the existing constitutional order, in an attempt to guarantee the political stability in the country. So Aylwin did everything he could (clarification of the truth, moral rehabilitation and material compensation) except trial and punishment of most of the perpetrators: he called this 'justice within the possible'.

During his administration Aylwin faced two situations of extreme tension with the military, originating in his attempts to restore civilian authority over the armed institutions and to clear up some financial questions involving the Pinochet family. If one looks at the backgrounds of both confrontations, it is possible to assess the extent to which the military had linked its own institutional fate with General Pinochet's personal interests.

The first confrontation broke out following an investigation by a parliamentary commission into a series of irregular financial transactions (the so-called '*Pinocheques*') conducted by one of Pinochet's sons in the late 1980s that involved the army and other state institutions. On the evening of 19 December 1990, Pinochet suddenly decreed a state of highest alert and ordered the army to its barracks (*acuartelamiento*) across the entire country – all without previous consultation with the government, which was completely taken by surprise. The official version provided the next day by the high command of the army was that this military manoeuvre had been simply a 'liaison exercise' (*ejercicio de enlace*) to test the institutional readiness of the army to act. It was obvious, however, that the real object of this show of force was to warn the government to back off from what the high command perceived as 'persecution and harassment' of the army.

Despite the open clashes between the government and the military leaders, several informal mechanisms of negotiation functioned between them. Most of the conflicts did not even reach public view as they were successfully channelled and dissipated by a small number of senior governmental officials who possessed direct links to a couple of top military officers (who functioned as liaison) for the treatment of sensitive questions (Loveman 1995: 317; Fuentes 1996: 35).

The second major crisis in government–military relations occurred in May 1993 when Pinochet ordered the army to its barracks while President Aylwin was away for an official trip around Europe. This action (which lasted for five days) was accompanied by a high-profile meeting of the entire high command of the army (in full combat outfit) at the building of the armed forces, in front of the presidential Moneda palace. Outside the building some one hundred combat-ready black beret élite troops (*boinas negras*) were deployed with the backing of armoured vehicles. Chilean Vice-President Enrique Krauss, who was in charge of the handling of this crisis (known as the *boinazo*) ordered a series of urgent meetings between top government officials and high-ranking army officers to ease the tensions. The direct cause of this crisis was the reopening in Parliament of the investigation into the *Pinocheques* case, this time directly linking General Pinochet to this financial scandal.

These destabilising moves by the military need to be set against the fact that Aylwin, after abandoning the presidency, actually praised the role played by Pinochet during the democratic transition. In his opinion, Pinochet's presence was critical for maintaining the unity of the armed forces and avoiding the military insurrections by subordinate officers that plagued neighbouring Argentina during the 1980s (Loveman 1995: 318).

Government–military relations under Frei: towards a defence policy

From the start the government led by Eduardo Frei (1994–2000) made it clear that its main priority would be to foster the country's overall modernisation, stressing education, healthcare, infrastructure, and a deeper political and commercial integration of Chile with the world community. Frei was also determined to lower the profile of the human rights question by approaching it as a strictly legal matter that is the province of the judiciary system. Although new attempts would be made to eliminate still-existing authoritarian enclaves through a series of constitutional reforms, the new government wanted to avoid investing too much time and energy in long political and legislative battles that had proved to be ineffective in the past.

In the field of government–military relations, Frei decided to follow a strategy different from that of his predecessor. The question of military subordination to the political authorities received less attention, while emphasis was given to the constitution of larger and more formal spaces of cooperation between the government and the armed forces on defence matters. One of Frei's key civilian advisers on military issues described the conflictual nature of civil–military relations under Aylwin and the need for change in the following terms:

> the political authorities in the area of defence, with their relative lack of power, exercise[d] a certain vindictive logic of promotion of presidential authority over the Armed Forces. In consequence, defence debates focused on the question of who exercised power in that area, and not whether the functions and policies of defence were desirable on their own merit.... This

> debate over supremacy, equilibrium, or subordination led to an ongoing state of rivalry in civilian–military relations. … [T]he continual legal, institutional, or purely political conflicts finally led to the recognition that the focal points in civilian–military relations had to be changed [by] centr[ing] the debate on the military's own subject: defence policy itself. (García 2000: 175–6)

By placing defence policy at the centre of civil–military relations, the government forced all the actors involved in this area to adapt themselves in both political and technical terms. In addition, most of the conflict between the government and the armed forces in the period 1990–4 had been related to political issues about the authoritarian past, and not to questions related to professional development and future defence policies. Based on that experience, the government's expectation was that the call to jointly formulate an explicit non-partisan and consensual state defence policy for the years to come would get a good reception among the armed forces.

For this purpose, the government decided to expand the professional and technical expertise on military matters among the personnel of the Ministry of Defence and to establish for the first time a solid 'defence community'. Academic bodies such as FLACSO, CED and the universities, as well as the academic institutions of the armed forces, created new fora for the discussion of defence policy issues between civilian and military experts: workshops, conferences, lectures, and the publication of working papers and specialised journals.[6]

The creation of an active civilian–military defence community represented a critical requirement for working on a consensual basis on the elaboration of 'a book on national defence' to specify the objectives and mechanisms of Chile's defence policies (as well as radiating transparency on this issue at the regional level: Hunter 1998; Clark, 2000). The project to produce this book was organised in three phases. During the first phase a series of documents were prepared by civilian and military experts for further discussion. In the second phase a series of workshops was organised with the participation of representatives of the government, Parliament, the armed forces, the universities and private research institutes. In the final phase, an editorial committee was commissioned to write the book on the basis of the debates and conclusions generated by the workshops (Fuentes 1997: 171).

Despite this conscious attempt to reduce the tensions between the government and the armed institutions by directing attention strictly to defence issues, Frei still had to face severe civil–military crises in the latter part of his presidential term. Paradoxically, most of these crises were not originated by initiatives from the Frei government but were the result of verdicts of the judicial system and unforeseen events such as the detention of General Pinochet in London in October 1998.

The first major confrontation involved Chile's police force. A month after his installation a judge convicted seventeen *carabineros* of the kidnapping and killing of political opponents in the so-called *degollados* case, one of the most gross violations of human rights during the period of authoritarian rule.[7] In his verdict, the judge implicated the Chief of *Carabineros*, General Rodolfo Stange, who in previous years had attempted to cover up police involvement in those crimes. President Frei formally asked Stange to resign but Stange refused to honour this request and the existing legislation did not allow the President to dismiss the commanders-in-chief of the armed institutions. As retaliation, the government held up the processing of a police promotion list and continued for months to pressure Stange to resign, until he finally went into retirement in October 1995 (Loveman 2001: 333).

Another difficult situation for the Frei administration came in May 1995 when the Supreme Court sentenced General Manuel Contreras, former head of the Chilean intelligence agency (DINA), and Colonel Pedro Espinoza, his second in command, to seven and six years in prison, respectively. They were found guilty of plotting the assassination of Orlando Letelier in September 1976.[8] A few days after the sentence, however, the army unexpectedly brought Contreras to the naval hospital in Talcahuano, arguing that he required medical attention. The army also protested against the court's 'arbitrary resolution' and demanded special treatment for these officers as their personal security would be at risk in an ordinary prison. Finally, the army used the crisis to demand a final political solution to the *Pinocheques* case, an increase in the military budget, and the transfer of imprisoned military personnel to army custody. Colonel Espinoza entered the prison on 19 June. Three days later some 300 officers demonstrated (in civilian clothes) in front of the Punta Peuco prison (the incident became known as the *peucazo*) to show their solidarity. This constituted a strong warning to the government. After a series of negotiations, the government agreed to open a special prison exclusively for military personnel at Punta Peuco, near Santiago. Furthermore, the government allowed the army to share custody of the prisoners with the *gendarmería* and announced a salary rise for armed forces personnel in the coming year. Finally, President Frei petitioned the State Defence Council[9] to suspend actions in the *Pinocheques* case for 'reasons of state' (Fuentes 2000: 129–30).[10]

Deep divisions among the *Concertación* partners emerged during Pinochet's last months as Commander-in-Chief of the army, before he had to leave this post on 10 March 1998. Some members of Parliament tried to bring constitutional charges against Pinochet for 'having put the stability of democracy in danger' by instigating the 'liaison exercise' of December 1990, the *boinazo* of May 1993 and the *peucazo* of June 1995. The explicit goal of this accusation was to prevent General Pinochet from being sworn in as a senator for life following his resignation as Commander-in-Chief of the army. The government lobbied *Concertación* members of Parliament to oppose this prosecution because it was considered 'inconvenient' for the consolidation of democratic rule in the country. Finally, prosecution proceedings under the constitution were rejected by 62 to 55 votes, with one abstention (Rojas 2001: 161–2).

Following Pinochet's resignation as Commander-in-Chief of the army[11] and his installation as a senator for life, the government had expected to be able to initiate a new chapter in its relations with the armed forces, and had hoped to develop a good working relationship with the new chief of the army, General Ricardo Izurieta. This general represented the more technocratically oriented part of the army and had no record of human rights abuses in the past. During his first public declarations, he made it clear that he wanted to bring the armed forces back to the path of professionalisation and modernisation, and to improve their public image.

Until October 1998, relations between the government and General Izurieta had clearly been improving, while Pinochet had almost no political presence at the Senate. The latter's spectacular detention in London on 16 October 1998, however, suddenly rearranged the entire political arena. One of the most critical questions emerging after his detention concerned the reaction of the Chilean armed forces. Although the military institutions expressed their total solidarity with their ex-Commander-in-Chief and roundly criticised Pinochet's arrest, they maintained a calm and subordinated attitude towards the Frei government. This was in line with the professional and institutional approach adopted in previous months by General Ricardo Izurieta. In this way, the Chilean armed forces openly backed the government's legal and diplomatic efforts to get Pinochet back to Chile. The armed institutions realised that if they antagonised the Chilean government they would lose the only possible defender of Pinochet's cause with access to the British and Spanish governments. During Pinochet's arrest, many high-ranking military officers – including General Izurieta – visited the old general in London to express the solidarity and support of his former comrades.

Government–armed forces relations came under stress during 1999 and 2000 as a result of the reopening of several legal cases against former top officers by some Chilean magistrates. In order to reduce tensions, Minister of Defence Edmundo Pérez Yoma inaugurated in August 1998 the so-called *Mesa de Diálogo*. This round-table colloquium was established with the cooperation of representatives of the armed forces and several representatives of civil society. For the very first time since the restoration of democratic rule in 1990, members of the armed forces, legal representatives of human rights organisations, and a group of highly respected 'wise men' from different religious and social backgrounds have held a prolonged series of difficult discussions. The main objective was to find ways to reactivate the process of national reconciliation, and particularly to establish the truth about the fate of the *desaparecidos*. Contrary to what many expected, the *Mesa de Diálogo* has survived its very difficult initiation, and has continued its work despite the political turbulence the country has experienced since Pinochet's detention in London.

Perhaps the most important consequence of Pinochet's detention, therefore, was the reopening of the national debate on the issue of human rights abuses under the military government. The radical left and many human rights groups immediately organised large public campaigns and demanded, through the mass media, the reopening of many legal cases against implicated military men. But the Frei government also sent some discreet signals to the judiciary, urging real action to demonstrate its independence and inclination to do something about the human rights issues. Certainly, this was related to international criticism of the alleged inability of Chile's judicial system to deal adequately with the human rights issues. Chilean human rights organisations still argue that the *Concertación*'s goal of achieving reconciliation among Chileans failed mainly because the question of human rights was not satisfactorily addressed by the Aylwin and Frei governments. In their opinion, Chile is paying the price for its attempt to cover up the past.

The Lagos government and the 'Pinochet affair'

When Pinochet returned to Chile on 3 March 2000 he encountered a political scenario that was quite different from the one he had left behind. The presidential victory of the Socialist Ricardo Lagos in January 2000 had made Pinochet's political and legal situation very uncertain.[12] Lagos had been for years one of Pinochet's most fervent opponents. As his plane landed at Santiago airport, discussion started on the possibility of prosecuting the former Commander-in-Chief in his own country. Three days after Senator Pinochet's return to Chile, judge Juan Guzmán sent the Santiago Appeal Court a request for the removal (*desafuero*) of his immunity.

Following his installation on 12 March 2000, President Lagos categorically stated that he would not search for a political solution to the question of human rights violations in the country (whether by a presidential decision or by holding a referendum), and that the fate of Senator Pinochet and all the military officers who might have been involved in those abuses would be entirely in the hands of the judicial system. This statement encapsulated two specific objectives. First, it rejected the suggestion made by some right-wing political leaders about the possibility of an agreement with the government on the pending constitutional reforms in exchange for respecting Pinochet's parliamentary immunity. Second, it sent a strong signal to his supporters, as well as to the right wing and the extra-parliamentary left, that exercising pressure on him would be meaningless, as the 'Pinochet affair' had now been expelled from the political arena and placed entirely in the judicial sphere. By adopting this position, Lagos was able to maintain for a while the political stability in the country and gradually to improve government–military relations. The decision by the Santiago Appeal Court to remove Pinochet's immunity on 8 August 2000 immediately strained government–military relations, however, and new calls were issued from the right wing for a political solution to the Pinochet affair.[13] Since the removal of Pinochet's immunity, the right-wing parties have adopted a more confrontational position *vis-à-vis* the Lagos government.

President Lagos opted to develop a personal relationship with General Ricardo Izurieta by organizing regular meetings on a very informal basis. This generated in the beginning a constructive relationship between both leaders that permitted the discussion of a series of sensitive issues in a direct way. They agreed that the *Mesa de Diálogo* initiative could represent the beginning of a more lasting solution for the question of human rights. Following Pinochet's return to Chile this initiative had been almost completely paralysed and many people expected it should soon end in total failure. However, the rapid improvement in relations between the Lagos government and the military leadership made this historic agreement possible. On 12 June 2000 the Chilean armed forces recognised for the first time since the 1973 coup the human rights abuses committed during their regime. They also promised to gather and to provide all the information available within the armed institutions about the location of the bodies of the *desaparecidos* within a period of six months (later extended for another month).

The unexpected decision taken by judge Guzmán on 1 December 2000 to prosecute General Pinochet visibly strained the political situation in the country. Some senior officers declared to the press that this decision could endanger the efforts deployed by the armed forces to gather the required information for the *Mesa de Diálogo*. General Izurieta was pressured by the armed institutions to adopt a harder stand against the government and even to withdraw all participation from the *Mesa*. In the end, Izurieta decided to honour his agreement on the elaboration of the report and its official presentation in the early days of 2001. The decision to prosecute General Pinochet represented a *de facto* invalidation of the 1978 amnesty law, as it no longer guaranteed the immunity of military officers, including Pinochet, from legal prosecution.

The *Mesa de Diálogo* represents the largest and most important direct involvement of various sectors from civil society in national affairs since the restoration of democratic rule in 1990. In addition, for the first time in Chile's democratic history, political parties did not play a direct role in an important national event, as they were deliberately not invited to participate in its deliberations. The *Mesa* initiative was strongly criticised by both Pinochetista circles and by sectors of the radical left. While the right-wing groups saw it as an act of treason, for the radical left it was a strategy to obtain a *punto final* for the human rights question in Chile. The *Mesa* initiative also produced a painful schism within the human rights movement itself. While some representatives accepted the invitation to participate at the *Mesa*, others emphatically rejected it. In the end, however, the *Mesa de Diálogo* survived all obstacles and reached its goal of obtaining the required information from the armed forces about the whereabouts of the *desaparecidos* and the location of the bodies.

On 6 January 2001 the armed forces handed President Lagos an extensive report concerning the fate of these people.[14] It is expected that this information will lead to the finding of the remains of about 200 *desaparecidos*. It is once again the judiciary that will be in charge of the excavations and of deciding if this information can lead to further legal prosecution of the people involved in these disappearances. Since the presentation of the report, however, frustration and disappointment has emerged among the public as many locations indicated by the armed forces proved to be wrong or inaccurate. In addition, human rights activists and the extra-Parliamentary left decided to prosecute the commanders-in-chief of several branches of the armed forces for 'obstructing the finding of the truth', accusing them of not having provided all the information they possessed about the *desaparecidos*. Although this accusation did not prosper in the courts of law, it seriously damaged government–military relations as the armed institutions felt abandoned by the Lagos administration's failure to support the commanders-in-chief unconditionally. Military leaders have expressed their regret at having collaborated in the *Mesa de Diálogo* initiative, as it had not produced the expected relief on the human rights question but rather a further escalation of left-wing attacks on the armed forces.

Concluding remarks

Government–military relations in post-authoritarian Chile continue to be dominated by events that occurred during Pinochet's regime (1973–90). In particular, the unresolved question of human rights abuses during those years and the fates of more than one thousand disappeared persons have hindered the achievement of a lasting national reconciliation among Chileans and the normalisation of civil–military relations. In contrast to the South African Truth and Reconciliation Commission, the Chilean Rettig Commission did not succeed in reducing the tensions in the country around the question of human rights violations committed by the former authoritarian regime, which continues to be at the centre of the national debate.

In the Chilean case civil–military relations have been strongly influenced by the balance of forces between the right-wing sectors of society (about 40 per cent) and the centre–left forces (almost 50 per cent). A not insignificant part of the population still defends the military coup of 1973 and the *oeuvre* of the Pinochet regime, and is against any prosecution of former member of his regime for human rights abuses committed in those years. In other words, the past and the existence of two antagonistic readings about the causes of the military intervention sustain Chile's divisions. Although South Africa is not entirely free of internal cleavages (in both ethnic and regional terms), much greater national consensus has been achieved about the need to concentrate on the present and the future of the nation.

The over-representation of the Chilean right in Parliament and the severe tensions the military issue produced among members of the House of Deputies and the Senate have made legislative supervision of defence and security activities impossible. Also, due to the extremely high sensitivity of any issue related to civil–military relations in Chile, there is an almost implicit agreement among politicians that these matters have to be conducted primarily by the President of the republic and his Minister of Defence.

The Chilean armed forces have adopted an institutional stand of unconditional support for their former Commander-in-Chief, General Augusto Pinochet. It can be said that until March 1998 General Pinochet, in himself, was a determinant factor in either the improvement or the worsening of government–military relations. But even after his replacement as Commander-in-Chief of the army he continued to be a central actor in Chilean politics, as became dramatically clear following his arrest in London in October 1998 and his return to Chile in March 2000. Since the decision by judge Guzmán in December 2000 to prosecute him, relations between the armed forces and the Lagos government have substantially deteriorated. The South African experience, where following the restoration of democratic rule the armed forces proved not to be afraid of radically readapting themselves to the new political scenario, compares favourably with the Chilean situation (cf. Le Roux 2000).

The economic difficulties Chile has been confronting since 1998 (mainly as a result of the Asian and Brazilian crises) have politically weakened the *Concertación* governments in their efforts to eliminate the authoritarian enclaves and to further democratise the country's legal and institutional structures. On the other hand, the growing rates of underemployment and economic insecurity among the population have redirected the attention of public opinion from the Pinochet case to their own problems of subsistence.

The *Mesa de Diálogo* initiative constitutes one of the few occasions on which civil society has been invited by the government to participate in one way or another in the discussion of an issue related to the military institutions. Previous to that initiative, the *Concertación* governments had shown marked fears about the possible overpoliticisation of the defence issue if civil society was allowed to play a more comprehensive role in these matters. Under these conditions, the most civil society has been able to do is to make use of its political freedom to protest against the human rights violations of the former military regime and to demand justice and the prosecution of the guilty. Unlike in South Africa, an active role for Chilean civil society in the formulation of the national defence agenda seems not to be a very realistic prospect in the coming years.

Chile possesses a strong legalistic tradition and actually most of the transition process so far has been conducted through legal arrangements. The fact the Chilean government has left the fate of Pinochet in the hands of the judiciary has helped to normalise the situation, in a sense. It is perhaps not an exaggeration to state that the fate of government–military relations, for the time being, is mainly in the hands of Juan Guzmán and the judicial system, who will have to decide whether to convict or to release the old general.

Chronology

1970	The Unidad Popular coalition led by Salvador Allende wins the presidential elections.
1973	*Coup d'état*. A military regime led by General Augusto Pinochet comes into power.
1978	An amnesty law is adopted in an attempt to impede any future legal prosecution of members of the armed forces for human rights abuses committed under military rule.
1980	A new constitution is adopted, limiting the prospects for a full restoration of democratic rule in the near future, as a series on non-democratic procedures were introduced and the armed forces obtained a tutelary hold on Chilean society.
1988	Pinochet loses referendum. This implies the organisation of general elections within 12 months.
1989	General elections. The democratic opposition organised around the *Concertación* coalition wins the elections and announces the imminent restoration of democratic rule in the country.
1990–4	Government of President Patricio Aylwin. Creation of Commission for Truth and Reconciliation to investigate the human rights violations under the military regime, but the 1978 amnesty law impedes the legal prosecution of members of the armed forces. Period of tense civil–military relations, as Pinochet remains Commander-in-Chief of the army.
1995–9	Government of President Eduardo Frei. Civil–military relations become less conflictive, but human rights issue is still not satisfactorily resolved. Pinochet is arrested in London, 1998; this strongly reactivates the discussion on the human rights abuses committed by the armed forces during his regime.
2000–1	Government of President Ricardo Lagos. Pinochet returns to Chile in March 2000. Soon after this, his parliamentary immunity is removed by the Supreme Court. The trial of

Pinochet creates severe tension in government–military relations. *Mesa de Diálogo* initiative provides a final report on the location of the remains of those who disappeared during the Pinochet years.

References

Cawthra, G. (1996) *Securing South Africa's Democracy: Defence, Development and Security in Transition*, Basingstoke: Macmillan.

—— (2000) 'Security transformation in post-apartheid South Africa', paper presented at the workshop on 'Security Structures and Democratic Governance', University of Witwatersrand, Johannesburg, 18–20 September.

Clark, K. M. (2000) 'Concepciones de la defensa nacional en Argentina y Chile: una comparación de los libros de defensa', *Fuerzas Armadas y Sociedad*, 15 (2): 39–51.

Díaz, J. L. (1998) 'Relaciones cívico-militares en 1997: otro hito en el complejo proceso de normalización', in FLACSO, *Chile 97: Análisis y opiniones*, Santiago: FLACSO, pp. 127–35.

Ensalaco, M. (1994) 'In with the new, out with the old? The democratising impact of constitutional reform in Chile', *Journal of Latin American Studies*, 26 (2): 409–29.

Fuentes, C. (1996) *El discurso militar en la transición chilena*, Santiago: FLACSO.

—— (1997) 'Militares en Chile: ni completa autonomía ni total sub-ordinación' in FLACSO, *Chile 96: Análisis y opiniones*, Santiago: FLACSO, pp. 165–81.

—— (2000) 'After Pinochet: civilian policies towards the military in the 1990s Chilean democracy', *Journal of Interamerican Studies and World Affairs*, 43 (3): 111–42.

García, G. (2000) 'National defence and the armed forces', in Toloza, C. and E. Lahera (eds.), *Chile in the Nineties*, Stanford: Stanford University Libraries, pp. 163–81.

Hunter, W. (1998) 'Civil–military relations in Argentina, Brazil, and Chile: present trends, future prospects', in Agüero, F. and J. Stark (eds.), *Fault Lines of Democracy in Post-Transition Latin America*, Miami: North–South Center Press, pp. 299–322.

Le Roux, L. (2000) 'Defence restructuring in the context of democratisation: actors and issues', paper presented at the workshop on 'Security Structures and Democratic Governance', University of Witwatersrand, Johannesburg, 18–20 September.

Loveman, B. (1991) 'Misión cumplida? Civil–military relations and the Chilean political transition', *Journal of Interamerican Studies and World Affairs*, 33 (3): 35–74.

—— (1995) 'The transition to civilian government in Chile, 1990–1994', in Drake, P. W. and I. Jaksic (eds.), *The Struggle for Democracy in Chile*, Lincoln: University of Nebraska Press, pp. 305–37.

Loveman, B. (2001) *Chile: The Legacy of Hispanic Capitalism*, New York: Oxford University Press, third edition.

Luckham, R. (1996) 'Faustian bargains: democratic control over military and security establishments', in Luckham, R. and G. White (eds.), *Democratization in the South: the Jagged Wave*, Manchester: Manchester University Press, pp. 119–77.

Ministry of Defence (1998) *Book of the National Defence of Chile*, Santiago: Ministry of Defence.

Remmer, K. (1991) *Military Rule in Latin America*, Boulder: Westview Press.

Report of the Chilean National Commission on Truth and Reconciliation (1993) Notre Dame: Notre Dame University Press, 2 vols.

Rojas, F. (2001) 'Civil–military relations in post-authoritarian Chile', in Silva, P. (ed.), *The Soldier and the State in South America: Essays in Civil–Military Relations*, Basingstoke: Palgrave, pp. 151–74.

Stepan, A. (1988) *Rethinking Military Politics: Brazil and the Southern Cone*, New Jersey: Princeton University Press.

Notes

1 I am grateful to Gavin Cawthra and Robin Luckham for their helpful comments on an earlier version of this chapter.

2 A recent survey conducted by the Catholic University of Santiago corroborated the persistence of this deep division among Chileans about the political past. It demonstrated that, while a section of the Chilean population blames left-wing extremism and the economic crisis under the Allende government for precipitating the military intervention, the left and human rights organisations regard the armed forces and their ambition for power as solely responsible for the destruction of the old democratic system (*La Tercera*, 12 May 2001).

3 Article 90 of the 1980 constitution states that 'The armed forces ... exist solely for the defense of the homeland, are essential for national security, and guarantee the institutional order of the Republic.' Quoted in Rojas (2001: 157).

4 In the original design, the armed forces possessed a majority of votes in the National Security Council, as it was formed by three civilians (the President, the president of the senate, and the president of the Supreme Court), and four representatives of the armed institutions (the chiefs of the army, air force, navy, and *Carabineros*, Chile's militarised police force). The inclusion of the Comptroller General (*Controlador General de la República*) in the NSC ensured that an equilibrium between civilians and military men was achieved.

5 His successor, Patricio Aylwin, was later not allowed to make use of the same right, as the same constitution establishes that only those presidents who have governed the country for six consecutive years are entitled to become senators for life (while Aylwin had served for only a four-year term, as the constitution stipulates).

6 For instance, the academic journal *Fuerzas Armadas y Sociedad*, published by FLACSO, has provided a strategic forum for dialogue between civilian and military experts on defence issues.
7 In 1986 a special commando of *Carabineros* assassinated (by slashing throats) a group of human rights activists and members of the Communist party.
8 Letelier was Minister of Foreign Affairs under the Allende government and a prominent leader of the Chilean opposition to Pinochet in exile. He was murdered by a car bomb in a street in the centre of Washington, DC. As a result of strong US pressure on Pinochet, the Letelier case was explicitly excluded from the 1978 amnesty law.
9 The State Defence Council is a decentralised public service body under the direct supervision of the President and independent of the ministries. It is charged with the juridical defence of the interests of the Chilean state. It is thus quite a different institution from the National Security Council,
10 General Contreras finally went to jail on 21 October 1995.
11 During the farewell ceremony for the Commander-in-Chief at the Bernardo O'Higgins military academy, Pinochet was unexpectedly declared by the army 'Commander-in-Chief *emérito*', a tailor-made title which was given him to stress the readiness of the army to protect their former chief in the future. The Ministry of Defence was not informed beforehand of this announcement.
12 See 'La agenda militar laguista', *La Tercera*, 18 January 2000.
13 Judge Guzmán prudently decided to delay the further prosecution of Pinochet until October, as September is politically a very sensitive and tense month in Chile. Most of the troublesome dates are concentrated in this month: 4 September (commemoration of the triumph of Salvador Allende in the presidential elections of 1970); 11 September (commemoration/celebration of the 1973 *coup d'état* and the death of Allende); and 19 September (the day of the armed forces).
14 In the official statement made by the armed forces at the presentation of their report they indicated that 'the reinterpretation of the 1978 amnesty law, in terms which are not related to the original purpose of providing political and social peace, has had a negative impact on the efforts made by the armed institutions, but has also affected negatively the basis for national reconciliation'. *La Tercera*, 21 January 2001.

6

Political Armies, Security Forces and Democratic Consolidation in Latin America

KEES KOONINGS

The aim of this chapter is to analyse the legacy of political armies and military regimes in Latin America, their relationship to the recent process of democratisation, and the overall problem of violence and insecurity under formal civil rule. The core proposition is that although the advance of democratic politics and civil governance has reduced the role of political armies over the past decade and a half, their legacies of coercion and arbitrary violence have not been completely erased. Indeed, the paradox emerges that formal democracy has been setting the stage for the proliferation of new forms of violence and insecurity that democratically elected governments have found hard to restrain.

First I discuss the legacy of political armies in Latin America and the morphology and dynamics of institutional military rule, especially in the post-Second World War period. Special attention will be paid to the militarisation of politics and to the systematisation of state-induced violence and terror. Then I will look at the role of the military within the process of democratic transition and consolidation in Latin America since 1980. The initial driving forces away from authoritarian rule had as much to do with the failure of the security forces to sustain dictatorships and militarised politics, as with the democratisation strategies of the (civil) political opposition. This has led to a variety of 'transition scenarios' in which the military tried to maintain control or seek protection for prerogatives and against retaliation.

This has led in a number of Latin American countries to a more or less enduring presence of the security forces (especially the army and the intelligence services) in domestic politics. The subsequent two sections analyse the problem of redefining civil supremacy over the security forces in two key areas: prerogatives and tutelary powers of the armed forces within domestic politics, and the complicated legacy of human rights violations committed during the military dictatorships and civil wars. This legacy of the past has deeply affected the institutional and political foundation of civilian governance. In addition, as I will argue in the final two sections of this chapter, new forms of violence and the emergence of a growing variety of 'armed actors' in the region contribute to ongoing fear and insecurity, casting long shadows over the prospects for full democracy in the region.

Political armies and state violence

During the first century of independent statehood, most Latin American countries were marked by a fragile state monopoly over the legitimate means of coercion. Throughout the better part of the nineteenth century, weak postcolonial élites contended with regional militiamen (*caudillos*) for control of the state and its territory. After 1870, state formation and nation building became the project of national rural, urban commercial and political élites. This led, in most cases, to civil-dominated oligarchic republics that rested partially on the deployment of violence to secure élite hegemony and to deal with occasional tensions arising from social exclusion. This type of violence can be called 'patrimonial' because it was to a large extent privatised (especially in rural and peripheral areas). Public security forces were being built up in this period, but, until the 1930s, police forces remained fragmentary in form, existing alongside a large number of other, often paramilitary, bodies or semi-private militias. The military embarked upon a gradual course of 'modernisation' which made it an early driving force in the quest for national unity, more centralised state control, and overall economic and social development.

Against this background it can be understood that Latin America became the cradle of an early and long-standing legacy of so-called 'political armies'. From the late nineteenth or early twentieth century onward, professionalising armed forces sought an active institutional role and doctrinal position in national politics in most Latin American countries (Nun 1967; Nunn 1992, 2001). The military nurtured new ideas for nation-building projects, alongside populist-nationalist political leaders, intellectuals, trade unions, and in some cases urban entrepreneurs. In Latin America this has usually been expressed in terms of the military guarding over 'permanent national objectives', rather than being involved in factional politics or the pursuit of particularistic interests (Arseneaux 1999; Fitch 1998; Loveman 1994, 1999; Rial 1990; Rouquié 1989). The military regarded itself as the protector of the nation and the state on behalf of the people, and this became the birthright principle of Latin American political armies.[1]

In the post-Second World War period specific strategies of 'security and development' were given a doctrinal format, which Stepan (1976) has called 'new professionalism'. New professionalism lay at the core of the 'competence principle'. From the 1950s onwards, a distrust of populist radicalism came to prevail among most Latin American military establishments. Boosted by US military and police assistance from the 1950s onwards, and confronted by the Cuban revolution of 1959 and the mushrooming guerrilla movements it inspired in the 1960s, the notion of civil inadequacy was sharpened into a perception that any non-submissive civilian sector was a direct threat to the state and the nation.

It is thus possible to see the consolidation of Latin American political armies as the combination of two parallel processes: the development of a pro-interventionist body of doctrine and expertise (new professionalism, the competence principle), and the evolution of a military perspective on nation building and the necessary means of political control and support (the military quasi-party, the principle of civil inadequacy). In a number of countries these dynamics eventually led to protracted periods of direct military rule, state terrorism, insurgent violence and (low-intensity) civil war.[2] Although there have been important differences among individual Latin American cases, a number of key features of the dictatorships of the 1960s–70s can be discerned.

A first feature was the closure of the political arena and the militarisation of key areas within the state structure. In Brazil and the Southern Cone countries, the armed forces took over the executive branch through *juntas* or military presidents endorsed by the armed forces. Legislatures and political parties were either disbanded (Argentina, Chile) or severely curtailed (Brazil). Real or perceived political opponents were suspended, silenced, exiled or 'disappeared'. In Argentina and Brazil, the military substituted itself for civil and political society as high-level officers deliberated political issues. National intelligence and national security agencies became pivotal in safeguarding internal political control (both within the state apparatus and within society at large) and were important sources of strategic thinking on a wide array of policy issues.

The second common feature was the concept of 'internal warfare'. Directly derived from the tenets of new professionalism, the idea that the armed forces took power to deal with an exceptional threat to state and nation legitimised the military takeovers. Subsequently it became a central part of the strategy of these regimes and, in retrospect, their most notorious characteristic. A basic distinction can be made between the low-intensity but pervasive state terrorism in Brazil and the Southern Cone, and the open civil wars waged in Central America, especially El Salvador and Guatemala. In both, however, the military itself systematically referred to 'warfare' when describing the activities of its repressive apparatus. In Brazil and the Southern Cone countries, repression was meted out not only against known adversaries but also to instil fear among certain sectors (organised labour, students, intellectuals, peasants) and within society as a whole (Corradi *et al.* 1992; Koonings and Kruijt 1999). Open civil war in Central America followed the same basic pattern of conflict (leading to even larger numbers of victims), but faced a well-organised armed opposition.

The third common feature was the development of 'national security doctrine', in which political interventionism, militarisation of the state and internal warfare were brought together. Such doctrine not only provided an ideological underpinning for military rule, it also inspired an elaborate pseudo-legal system of repression and control, formalising the internal politico-military orientation of the Latin American armed forces (Fitch 1998; Zagorski 1992). In addition, military regimes made explicit connections between national security, political control, and projects for national development. Latin American security thinking, with strong roots in early European geopolitical as well as US notions of 'counterinsurgency and civic action', tended to visualise security as an integrated concept with not only a military but also an economic and social dimension. Economic progress and social integration were generally seen as key preconditions for the avoidance or neutralisation of insurgency. This military concern with the economic and social dimensions of development was especially prominent in the larger South American countries. There were, however, important differences in the way military regimes worked this issue out. For instance, the Brazilian military deepened state-led import substitution industrialisation, while their Chilean counterparts opted for neoliberalism and export promotion.

A final aspect was the distortion of law enforcement and the maintenance of public order. Especially in countries which experienced prolonged authoritarian rule, state repression, or civil war, the police force and the justice system were subordinated to military control and the overriding priority of national security against internal enemies (Chevigny 1995). In many cases, the police became auxiliary forces of repression, responding to military commanders rather than civil authorities and using arbitrary violence under conditions of impunity, to the detriment of law enforcement and the protection of citizenship rights. It has been widely documented that police violence mostly affected the poor and excluded segments of society (Pinheiro 1991, 1996). Police and other security forces often engaged in clandestine or even criminal activities, veiled from public scrutiny by the general climate of censorship, arbitrariness and impunity.

Democratic transitions and the military

From the late 1970s, the institutional dictatorships in South America started to show fissures and cracks. In due course, civil governments also began to emerge in Central America, notably in Honduras, El Salvador and Guatemala. By the 1990s the emphasis had shifted towards the mechanisms and conditions of democratic consolidation as, with a few exceptions, elected civilian governments were installed and were regularly succeeded by other elected civilian governments. This is not the place to dwell on the various stages and dimensions of democratic transition and consolidation.[3] Here I shall discuss only the role of the security forces, especially the military, in democratic transitions.

In the Latin American transition scenarios a number of variables were in play. Prolonged military rule eroded the institutional integrity of the Latin American armed forces. This tendency could only partially be countered by doctrines of internal warfare, as fighting against the internal enemy was conducted in ways that did not at all resemble the notions of battlefield valour and institutional competence of the armed forces. The dirty work of counterinsurgency was often relegated to specific units or branches within the security forces, whose involvement in repression and human rights violations not only came to be seen as unworthy of real soldiers, but also fragmented lines of command and control within the security forces themselves. In addition, involvement in human rights violations created an increasingly complex 'extrication problem' for security forces that feared they would be held accountable by civilian governments. A final element of institutional erosion was military involvement in rent-seeking schemes and corruption, undermining the credibility of regimes and their dedication to the national interest.

A second factor contributing to the weakening and demise of military rule was the erosion of the legitimacy of authoritarian regimes. It has to be stressed that even the most severe military regimes in Latin America were concerned, from the outset, with legitimising their control of state power and pursuit of military policies. In a number of cases, this was done by referring to the dictatorship as a 'revolution' (Brazil, Peru), or as an overdue process of national reorganization (Argentina, Chile). Additional legitimisation was sought in the perennial battle against radical or Marxist subversion. In Brazil and the Southern Cone, economic development and (middle-class) material well-being also became important ingredients of legitimacy, binding societal allies such as landowners, entrepreneurs and the urban middle classes to the regime project. But prolonged military rule tended to erode this legitimacy and led to the defection of civilian allies, especially where they became estranged by the concentration of power in the hands of increasingly unpopular and isolated military *juntas*. In addition, the inability of military regimes to build a stable mass political base for their rule, such as a movement or a party, eroded their political position. Legitimacy problems also tended to sharpen internal dissent and factionalism within military regimes themselves, that could be played upon by the opposition.

On the political plane, the rise of mass-based societal and political oppositions has been a key factor in successful transitions. The locus of legitimacy shifted from the dictatorship to the broad-based civil opposition in countries such as Peru, Brazil and Chile, where a wide array of social and protest movements linked up with the (formally neutralised or severely constricted) party system to present alternative political platforms. The latter generally incorporated the restoration of political freedom and pluralism, and the reestablishment of human and citizenship rights, which also implied a critique of the conservative and exclusionary nature of the military-backed development model. This resurgence of feasible and trustworthy political alternatives eased the way into power of civilian oppositions. If they could demonstrate a track record of peaceful institutional tactics and skilful, moderate negotiation, this further widened the fissures in military regimes and ate into their legitimacy and support base. In Central America a fledgling process of democratisation had a similar effect, to the extent that it created the starting conditions for peace negotiations.

Last, international pressure for democracy and human rights (notably stronger after the end of the Cold War) served to isolate authoritarian regimes and to strengthen domestic civilian opposition. Even hard-boiled military regimes became weary of perpetual ostracism and pariah status in the development community of multilateral banks and bilateral donors. International pressure came not only from (some, not all) democratically governed nations in the North, but also from their public opinion and civic associations. The international community played an especially important role in the Central American peace process (Arnson

1999). Also, countries of recent re-democratisation generated democratic peer pressures within their own ranks: examples are the Esquipulas peace initiative in Central America; protest within the MERCOSUR area against Oviedo in Paraguay; and the regional condemnation of authoritarian repression in Peru and Ecuador.

But does this mean that democratic transition and consolidation in Latin America have effectively ended the cycle of political armies, or the military and security forces' involvement in domestic politics? And if so, do popularly elected civilian governments now effectively control security forces on the basis of the rule of law and democratic civil–military relations? In the next two sections, I shall try and take a detached look at the question of the security forces under civil rule in post-authoritarian Latin America, focusing on two aspects: first, the problem of military prerogatives (political and institutional) and military tutelage; and second, the delicate problem of the legacy of human rights violations by military regimes and the ensuing problem of impunity, which casts a shadow over efforts at reconciliation and the reinsertion of the military institution into a legitimate democratic order.

Civil rule and military tutelage

During the transition process, Latin America's political armies went to great lengths to preserve a series of prerogatives that would insulate them from civil control and assure as far as possible their capacity to influence domestic politics under formal civil-democratic governance. These prerogatives emanated both from the ability of outgoing authoritarian regimes to set the terms for the post-dictatorial institutional order and from the long history of active militarism as an integral part of political culture in most Latin American countries (Stepan 1988: 94–8; Kruijt and Koonings 1999: 15–19; Kruijt 2001).

When a structure of prerogatives has been used to maintain permanent supervision and guidance over politics and policy making, it is possible to speak of a tutelary situation or a 'veto regime'. The military has retained direct access to power and decision making, and many trappings of the former military regime have survived. Notably, the policy making and control roles of intelligence services and military academies have been retained, together with the active presence of the military in the cabinet and mandatory advisory or consultative bodies, such as the National Security Council (Brazil until 1990, Chile) or the Guatemalan Estado Mayor Presidencial (Supreme Presidential Staff, EMP). The military has retained substantial control over the formulation of policy, using the intelligence system as its main vehicle. In countries such as Chile, Peru, Guatemala and Brazil (at least until 1989), elected or appointed presidents have been strongly influenced by their intelligence advisers. In Chile, military moderatorship has been institutionally anchored in so-called 'authoritarian enclaves' (a powerful military-dominated National Security Council and non-elected senators and Supreme Court justices appointed by Pinochet). These were entrenched by the prevailing legalism of Chilean political culture, the artificial veto given to pro-military forces in Congress, as well as the *de facto* autonomy of the military institution (Agüero 2002; Rojas 2001; Silva in this volume). In Guatemala, defence ministers have had an army general as presidential chief-of-staff and chief of the EMP. Civilian presidents Cereso, Serrano, De Leon Carpio and Arzú continued to receive 'consultative briefings' on long-term national development and security priorities, as perceived by the army. In Peru, president Fujimori's intelligence chief Vladimiro Montesinos, acted for ten years (1990–2000) as virtual president of the national intelligence system in close connection with the military leadership (Kruijt and Tello 2002).

A second element of military prerogatives in most Latin American countries has been military predominance over the national and local police. It has been common for army officers to hold sensitive posts in the police hierarchy, and the political responsibility for the national police is often a matter of civil–military power distribution. Sometimes an army general has been Minister of Interior Affairs or Public Safety, whilst in other cases the vice-minister or the national police director has been a former army officer. In some countries, (Guatemala for instance, at least prior to the post-1996 police reform) the police have been subordinated to the military not only at the national, but also at regional and local levels; the local police have had to coordinate, in detail, with local army commanders, and have depended completely on army intelligence. Furthermore, the military logic of indiscriminate stigmatisation of adversaries has also characterised police forces, with serious consequences for their ability to ensure the rule of law.

A third aspect of the continued influence of the military in Latin America has been that it has often acted as the sole representative of national public authority in remote areas. The army or in some cases the navy or air force have taken on the provision of public services, such as the construction of infrastructure, transportation and health-care, as well as routine public administration. After the 1950s, this was amplified through so-called 'civic action' strategies, which were seen as an explicit supplement to counterinsurgency warfare. Civic action has been reinvented in post-authoritarian Latin America, for instance where the military is assigned to services like environmental control.

Finally, in some countries, the military has developed into an economic stakeholder or even a revenue seeker. In countries like Ecuador or Guatemala, the armed forces have set up a variety of business ventures. In many more countries active or retired officers have found careers in the private or parastatal sectors. In other cases, notably Chile and Ecuador, the military appropriates a fixed proportion of annual export revenues from natural resources. This economic role is often justified in terms of the military's limited budgetary allocations, for which direct revenues then function as a substitute, sometimes even with open civilian consent.

Closely linked to the problem of military prerogatives is the issue of reformulating military 'missions' or 'role orientations'. As we have seen, the new professionalism generated military role expansion to deal with domestic opponents, and pushed the armed forces towards political intervention and direct military rule, precisely as a legitimate option from a doctrinal and institutional point of view. Democratising civil–military relations would therefore imply that armies become depoliticised by excluding such role expansion from their mission statements.

Yet in the case of Latin America, there are few signs that such a mission reformulation towards an apolitical Huntingtonian professionalism is imminent or easy to bring about, despite the fact that the end of the Cold War has made anti-communism obsolete. Indeed, the mission statements of the armed forces, stripped of Cold War rhetoric, remain inward-looking and broad-brushed. To be sure, it has become fashionable to champion old 'professional' tasks such as technological upgrading, territorial defence, or participation in UN peacekeeping. Yet at the same time missions and roles retain strong elements of national guardianship, the constitutionally sanctioned right to intervene to protect the national interest, a military view of domestic order and stability, developmentalism, and civic action. Threat perceptions have been adapted to the post-Cold War context: the internal enemy of 'Marxist subversion' has been traded in for more diffuse and morally defined dangers to national goals: 'narco-terrorism', Maoist guerrilla warfare, ethnic tensions and poverty-induced unrest have been cited as potential threats meriting continued attention by the military (Marcella 1994; Rial 1994).

The military and the legacy of human rights violations

A crucial problem for post-authoritarian civil–military relations in Latin America has been how human rights violations committed by the security forces during the dictatorships are dealt with under democratic governance. This issue is not only relevant to the immediate problem of military acceptance of democratic rule. It affects longer-term issues, such as the reconciliation of antagonistic groups and ideas around post-authoritarian civil and institutional reconstruction, as well as the ongoing problem of the rule of law and impunity. It is widely held that long-term consolidation of democracy in Latin America is impossible without addressing the legacy of human rights violations, not only because this is the key to durable reconciliation of past antagonisms, but also in order to restore basic trust between the citizens and the security forces.

The prospect of being held accountable for the conduct of 'dirty wars' has been a key component of the so-called 'extrication problem' faced by the military during transitions. In all cases (with the initial exception of Argentina) the military, while still in power, tried to get around this problem by institutionalising impunity through so-called amnesty legislation. Safeguards were sought in the overt or covert pacts made as part of the various transition processes, in some cases leading to 'full stop' legislation barring any prosecution of perpetrators of state terror.

However, in a number of countries, human rights-focused civil bodies (such as the Catholic Church), or official truth commissions have produced detailed accounts of political assassinations, disappearances, torture and the like.[4] These reports have served to ensure public and international awareness of human rights violations. But the security forces have remained by and large hostile to their findings and have mounted strong legal and political challenges to the reports.

Democratic governments themselves have been slow in insisting on accountability for human rights violators, whether from fear of military backlash, due to ongoing military tutelage, out of concern with other priorities, or because of lack of political interest. In countries where the military has maintained relatively high levels of cohesion and support (such as Chile, Guatemala, and to a lesser extent Brazil) addressing human rights issues has remained difficult. Only in Argentina did the first civilian government, headed by Raúl Alfonsín of the Radical Civic Union party, take swift judicial action against the military leadership responsible for state terror and the disastrous conduct of the Malvinas/Falklands war. Yet, during the late 1980s and early 1990s, three military revolts forced the shortening of the penalties imposed on the junta leaders and eventually the promulgation of a full-stop law by Alfonsín's successor, the Peronist Carlos Menémm. In Uruguay, full-stop legislation was agreed by a popular referendum. In Chile, the armed forces rejected any legal action against military involved in the repression, while in Guatemala the security forces lashed out after the publication of the two Truth Commission reports, leading to the assassination of Bishop Gerardi, the coordinator of the REMHI investigation.

However, things seem to be changing (though slowly) with respect to the legacy of human rights violations. International pressures have started to play a significant role, and this has strengthened the hand of domestic forces calling for justice and the end of impunity. In Brazil, the social-liberal government headed by Fernando Henrique Cardoso has since 1994 begun to address the rights of victims of repression, providing financial compensation and pensions, therewith recognising the responsibility of the state for human rights violations in the 1960s and 1970s (Koonings 1999: 215–16). Nevertheless the 1979 amnesty law precludes persecution of involved members of the security forces. In Argentina, a new generation of commanding officers has appeared more willing to acknowledge military responsibility for illegal actions during the dirty war. In Argentina as well as Chile, prosecutors have taken cases to the court that are not covered by the amnesty or full-stop laws, such as the abduction of children of victims, or crimes against humanity. International legal action has been important in preparing the ground, with Pinochet's arrest in London in 1998 being the *cause célèbre*. After his return to Chile, the Supreme Court nullified Pinochet's immunity as senator. The case against the former dictator was only halted in July 2001 for health reasons. In Guatemala, rural communities have filed indictments in the Guatemalan justice system for genocide against former dictators Lucas García and Ríos Montt (the latter currently president of the national Congress). Likewise former junta leader Jorge Videla has been indicted by an Argentinian prosecutor for his involvement in Operation Condor, an international scheme under which political opponents of the dictatorships in Argentina, Bolivia, Brazil, Chile, Paraguay and Uruguay during the 1970s were persecuted.

In sum, the human rights issue is far from being resolved, and remains highly relevant for civilian control of the security forces. Even more important, the search for justice, truth and eventual reconciliation continues as part of a more general reconstruction of national consensus, democratic institutionality and rule of law in Latin America.

The 'new violence' of non-state armed actors

Most discussions of the role of security forces under democratic rule in Latin America have focused on the legacy and continuing presence of political militarism. This is understandable given the historical preponderance of this phenomenon during the past century. However, an increasingly important aspect of democratic consolidation has been the continuation and even further spread of political and social violence.

In theory, full democratic consolidation would not only mean the subordination of the security forces under civil rule, but also the effective maintenance of the state's monopoly of the means of coercion and its deployment to secure public order, the rule of law, and citizenship rights on the basis of accountable norms and procedures. This ideal type is far from established in many Latin American countries. Instead, violence has continued even in countries where democracy has made considerable headway.

Elsewhere we have dubbed this phenomenon the 'new violence', although many of its manifestations are in fact far from new (Kruijt and Koonings 1999: 12). The basic empirical characteristic of the new violence is that it is increasingly widespread and no longer a resource only of élites or security forces, and its 'newness' contrasts with the norms and expectations derived from the democratisation process (Peralva 2000). Another characteristic is its variety: it subsumes different forms of violence, such as everyday criminal and street violence, riots, social cleansing, private account settling, police arbitrariness, paramilitary activities, guerrillas, etcetera. This makes it hard to capture the new violence in a satisfactory explanatory framework.

Still, a number of causal factors can be mentioned. Firstly, the combination of two long-term problems, namely the syndrome of inequality and social exclusion (often called structural violence) plaguing Latin American societies throughout their existence, and the legacy of particularism in applying justice and the rule of law. This combination produces a manifest discrepancy between demands for rights and justice generated by overall economic and social change and democratisation, and the capability of a given social system to deliver. With the demise of authoritarianism and a police-state approach to public order, a Pandora's box has been opened. Violence, a resource that benefited élites and regimes in the past, allowing them to evade accountability, has become an option for an increasing variety of social actors. The continuing difficulties of disentangling domestic law enforcement from its militaristic, politicised and arbitrary authoritarian past does little to increase the legitimacy of public authorities. Indeed, arbitrary violence by state agencies such as the police still reinforces a militaristic understanding of public order. The 'enemy' is no longer the former political and ideological opponents of military regimes, but rather those socially excluded by class and colour. Arbitrary violence has been unleashed against second-class citizens stigmatised as 'marginal' or 'dangerous' classes. It should come as no surprise that members of these classes themselves resort to violence through criminal activities, vigilante justice, or even violent acts of social redistribution.

In addition, there are specific legacies of authoritarianism itself. The militarisation of the security forces and their conception of internal order have reinforced patterns of conflict that have survived into the recent era of democratic politics. This has in some cases led to 'dirty wars' waged directly by the security forces under the formal control of democratic governments (as in Peru, El Salvador and Guatemala), or to repression and terror by paramilitary forces and death squads with no official but often very real informal connections to state security forces or to economically and politically powerful social sectors. Such forces by their very nature escape control by democratic governments. Almost by definition they contribute to the 'unrule of law' and to 'uncivil society' (Méndez, O'Donnell and Pinheiro 1999; Payne 2000). Sometimes these forces have become linked to large-scale organised crime, supplying both the means (notably in the form of drug money) and the motive to undermine the state's monopoly of means of violence.

It would go beyond the scope of this chapter to give an exhaustive overview of the manifestations of this violence and the armed actors involved in it.[5] For the purpose of brevity I group them in three categories that are, however, in practice closely linked. First there are the official security forces themselves. Military, paramilitary, intelligence and police agencies continue to operate outside the rule of law, subordinating law enforcement to their own political and other interests, operating in conditions of arbitrariness and impunity. Sometimes, they have been linked to informal murky armed actors (such as death squads or civil patrols) engaged in the repression of political opponents, human rights activists, peasants, trade unionists, etcetera. Such violence is thus often a direct projection of the authoritarian past into the democratic present.

The second category of armed actors can be put in the realm of 'extra-legal violence', including a wide array of criminal and social violence having political ramifications. Large-scale organised crime, linked to the international drug trade, has created parallel systems of violence and order in countries such as Colombia and Mexico. This logic has been reproduced on a smaller scale by the drug bosses and their gangs in the Brazilian *favelas* or by the *maras*, the criminal youth gangs in several Central American countries. These armed actors fill up the voids left by the failure of the rule of law and thrive in an overall climate of impunity, which in turn fosters vigilante and mob justice in poor neighbourhoods and rural communities.[6]

Finally, guerrilla forces and armed oppositions continue to employ violence, despite their seeming marginalisation in the post-Cold War period. Conventional guerrilla groups have indeed become scarce in Latin America after 1990 (Gaspar 1997). In Peru, Shining Path and the *guevarista* Tupac Amaru revolutionary movement have been significantly weakened, while the Central American guerrillas have been transformed into political movements following the peace settlements in the region. Only in Colombia do left-wing guerrilla armies still bring significant military power to bear against state and paramilitary forces. The 'postmodern' guerrilla movement of the EZLN in Southern Mexico has hardly done any fighting at all and should rather be seen as a guerrilla-ignited social movement pursuing basic social and political reforms, including greater dignity for Mexico's long-ignored indigenous populations. Elsewhere some 'radicalising' social movements have discovered that force may be employed to back up economic or social claims. Clear examples are the tactics of the landless workers' movement in Brazil or Ecuador's indigenous movement in the 1980s and 1990s.[7]

Not surprisingly these movements have been cited among the new security threats identified by the military and police in these countries. In several cases there has been right-wing counter-reform political violence as well, most notably in Nicaragua, El Salvador, Colombia, Argentina and Brazil.[8]

Democracy, security forces and violence: three Latin American scenarios

The related problems of weak democratic control of the security forces and the spread of political violence in Latin America have cast shadows over the very future of democracy and the rule of law. However, important differences in kind and degree exist among countries of the region. In this final section I will outline three current configurations or scenarios for the post-Cold War period, each representing a specific interplay between the reshaping of the political role of the military and security forces and the continued political violence under formal democratic rule (Koonings and Kruijt 2002). Each scenario is illustrated with specific country cases: Brazil; Guatemala; and Peru and Colombia.[9]

The first scenario takes the *withering away* of political armies as its point of departure. If the forces working against the classical project of military politics are strong enough, this can potentially lead to the gradual demise of military involvement in politics to the benefit of democratic consolidation. Such forces include the stability and legitimacy of democratic politics itself, together with the strengthening of civil society and public acceptance of the notion that democracy offers the best prospects for economic development, social participation and the rights of citizens. Political violence in this scenario is therefore typically seen as a *problem of governance* set against the background of inequality and social exclusion. Civil and democratic authorities are not themselves contested, but their effectiveness in assuring civil order and the rule of law is perceived as limited due to political or institutional defaults of the system.

The second scenario is grounded upon the notion that the political role of the military and security forces has been preserved through *institutionalised modification*. The political role of the military continues to be anchored in its formal institutional position through tutelary powers or notions of 'guided democracy'. In this scenario political armies maintain their influence, whilst altering their political profile, for instance by identifying new threats to national unity, or creating new missions like humanitarian aid, environmental control, crime fighting, or the 'war on drugs'. The preservation of a political army may in turn preserve or create spaces for official or unofficial extra-legal violence. Coercion, intimidation, and repression by the security forces themselves or by their hidden allies continue to serve political ends dictated by a military perception of the social and political order. Democracy may ultimately be reduced to a shallow outer shell.

Finally, I suggest a *perversion and corruption scenario* of militarised politics and the proliferation of violence. In this scenario, armed actors exert a *de facto* control of social and political life, which is in marked contrast to a formal institutional framework of democratic governance and the rule of law. Here a further distinction can be made. On one hand there is deliberate 'regime-induced' perversion of the political process. The regime itself has no substantial democratic content, only maintaining democracy's outer appearances. It becomes corrupted through the displacement of power from civil and political society to hidden networks of coercion and intimidation organised by the 'dark side' of the state. On the other hand there is a separation opening up between the formal polity, which may be genuinely democratic, and the realm of violence and fear, marked by the proliferation of armed actors. Procedures and rights organised in the former are made meaningless in the latter. Under such conditions, arbitrariness and violence is ultimately bound to creep into the domain of democracy, with the rule of law becoming subjugated by the rule of force.

Brazil: the unrule of law in a restored democracy

Until 1990, Brazil seemed to fit the 'institutional modification' scenario rather than the 'withering away' one. The first civilian government after 21 years of military rule (1964–85) was indirectly selected in an electoral college and was headed by José Sarney, who had been for a long time one of the key figures in the military-supportive ARENA party. Due to the disastrous economic performance of his administration and widespread personalism and corruption, the Sarney government soon became enormously unpopular within Brazil's increasingly fragmented political society. Meanwhile, the military preserved its fully fledged tutelary power. As a result, the Sarney government sought the support of the military institution; the military, in turn, used its clout to carve out prerogatives in the new constitution adopted in 1988.

The direct election of Sarney's successor in 1989 set the stage for a remarkable redressing of civil–military relations. Electoral politics as well as the deteriorating status of the armed forces moved the military gradually to the margins of political life (Hunter 1997; Castro 2002). Soon after the inauguration of the second civilian government of Fernando Collor in 1990, important building blocks of military tutelage were removed, such as the National Security Council and the National Intelligence Service, placing internal intelligence and security under civilian control. Military involvement in non-military affairs was ended after a last and unsuccessful effort to deploy the army in urban crime fighting in Rio de Janeiro in 1994. Military concerns such as the nuclear research programme or the Amazonian defence programme were abolished or scaled down. Efforts were made to reorient the armed forces towards tasks such as territorial defence and international peace-keeping and to increase civilian competence in these matters.

The corruption scandal of 1992 that led to the abdication of President Collor did not provoke significant military unrest, nor did the erratic behaviour of his interim successor, Itamar Franco. Fernando Henrique Cardoso, who won the presidency convincingly in both the 1994 and 1998 elections, took further steps to depoliticise the military. The most historically unique of these was the abolition of the five remaining military ministerial posts in the cabinet and the creation of a civilian-headed Ministry of Defence in 1998. Other advances made by the Cardoso government included (as already mentioned) an official committee to investigate the fate of disappeared persons and recognition of state responsibility for assassinations and disappearances during military rule, despite clamorous military opposition.

In more general terms, the dynamism of the democratic process in Brazil seems to have diminished both the political aspirations and political space of the military, despite the constitutional provision that the armed forces may intervene to protect the institutional order at the request of any of the three constitutive powers (executive, legislative, judiciary). The vitality of the electoral process and the gradual strengthening of civil society have precluded the 'knocking on the barracks' door' so characteristic of pre-1964 politics. In addition, as Castro (2002) argues, the military has been losing the 'battle of memory'. Not only has military symbolism been greatly reduced within the national symbolic universe, but the armed forces' views are increasingly isolated from mainstream opinion with respect to the past 'anti-subversive battle'.

However, the spread of extra-legal violence has cast a shadow over democratic consolidation and the demise of Brazil's political army.[10] Social confrontations in the 1980s and 1990s, such as strikes, land invasions and the like, have often led to violence, mostly initiated by police forces, private gunmen or sometimes by protesters. Privatised violence remains a resource in 'backland politics' or frontier regions. Most dramatically and visibly, the unrule of law has taken hold of the poor and peripheral areas of the large cities, particularly Rio de Janeiro and São Paulo. Here we witness the collapse of the rule of law and the fragile imposition of parallel forms of 'order' on the basis of violence (Leeds 1996). State and municipal police regularly employ violence in their 'war' against the poor and coloured urban underclass; indeed, they may be actively associated with criminal networks through corruption and the small arms trade. Criminal groups control most of the *favelas* (shantytowns). Order is founded upon intimidation to serve the almost 'feudal' notions of territoriality of the drug lords, to be defended against both security forces and rival gangs. In the interstices of the unrule of law, various forms of private justice have flourished, reflecting local-level hierarchies of status and power.

In response, the Brazilian state has made electorate-driven but mostly ineffective efforts to control crime, reform the police and the judiciary, and to promote citizenship rights. The problems are publicly regarded primarily as governance issues, to be addressed through eliminating specific areas of 'incompetence' or 'corruption' within the security and judicial sectors. Nevertheless, few would doubt that they cannot be solved without addressing the fundamental issue of social exclusion that permeates Brazilian society.

Guatemala: military guardians of a 'strategic peace'

The 'institutional modification' scenario implies that the military retains considerable doctrinal coherence and institutional capacity for intervention in politics, even if elected civilian governments have replaced direct military rule. It also implies that the military still claims considerable support for its past political performance and present political prerogatives. In sum, it entails a refurbishing of moderator or veto-type political armies under post-Cold War conditions, in which 'anti-communism' is obsolete and 'democracy' is the dominant norm.

In Latin America, Guatemala provides the clearest example. The military reached the limits of hard-boiled counterinsurgency warfare at the end of the 1970s. This led to the elaboration of a 'military–political project' that envisaged a stable form of 'protected democracy' once the insurgency had been dealt with effectively (Rosada-Granados 1999). With this project the military built upon the already far-reaching militarisation of politics and public administration achieved during the civil conflict since the 1960s. Between 1982 and 1985, the armed forces gained a strategic victory over the guerrilla forces of the URNG, through a combination of ruthless terror ('bullets'), civic action ('beans'), and mobilisation of the rural population in mandatory civil patrols.

Following constitutional reform and the installation of elected civil government in 1984–5, the military explicitly deepened its supervision of the civilian sector through a system known as 'co-governance'. The newly established Centro ESTNA, a high-level military study and training institution, refurbished military control of politics under the 'national stability thesis' that made democratic governance dependent on military supervision. Although notions of civil government, democracy and human rights were accepted as part of the Guatemalan polity, they remained subordinated to the military mission of countering threats to political and institutional stability. Such threats included the ongoing presence of armed guerrillas, rising crime, civil society opposition, and indigenous mobilisation. The military maintained control of internal intelligence, police operations, and overall policy guidance through the Estado Mayor Presidencial.

The peace process that accelerated from the early 1990s onward only gradually and incompletely amended the military co-governance project. The peace process enjoyed strong international support and gave an increasing role to civil society organisations. The failure of President Serrano's military-backed self-coup in 1993 led to the appointment of the human rights ombudsman De Leon Carpio as the new President. The agreement on the 'role of the security forces in a democratic society', which was part of the peace accord finalised in 1996, defined a non-political role for the military and called for the abolition of tutelary instruments such as military intelligence and the EMP. The same agreement also stipulated the creation of a new national civilian police force (Azpuru 1999; Glebbeek 2001).

On the other hand, as Schirmer (1998, 2002) argues, the sheer clout of the Guatemalan military precluded its effective removal from power sharing. The termination of military control of intelligence was delayed, as was the abolition of the EMP. The military continued to play a role in domestic policing. The armed forces vehemently opposed the findings of the Commission for Historical Clarification and the Church's Report on Historical Memory: these investigations had attributed the overwhelming majority of human rights violations and war crimes to the military and its related paramilitary forces and civil patrols. Currently (March 2002), the military is still thwarting the investigation and prosecution of the perpetrators of the assassination of Bishop Gerardi almost three years ago. The continuing fragility of Guatemalan politics, at present exemplified by the delicate stalemate between President Alfonso Portillo and Congress leader Efraím Ríos Montt, contributes little to the strengthening of civil power *vis-à-vis* a truculent military. Furthermore, as exemplified by the Gerardi case, there are numerous indications of links between the formal security forces and clandestine violent groups (MINUGUA 2001: 15–17).

Peru and Colombia: the politics of coercion

Peru and Colombia serve as examples of perversion 'from above' and 'from below', respectively. In Peru, the failure of democratic governance during the 1980s led to the authoritarian-populist project of the elected Fujimori government. This regime not only openly bypassed established democratic procedures but also created and managed a clandestine network of extortion, intimidation and violence, to which even the country's reform-minded political army was subordinated. In Colombia, formal politics seemingly became less oligarchic and more open during the past two decades; and there is no historical tradition of open military rule (with the exception of the 1953–7 *junta* of Rojas Pinilla during *La Violencia*). Yet non-state armed actors have precipitated a virtual state collapse and have laid siege to civil society. As a result, coercion reigns supreme in large parts of the country.

The restoration of democracy in Peru in 1980 followed a cycle of reformist military rule. It also marked the beginning of the 'lost decade' of the 1980s, a period of economic decline, growing poverty, widespread informalisation and social exclusion (Kruijt 1994, 1996). This was the background to one of the most obscure and violent conflicts in recent Latin American history with the sudden appearance of the Maoist guerrilla movement Shining Path on election day in 1980. Shining Path developed an ultra-orthodox Maoist doctrine and a long-term military strategy to encircle and defeat the state in two to three generations. The conflict lasted almost 14 years, more or less ending after the capture of its leader, Abimael Guzmán, in September 1992.[11]

The war against Shining Path contributed to the disintegration of the Peruvian political army, as well as being a key factor in the de-legitimisation of civil democratic politics during the 1980s. In 1982, after two years of ineffective police counter-measures against the 'bandits and terrorists', the military entered to conduct a violent dirty war in emergency zones, militarising large parts of the Andean highlands. Its counterinsurgency role was resented by a military establishment still mindful of the reformist nation-building project of the Velasco regime. The final year of the Alan García government (1985–90) and the first three years of the Fujimori presidency brought the rise of paramilitary forces and death squads. In rural conflict zones an effective counter-strategy was based on a more balanced approach: counterinsurgency alongside civic action and the expansion of *rondas campesinas* (counterinsurgent peasant militias) (Basombrío 1999; Fumerton 2001; Kruijt 1999).

The unfolding drama of the 1980s set the stage for the final corruption not only of the army but also of the entire system of civil–military relations and democracy (Kruijt and Tello 2002). In the 1990 presidential elections the unknown anti-politician Alberto Fujimori succeeded in defeating the political establishment. Immediately he embarked upon a peculiar political career, welding *chicha* (popular) streetwise personalism with orthodox economic austerity and hard-boiled counterinsurgency. In April 1992 Fujimori carried out his self-coup, removing constitutional barriers to the exercise of his presidential powers, which enjoyed popular support because it played upon popular resentment of the political establishment. This was followed, five months later, by the tracking down and arrest of Guzmán. The Fujimori regime developed into a civilian dictatorship that rested on three pillars: the personal political shrewdness of Fujimori, the murky network of corruption, blackmail and control set up by its security adviser and intelligence chief Montesinos, and the support of the armed forces supreme command. It may be called a civilian dictatorship because it was increasingly authoritarian in practice, although Fujimori engineered popular legitimacy through referenda and elections. It remained civilian while still being able to count on important military support, because Fujimori and Montesinos maintained control of the military institution through surveillance carried out by SIN (National Intelligence System), manipulation of appointments and dismissals, and blackmail. Here lies the perversion and the corruption of this particular scenario: the military became part of a wider system of official corruption, crime and repression resembling on an even more grandiose scale the praetorian dynasties of the past in countries like pre-1959 Cuba, pre-1960 Dominican Republic, pre-1979 Nicaragua or pre-1990 Paraguay.

In this process, the Peruvian military was not only subordinated to an authoritarian-populist civilian regime, but also participated in a logic of repression, paramilitarisation and political violence, drug trafficking, blackmail and corruption. The last vestiges of the erstwhile nationalist and reformist political army that sought nation building and social development fell into shambles. It was persistent popular protest and the unravelling of the Montesinos racket (in which opposing military elements might have played a part) that eventually brought down the Fujimori regime at the end of 2000.

Colombia, in turn, can claim the sorry status of combining the new violence and the proliferation of armed actors in a singular scenario of institutional degeneration. Colombia is often cited as one of the few examples of prolonged and stable, albeit oligarchic, democratic governance in Latin America. Indeed, it did not know a political army in the sense discussed in this chapter. After a century of intermittent warfare between regional factions and followers of the Liberal and Conservative parties, it entered a period of relative tranquillity between 1900 and 1948, marked by civil rule and the alternation in power of the two parties. The second half of the past century, however, was characterised by a crescendo of violence. This started with the infamous *Violencia* from 1948–58, which was a mixture of inter-party violence, local feuding and banditry. Although it was formally ended by an élite settlement in 1958, it paved the way for the progressive erosion of institutionality and the installation of endemic violence that soon transcended the political domain to acquire economic, social and cultural connotations. From the 1960s, Marxist guerrillas evolved from the radical liberal protagonists in *La Violencia* to form the FARC, ELN and other armed groups. The National Front bipartisan coalition, formed after the 1958 settlement, reacted with the declaration of a permanent state of siege that lasted until 1982. This gave the military ample powers to conduct counterinsurgency warfare (which they handled far from competently) and led to partial militarisation of local administration in the conflict zones. Yet the military had neither the incentive nor the inclination to assume state power directly itself.

During the 1980s, two contradictory processes evolved. On one hand, increased political party competition and civil society activism deepened democracy, leading to a quite innovative new constitution adopted in 1991. On the other hand, violence escalated, first through large-scale organised crime related to drugs, and then through the rise of the paramilitaries. The latter started as an élite reaction to kidnappings by guerrilla commandos, but developed into a para-institutionalised force for the defence of large landed properties (many of which had been acquired by drug lords).[12] Following their eventual unification as the United Self-Defence Forces of Colombia (AUC), paramilitary units turned to systematic social cleansing campaigns in connivance with the regular army. They terrorised local and rural populations in a territorial struggle with guerrilla forces, as well as removing people from areas coveted by their paymasters. The guerrillas responded by developing their own cash nexus of drug and extortion money.

As a result, the Colombian state has lost its monopoly of the means of coercion over significant parts of its territory. Violence in Colombia has become banalised, to use the expression of Pécaut (1999), becoming a routine way of settling accounts, pursuing social mobility, asserting identities, advancing economic interests or carving out political positions. The state has failed, so far, to initiate a successful strategy of peace, reconciliation, and social reform, despite a number of attempts. Those willing to accept past peace arrangements and to enter institutional politics have been systematically punished by the ruthless violence of the intransigent armed actors. There are fears that Plan Colombia, under which the government is attempting to deal with the crisis, will lead to further militarisation of the violence. Events after 11 September 2001 have further enhanced the government's intransigency towards what has promptly been relabelled 'terrorism'. In February and March 2002, FARC stepped up violence against representatives of political society. The Pastrana administration formally abandoned peace negotiations and set in motion a military offensive against the FARC-held enclave. It can be assumed that these events will contribute little to the reassertion of legitimate governance against the 'forces of insecurity'.

Conclusion

To summarise, against the background of fragmented and particularist state formation until the early twentieth century, a strong tradition of political armies developed in Latin America. This phenomenon was built into the political structures of a number of countries from the 1930s as part of modernisation and the advent of mass politics. After 1960, institutional military dictatorships were established in countries where the earlier populist or democratic political order broke down under the weight of economic stagnation, social confrontation and crises of governability. The ensuing bureaucratic-authoritarian regimes pursued a comprehensive strategy of militarisation of the state and widespread violence against 'internal enemies' in dirty wars or protracted civil conflicts.

This has set the stage for the current paradox of democratic control of the security forces in Latin America. On one hand, the experience of authoritarianism, state terror and civil war eventually broke down, making way for widely supported democratisation processes. Accountable civil governments have been established throughout the region, establishing civil–military relations on a new footing of civil control and military non-political professionalism. Yet, on the other hand, the military has maintained a considerable role in domestic politics through its capability to preserve professional prerogatives, retain a broad political role, and evade accountability for human rights violations.

As argued in this chapter, the outcome has been variegated. In countries where the democratic process has been stable and legitimate, the role of political armies has diminished considerably, especially where the legacy of military rule has been evaluated negatively, as in Brazil and Argentina. In other cases, however, democratic politics has been weaker, while the military has maintained a modified institutional involvement in domestic politics: Guatemala is the clearest example. A third outcome, exemplified by Peru during the 1980s and 1990s, has been the transformation of political armies into corrupted support structures of perverted regimes that maintain only the outward appearance of democratic governance. In sum, civil democratic control of the military and security forces has by no means been a certain outcome of the demise of dictatorships, all the more where the spread of new forms of violence has jeopardised the rule of law, a key condition for democratically organised security.

References

Agüero, F. (2002) 'A political army in Chile: historical assessment and prospects for the new democracy', in Koonings, K. and D. Kruijt (eds.), *Political Armies. The Military and Nation Building in the Age of Democracy*, London: Zed Books.

Agüero, F. and J. Stark (eds.) (1998) *Fault Lines of Democracy in Post-Transition*

Latin America, Coral Gables: North–South Center Press.

Arnson, C. J. (ed.) (1999) *Comparative Peace Processes in Latin America*, Washington and Stanford: Woodrow Wilson Center Press and Stanford University Press.

Arseneaux, C. L. (1999) 'The military in Latin America: defining the road ahead', in Buxton, J. and N. Phillips (eds.), *Developments in Latin American Political Economy. States, Markets and Actors*, Manchester and New York: Manchester University Press, pp. 93–111.

Azpuru, D. (1999) 'Peace and democratization in Guatemala: two parallel processes', in Arnson, C. J. (ed.), *Comparative Peace Processes in Latin America*, Washington and Stanford: Woodrow Wilson Center Press and Stanford University Press, pp. 97–125.

Basombrío, C. (1999) 'Peace in Peru: an unfinished task', in Arnson, C. J. (ed.), *Comparative Peace Processes in Latin America*, Washington and Stanford: Woodrow Wilson Center Press and Stanford University Press, pp. 205–22.

Benevides, M-V. and R-M. Fischer Ferreira (1991) 'Popular responses and urban violence: lynching in Brazil', in Huggins, M. K. (ed.), *Vigilantism and the State in Modern Latin America. Essays on Extralegal Violence*, New York: Praeger; pp. 33–46.

Castañeda, G. A. Palacio (1991) 'Institutional crisis, parainstitutionality, and regime flexibility in Colombia: the place of narcotraffic and counterinsurgency', in Huggins, M. K. (ed.), *Vigilantism and the State in Modern Latin America. Essays on Extralegal Violence*, New York: Praeger, pp. 105–24.

Castro, C. (2002) 'The military and politics in Brazil, 1964–2000', in Koonings, K. and D. Kruijt (eds.), *Political Armies. The Military and Nation Building in the Age of Democracy*, London: Zed Books.

Chevigny, P. (1995) *Edge of the Knife. Police Violence in the Americas*, New York: The New Press.

Collier, D. (ed.) (1979) *The New Authoritarianism in Latin America*, Princeton: Princeton University Press.

Corradi, J. F., P. Weiss Fagen and M. A. Garretón (eds.) (1992) *Fear at the Edge. State Terror and Resistance in Latin America*, Berkeley: University of California Press.

Domínguez, J. I. and A. F. Lowenthal (eds.) (1996) *Constructing Democratic Governance – Themes and Issues*, Baltimore and London: Johns Hopkins University Press

Fernandes, H. Rodrigues (1991) 'Authoritarian society: breeding ground for *Justiceiros*', in Huggins, M. K. (ed.), *Vigilantism and the State in Modern Latin America. Essays on Extralegal Violence*, New York: Praeger, pp. 61–70.

Fitch, J. S. (1998) *The Armed Forces and Democracy in Latin America*, Baltimore: Johns Hopkins University Press.

Fumerton, M. (2001) '*Rondas campesinas* in the Peruvian civil war: peasant self-defence organisations in Ayacucho', *Bulletin of Latin American Research*, 20 (4): 470–97.

Gaspar, G. (1997) *Guerrillas en America Latina*, Santiago: FLACSO–Chile (Nueva Serie FLACSO).

Glebbeek, M-L. (2001) 'Police reform and the peace process in Guatemala: the fifth promotion of the National Civilian Police', *Bulletin of Latin American Research*, 20 (4): 431–53.

Hammond, J. L. (1999) 'Law and disorder: the Brazilian landless farmworkers' movement', *Bulletin of Latin American Research*, 18 (4): 469–89.

Higley, J. and R. Gunther (eds.) (1992) *Élites and Democratic Consolidation in Latin America and Southern Europe*, Cambridge: Cambridge University Press.

Hunter, W. (1997) *Eroding Military Influence in Brazil – Politicians against Soldiers*, Chapel Hill: University of North Carolina.

Koonings, K. (1999) 'Shadows of violence and political transition in Brazil: from military rule to democratic governance', in Koonings, K. and D. Kruijt (eds.), *Societies of Fear: the Legacy of Civil War, Violence and Terror in Latin America*, London: Zed Books, pp. 197–234.

—— (2001) 'Armed actors, violence and democracy in Latin America: introductory notes', *Bulletin of Latin American Research*, 20 (4): 401–8.

Koonings, K. and D. Kruijt (2002) 'Military politics and the mission of nation building', in Koonings, K. and D. Kruijt (eds.), *Political Armies. The Military and Nation Building in the Age of Democracy*, London: Zed Books.

—— (eds.) (1999) *Societies of Fear: the Legacy of Civil War, Violence and Terror in Latin America*, London: Zed Books.

Kruijt, D. (1994) *Revolution by Decree. Peru 1968–1975*, Amsterdam: Thela Thesis Publishers.

—— (1996) 'Peru: the state under siege', in Millet, R. L. and M. Gold-Biss (eds.), *Beyond Praetorianism. The Latin American Military in Transition*, Miami: North–South Center Press, pp. 261–89.

—— (1999), 'Exercises in state terrorism: the counter-insurgency campaigns in Guatemala and Peru', in Koonings, K. and D. Kruijt (eds.), *Societies of Fear: the Legacy of Civil War, Violence and Terror in Latin America*, London: Zed Books, pp. 33–62.

—— (2001) 'Low intensity democracies: Latin America in the post-dictatorial era', *Bulletin of Latin American Research*, 20 (4): 409–30.

Kruijt, D. and K. Koonings (1999) 'Introduction: violence and fear in Latin America', in Koonings, K. and D. Kruijt (eds.), *Societies of Fear: the Legacy of Civil War, Violence and Terror in Latin America*, London: Zed Books, pp. 1–30.

Kruijt, D. and M. del Pilar Tello (2002) 'From military reformists to civilian dictatorship: Peruvian military politics since the 1960s', in Koonings, K. and D. Kruijt (eds.), *Political Armies. The Military and Nation Building in the Age of Democracy*, London: Zed Books.

Leeds, E. (1996) 'Cocaine and parallel politics in the Brazilian urban periphery: constraints on local-level democratization', *Latin American Research Review*, 31 (3): 47–84.

Loveman, B. (1994) 'Protected democracies and military guardianship: political transitions in Latin America, 1978–1993', *Journal of Interamerican Studies and World Affairs*, 36 (2): 105–90.

—— (1999) *For la Patria: Politics and the Armed Forces in Latin America*, Wilmington: SR Books.

Marcella, G. (1994) 'Warriors in peacetime: future missions of the Latin American armed forces', in Marcella, G. (ed.), *Warriors in Peacetime. The Military and Democracy in Latin America*, Ilford (Essex): Frank Cass, pp. 1–33.

Martins, J. de Souza (1991) 'Lynchings – life by a thread: street justice in Brazil, 1979–1988', in Huggins, M. K. (ed.), *Vigilantism and the State in Modern Latin America. Essays on Extralegal Violence*, New York: Praeger, pp. 21–32.

McClintock, C. (1998) *Revolutionary Movements in Latin America. El Salvador's FMLN and Peru's Shining Path*, Washington: United States Institute of Peace Press.

Méndez, J. E., G. O'Donnell and P. S. Pinheiro (eds.) (1999) *The (Un)rule of Law and the Underprivilieged in Latin America*, Notre Dame: University of Notre Dame Press.

MINUGUA (2001) *Duodécimo informe sobre derechos humanos de la Misión de Verificación de las Naciones Unidas en Guatemala*, Guatemala, September, consulted at www.minugua.guate.net

Nun, J. (1967) 'The middle class military coup', in Véliz, C. (ed.), *The Politics of Conformity in Latin America*, Oxford: Oxford University Press, pp. 66–118.

Nunn, F. M. (1992) *The Time of the Generals. Latin American Professional Militarism in World Perspective*, Lincoln and London: University of Nebraska Press.

—— (2001) 'Foreign influences on the South American military: professionalization and politicization', in Silva, P. (ed.), *The Soldier and the State in South America. Essays in Civil–Military Relations*, Basingstoke: Palgrave, pp. 13–38.

O'Brien, P. and P. Cammack (eds.) (1985) *Generals in Retreat. The Crisis of Military Rule in Latin America*, Manchester: University of Manchester Press.

O'Donnell, G. (1973) *Modernization and Bureaucratic-Authoritarianism: Studies in South American Politics*, Berkeley: Center for International Studies, University of California.

O'Donnell, G. and P. C. Schmitter (1986) *Transitions from Authoritarian Rule: Tentative Conclusions about Uncertain Democracies*, Baltimore: Johns Hopkins University Press.

Palmer, D. S. (ed.) (1992) *The Shining Path of Peru*, New York: St Martin's Press.

Payne, L. A. (2000) *Uncivil Movements. The Armed Right Wing and Democracy in Latin America*, Baltimore and London: Johns Hopkins University Press.

Pécaut, D. (1999) 'From the banality of violence to real terror. The case of Colombia', in Koonings, K. and D. Kruijt (eds.), *Societies of Fear: the Legacy of Civil War, Violence and Terror in Latin America*, London: Zed Books, pp. 141–67.

Peralva, A. (2000) *Violência e Democracia: O Paradoxo Brasileiro*, São Paulo: Paz e Terra.

Pinheiro, P. S. (1991) 'Police and political crisis: the case of the military police', in Huggins, M. K. (ed.), *Vigilantism and the State in Modern Latin America. Essays on Extralegal Violence*, New York: Praeger, pp. 167–88.

—— (1996) 'Democracies without citizenship', in *Injustice for All. Crime and Impunity in Latin America. NACLA Report on the Americas*, 30 (2): 17–23.

Remijnse, S. (2001) 'Remembering civil patrols in Joyabaj, Guatemala', *Bulletin of Latin American Research*, 20 (4): 454–69.

Rial, J. (1990) 'The armed forces and the question of democracy in Latin America', in Goodman, L. W., J. S. R. Mendelson and J. Rial (eds.), *The Military and Democracy. The Future of Civil–Military Relations in Latin America*, Lexington, Massachusetts and Toronto: Lexington Books, pp. 3–21.

—— (1994) 'Civil–military relations in the transition to and the consolidation of democracy in Latin America', in Marcella, G. (ed.), *Warriors in Peacetime. The Military and Democracy in Latin America*, Ilford (Essex): Frank Cass, pp. 34–55.

Rojas, F. (2001) 'Civil–military relations in post-authoritarian Chile', in Silva, P. (ed.), *The Soldier and the State in South America. Essays in Civil–Military Relations*, Basingstoke: Palgrave, pp. 151–74

Rosada-Granados, H. (1999) *Soldados en el poder. Proyecto militar en Guatemala, 1944–1990*, Amsterdam: Thela Thesis Publishers (Latin America Series, 15).

Rouquié, A. (1989) *The Military and the State in Latin America*, Berkeley: University of California Press.

Schirmer, J. (1998) *The Guatemalan Military Project. A Violence Called Democracy*, Philadelphia: University of Pennsylvania Press.

—— (2002) 'The Guatemalan politico-military project: whose ship of state?', in Koonings, K. and D. Kruijt (eds.), *Political Armies. The Military and Nation Building in the Age of Democracy*, London: Zed Books.

Stepan, A. (1976) 'The new professionalism of internal warfare and military role expansion', in Lowenthal, A. F. (ed.), *Armies and Politics in Latin America*, New York and London: Holmes and Meier, pp. 244–60.

—— (1988) *Rethinking Military Politics: Brazil and the Southern Cone*, Princeton: Princeton University Press.

Wouters, M. (2001) 'Ethnic rights under threat: the black peasant movement against armed groups' pressure in the Chocó, Colombia', *Bulletin of Latin American Research* 20 (4): 498–519.

Zagorski, P. (1992) *Democracy vs. National Security. Civil–Military Relations in Latin America*, Boulder: Lynne Rienner.

Notes

1 'Birthright' means that political armies see themselves as uniquely placed to supervise national destiny because of their real or perceived role in nation building (independence, revolution, or modernisation). 'Competence' means that political armies see themselves as particularly qualified to take on political and administrative responsibilities, while 'civil inadequacy' refers to the notion that civilian politicians are not up to those same tasks due to particularistic interests, factionalism or radicalism, or simply lack of 'patriotism'. See Koonings and Kruijt (2002).

2 I refer to what are generally labelled 'bureaucratic-authoritarian' regimes (see O'Donnell 1973; Collier 1979; O'Brien and Cammack 1985 for a critical assessment) as well as to the authoritarian regimes that waged a civil war against armed opposition in Central America.

3 A huge literature is available on democratic transition and consolidation. See O'Donnell and Schmitter (1986), Higley and Guenther (1992), Domínguez

and Lowenthal (1996), Agüero and Stark (1998).

4 For instance, the *Nunca Mais* report of the Brazilian Bishops' Conference (1984), the CONADEP *Nunca Más* report in Argentina (1986), the Rettig Report in Chile (1993), and the reports of the formal Commission for Historical Clarification (CEH) and the Church's Report on the Restoration of Historical Memory (REMHI), both in 1999.

5 See Koonings (2001) and the case studies in that volume by Fumerton (2001), Glebbeek (2001), Remijnse (2001) and Wouters (2001).

6 See Benevides and Ferreira (1991), Fernandes (1991), Martins (1991). See also Chevigny (1995).

7 Hammond (1999) makes this point with respect to the Brazilian landless workers' movement (MST).

8 See the thorough analysis by Payne (2000) of the Brazilian Rural Democratic Union, a landowners' association with paramilitary dimensions set up to counter the threat of land reform and MST invasions after 1985. She also refers to the Argentinian *Carapintadas* (the military rebels of the late 1980s and early 1990s) and the Nicaraguan *Contras* in the same study.

9 It is of course obvious that these are ideal types. Elements of all three scenarios can easily be found in these cases, and indeed throughout Latin America. Neither are scenarios irreversible. Take, for instance, the recent downfall of Fujimori in Peru, followed by a national effort to restore political institutionality. Other examples of the 'withering away' scenario could be Argentina, Bolivia, Uruguay, Honduras and Panama; for the 'institutional modification' scenario Chile, Ecuador and Venezuela (under Chávez); for the 'perversion and corruption' scenario Paraguay, Surinam, and maybe El Salvador and Nicaragua.

10 I follow here my earlier argument set forth in Koonings (1999).

11 The literature on Sendero Luminoso is extensive. See Palmer (1992) and McClintock (1998) for overviews.

12 See Castañeda (1991) for the notion of 'para-institutionality'.

III

Democratic Control and Security Sector Transformation in Conflict-Torn Societies

7

Democratisation and its Enemies
The Algerian Transition to Authoritarianism, 1988–2001

FRÉDÉRIC VOLPI

In the late 1980s, the Algerian democratic transition was one of the first processes of political liberalisation in the Islamic world to embody the principles of the 'Third Wave' of democratisation.[1] Yet, Algeria soon became a dramatic example of how this process of democratisation could drive a polity toward the brink of disaster. As political disagreements escalated in a climate of social mistrust, the main actors of the democratic transition – the state political élite, the military officers, the Islamic fundamentalists and the democrats – unwittingly created a political dynamic that drove social groups further and further away from a consensus on the state and on governance. These events illustrated how tenuous was the link between a liberal order and a democratic system, and how easily a democratic transition unattended by able (domestic and foreign) political actors could turn any potential benefit into lasting impediments (Volpi 2002). But to understand fully why the Algerian democratic transition failed, one must realise first how fortuitous was its 'birth'. The changes in the polity were not brought about by a well-thought-out liberalisation of the country's institutions by Algeria's 'socialist' regime, but by a series of bungled efforts at maintaining political order whilst reforming the economic system. More than any specific demands for democracy, it was the failure of the army to impose order and the failure of the patronage networks of the state party to keep in check the social demands of the population that kick-started the transition.[2]

Until 1988, Algeria had been ruled by a (relatively) mild authoritarian Arab socialist regime that managed to keep the political demands of the population under control by providing social and economic development (Ruedy 1992). From the mid-1960s to the mid-1980s, the country was governed by the FLN (Front de Libération Nationale –

National Liberation Front), the nationalist movement that had wrested Algeria from its French colonial masters. From the very beginning, the military imposed its stamp on the country, as Colonel Boumediene, then Defence Minister, took control of the regime after a brief internal struggle which led to the eviction of President Ben Bella. Boumediene set up Algeria's economic policy of Soviet-style heavy industrialisation and financed it with the country's oil and gas resources. By the time of his death, in 1978, it had become evident that central planning and investment in heavy industry were not the best answers to the country's economic needs, as growth stagnated and social development levelled off. Following a brief struggle for influence between party cadres and military officers, Colonel Chadli Benjedid was nominated by the FLN in 1979 to be the country's new President – demonstrating once more the strength of the institutional linkages between the party and the army (Zartman 1987; Leveau 1993). Within a few years, Chadli's efforts to introduce a degree of economic liberalisation had squandered the country's wealth. The increased appetite of Algerians for imported consumption goods increased the country's debt burden. When the price of oil fell sharply in the mid-1980s, the country was confronted with a growing debt crisis and a slump in industrial production as state investments plummeted. Unemployment rose, inflation hit, food shortages became common and it was no great surprise that in the late 1980s the regime should seek to divert people's attention from the country's disastrous economic situation by giving in on the issue of political freedom. What the regime did not plan well enough, however, was how much to give, to whom, in which order and with what safeguards.

A main cause of the failure of the 1988 democratic transition was merely the ending of a bout of political good fortune (or *Fortuna*, to re-use a term from Machiavelli that has found a new meaning in contemporary analyses of democratic transitions).[3] In causal terms, the inability of the main social and political actors who started the transition to devise effective political procedures and institutions ensured that the drive toward liberalisation lost its momentum as soon as it ran into difficulties. Furthermore, the lack of involvement by the international community – Western democracies and international financial organisations – ensured that the poor skills displayed by the Algerian political élite at the time were not compensated for by guidance from abroad.[4] When the political disagreements between the main actors of the democratic transition turned violent, a recourse to the military and to the 'certainties' of authoritarianism appeared to be the right choice for many Algerians (and, to some extent, for the international community).

Both government and opposition quickly deserted the political field and reverted to what they knew best, extra-political strong-arm tactics, in order to voice their demands and make themselves heard. Although the armed forces were much better than the rest at this ruthless game, they knew no better than the political actors how to diffuse the social and ideological conflicts that had undermined the democratic transition. In this context, it was the army's own strong-arm tactics that allowed popular discontent to spin out of control. At the time of writing, the vicious civil conflict that began in 1992, when the military leadership halted the electoral process, is still ongoing and has already caused 100,000 deaths.

The first part of this chapter will look at the crucial changes that occurred during the Algerian democratic transition and at the rationale of the process of liberalisation. I argue that the underlying causes of the failure of this political process were the lack of serious understanding of the political mechanisms that were set in motion at the beginning of the transition and, consequently, the lack of appropriate planning for building new and effective political institutions. It is shown that, instead of contributing to a reform of the political system, the last few months of the democratic transition and the aftermath of the coup further undermined the pre-existing institutional framework and paved the way for the country's descent into a violent state of anarchy. The second part of the analysis deals with the civil conflict that erupted at the end of the democratic transition. It gives an account of the principal actors of the civil war and of the mechanisms that permitted the spread and entrenchment of political violence. It is argued that popular resentment was channelled towards supporting the Islamic guerrilla movement because of the harsh repressive tactics utilised by the new military rulers of the country. In Weberian terms, the Algerian regime weakened its moral claim to using legitimate violence by its own actions, and it was hindered in the longer run by the Islamic guerrillas' direct challenge to its monopoly of violence. In the final section, I conclude with some reflections on the political lessons that can be gained from the failed Algerian democratic transition. I highlight the role that pseudo-democratic procedures have in the reproduction of the current authoritarian structures of the regime, and I assess the prospects for democracy in the polity.

The army in politics: continuity and change 1988–92

Between 1988 and 1992 the Algerian army risked losing the political and economic privileges it had gained during the war of decolonisation

(1954–62) and the 'Arab socialist' period (1962–88) (Mortimer 1996; Entelis 1999). Yet, by the end of the democratic transition, the military had not only managed to retain its privileges but had also increased its power by playing on domestic and international fears that its demise would usher in an Islamic fundamentalist regime. If the Algerian democratic transition played into the hands of the army, however, it is not principally because of the purposeful efforts of ill-intentioned military leaders. These outcomes were produced by the miscalculations and misdemeanours of (civilian) social and political actors who failed to create the necessary conditions for their own success and for the success of democracy. The causes of these rapid reversals of fortune and the mechanisms that created this infelicitous relationship between the military institution and the political/civil society are encapsulated in three political events which mark the beginning, the stalling and the collapse of the democratic transition. These are the 1988 October riots, the summer of 1991 crisis and the January 1992 *coup d'état*.

The 1988 riots

In October 1988, the worsening of the economic situation in Algeria triggered a spate of food riots that seriously challenged the authority of the ruling 'socialist' regime. Besides the economic crisis, the proximate causes of the October riots were an ill-applied repression by the security apparatus and the aloof attitude adopted by the political authorities *vis-à-vis* the protesters. In Algiers, as Charef (1994) reports, popular anger was initially fuelled by the actions of the police, who shot dead several young demonstrators on the first day of what were until then very limited disturbances. As the protest gathered momentum, the government decided to impose a state of emergency in the Algiers region and to call in the army to reestablish order. Unfortunately, the very unpreparedness of the troops to deal with a popular protest and street demonstrations ensured that the protest marches often turned into a bloodbath. These clashes were especially violent outside the Algiers region, where the regime was not expecting any demonstrations and where the armed forces had to be deployed hastily in response to a new wave of rioting. Not only was the repressive apparatus taken by surprise by the rapidity with which the protest spread, but internal disagreements on how to tackle the protest also undermined the effectiveness of the repression. The ruthless – several hundred protesters were killed in less than a week – yet ineffective intervention of the army made the military institution highly unpopular and further undermined the authority of the regime. By the time the Algerian President offered an 'olive branch' to the demonstrators in the form of the promise of a democratic opening, the cohesiveness of the regime and of its repressive apparatus had been seriously tested.

The political consequences of the October riots were a strengthening of the authority of the political executive over the military. Because the wave of rioting ended when the President made the promise of political liberalisation, Chadli temporarily found himself in an advantageous position *vis-à-vis* the military establishment. Using the pretext of the disastrous army intervention and of the democratic opening, the President was able to remove from the military high command several dominant members of the old guard who could have questioned his political authority.[5] This constituted a striking reversal of fortune for the President, as at the beginning of the protest Chadli himself was blamed for the social and economic ills of the country, and the role of the army in politics was barely questioned. The President moved quickly to assert his authority by organising a referendum on his proposal for democratisation and on an extension of his political mandate. His personal authority was boosted by a (genuine) popular mandate, when he was re-elected President in a one-candidate election in November 1988 with over 80 per cent of positive votes and a participation rate near 90 per cent.

The process of political liberalisation launched by Chadli allowed the liberal wing of the FLN to start undermining the hold of the military on the government and the party. First, in February 1989, the political monopoly of the FLN was ended by the adoption (through a referendum) of a new constitution legalising multi-partyism. Then, arguing that the current unpopularity of the army constituted a liability for the government and the party, the President and the reformers induced the military officers to give up the seats in the governing body of the FLN that were reserved for them. This formal redefinition of the relationship between the army leadership and the political élite, as well as the internal reorganisation of the armed forces, was possible not merely because the military institution had been weakened by its own ruthless actions, but also because this redefinition of its institutional role had heightened the rivalries inside the military and was conducive to (political) infighting. These and later power struggles inside the armed forces did not reflect deep-seated ideological differences or different social outlooks; they were primarily based on personal disagreements between individual officers and on the competition between different patronage networks or 'clans' (Lavenue 1993; Volpi 2000a). Throughout 1989 and 1990, the army officers were too busy jockeying for position at the top of the military hierarchy to oppose effectively the reforms proposed by the liberal wing of the regime. Eventually, the formal distinction between the prerogatives of the army and those of the political executive was (re)affirmed in the summer of 1990 when Chadli demarcated the functions of the President from those of the Defence Minister and of the Chief of Staff.[6]

Despite these formal advances, it was clear by the end of 1990 that the efforts of the reformers had slackened and that they did not go all the way to eliminating military influence from the political decision-making process. The level of politicisation of the army remained high and strong informal alliances were maintained between the conservative faction in government and high-ranking officers. The reformers were able neither to impose a new code of conduct on military–civilian relations nor to create a new consensus on this issue. Even at the institutional level, the President did not seize the opportunity to place the military firmly under the control of a civilian leadership. Instead, the newly created post of Defence Minister had been offered to one of Chadli's allies in the military, General Nezzar. Whilst it is obvious that the promotion of a well-known General to this position ensured that the Ministry of Defence had an authority over the military which it might not otherwise have had (initially at least), it is also clear that the reformers failed to take full advantage of the loss of confidence and nerve of the military establishment at that time. In any process of transition from authoritarianism, it is never obvious *a priori* when to push for rapid and thorough transformations and when to permit new arrangements to fall into place.[7] But looking back on the 1988–91 period, it is now clear that the Algerian reformers erred on the side of complacency and not of radicalism. And this mistake was soon to prove very costly, for them and for the polity.

The 1991 crisis

By 1991, the army had begun to recover its internal cohesion and a sense of purpose. At the same time, the government and the FLN had become increasingly unable to deal with the political consequences of the process of democratisation, and especially with the success of the Islamic opposition led by the FIS (Front Islamique du Salut – Islamic Salvation Front). The tension between the political executive and the military institution resurfaced in the summer of 1991 after a series of bungled efforts by the FLN and the FIS to secure more favourable outcomes for themselves in the impending parliamentary elections. The outgoing FLN-dominated Parliament redesigned the electoral boundaries to give greater weight to the rural vote (which tended to go in their favour) at the expense of the urban electors (who were more likely to be pro-FIS). Unsure of the size of the Islamic vote, the FIS called up street demonstrations and a general strike to force Parliament to backtrack on its proposal. This pre-electoral bickering started up a wave of protests and a political clampdown that redefined the relationship between the government and the army for the worse. As the police proved unable to cope with the upsurge in street demonstrations in Algiers, the army was given a convenient excuse to once again take centre-stage in Algerian political life. With the approval of the President, the Defence Minister overrode the authority of the Prime Minister (who was still trying to reach a negotiated agreement with the FIS) and ordered the troops to suppress the protest. A state of emergency was declared for a three-month period and the principal leaders of the FIS were arrested (Roberts 1994).

The President had found it expedient to use the might of the military to put down the FIS protest and to weaken its electoral machinery. At that time, Chadli still hoped to play a major role in Algerian politics by presiding over what he hoped would be a coalition government with a fragile parliamentary majority. He calculated that a limited repression of the FIS would reduce the (too great) appeal of the Islamic party and would prop up the FLN and other liberal/secular political parties. This choice of tactics, however, was quite an upset for the reformers inside the regime – leading to the resignation (probably forced) of the liberal Prime Minister, Mouloud Hamrouche – and for the democratic parties, who realised that this intervention by the army set a dangerous precedent for Algerian democracy. This episode gave the army another taste of power at a crucial time and it increased the confidence of its leadership. Although this period of unrest did not formally redefine the process of democratisation – despite repeated demands by the military to this effect – it reintroduced some ill-boding practices that had not been used since the beginning of the political opening. In the Islamic camp, even as the FIS returned to electoral campaigning with a new (provisional) leader, Abdelkader Hachani, dissent grew in the ranks. At the congress of Batna, in August 1991, several members of its executive committee were excluded from the party for advocating an end to participation in the electoral process and preparation for extra-political actions (armed struggle) (Volpi 2000b).

The spate of military actions and the resignation of the Prime Minister showed the fragility of the new political institutions and of the mechanisms that were supposed to define the respective authorities of the state executive, the legislature, and the military. After the intervention, many inside the regime and in the opposition felt that the armed forces were once more in the ascendancy. The powers given to the army during the state of emergency meant that the military institution had formally regained (some of) the political functions that the democratic transition was meant to take away from it. This deepened the rift inside the regime between reformers (in favour of a deeper liberalisation and an accommodation with the Islamic fundamentalists) and the conservatives (in favour of a 'pacted' transition with the military and of further restrictions imposed on Islamic parties). Amidst this turmoil, the President gained a reputation for indecisiveness. In the end, Chadli's miscalculated support for the army not only proved insufficient to revitalise the FLN but also placed himself and the other political parties and actors in a weaker position *vis-à-vis* the military leadership. The summer of 1991 marked the beginning of the end for the democratic transition, as the processes which had led to a greater democratisation and accountability of the state institutions began to function in reverse. Instead of having a formal political liberalisation slowly changing informal authoritarian practices, it was these practices that began to overwhelm the democratic transition.

The 1992 coup

From the army's perspective, a main incentive for the *coup d'état* of January 1992 was the government's lack of advance planning of its response to a sweeping electoral victory of the Islamic fundamentalists. In December 1991, in the first round of the parliamentary elections, the FIS nearly won an absolute majority in Parliament and was poised to win all the seats it needed in the second round. A divided Algerian political class was caught up in a virulent public debate on how to deal with the FIS. The more secular and conservative social and political actors vociferously called for a halt to the process of democratic transition, with the help of the army if necessary. Said Sadi, the leader of the small secular-'democratic' party, the Rally for Culture and Democracy (RCD) called for the cancellation of the elections and declared boldly that his party was ready to take upon itself full responsibility for the consequences. At the same time, a 'National Committee for the Safeguard of Algeria' was created under the impetus of Benhamouda (the leader of the very official Algerian Workers' Union), and it called upon the army to stop the Islamic fundamentalists (Willis 1996; Volpi 2000b). At that time, both popular and institutional support for the President and the reformers were weak due to the electoral defeat of the regime at the hands of the Islamic opposition. Considering the scale of the Islamic victory, the President could not assume the role of arbiter between the secular and religious currents in Algerian society. Worse still, his unsteady political line had led the military to believe that Chadli would not be able to rein in the Islamic fundamentalists if they decided to use their legislative powers to drastically reform (and reprimand) the military institutions. The army leadership, strengthened by the support that it now received from conservative politicians and the more secular segments of society, and playing upon the fact that it had already assumed control during a situation of crisis a few months earlier, made a bid for power. A coalition of military officers led by General Nezzar, the Defence Minister, induced the President to resign. Haunted by his military past and the repression he had authorised earlier against the Islamic fundamentalists, Chadli was not in a position to stand against them. Then Chadli resigned and the army officers called in a new civilian political leader, Mohamed Boudiaf (a former leader of the war of decolonisation living in exile), to serve as (temporary) President.

During these events, the reaction of the international community was conspicuously muted. Whilst neighbouring North African countries, worried by the influence of Islamic fundamentalist movements at home, quickly rallied behind the new military-backed Algerian regime, Western democracies remained silent. The United States and France declared themselves 'preoccupied' and 'worried' by the situation in Algeria, but they did not need to be pressed to follow the advice of the Egyptian President 'not to interfere' (*Le Monde*, 16 January 1992). Only several weeks after the military had taken over (and several rounds of repression later) did the European Union and France begin to suggest (timidly) that the democratic process should be restarted.[8] The 'hands-off' approach adopted by the international community was an indirect consequence of its earlier lack of involvement in the Algerian democratic transition. Not only had Western democracies not been a factor in the initiation of this liberalisation process, but they had not taken steps to ensure that they were appropriately involved in its consolidation (via electoral education, support for democratic parties, etcetera). Just like the Algerian reformers, foreign players had failed to realise how fortuitous the initial democratic transition had been and, consequently, they did not devise contingency strategies to support the democratic process in case of difficulties. They, too, failed to create propitious conditions for the consolidation of democracy in Algeria. And when the democratic process was put in jeopardy by this dual problem of ineffective institutional reforms to keep the military in check and a lack of popular consensus in favour of regime change, all the international community appeared able to do was to witness the transition falling apart and engage in an (external) damage limitation exercise. By the time the military takeover was on the cards, it is unclear whether the use of selective sanctions against the Algerian regime could have had a significant impact. Nonetheless, the reluctance of Western democracies to get involved in this affair sent a very ambiguous message to the Algerian citizenry and to all the parties involved in this struggle for power.

The civil conflict: the Islamic guerrillas, the militias and the army

The wave of popular agitation that followed the military takeover did not quietly subside after a few weeks of street demonstrations. Instead, the groundswell in anti-government feelings fuelled an upsurge in guerrilla activities from newly created underground Islamic fundamentalist networks. The dramatic political transformation that occurred at the heart of the Algerian regime at the start of 1992 had induced a power shift in the Islamic camp, from the moderates to the radicals. This transformation ensured that, from then on, 'revolutionary' politics became the preferred option of the Islamic fundamentalists to seize state power. The following account highlights the socio-economic and ideological basis of the support for the Islamic guerrillas, the pro-governmental militias and the army during the core period of the conflict, from 1992 to 1999.

The Islamic guerrillas

The striking fact about the Islamic guerrilla movement in Algeria in the 1990s is that it held such sway over a country which, for decades, had only experienced a mild Arab socialist regime and which had had a relatively inconspicuous Islamic revival in the 1980s (Burgat 1988). This ruthless Islamic guerrilla movement appeared to have come out of nowhere and to have rapidly colonised most parts of Algerian society, deeply transforming everyday social relations. In retrospect, it is easy to see that this upsurge in political violence was a direct consequence of the Algerian regime's return to authoritarian rule. In 1992, the military intervention created a situation of crisis in which the state and its subjects were no longer able to find a compromise on the basis of the previous 'Arab socialist' consensus and not yet able to reach a consensus on a democratic basis. After the coup, deprived of the veneer of legitimacy that previously characterised its rule, the regime appeared even more ruthless and arbitrary than before – even when it used the same political tropes as before. In the end, it was the actions of the population themselves that helped to turn what were until then authoritarian-populist policies into a violent and anarchic social order. The pro-Islamic camp, in particular, was seriously disorganised at the beginning of the upheaval. The political structures of the FIS had been quickly dismantled by the army, and the party cadres had been unable to devise an effective political response. Yet, by removing the leadership of the FIS and suppressing the party – some 15,000 FIS members were placed in administrative detention in Saharan prison camps in 1992 – the army merely ensured that the groundswell in pro-Islamic sentiments could not find an institutionalised political voice. As a result, political authority rapidly moved away from the FIS and towards more radical Islamic groups which had remained thus far on the margins of politics (but which were better organised to withstand repression).

The disappearance of the FIS permitted the re-emergence of the leaders of the Bouyali faction (a small group of Islamic fighters in the 'brigand of honour' tradition that operated in Algeria in the mid-1980s) and of the 'Afghans', the Algerians who had fought or trained for the war in Afghanistan in the 1980s (Carlier 1995; Labat 1995). Because they benefited from the support of a disgruntled Algerian citizenry, these groups were able to organise a counter-repression directed against the army and the representatives of the state. Although active guerrilla forces only numbered 2,000–3,000 men at the beginning of the conflict, these groups were able to evade state repression (to some extent), and to score some successes against the security forces. Nonetheless, they lacked a coherent political and military strategy. In practice, these groups often operated independently of one another and devised their tactics on a day-to-day basis. Within a few months, as the indiscriminate police and army repression continued, these early guerrilla groups gave birth to new armed groups, principally made up of young Islamic converts who had developed their interpretation of Islam in the context of a life or death struggle against the regime. This state of affairs favoured the emergence of pockets of radical Islam – more radical than what was proposed by the FIS – throughout the country. Unavoidably, without the moderating influence and long-term vision of a well-established Islamic political leadership, the cycles of repression by the security forces and counter-attacks by the guerrillas created an upward spiral of violence. By 1993, radical Islamic groups such as the GIA (Groupements Islamiques Armés – Armed Islamic Groups) decided to take action not only against the security forces and their supporters, but also against civilians (including foreign nationals whose governments' inaction was perceived to be indirectly helping the military-backed regime) (Dévoluy and Duteil 1994; Willis 1996). This radicalisation of the conflict meant that it was becoming increasingly difficult for ordinary Algerians to remain politically non-committed. Their dilemmas came sharply into focus in 1995 when the regime proposed to hold a presidential election and the GIA responded by saying that it would consider as apostate (hence punishable by death) anyone who participated in the electoral process.

Despite an escalation of the violence, it became clear by the mid-1990s that there would be no rapid military or political solution to the conflict. Although the size of the guerrilla forces had progressed steadily – to about 20,000 men in 1993 (logistic networks included) and up to 40,000 in 1994 with the creation of the armed wing of the FIS, the AIS (Armée Islamique du Salut – Islamic Salvation Army) – the guerrillas were only able to reach a stalemate with the military (Martinez 1998). The guerrillas' rise to power was halted primarily by their own failure to organise the rebellion and to stop the infighting that had broken out between the various factions in late 1993. After 1995 their numbers levelled off – around 10,000 active fighters were more or less evenly split between the GIA and its allies and the AIS organisation.[9] The Algerian population realised that if the guerrillas could not topple the military-backed regime, the army could not fully eradicate the guerrilla groups either. As the political and military quagmire deepened, popular support for the guerrilla movement and for the regime became more instrumental. People learnt to switch allegiances according to the circumstances. Hence, in the second half of the 1990s, the political content of the struggle slowly evaporated and a more instrumental approach to the conflict developed, based on spoils. Until then, the guerrilla groups had principally targeted government assets to sustain their own war effort financially. As these resources became exhausted and the regime was not replacing them, they had to turn to the private sector for support. This corresponded to the time the Algerian regime launched its programme of privatisation and restructuring that was part of the IMF debt-rescheduling package. In this context, the racket of small local businesses and the setting up of roadblocks on communication axes to hold travellers to ransom and steal goods became the main methods of financing the rebellion. As Luis Martinez pointed out, this introduced a new logic into the conflict, based on profiteering from the war economy (Martinez 1998). Increasingly, it became difficult to draw clear boundaries between the politically motivated actions of the guerrilla groups and their more 'mundane' activities as organisers of the black market. The guerrillas' business even benefited from the process of economic liberalisation and privatisation, as this allowed the armed groups to use their war booty to buy or set up their own (legal) enterprises. Overall, this situation ensured that, despite the risks, the armed groups continued to be a source of 'opportunities' for impoverished young Algerians.[10] The guerrilla movement became just another 'business', as guerrillas competed with organised crime and the militias to gain control of a booming informal economy.[11]

The militias

The militias became an important player in the Algerian conflict in 1995 when the government actively encouraged their formation in those parts of the countryside under the sway of the Islamic guerrillas. The militia phenomenon had started a year earlier in Kabylia where, historically, the hold of the Islamic movement was tenuous,[12] but where armed Islamic groups had set up base camps after the coup to use the protection offered by this mountainous region. Because the army was unwilling and/or unable to divert its limited resources to protecting the civilian population in the (politically and economically less important) Algerian countryside, the militias became (with the guerrillas) the main source of 'law' enforcement there. Once the militias were officially endorsed by the Algerian regime, they received substantial amounts of financial and material help from the government in exchange for their policing role. Created in 1995, on the basis of a previous 10,000-strong rural police force, the paramilitary forces had grown by 1997 to an estimated 200,000 men in arms – including 2,313 communal guard units and approximately 5,000 'patriot' units or 'self-defence groups' (Bariki 1995; *Monde Arabe*, 1998).[13]

Rapidly, the militias became involved in the informal economy and protection rackets, alongside the guerrillas and organised crime. Many militiamen joined the militias because of their desire for revenge for the misdeeds of the guerrillas or because of their desperate need for protection, but many others joined because of the financial opportunities the job offered (Martinez 1998). The combination of ruthless economic competition and blood feuds ensured that the occasions for violent clashes multiplied and that an endemic form of social violence resulted, which was far less controllable by the state authorities – even though it was no direct threat to their leadership. Fortunately for the Algerian regime, the restricted economic opportunities available in the countryside limited the ability of the militias to raise their political profile. Like the guerrilla groups, they could only take advantage of small import–export businesses and transport companies. This allowed the central government and the army to keep them in check by offering modest social and financial rewards in return for their obedience.[14] The fighting over territory between guerrilla groups and militias was important when the militias were first created but it slowly subsided as both camps reached informal agreements to avoid unnecessary bloodshed. Guerrilla groups and militias learnt to live side by side, 'peacefully', in a precarious environment. With tacit agreements in place, the guerrilla groups could discreetly raise their 'Islamic taxes' and use the commercial facilities of the towns under the control of the militias, while the militiamen avoided creating unnecessary problems for themselves and their families, and kept the profile of the guerrillas low (thereby pleasing their patrons in the central administration).

The formation of the militias coincided with and reflected the displacement of conflict from the towns and suburbs into the countryside – particularly the Mitijda plain just outside Algiers, the Ouarsenis mountains, and the easternmost part of the country, near the Moroccan border. After 1996, the violent showdowns that led to large-scale massacres of civilians resulted from the combination of two main factors. The first component in this drama was the attempt by guerrilla groups to expand their territory or, conversely, the attempt by the army to wipe out guerrilla activities in specific locations. Both efforts meant that the delicate local balance between guerrillas and militiamen was temporarily upset and that revenge killings by one party or the other (or both) were re-ignited.

The second element that came into play was the development of protection rackets, by both militias and guerrilla groups, which re-started long-running blood feuds or set new ones in motion. Whatever the political motives for the formation of these armed groups might have been, their slow transformation into organised criminality meant that they often targeted civilians not because of their political activities but because of their involvement in black market activities. In both cases, the traditional divisions of the rural population into clans meant that disputes between militiamen and guerrillas (or even disputes between guerrilla groups and between militias) were often settled with regard to kin – hence, the wiping out of entire families or villages. The incidents of August 1997 in the village of Ain Hamra were a typical instance of these clashes – albeit with unusually high media coverage. When a section of the militia of a neighbouring village was decimated by a bomb placed near Ain Hamra, the rest of the militia launched a punitive campaign against the families in the village who were known to have relatives with the guerrillas. Their houses were burnt down and the men who happened to be at home were executed.[15]

Today, it is clear that, if the militarisation of the Algerian countryside hindered the activities of the guerrillas, it also made it more difficult to police. This social violence does not merely reflect the political opposition between the supporters of the regime and those of the Islamic fundamentalists. It is a situation of generalised mistrust, making it far more difficult for the military-backed regime and the Islamic opposition to reach an agreement that can be implemented locally, simply on the basis of a formal political consensus.

The army

The key player in the Algerian civil conflict is the army. Between 1992 and 1998 in particular, the struggle for power among the coup leaders was instrumental in ensuring that the political situation remained in deadlock. In the early stages of the conflict, because of a low level of popular support and a lack of political allies, the main difficulty for the army was that it had to impose physically most of the policies it wanted to implement. This stretched its financial, material and human resources to the limit. Its dominion over the country was therefore limited and many parts of the towns (the suburbs) and of the countryside were simply no-go areas for the regime. This was not because of a lack of military personnel *per se*, but because the troops were principally composed of ill-trained and disabused young conscripts who could not be relied upon to combat highly motivated guerrilla forces.[16] Initially, the army's inability to act decisively and effectively to control the Islamic upheaval was tightly connected to the fact that the military did not know what to do politically and economically to improve the situation of the country. At best it knew what it did not want: a Parliament and an executive controlled by the Islamic fundamentalists. But there had been no 'foundational' logic to the coup. The military did not want to replace the democratic process by a 'better' political system; they merely wanted this process to have a different electoral outcome. Hence, in the ensuing months and years, the military-backed government continued to use, somewhat unconvincingly, a democratic rhetoric to justify its actions.[16]

This lack of coherent strategy was illustrated by the constant changes of administrative and economic policies devised by the provisional government. In the first half of 1992, under Boudiaf's political leadership, the government was bent on achieving a swift reconstruction of the political institutions and a rapid economic liberalisation. But after Boudiaf's assassination in June, the provisional government reverted to a well-tried 'socialist' model of development and halted or cancelled previous liberal measures – thereby losing the confidence of foreign investors and lenders.[18] A year later, the attempt to restart the economy according to socialist principles had clearly backfired, and the financial situation of the country (and of the army) went from bad to worse. The disastrous policies of the provisional government, coupled to internal struggles in the army, ensured that the guerrilla movement continued to thrive and that the population continued to be disaffected with the country's 'official' institutions (even more so because the main political parties of the democratic transition – the FIS, the FLN and the FFS (Front des Forces Socialistes) – kept questioning the legitimacy of the regime).

In the summer of 1993, these politico-economic mishaps and the lack of progress made in the struggle against the Islamic guerrillas triggered a reorganisation of the military leadership. A new structure of power began to emerge with General Lamari gaining the upper hand inside the army's high command. He was promoted Chief of Staff in July 1993, as his strategy for combating the guerrillas with special 'anti-terrorist' units began to gain acceptance. At the same time, General Zeroual was recalled by Nezzar and offered the post of Defence Minister. Zeroual used his position to launch the rebuilding of political institutions and to open negotiations with the imprisoned FIS leaders. By 1994 Nezzar had been forced to retire and Zeroual and Lamari formed a power duopoly. They agreed on economic liberalisation and on a debt-rescheduling package devised by the IMF that allowed the Algerian state to receive much-needed financial support.[19] Lamari used the funds made available by the international financial organisations to reinforce the position of the army in all the main urban areas – progressively chasing the Islamic guerrillas from the suburbs – and to protect the oil fields in the Sahara, where special exclusion zones were created in 1995. The anti-terrorist force, which began with 15,000 men in 1993 and reached 60,000 men by 1995, served not only to contain the guerrilla threat but also as the basis of Lamari's power in the military institution.

Zeroual took charge of reestablishing a dialogue with the political opposition and reconstructed 'independent' political institutions – a presidential election was held in 1995 and local and parliamentary elections in 1997. All these electoral contests were 'won' by Zeroual and his newly created party the RND (Rassemblement National pour la Démocratie – National Rally for Democracy), after much tampering with the ballot boxes.[20] By simultaneously ensuring that they remained the main engine of institutional reform and by monopolising the main economic resources of the country (oil and gas), the military leadership was able to overcome the political and military challenge of the Islamic fundamentalists. Although the armed forces sacrificed a great deal of their legitimacy – especially their claim to have the monopoly of legitimate violence – and brought many hardships upon the Algerian polity, they managed to ensure that these failings could not be used against them by the opposition.

By 1997, most opposition political parties and the main guerrilla groups had resigned themselves to reaching a truce with the military-backed regime, on the terms set by the army. These conditions included a veto on the re-legalisation of the FIS, as well as amendments to the constitution that allowed President Zeroual to nominate one-third of the Senate (such appointees, mostly former civil servants and retired army officers, gave the military a blocking minority in the Senate, ensuring that they could repeal any law voted by Parliament). Inside the army leadership, however, the struggle for supremacy continued until 1998, when the power duopoly collapsed in favour of Lamari and Zeroual was forced to resign. A new civilian leader, Bouteflika, was pushed forward by the military and 'won' a presidential election in 1999 in which he was the sole candidate. His opponents withdrew on the eve of the poll as the security forces once more began to tamper with the ballot boxes (Volpi 2000a). This ungainly election secured Lamari's position at the heart of the Algerian regime by ensuring that the new President remained dependent on the support of the military for his political survival. Lamari also secured the independence of the armed forces by cancelling, in all but name, the post of Defence Minister, thereby making the military institution even more impervious to civilian control. This stranglehold also means that since the election of Bouteflika and the signing of the peace accord with the AIS the political situation has been in deadlock. In particular, the military has repeatedly blocked, via the Interior Ministry, the legalisation of a moderate Islamic party – led by Taleb Ibrahimi, a main challenger in the 1999 presidential race until his retirement – capable of representing the political aspirations of a large segment of the Algerian citizenry. Despite the revival of guerrilla activities in the second half of 2000 and the anti-government riots in Kabylia in the spring of 2001, the military minders of the Algerian regime consider the political situation settled and in need of no further change. This is a view that they are likely to retain in the near-to-medium term unless a dramatic event occurs in the polity (such as nation-wide riots), in the military (an internal coup, perhaps) or on the international scene (the imposition of sanctions, for example).

Conclusion: the role of the military in a pseudo-democracy

In Algeria, the military was involved in a complex redefinition of the country's political structures. These transformations laid the foundations for the durable involvement of the military in the political social and economic organisation of the polity. In less than five years, the army changed from being the main protector of the country against external aggressors – and a main component of the one-party system – to being briefly the subservient security apparatus of a democratic polity and, finally, the shadowy ruler of the country and the (more or less successful) guarantor of its internal peace. In the last few years, however, what the Algerian military best exemplified, both by its successes and by its failures, was the role that a security apparatus could play in a nominally democratic system (or pseudo-democracy). In the developing world, the presence of loci of authoritarianism in 'new democracies' is not an unusual state of affairs (O'Donnell 1994, 1997; Linz and Stepan 1996; Bratton and van de Walle 1997).[21] What is noteworthy about the organisation of the Algerian polity today is that the manipulation of the democratic process by the military is so blatantly known, and yet working. Not only do the armed forces possess extremely large discretionary powers in all domains (in terms of a state of emergency in place since 1992), but they also intervene recurrently on a massive scale to ensure the reproduction of these political arrangements. Such interventions, which have occurred in all the elections held since 1995, are partly to protect the population from intimidation by the guerrillas, and made partly to stuff the polling booths with the 'appropriate' voting slips.

Initially, what gave power to the army was the lack of political vision and skills betrayed by the country's political representatives. Now, the military remains in place because it has devised a (so far) successful strategy to use 'democratic' politics as an instrument of social control. By pretending to be committed to democratic politics at all but the most inopportune times – during elections – the military is able to use procedural democracy against the political actors who best express the wishes of the Algerian citizenry. Typically, after a rigged election, once the country's 'democratic' institutions are occupied by the supporters of the military, these 'democratically elected' officials vow never to allow the army to use such inappropriate methods ever again. In the meantime, however, these dubious political 'representatives' use their institutional prerogatives to force the political opposition into complying with the fair procedures of institutions that they have come to control via unfair means. They are therefore able to oversee the (legal) political opposition up to the next electoral contest, when another temporary democratic breakdown is engineered by the military (and when similar results are obtained using a new set of conservative politicians).

Using these tactics, the only problem that the armed forces currently have is that they need to keep upgrading their understanding of the various political movements in order to be able to deal effectively with an increasing number of political actors in an increasingly complex political environment. As time passes and the sense of urgency created by the 1992 *coup d'état* disappears, the military leadership must increasingly confront the demands of the citizenry for a more meaningful and effective organisation of the political system. To do so they must co-opt new political actors who express these concerns, whilst at the same time not giving them the capacity to undermine their leadership. Their ambiguous attitude towards Taleb Ibrahimi, a former FLN Foreign Minister now embodying the hope of many Islamists, reflects the limited political openness that they try to retain. Ibrahimi was vetted to participate in the 1999 presidential election to give the contest greater credibility, but then refused authorisation to create his own political party in 2000 because this was judged to be potentially destabilising for the rest of the political class.

In the longer term, however, it is unavoidable that a more workable division of power between the military (and their conservative allies), the Islamic fundamentalists and the democrats will be needed. This is not a result which can be produced by the kind of winner-takes-all elections that now characterise Algerian 'democracy'. Instead, it can only be the outcome of a concerted effort at dialogue by all three groups of political actors – something the military could authorise in Parliament without risk, because of the blocking majority they retain in the Senate. Having just succeeded in fighting off an armed challenge by Islamic guerrillas, however, the armed forces are not ready to embark on a course of liberal/democratic reforms just yet. The military leadership may well realise that in the current political context neither a rapid economic recovery nor a swift abatement of social violence is likely to happen, but they are still unwilling to make any concession that would resemble an admission of defeat. Furthermore, their access to international finance and to the oil rent gives the military-backed regime a comfortable financial breathing space and permits it to control the social and political situation for the moment.

The prospects for the future of democracy in Algeria's polity are not very good. The nuclei of authoritarianism that emerged during the civil conflict are likely to become entrenched and the political class, deprived of any real power, is likely to continue to focus on short-term solutions and personal enrichment. It cannot be known now whether, had the FIS been allowed to take power in 1992, the more moderate Islamic leaders would (or could) have pushed forward a democratic and reformist agenda, in alliance with a secular democratic party like the FFS and the reformers of the FLN. Nonetheless, a similar alliance is the only means today to secure the future for democracy in Algeria. Only such a joint enterprise can hope to delimit the respective areas of political authority of the army, the executive, the legislative, and the judicial and religious system, as well as a workable method of transfer of power (and sequencing of political reforms). But it remains to be seen whether nationalists, democrats and Islamists, still so divided along nationalistic, secularist and religious fault-lines, can – or even want to – produce a joint effort to undermine the authoritarian tendencies of the regime. The continuing deterioration of the institutional framework, and the cynicism that increasingly characterises the relationships between politicians/civil servants and the population, also mean that the longer they wait the more formidable their task will be. The more people get used to a high level of social violence and inequity, and the more the state rules in an arbitrary manner, the less a political system based on anything like deliberative processes and democratic accountability is likely to be created endogenously. In the medium to longer term, therefore, even with the emergence of a new inspirational leader, or a massive revival of interest (and effective support) from the international community, or, more realistically, a reorganisation of the military élite, there is no guarantee that an end to this particular authoritarian rule will permit the emergence of a liberal democratic system. So far, the military has been able to stop all genuine attempts at transforming the political organisation of the Algerian state. If a new leadership permits changes to take place, either by design or by mistake, it is likely that the social forces unleashed will not be any more 'enlightened' or tame than they were in 1988 or 1992 (the rule of the army being precisely what has prevented political and social movements from maturing). It is likely that, partly through design (on the part of the nationalist or Islamic radical forces) and partly through sheer incompetence, democratisation, when it occurs, will again be hectic in Algeria.

Chronology

1954 The Algerian war of decolonisation begins.
1962 Algeria becomes independent.
1963 The FLN becomes state party.
1965 Colonel Boumediene stages a successful *coup d'état*.
1967 Failed *coup d'état* by Colonel Zbiri.
1971 Nationalisation of the oil and gas sector.
1978 Death of President Boumediene.
1979 Colonel Chadli Benjedid is nominated President.
1980 'Berber Spring': violent protest in Kabylia by ethnic Berbers.
1986 Food riots in Constantine and Setif.
1988 The 'October riots': nation-wide anti-government protests; rewriting of the constitution to allow multi-partyism.
1989 Creation of the FIS by Abassi Madani and Ali Belhadj.
1990 Victory of the FIS in local elections.
1991 FIS general strike, army intervention and arrest of the FIS leaders; FIS takes a commanding lead in parliamentary elections.
1992 Removal of President Chadli Benjedid; The High Security Council suspends the electoral process and declares a state of emergency (still in place at the time of writing); the FIS is officially banned and Madani and Belhadj are condemned to twelve years in jail.
1993 General Lamari becomes Chief of Staff. General Zeroual becomes Defence Minister; foreign nationals are targeted by Islamic guerrilla groups.
1994 Zeroual is nominated head of state; Algeria signs structural agreement package with the IMF.
1995 The main opposition political parties boycott the presidential election; Zeroual is elected President.
1996 The FLN and Hamas (moderate Islamists) enter a coalition government.
1997 Massacres of civilians by Islamic guerrillas and (allegedly) the army; the RND (Zeroual's party) wins Parliamentary elections amidst allegations of widespread fraud; the AIS, the main Islamic guerrilla organisation, declares a ceasefire.
1998 Wave of anti-government riots in Kabylia; Zeroual resigns from presidency.
1999 Presidential race won by Abelaziz Bouteflika after all the other candidates had withdrawn; the AIS proposes to disband in exchange for general amnesty; Bouteflika's peace plan approved

by referendum – the AIS disbands.

2000 Taleb Ibrahimi's party (moderate Islamists) is denied legal recognition; revival of guerrilla activities and massacres of civilians.

2001 Wave of violent anti-governmental protests in Kabylia.

References

Abada, K. (1994–5) 'Armée: la fin d'un mythe', *Les Cahiers de l'Orient*, 36–37.

Bariki, S. (1995) 'Algérie: chronique intérieure', *Annuaire de l'Afrique du Nord*, 35.

Bormeo, N. (1992) 'Democracy and the lessons of dictatorship', *Comparative Politics*, 24 (3).

Bratton, M. and N. van de Walle (1997) *Democratic Experiments in Africa: Regime Transitions in Comparative Perspective*, Cambridge: Cambridge University Press.

Burgat, F. (1988) *L'Islamisme au Maghreb*, Paris: Karthala.

Carlier, O. (1995) *Entre Nation et Jihad: Histoire Sociale des Radicalismes Algériens*, Paris: Presses de Science Po.

Charef, A. (1994) *Algérie: Le Grand Dérapage*, Paris: Éditions de l'Aube.

Dévoluy, P. and M. Duteil (1994) *La Poudrière Algérienne: Histoire Secrète d'une République sous Influence*, Paris: Calmann-Levy.

Diamond, L. (1996) 'Is the third wave over?', *Journal of Democracy*, 7 (3).

Dunn, J. (1996) 'How democracies succeed', *Economy and Society*, 25 (4).

Entelis, J. P. (1999) 'State-society relations: Algeria as a case study', in Tessler, M., J. Nachtwey and A. Banda (eds.), *Area Studies and Social Sciences: Strategies for Understanding Middle East Politics*, Bloomington: Indiana University Press.

Fontaine, J. (1996) 'Les résultats de l'élection présidentielle du 16 novembre 1995', *Monde Arabe Maghreb-Machrek*, 151.

—— (1997) 'Résultats et évolution des forces politiques', *Monde Arabe Maghreb-Machrek*, 157.

Huntington, S. P. (1991) *The Third Wave: Democratization in the Late Twentieth Century*, Norman: University of Oklahoma Press.

Labat, S. (1995) *Les Islamistes Algériens: Entre les Urnes et le Maquis*, Paris: Éditions du Seuil.

Lavenue, J. J. (1993) *Algérie: La Démocracie Interdite*, Paris: L'Harmattan.

Leveau, R. (1993) *Le Sabre et le Turban*, Paris: François Bourin.

Linz, J. L. and A. Stepan (1996) *Problems of Democratic Transition and Consolidation: Southern Europe, South America and Post-Communist Europe*, Baltimore: Johns Hopkins University Press.

Luckham, R. (1996a) 'Faustian bargains: democratic control over military and security establishments', in Luckham, R. and G. White (eds.), *Democratization in the South: the Jagged Wave*, Manchester: Manchester University Press.

—— (1996b) 'Democracy and the military: an epitaph for Frankenstein's monster?', *Democratization*, 3 (2).

Martinez, L. (1998) *La Guerre Civile en Algérie, 1990–1998*, Paris: Karthala.

Mortimer, M. (1996) 'Islamists, soldiers and democrats: the second Algerian war', *The Middle East Journal*, 50 (1).

O'Donnell, G. (1994) 'Delegative democracy', *Journal of Democracy*, 5 (1).

—— (1997) 'Illusions about consolidation', in Diamond, L., M. Plattner, Y. Chu and H. Tien (eds.), *Consolidating the Third Wave Democracies*, Baltimore: Johns Hopkins University Press.

O'Donnell, G. and P. Schmitter (1986) 'Tentative conclusions about uncertain democracies', in O'Donnell, G., P. Schmitter and L. Whitehead (eds.), *Transitions from Authoritarian Rule: Prospects for Democracy*, Baltimore: Johns Hopkins University Press.

Piscatori, J. (1991) 'Religion and realpolitik: Islamic responses to the Gulf War', in Piscatori, J. (ed.), *Islamic Fundamentalisms and the Gulf Crisis*, Chicago: American Academy of Arts and Sciences.

Roberts, H. (1994) 'From radical mission to equivocal ambition: the expansion and manipulation of Algerian Islamism', in Marty, M. E. and R. S. Appleby (eds.), *Accounting for Fundamentalisms: the Dynamic Character of Movements*, Chicago: University of Chicago Press.

Ruedy, J. (1992) *Modern Algeria: the Origins and Development of a Nation*, Bloomington: Indiana University Press.

Volpi, F. (2000a) 'Democracy in Algeria: continuity and change in the organisation of political representation', *Journal of North African Studies*, 5 (2).

—— (2000b) 'Algeria between revolution and democracy (1988–1999): Islamic fundamentalism and political change at the end of the twentieth century', unpublished PhD thesis, Cambridge University.

—— (2002) 'Language, practice and the possibility of a transnational liberal-democratic *ethos*', *Global Society*, 16 (1).

Willis, M. (1996) *The Islamist Challenge in Algeria: a Political History*, London: Ithaca.

Yefsah, A. (1995) 'L'armée sans hidjab', *Les Temps Modernes*, January–February.

Zartman, W. (1987) 'The military in the politics of succession: Algeria', in Harbeson, J. W. (ed.), *The Military in African Politics*, New York: Praeger.

Semi-official documents

Conseil National Économique et Social (CNES) (1996) *Rapport de la Sixième Session Plénière*, Algiers.

Conseil National Économique et Social (CNES) (1997) *Situation de la Communauté Algérienne à l'Étranger*, Algiers.

Conseil National Économique et Social (CNES) (1998) *Le Système des Relations de Travail dans le Contexte de l'Ajustement Structurel*, Algiers.

Reports

Amnesty International (1996) 'Algeria: Fear and Silence', London.

Economist Intelligence Unit (1995/1996) 'Algeria: Country Risk', London.

Monde Arabe Maghreb-Machrek (1998) 'Chronologie: Algérie', Paris.

Newspapers
Le Monde (France).
Actualité-Algérie.
El Watan (Algeria).
La Tribune (Algeria).

Notes

1 Concerning the 'Third Wave', see particularly Huntington (1991) and compare Diamond (1996).

2 I use the terms army and military interchangeably as the air force and the navy played no significant role in the contemporary (or any earlier) conflict, and because the other branches of the security apparatus (the *gendarmerie*, the police and the secret police) have increasingly come under the control of a military high command dominated by the army leadership.

3 On the reactualisation of *Fortuna*, see particularly O'Donnell and Schmitter (1986).

4 Very practical reasons prevented the international community from devoting much attention to Algeria, as the transition ran into difficulties at a very inopportune time: during the Gulf War. But there were also more ideologically construed reasons for this inaction that had to do with the fact that Western powers were reluctant to get involved in a transition in which Islamic fundamentalists were the main political players. On these issues see Piscatori (1991).

5 The principal losers in this reorganisation of the military leadership were the head of the military high command (General Belouchet), the head of security (General Ayat), the commander of the ground forces (General Abderrahim) and the commander of the Algiers military region (General Attailia).

6 The positions of President and Defence Minister had been *de facto* merged since the 1965 coup by Colonel Boumediene (then Defence Minister), while the prerogatives of Chief of Staff were abolished after the 1967 attempted coup by Colonel Zbiri, the then Chief of Staff.

7 The precise mechanisms that underpin a lasting civilian control of the military are not yet fully understood today even in well-established democracies. On these issues see Luckham (1996a, 1996b), Dunn (1996), Bormeo (1992).

8 The European Union insisted that the Algerian authorities 'do all they can to restore a normal institutional life in Algeria by allowing all concerned parties to establish a peaceful dialogue and the democratic process to continue unhindered' (*Le Monde*, 25 January 1992). The French President declared that France 'wishes to maintain and develop her relations with Algeria in so far as the principles that she judges essential, progress towards democracy and respect of human rights, are respected' (*Le Monde*, 28 January 1992).

9 By the end of the decade, only Hassan Hattab's Group for Combat and

Preaching (estimated strength: 500–1,000 men) would have retained a consistent policy of political and military opposition to the regime (*La Tribune*, 2 May 1999, *La Tribune*, 9 August 1999).

10 A situation illustrated by the fact that even after the 1997 ceasefire of the AIS and the 1999 general amnesty, violence linked to armed groups (of any persuasion) remained rampant in Algeria.

11 By 1996, nearly one million Algerians (about twenty per cent of the country's workforce) worked in the informal sector, and nearly half of the country's monetary supply circulated outside the (state-controlled) banking sector (Conseil National Économique et Social (CNES) 1996; CNES 1997; CNES 1998).

12 In the December 1991 Parliamentary elections, in the district of Tizi-Ouzou, the regional capital of Kabylia, the FIS received less than 10,000 votes while the main Kabyle/democratic party, the FFS (Front des Forces Socialistes – Socialist Front) received nearly 150,000 votes (*Algérie-actualité*, 9–15 January 1992).

13 The relationship between the relatively well-organised and well-supervised 'communal guards' and the 'self-defence groups' (which act much more like private security companies) is closer than one might expect. Members of the communal guards often form or join self-defence groups whenever government funding dries up or when they disagree with the administration's policies.

14 An exception may be made for an *independentist*-inclined region like Kabylia, where militias linked to regionalist political parties did help to weaken the grip of the central government in the area – as the recurrence of waves of anti-government protests there illustrate.

15 On this occasion, the people involved were given a high-profile trial – a tentative attempt by the government to display the fairness and effectiveness of its justice system after allegations of complicity in the killings had damaged the regime's image. More routinely, these incidents were discreetly treated by local army commanders or military tribunals. On this type of exaction see Amnesty International (1996) and Volpi (2000b).

16 Because the Islamic fundamentalists had not made serious inroads into close-knit officer circles, the Algerian army managed to retain its cohesion. Officially, only 90 members of the armed forces were court-martialled in 1992 in connection with the Islamic insurrection. (But despite this resilience, the number of new conscripts entering the ranks continued to plummet.) See Yefsah (1995); Abada (1994–5).

17 This lack of ideas was apparent in a 1998 speech by Zeroual, in which he proudly claimed that while in 1992 Algeria was about to be 'sacrificed on the altar of a supposed democracy', in 1998 this danger had subsided and had been replaced by 'a return to the kind of democracy Algerians could legitimately aspire to' (*El Watan*, 12 September 1998).

18 Boudiaf's assassination may or may not have been engineered by a faction within the military that was upset by his anti-corruption campaign. Public opinion, however, was in no doubt that the army was involved in his assas-

sination, and this alone seriously weakened the political authority of the regime (Dévoluy and Duteil 1994).

19 The IMF deal signed in May 1994 provided the Algerian regime with a $1 billion stand-by loan and paved the way for a $5 billion debt rescheduling deal by the Paris Club (institutional creditors) that almost halved the debt-service ratio of the country. The financial wealth of the regime was further secured in March 1995, when Algeria renegotiated an IMF extended-facilities loan guaranteeing another $1.8 billion a year over a three-year period. In addition, the Paris Club authorised another $5 billion rescheduling of the Algerian public debt and the London Club (private investors) authorised a $3 billion rescheduling of the Algerian private debt (Economist Intelligence Unit 1996).

20 In 1995, the official turn-out was announced as near 75 per cent, and Zeroual was declared President-elect with more than 60 per cent of the votes. The moderate Islamic leader, Nannah, was accorded 25 per cent of the vote and the Kabyle 'democrat' Sadi nearly 10 per cent. In 1997, the RND 'won' over 40 per cent of the Parliamentary seats, the Movement for a Peaceful Society (MSP) (Nannah's party) 18 per cent, the FLN 17 per cent, Ennahda (moderate Islamic fundamentalists) 9 per cent and the two Kabyle/democratic parties, FFS and RCD, 5 per cent each (Fontaine 1996, 1997).

21 In the region, the informal influence of the military in the political system is an entrenched feature of a semi-democratic state like Turkey, which Algeria now tries to emulate.

8

The Security Establishment in Sri Lanka
A Case for Reform

JAGATH P. SENARATNE[1]

Throughout the last two decades Sri Lanka has been convulsed by violent insurrections. A social class-based insurrection resulted in the loss of about 60,000 lives between 1987 and 1990. The Tamil secessionist insurrection, which began in 1972 and escalated to a qualitatively higher level from 1983 onwards, has also led to the loss of at least 60,000 lives, half of them civilians (National Peace Council 2001: 5). Tens of thousands have been injured and approximately 800,000 remain internally displaced. The full horror and human costs of the conflict can barely be glimpsed in such statistics.

Sri Lankan society is composed of diverse ethnic groups. Religion and language, singly or combined, are the primary markers of ethnic identity. The four major ethnic groups in the island are the Sinhalas (74 per cent of the population), Sri Lanka Tamils (12.7 per cent), upcountry Tamils (5.5 per cent), and the Muslims (7.1 per cent).[2] In terms of religious distribution the main divisions are as follows: Buddhists (69.3 per cent), Hindus (15.5 per cent), Muslims (7.6 per cent), Christians (7.6 per cent), and other religions (0.1 per cent).[3]

Ethnicity and class underlie intra-state conflict in Sri Lanka. Both ethnic and class competition have been evident at least from the early nineteenth century.[4] The arenas and intensity of competition have increased over time along with the increase in population and the increasingly complex social divisions which have emerged in tandem with modernity. Yet prior to the insurrections of the past two or three decades, ethnic and class competition crossed the threshold into mass violence only during (relatively rare) periods of rioting, strikes and civil disorder.

All ethnic groups contain class divisions. Or, stated in another way, all classes contain ethnic divisions. Neither ethnicity nor class can be derived from the other, and neither should be given analytical preference. Ethnic identity in Sri Lanka is a combination of religion, language and some elements of culture (including socialisation), combined with collective economic interests. While economic interests are an important constituent element of ethnic identity, the yearning for political rights, collective security and the space for social and cultural expression are no less significant. Ethnic identity has evolved through time in tandem with political mobilisation. The actions of the state (including military and police actions) have also influenced this evolution. Class identity stems from complex processes of class formation which have accompanied complex changes in the economy over centuries. These were accelerated by the shift from state welfare capitalism to the liberalisation of the economy and market-driven growth from 1977 (see Lakshman 1997: 7–12).

The collective interests of ethnic groups and classes are articulated in complex ways through the political party system, although on the whole left-wing, class-based political parties have been less successful than ethnic political parties. All the major ethnic groups are mobilised politically through parties. The two major political parties – the United National Party (UNP) and the Sri Lanka Freedom Party (SLFP) – are identified with the Sinhalese, even though they both have had numbers of Muslim and Tamil supporters. Although they have attempted to project themselves as incorporating all ethnic groups, both have had to respond to the electoral gravitational pull of the Sinhalese electorate. When first established in 1946 the UNP was able (to a limited degree) to incorporate members of all ethnic groups, although the leadership of the party was, of course, in the hands of Sinhalese. In contrast, the SLFP began in 1951 on an unequivocal pro-Sinhalese platform, which was phenomenally successful among Sinhalese voters in 1956. The UNP could not remain unaffected by the SLFP's success. Over the following turbulent decade the UNP gradually lost its multi-ethnic orientation in response to the competition posed by (and the need to emulate) the SLFP. The UNP and the SLFP have continued to compete for the votes of the Sinhala electorate, often accusing each other of 'betraying' Sinhala interests and thereby adding to the difficulties of arriving at compromises with the other minority ethnic communities. The emergence of Tamil and Muslim ethnic parties has further intensified the association between the UNP–SLFP duo and the Sinhala electorate.

Faced with the reality of political power becoming more and more concentrated in the hands of the Sinhalese after Independence, Sri Lanka Tamils have also mobilised politically along ethnic lines. The parties of the 1950s were the Illankai Tamil Arasu Kadchi (ITAK or Lanka Tamil State Party, otherwise known as the Federal Party), and the Tamil Congress (TC). Through subsequent schisms and amalgamations the Tamil United Liberation Front (TULF) emerged in the 1970s as the foremost parliamentary party of the Sri Lanka Tamils. The Tamil secessionist tendency spawned many Tamil guerrilla groups in the 1970s and early 1980s, including the Liberation Tigers of Tamil Eelam (LTTE), the Eelam Revolutionary Organisation of Students (EROS), the Tamil Eelam Liberation Organisation (TELO), the People's Liberation Organisation of Tamil Eelam (PLOTE) and the Eelam People's Revolutionary Liberation Front (EPRLF). But of these only the LTTE has continued to prosecute the secessionist insurrection.

Upcountry Tamils have a unique trade union-cum-political party called the Ceylon Workers' Congress (CWC), which has worked in several coalition governments to further their collective interests. Until the 1980s, the Muslims found political representation within the UNP and (to a lesser extent) the SLFP. Although many Muslims continue to support these two parties, from the mid-1980s a number of Muslim ethnic parties have emerged, among which the Sri Lanka Muslim Congress (SLMC) is the most prominent.

In the 1950s and 1960s two left-wing parties – the LSSP (Lanka Sama Samaja Party) and the CP (Communist Party) – had some support among the urban working class, but were unsuccessful in the face of escalating ethnic mobilisation. From the mid-1990s the Janatha Vimukthi Peramuna (JVP, Peoples' Liberation Front) has transformed itself from an insurrectionary movement into the main left-wing party. Its attempts to mobilise people across ethnic lines have been largely unsuccessful, and its support base remains predominantly Sinhala. In sum, where ethnic identity is pitched diametrically against class, it is ethnic identity that has usually emerged victorious. This does not mean that class identity and consciousness have ceased to exist, merely that they have been overdetermined by the strength of ethnic mobilisation.

Sri Lanka is a country with scarce resources, a growing population, and a relatively underdeveloped economy. Both ethnic groups and social classes compete for all manner of resources – land, water, credit, employment, education, urban space and housing. This competition manifests itself in the marketplace, in government departments, between government officials and the public, in schools, in public debates in newspapers, in neighbourhoods, in universities, and in numerous other contexts.

There is also intense competition between ethnic groups for political representation and power. From independence Sri Lanka has been unable to devise a stable and sustainable constitutional framework within which this competition can be regulated in a peaceful and democratic manner (Coomaraswamy, forthcoming). The country has to date functioned under three different constitutions and is, at present, contemplating the enactment of its fourth. This 'constitutional restlessness' is symptomatic of so far irreconcilable disagreements between and within the ethnic groups.

The purpose of this chapter is to assess, first, the actions of Sri Lanka's security establishment in relation to the Tamil insurrection; second, the direct and indirect consequences which flowed from these actions; and, third, the case for security sector reform.

Security problems of postcolonial Sri Lanka: class and ethnic insurrection

The armed forces of Sri Lanka were created soon after independence in 1948: the Ceylon Army in 1949, the Royal Ceylon Navy in 1950 and the Royal Ceylon Air Force in 1951.[5] The British government and military forces played a vital role in their creation and initial recruitment. All were fashioned along British lines, inclusive of their organisational structures, uniforms, regimental insignia, training, weapons and equipment. The initial establishment was minuscule by present-day standards: an army of approximately 4,000, a navy of 1,500, and an air force of 1,000. These numbers increased gradually over the subsequent decades. However, the escalation of the Tamil secessionist insurrection initiated major expansions from 1984/5 in military personnel, military expenditure, new weapon systems and operational activity. All this was despite unbroken civilian governance during the postcolonial period, although there have been times – the most serious being the attempted coup of 1962 – when sections of the officer corps have contemplated intervention.

The Sri Lankan armed forces have only been deployed to deal with internal problems, and have never been involved in international conflicts. All their early active deployments entailed assistance to the police during breakdown of public order ('aid to the civil power', also referred to as internal security (IS) duties in line with British operational doctrine). Into this category fell the internal security deployments of 1953 (countering working-class agitation), 1956 and 1958 (suppressing and containing anti-Tamil riots), 1961 (suppressing widespread Tamil civil disobedience), 1977 (suppressing and containing anti-Tamil riots) and 1983 (suppressing the anti-Tamil pogrom-cum-riots after an initial failure to act). In addition to these short deployments, a relatively small proportion of the security forces were actively deployed between the early 1950s (Muttukumaru 1987: 158 and Sri Lanka Army 1999: 62) and the late 1970s (Sri Lanka Army 1979: 154) on anti-illicit immigration and anti-smuggling duties in the North.

Far more serious violence occurred during the two JVP insurrections. The first (in 1971) was relatively easily suppressed in six weeks, although with the loss of 5,000–10,000 lives. The second (mid-1987–1989) was more protracted, lasting two and a half years and resulting in about 60,000 deaths and disappearances. Many human rights violations occurred, including extra-judicial killings, 'disappearances', torture and incommunicado detention. These also brought about a considerable deterioration in the conduct of the military and security forces, which carried over to their conduct against the Tamil secessionist insurrection. The second JVP insurrection effectively ceased at the end of 1989, more than 12 years ago, and the JVP has entered mainstream politics with a significant (though minority) representation in Parliament.

The Tamil secessionist insurrection, however, has dwarfed all the other security problems faced by the postcolonial state, being by far its most serious politico-military challenge. The political alienation of Tamils – the fundamental factor in the secessionist insurrection – began in the 1950s and gradually developed in the 1960s. The actively armed phases of the insurrection commenced in 1972 at low levels of violence (it was only in 1979 that the government introduced legislation to ban secessionist movements). But after the 1983 anti-Tamil pogrom-cum-riots, the insurrection escalated to a qualitatively higher intensity. As of early 2002, the insurrection has been militarily active for 30 years, except for short periods of peace negotiations.

The Tamil insurrection aims to establish a separate state called Tamil Eelam in the Northern and Eastern Provinces of Sri Lanka, thus repudiating the territorial and political unity of the Sri Lankan state. It is a complex politico-military process arising from ethnic competition and violence between Sri Lanka Tamils and Sinhala exclusivists and the (Sinhala-dominated) postcolonial state. However, it has been intensified through the security force's efforts to counter the insurrection through the massive (and ill-conceived) use of force. It cannot be overemphasised that the military increases referred to earlier have *all* been directly related to this insurrection.

The insurrection has undergone many internal changes over the last three decades. The militant secessionist tendency initially originated and grew within the womb of democratic Tamil political parties like the Federal Party and the TULF (Tamil United Liberation Front). The embryonic guerrilla movements of the early 1970s started with a handful of Tamil youths armed with revolvers and shotguns. By 1983 the five main groups – LTTE, EROS, TELO, PLOTE, and EPRLF – were established, to a considerable extent, because of the perceived (and actual) ineffectiveness of Tamil parliamentary parties.[6]

During the years immediately after the 1983 riots there was a marked increase in the number and activities of Tamil guerrilla groups. Numerous conflicts occurred within and between them, and internecine violence finally eliminated all but the original five.[7] In 1987, under the Indo-Lanka Accord, all the armed groups except the LTTE agreed to search for a solution for the Tamil people's problems within an undivided Sri Lankan state. In October 1987, fighting began between the LTTE and the Indian forces and the LTTE became the sole military expression of Tamil secessionism (Senaratne 1997: 89–102; Kadian 1990; Sardeshpande 1992; and Gunaratna 1993). From 1987 it has been the LTTE alone that has prosecuted the insurrection. International sources estimate that in 2000/1 the LTTE had 6,000–7,000 armed, combat-experienced cadres at its disposal (SIPRI Yearbook 2001: 62). It is the author's estimate, however, that the figure is closer to 10,000, and they are supported by many thousands more part-time supporters who provide numerous types of assistance, including logistical and medical back-up, food-preparation, administration, vehicle and weapon repair, and intelligence.

The Tamil secessionist insurrection has outlasted numerous political, diplomatic, and military developments in both Sri Lanka and India during these decades,[8] as well as four Sri Lankan governments, namely 1970–7 (SLFP coalition), 1977–88 (UNP), 1989–94 (UNP), and 1994–2001 (SLFP coalition). Since a new UNP government took office in January 2002 a ceasefire has been agreed, and complex negotiations have begun between the government and the LTTE.

From a political–military operational perspective the most important characteristic of the Tamil insurrection in general, and the LTTE in particular, has been the ability to wage protracted guerrilla warfare. Further, the LTTE has demonstrated over the last ten years its capacity to face – and on some occasions defeat – the Sri Lanka army in conventional-type military operations. Such warfare has fully extended the coercive resources of both the Sri Lankan state (from 1972 onwards) and the Indian state (during 1987–90). It is also this ability to wage protracted guerrilla warfare that has differentiated the Tamil insurrection from the two JVP insurrections.

By this I do not mean to imply that the LTTE were experts in guerrilla warfare from their beginnings in the early 1970s. On the contrary, their initial actions were predictably amateurish, and they made many mistakes. But as the insurrection unfolded and the political mobilisation of the Tamil people continued, the characteristics of protracted guerrilla warfare gradually evolved. The LTTE has been able to manoeuvre and counter-manoeuvre in relation to each new challenge it has faced, making optimum use of its military and political capabilities as well as its international and popular support.[9]

Moreover, the trajectory of the insurrection has been profoundly influenced by acts of commission and omission on the part of the Sri Lankan state and its security forces regarding political reform, military strategy and operations, reconciliation and reconstruction, internal displacement and human rights. This dialectical interaction needs emphasis, as otherwise an erroneous impression might be created that the insurgents were omnipotent, and followed a preconceived strategy from the start, a picture that is far from reality.

Sri Lanka's security establishment

The country's security establishment comprises the National Security Council (NSC); the Ministry of Defence (MoD), the army, navy, and air force; the police and its Special Task Force (STF); the intelligence organisations; and the 'Home Guard' militia. The apex body is the NSC, informally in existence from at least the early 1970s. It is the most important policy-making body and consequently has a great impact on all matters pertaining to security. The President – who is head of state, head of government and Commander-in-Chief – is chairperson of the NSC. The NSC also includes the Deputy Minister for Defence, the secretaries to the President and MoD, the armed forces and police commanders, and the directors of the intelligence services. There is a high degree of civilian governmental (or more accurately presidential) control. Until the change of government in 2002, the President was the Minister of Defence, with the Deputy Minister reporting directly to her. All the important security-related policies and strategies of the government are discussed at the NSC, and after discussion the President takes the decisions which are passed on to the armed forces and police to be implemented. The respective force commanders are the principal advisers to the NSC on matters pertaining to their departments.

The Ministry of Defence has responsibility for the army, navy, air force and, prior to January 2002, the police, being responsible for all promotions, appointments, budgetary allocations and procurements. In January 2002 the new UNP government brought the police under a newly created Ministry of the Interior, in order to make the police more accessible to the public and separate it from the harsher ethos of the MoD.[10] By and large the new policy is welcome, yet in the context of internal conflict the police will continue to be deployed on a wide range of internal security duties. The Ministry of Justice is also closely associated with the security establishment. It is responsible for drafting regulations and legislation – such as Emergency Regulations under the Public Security Ordinance and the Prevention of Terrorism Act (PTA) – and prosecutions, if any, of armed forces and police personnel. The financial requirements of the different institutions under Ministry of Defence control are collated, reviewed and negotiated with the Ministry of Finance, which remains the ultimate authority on the release of financial resources.

There is little parliamentary supervision of the military and intelligence services and neither does the constitution provide for any such role. Controversial issues which have arisen periodically – such as military defeats, allegations of corruption or allegations of human rights violations – have been debated in Parliament and in the media and these debates have served to inform the public. At all other times the security establishment has been left largely under the unsupervised control of the executive and the MoD.

The army, navy, air force and police are organised as separate departments with their respective commanders as their chief executive officers. The army is the dominant organisation and its dominance – due to its size, omnipresence and the tactical context of the North and East – has increased over the years. However, the MoD has good overall control of these institutions via the operational, financial, promotion and administrative mechanisms at the disposal of the Minister, his deputy and the secretary to the MoD.

With the escalation of internal conflicts in the 1980s and 1990s the intelligence apparatuses of the state also underwent considerable change. Up to 1994/5 the primary intelligence agency was the National Intelligence Bureau (NIB) which was part of the police. During the PA (People's Alliance) government of 1994–2001 the NIB was dismantled and two new intelligence organisations were created in its place: the Directorate of Foreign Intelligence (DFI) and the Directorate of Internal Intelligence (DII). However, both the DFI and DII are under the control of the MoD. The police have responsibility for the Criminal Investigation Department (CID) and Terrorism Investigation Division (TID) and these too have some intelligence-gathering capabilities in addition to their criminal investigative functions. The Special Task Force (STF) – created in 1984 after the 1983 riots and colloquially referred to as the 'police commandos' – is part of the police establishment but in training, capabilities and operational role it is identical to an army commando-type regiment. The army's Military Intelligence Corps was created in 1990, and its command and control body, the Directorate of Military Intelligence (DMI), is a component of the general staff at army headquarters. The navy and air force do not have separate intelligence directorates, but have small 'air intelligence' and 'naval intelligence' departments built into their directorates of operations.

Once overall strategy is decided at the NSC each armed force is responsible for implementing the missions falling within its purview. Any operation requiring the coordinated effort of more than a single armed force is conducted as a 'joint operation'. The army is invariably responsible for preparing operational plans, while sea-borne and aerial logistics operations are the responsibility of the navy and air force. The general staff at army headquarters in Colombo, through its directorate of operations, prepares plans and orders in close consultation with divisional field commanders of the divisions deployed in the North and East. In sum, overall control of the use of military force extends downwards from the President and the NSC to divisional and unit commanders. In terms of implementing military operations this formal command structure still works reasonably well.

The security establishment's attempts to counter secessionist insurrection (1979–2001)

From 1978/9, state security planners began to take serious note of the secessionist insurrectionary activity under way at a low intensity in the Jaffna peninsula from 1972. The then President, J. R. Jayewardene, placed Jaffna under military rule in July 1979, and sent a brigade-strong army contingent to Jaffna with orders to 'wipe out terrorism' in six months. It duly carried out a series of repressive internal security operations and in December 1979 its commander reported to President Jayewardene that the mission had been completed successfully. This was far from the case, since the insurgents had merely made a tactical retreat. Insurrectionary activity gradually built up during 1981–3, and following the anti-Tamil pogrom-cum-riots of July 1983, escalated to qualitatively higher levels, from which it has not declined since. These riots proved immensely beneficial to the secessionist cause, and served to swell the guerrilla organisations with thousands of new recruits.

From 1983 to 1987 the government carried out a series of military 'cordon and search' and internal security operations, but the insurrection increased in intensity amidst internal displacement, detentions, some extra-judicial killings and disappearances. Some efforts were made to address Tamil political grievances, but these were largely futile. In May–June 1987 the government embarked upon a large military operation (Operation LIBERATION) in the Jaffna peninsula. Although it made tactical gains, in terms of overall strategy it was a failure, since it precipitated direct Indian intervention in July 1987 via the Indo-Lanka Accord.

The Indian intervention was the culmination of a 'two-track' policy whereby the Indian government covertly assisted secessionist insurgent groups while concurrently pressuring the Sri Lanka government to make concessions (see Senaratne 1997: 89–102). As a part of the terms of the Accord the Sri Lankan armed forces were compelled to retreat to the positions from which they launched the operation.

After a few months of peace, hostilities between the Indian forces and the LTTE began in early October 1987 and were to continue until 1990. Efforts at political reform, including the Thirteenth Amendment to the constitution and the creation of provincial councils, once again proved fruitless.[11] While the main north-eastern cities such as Jaffna, Trincomalee, Batticaloa, and Amparai and many other smaller urban centres were controlled by the Indian forces, the LTTE withdrew into the jungles in the North and East and carried out guerrilla operations. In June 1989 the LTTE and Sri Lanka agreed to a ceasefire, whereupon the Sri Lankan President requested the Indian government to withdraw its forces, and they left the island in March 1990.

Three months later, in June 1990 the LTTE re-ignited the insurrection, and the subsequent four years saw the heaviest fighting experienced up to that time. Despite a large number of military operations and the killing of considerable numbers of LTTE cadres, the UNP government's attempts to suppress the LTTE proved unsuccessful.

In late 1994 a new government, the Peoples' Alliance (PA, a coalition led by the SLFP) came to power. This new government attempted negotiations but once again these proved fruitless. The LTTE withdrew from a ceasefire in April 1995, and fighting between the LTTE and the security forces escalated. The government's several attempts to formulate a political reform package were frustrated. Military operations during

1995–2001 were of an unprecedented high intensity. During Operation RIVIRESA (the government's capture of Jaffna peninsula) the LTTE fought on a semi-conventional basis and ultimately withdrew to the Vanni area of the Northern Province – the largely jungle area immediately south of the Jaffna peninsula. During Operation JAYASIKURU the government attempted to capture the main road running through the centre of the Vanni, but during two and a half years (from May 1997) the LTTE successfully resisted. From November 1999 to May 2000 the LTTE launched a counter-offensive, which in the southern Vanni pushed the army back to where it had started in 1997, and in the north overran the Elephant Pass army base and came near the outskirts of Jaffna city. By 2001 the LTTE's defences in the peninsula had stabilised, and in effect the area south of Eluthumadduval on the Jaffna peninsula and north of Vavuniya fell completely under its control.

In sum, the actions of the military and security forces over these 18 years have been largely counterproductive. Although considerable numbers of insurgent cadres may have been eliminated, the political–military phenomenon that is the insurrection itself has grown from strength to strength, and has gained considerable popular support. The primary reason is that none of Sri Lanka's governments were able to formulate and implement political reforms on behalf of which appropriate military–civilian counterinsurgency operations could be used. On the contrary, during the 11-year period from 1990 to 2001 a large number of 'search and destroy' and 'territory capture' military operations were carried out, displacing hundreds of thousands of Tamil civilians and accompanied by widespread human rights violations. These only increased the secessionist movement's popular support among the Tamil people.

It needs to be kept in mind that running parallel to its military operations the LTTE was quick to exploit government errors. LTTE political cadres carried out and continue to perform a great deal of political mobilisational work among Tamil civilians, in areas under government control as well as those under its own direct authority. The LTTE military cadres have developed fighting capabilities at sea and against aircraft; on land the LTTE has developed more potent quasi-conventional military capabilities. The organisation has comprehensively penetrated the Tamil community and any Tamils who oppose the LTTE are dealt with ruthlessly. The Tamil diaspora has been systematically organised and generates large amounts of funding with which arms and other equipment are purchased. Thus the LTTE has evolved into a formidable political–military organisation fully capable of exploiting the military weaknesses and political failures of successive governments.

Cumulative consequences of insurrection and government counteractions (1983–2001)

Government, military and security force errors and lost opportunities over the past 18 years have had widespread ramifications for society and the state, bringing the country to its present precarious political, military and economic condition.

Impacts upon Tamil civilians

Tamil civilians have been subjected to massive human rights violations. Sinhalese and Muslim civilians have also suffered during these years, primarily due to the 'ethnic cleansing' tactics of the LTTE in the Jaffna peninsula and the Eastern Province. While not in any way belittling the suffering of the latter I will concentrate on Tamil civilians because their mistreatment is the primary cause for the intractability of the insurrection.

The insurrection has both arisen from and reinforced the inexorable alienation of large numbers of Tamil people from the (Sinhala-dominated) postcolonial Sri Lankan state. The government's primary objective should have been to develop policies to regain the allegiance of the constituency from within which the insurgent movement arose, the Tamil people. The security of Tamil people should have been a fundamental concern; the government should not only have protected and assisted Tamil civilians, but also have been seen to be doing so. For example, the fact that the 1983 pogrom-cum-riot was not brought under control until six to seven days after rioting began was a huge dereliction of the fundamental duty of any state, namely the security of life and limb of its citizens. None of the country's governments has expressed official regret at the emigration of hundreds of thousands of Tamils over the last 20 years. The Tamil people should have been reassured of their status as citizens of Sri Lanka and policies should have been designed to wean them away from secessionist politics. Military and police operations, which subjected Tamil civilians to collective 'punishment' have been completely counterproductive.

The armed forces and police have been responsible for many violations across the entire spectrum of human rights abuse.[12] There have been widespread internal displacements of Tamil people as a result of misconceived and erroneous security policies. These have politically alienated many Tamil civilians. In areas under government control torture, extra-judicial killings, disappearances and deaths in custody have been common. In the course of military operations Tamil civilians have suffered death, injury, loss of property and livelihood. Rape has been widespread and a cause for constant fear and apprehension within the Tamil community. There is compelling evidence that large numbers of the Tamil community has been traumatised at a mass psychological level (see Somasundaram 1998).

Given a context of effective impunity the vast majority of human rights violations have gone uninvestigated and unpunished. Very few prosecutions have been launched by the Attorney General's department. To be sure, some fundamental rights cases have been filed in the Supreme Court by civilians who have been tortured or unjustly incarcerated and the Court has given redress to complainants able to come to Colombo and gain access to legal assistance. But the vast majority of Tamil civilians affected by human rights violations cannot find redress because of poverty, ignorance, distance from Colombo and lack of legal aid. The perpetrators of numerous extra-judicial executions and 'disappearances' in the North and East have operated with impunity, increasing the alienation of large sections of Tamil people from the government.

Political consequences

The military and security force strategies have had numerous direct and indirect macro-political consequences, of which the political alienation from the state of a large proportion of Tamils is the foremost. This alienation has developed to such an extent that a considerable number of Tamils consider themselves a separate nation that requires a state of its own. A second macro-political consequence has been the political weakening of the Colombo-centred, unitary, Sinhala-dominated post-colonial state. A new state structure, which includes a great deal of devolution – be it asymmetric devolution, federal or confederal – is needed if the state is to remain even loosely united.

Economic consequences

The heavy economic costs of the conflict during the period 1984–96 have been documented in a study published by the Institute of Policy Studies (IPS), Colombo. Total direct government military expenditure over this period was Rs287.5 billion,[13] rising to 6 per cent of GDP and 21.6 per cent of the government budget by 1996. Total direct and indirect costs of the conflict[14] were Rs1,168 billion[15] (US$21 billion),[16] which is a huge burden for a relatively poor Third World country to carry. It should be noted that the above figures do not include the five-year period 1997 to 2001, when many further military operations took place and enormous additional costs were incurred.

Table 8.1 Defence expenditure, 1982–96 (selected years)

	Defence expenditure as % of GDP	Defence expenditure as % of total government expenditure
1982	1.1	3.1
1985	3.5	10.2
1988	4.8	14.3
1990	4.5	14.6
1993	4.2	14.7
1996	6.0	21.6

Source: IPS 1999: 4.

In 2000–1 a sequence of events occurred that brought the economic crisis to a head. First, the LTTE's defeat of the army's attempt to open a land route through the Vanni, and its capture of significant territory in the Jaffna peninsula in 1999–2000 resulted in heavy losses in men and equipment, and compelled the government to increase military expenditure dramatically by US$350 million.[17] This unscheduled expenditure decreased funds available for development and was also responsible for a large increase in public debt (*Daily Mirror*, 12 February 2002, 'The huge public debt burden').

Second, in July 2001 the LTTE attacked Sri Lanka's sole international airport and destroyed many civilian passenger aircraft and air force helicopters and attack aircraft. This attack led to increases in international insurance premiums and grievously affected the country's export and import trade. Simultaneously, the global recession had begun to affect the country's highly export-oriented economy.

Third, hit by the deepened global recession after the attack on the USA on 11 September, in the latter part of 2001 the country underwent a period of negative growth for the first time since the Great Depression of the 1930s. By early 2002, the country was in serious economic difficulties with the public debt at Rs1,414 billion, exceeding GDP by 13 per cent (*Daily Mirror*, 12 February 2002, 'The huge public debt burden'). The country's security policies have thus resulted in an unprecedented economic crisis.

Increase in security establishment capability and size

During the last two decades the armed forces have been completely transformed in tactical capability, weaponry and size, although in terms of doctrinal and strategic capabilities, there has not been a commensurate development. In 1983 the armed forces operated in platoon and company-sized units and no operations involving even a battalion-sized group were conducted. With the escalation of the insurrection this changed, and increasingly large military formations were involved in 'clearing' and 'search and destroy' operations in the North and East. The Indian forces (1987–9) carried out brigade-scale operations. With the re-ignition of the insurrection in 1990 the war entered a period of 11 years during which, except for brief periods of peace talks, security forces and the LTTE were involved in continuous fighting. Over a hundred military operations utilising at least two or more battalions and thousands of smaller operations were conducted in the North and East. The largest operations since 1995 have seen the deployment of up to three divisions, and during Operation JAYASIKURU in 1997–8, five divisions (each Sri Lankan division has a nominal strength of approximately 9,000) were involved in the (unsuccessful) operation.

The military and security forces have also increased greatly in size. While reliable figures are difficult to obtain the following figures for the army and the air force illustrate the scale of the increases. In 1983 the army had a total of 13,421, which by 1998 had increased to 125,616 (Sri Lanka Army 1999: 906–7), an increase of 837 per cent over 15 years. In 1985 the air force had a total of 5,206, which by 1997 had increased to 16,297 (Senaratne 1998a: 84 and 240). Numbers in the police and navy are estimated at 88,600 and 18,000 respectively (International Institute for Strategic Studies (IISS) 2001: 169). This gives a grand total of approximately 248,500 in the armed forces and police.

Since 1990 Sri Lanka has procured a wide range of military hardware from Chinese, ex-Soviet, Israeli and (in very limited quantities, due to supply restrictions) Western sources. These have included T-55 main battle tanks, armoured personnel carriers, large calibre artillery, naval fast-attack craft, transport and attack helicopters, transport aircraft and F-7, Kfir and MiG-27 jet ground attack aircraft. Concurrently with these large weapon systems, the armed forces have received tens of thousands of infantry weapons, machine guns, rocket-propelled grenades, light mortars, etcetera.

In the final analysis, however, it needs to be emphasised that in spite of the accumulation of military hardware, the increase in personnel and the resort to large-scale military operations, *no decisive impact has been made on the secessionist insurrection.* Indeed the LTTE is stronger than it has been at any earlier stage of its existence. At present the misconceived and erroneous large-scale military operations favoured by Sri Lankan governments and the military are economically impossible for the country to sustain.

The LTTE and the security forces, early 2002

As of February 2002 a ceasefire exists between the government and the LTTE. The military situation in the North and East is as follows. In the Jaffna peninsula government forces control Jaffna city, the islands to the west and the territory down to the Kilali–Eluthumadduval–Nakarkoyil line. In April–May 2000 the LTTE overran the strategically important army base at Elephant Pass and even reached the outskirts of Jaffna city. However, government counter-attacks and the LTTE's over-extension, ironically similar to the government's own conduct a few months earlier, compelled the LTTE to withdraw to the Kilali–Eluthu-madduval–Nakarkoyil line. Both the LTTE and the government forces have constructed new defences, which at present are holding. Both forces are heavily armed and operating in a quasi-conventional mode. The approximately 30,000 strong government forces in Jaffna have to be supplied by sea and air, as there is no land route from Jaffna peninsula to the rest of the country. This expensive and, in the long run, unsustainable logistic supply system contributes to the drain on the economy.

The territory south of the peninsula – the Vanni region – is under LTTE control as far as the Mannar–Vavuniya–Welioya line, more than 100 kilometres south of the peninsula. In the Vanni area the LTTE is in control of a large area of land and approximately 400,000 Tamil people. It is also politically and militarily active in and around Mannar, Vavuniya and Welioya areas in small guerrilla units, but can, if necessary, aggregate in large numbers for offensive and defensive missions. Large government forces in this area strive to restrict LTTE cadres from moving between the East and the North.

In the Eastern districts of Trincomalee, Batticaloa and Amparai the LTTE is in control of large areas of the hinterland while government forces control the main towns – mostly along the coast – and some of the main roads. The LTTE operates in a guerrilla mode but can launch large attacks when it chooses to do so. Government-controlled areas are termed 'cleared areas' and LTTE-controlled areas 'uncleared areas'. However, every Tamil-populated village and town in the East is penetrated by the LTTE administrative-cum-surveillance system. In the areas directly under LTTE control this system is overt, whilst elsewhere it is covert. This system monitors all activities of the Tamil civilian population (including its contact, if any, with government forces), maintains a network of informers, carries out punishments and assassinations and extracts taxes. In the vast jungle areas of the hinterland, the LTTE has hundreds of large and small camps. Political cadres radiate out from these and carry out incessant political mobilisation work amongst the Tamil people. Military cadres also recruit, train and operate from these camps. Except in major towns like Trincomalee, Batticaloa and Amparai, and some smaller towns, a situation of 'dual power' between government forces and the LTTE can be said to exist. The LTTE directly controls a significant area of the East and directly or indirectly most of its people. Whether living in so-called 'cleared' or 'uncleared' areas, any Tamil person is accessible to the LTTE, and government forces are unable, in any fundamental manner, to weaken this hold.

Incipient problems in civil–military relations?

Notwithstanding its multiple crises and conflicts, Sri Lanka has remained among the minority of Third World states in which civilian governance has prevailed unbroken since independence. This is especially noteworthy since the armed forces have been continuously deployed on active internal military operations from 1983. While there have been times when the military has contemplated exceeding its constitutionally sanctioned role, all these initiatives were abortive. The most serious instance was the attempted *coup d'état* of 1962 (Horowitz 1980; de Silva and Wriggins 1994: 113–20) and there was a further serious incident in 1966 (de Silva and Wriggins 1994: 154–6). Since then there have been occasional rumours and speculations in newspapers, but no prosecutions; civilian governance has prevailed.

After the 1962 coup attempt the ethnic composition of the armed forces in both the officer corps and the other ranks showed overwhelming Sinhala predominance, reflecting changed government recruitment policies. Thus the ethnic composition of the political élite and that of the armed forces have come to correspond with each other. Alagappa (2001: 8 and 19) holds that this ethnic 'correspondence' between the ruling political élite and the military has resulted in (to use Samuel Huntington's categorisation) 'subjective' control of the military (Huntington 1957). The Sri Lankan military's Sinhala–Buddhist ethos and that of ruling Sinhala politicians are one and the same.

Despite Sri Lanka's record of civilian governance one cannot be entirely sanguine about the future. The armed forces are now the largest component of state sector employees. They also have grievances in that they have been compelled to fight a protracted conflict with (at least until recently) no end in sight, and have had to absorb unprecedented casualties. In many conflict-torn developing countries where state security is a high priority, military and security bureaucracies have tended to acquire political influence and privileges behind a façade of apparent civilian control. Yet this has not so far been the case in Sri Lanka, where civilian governments have retained firm control of the military.

During the last 4–5 years under the former PA government, however, several trends have emerged which underscore the need for vigilance in civil–military relations. First, regular army personnel have sometimes been used to terrorise political opponents. For instance, during the general elections of December 2001, the Deputy Minister of Defence requested the services of a young officer and a platoon of soldiers, ostensibly for personal protection. On the day of the elections they were involved in the assassination of ten Muslim youths, all supporters of a rival Muslim politician (*Sunday Times*, 13 January 2002, 'The untold story of polls day terror in the hills'). Other soldiers attached to the Minister's bodyguard were allegedly involved in various election malpractices (*The Island*, 18 January 2002, 'Army personnel deployed to grab votes, says Minister Marapone'). This use of regular soldiers for election malpractices and killings is unprecedented, a violation of proper civil–military relations emanating not as is usual from the military side but from the side of the political leadership. However, the new UNP government has taken measures to prevent the future occurrence of such events by prohibiting the use of army personnel for VIP security (*The Island*, 27 January 2002, 'Over Kandy massacre: government ends army's role in VIP protection'). Moreover, the former Deputy Minister and two of his sons accused of being involved in the killings were remanded in February 2002 and face possible prosecution (*The Island*, 21 February 2002, 'Anuruddha remanded: enters hospital'; *Sunday Times*, 24 February 2002, 'Ratwatte sons, Lohan and Chanuka, surrender').

Another development was the conduct of the PSD (Presidential Security Division) during the last four or five years under President Kumaratunga. The PSD is responsible for the protection of the President and is a part of the police. Both under the PA government (and under the previous UNP governments) the PSD was under the direct command and control of the President's Office. From the perspective of ministerial responsibility this did not pose any difficulty, as the Minister of Defence was the President. The PSD's movements, deployments and general *modus operandi* are kept secret so as to facilitate the security of the President. It serves a vital function, especially in the context of the

LTTE's successful assassination of a serving Sri Lankan President (President Premadasa in May 1993) and the attempt to assassinate President Kumaratunga in December 1999, by an LTTE suicide bomber.

However, the manner in which the PSD was used during President Kumaratunga's tenure is a cause for concern. There is considerable evidence that it was involved in electoral violence and intimidation. Since the new UNP government took office the head of the PSD has been indicted in relation to a case of pre-election violence (*The Island*, 30 January 2002, 'Over complaint of threat on Hanguranketha OIC: warrant on PSD chief Nihal Karaunaratne'; *The Island*, 13 February 2002, 'PSD chief tenth suspect in Padiyapelelle pre-poll violence case'), in addition to investigations into its involvements in attacks against a newspaper editor, the assassination of a Tamil politician and attacks against government opponents (*The Island*, 13 February 2002, 'Top officials quizzed over release of guns to security firm'). All the above involvements had nothing to do with the primary role of the PSD, namely the physical protection of the President. On the contrary, they are more in line with the practices of an autonomous 'presidential guard'.

With the change of government in December 2001 both the above trends have been halted. Although these may have been aberrations, the ease with which they developed is cause for concern. One may hope that under the new government civil–military relations will revert back to their former (relatively) stable basis. Yet it is clear that civil–military relations need to be kept under close review.

Conclusions: towards reform of the security establishment

The above examination of the security establishment's actions and their repercussions reveal the following. First, Tamil civilians have been subjected to widespread human rights violations and hardship. This has been a strategic political–military error of the highest magnitude, alienating large numbers of Tamils from the Sri Lankan government and state, and fostering their support of secession. Second, the alienation of Tamil people and the secessionist insurrection have led to a crisis in the unitary, Sinhala-dominated, Colombo-centred postcolonial state. In its present form the Sri Lanka state is not viable and fundamental political restructuring is mandatory. Third, the economy has been grievously affected to the extent that by 2001, and into early 2002, it was in the grip of the worst economic crisis of the entire postcolonial era. In this context it is strongly suggested that reform of the security sector is indispensable in contemporary Sri Lanka. The recent debate and discussion of security sector reform[18] in development circles provides a suitable entry point to begin thinking about a reform programme for Sri Lanka. Yet it must be clearly understood that prior to any security sector reform the government needs to recognise the fundamental grievances that drive the Tamil insurrection, and to address them through appropriate political and constitutional reforms.

The security establishment has conducted a very large number of military operations, invested in new weaponry and increased personnel in its efforts to counter the secessionist insurrection. Ever-increasing amounts of military hardware and personnel have been 'thrown' at the insurrection in conventional military operations. Instead of the insurrection being 'countered', however, the exact opposite has happened: it has increased in intensity.

Deep-seated errors of security policy making, at the highest levels of doctrine, conceptualisation and strategy formulation – along with many inadequacies at the level of operations and military tactics – underlie the security miasma within which Sri Lanka finds itself. Hence, one of the primary tasks for a programme of security sector reform is to formulate the correct doctrines and conceptual bases for the use of military force in intra-state conflict, and to develop the institutional capacities of the state to carry them out and review them on a continuous basis.

A second area in need of reform is that of military expenditure and procurement. During the last 18 years various weapon systems have been procured and numerous questions have been raised about their procurement. Procedures to ensure transparency and accountability in weapons and equipment procurement are an urgent necessity. Adequate supervision and auditing procedures are all the more essential in a context where military expenditure has increased inexorably, and by 2002 had become unsustainable.

Third, the question of civil–military relations needs careful consideration, especially as the armed forces have accumulated a sense of grievance due to the protracted conflict they have been compelled to fight and the casualties they have absorbed. The misuse of military personnel by politicians, described earlier, adds to the problems which could arise in the future. While such misuse has, for the present, been curtailed, reforms in a number of areas need to be considered.

A major reform priority is greater parliamentary supervision. Under the new UNP government both the Prime Minister (in overall control of all the ministries) and the Minister of Defence are parliamentarians.

While this is a definite improvement compared with the previous situation where the President was in sole control of the armed forces and police (with a Deputy Minister serving under her), the Prime Minister and the Minister of Defence are nevertheless both powerful members of the Executive.[19] To ensure greater supervision by Parliament as a whole, the armed forces and police need to be subject to effective review by parliamentary committees able to examine military expenditure and procurements in some detail.

A further area of reform is the need to strengthen the rule of law *vis-à-vis* the security establishment. This requires a more proactive judiciary and military justice system. Freedom of information and the active involvement of the press and civil society groups in security issues is essential for stable civil–military relations. Excessive (and largely redundant) secrecy breeds the conditions under which proper civil–military relations can be violated. The role of the press in uncovering the violations mentioned earlier and keeping the issues in the public's attention offers some room for optimism.

To conclude, over the last 18 or more years the security establishment in Sri Lanka has consumed a great deal of the wealth of the country – both in material and personnel – but the returns have been negligible. Reforms along the above lines are absolutely essential.

References

Alagappa, M. (2001) 'Introduction', in Alagappa, M. (ed.), *Coercion and Governance: the Declining Political Role of the Military in Asia*, California: Stanford University Press.

Amnesty International (1991) *Sri Lanka – the Northeast: Human Rights Violations in a Context of Armed Conflict* (ASA 37/14/91).

Amnesty International (1995) *Sri Lanka: Reports of Extra-judicial Executions during May 1995* (ASA 37/10/95).

Amnesty International (1999) *Sri Lanka – Torture in Custody* (ASA 37/10/99).

Amnesty International (2002) *Sri Lanka – Rape in Custody* (ASA 37/001/2002).

Asia Watch (1992) *Human Rights Accountability in Sri Lanka*, New York: Human Rights Watch.

Coomarasawmy, R. (forthcoming) 'The politics of institutional design – an overview of the case of Sri Lanka', in Bastian, S. and R. Luckham, *Can Democracy be Designed?*, London: Zed Books.

Department of Census and Statistics (1998) *Statistical Profile of Sri Lanka: A Statistical Compendium to Commemorate the 50th Anniversary of Independence in Sri Lanka*, Colombo: Department of Census and Statistics.

de Silva, K. M. (1986) *Managing Ethnic Tensions in Multi-Ethnic Societies: Sri Lanka, 1880–1985*, Lanham, New York and London: University Press of America.

de Silva, K. M. (1988) 'Nationalism and the state in Sri Lanka', in de Silva, K. M. *et al.* (eds.), *Ethnic Conflict in Buddhist Societies: Sri Lanka, Thailand and Burma*, London: Pinter Publishers and Colorado: Westview Press.

de Silva, K. M. and H. Wriggins (1994) *J. R. Jayewardene of Sri Lanka: a Political Biography, Volume 2: 1956–1989*, Colombo: Jayewardene Cultural Centre.

DFID (2000) *Security Sector Reform and the Management of Military Expenditure: High Risks for Donors, High Returns for Development*, report sponsored by Department for International Development (DFID).

Gunaratna, R. (1993) *Indian Intervention in Sri Lanka: the Role of India's Intelligence Agencies*, Colombo: South Asian Network on Conflict Research.

Hoole, R., D. Somasundaram, K. Sritharan and R. Thiranagama (1990) *The Broken Palmyra: the Tamil Crisis in Sri Lanka – an Inside Account*, California: Sri Lanka Studies Institute.

Horowitz, D. L. (1980) *Coup Theories and Officers' Motives: Sri Lanka in Comparative Perspective*, Princeton: Princeton University Press.

Huntington, S. P. (1957) *The Soldier and the State. The Theory and Politics of Civil–Military Relations*, New York, Vintage Press.

IISS (2001) *The Military Balance 2001–2002*, prepared by the International Institute for Strategic Studies (IISS), London: Oxford University Press.

IPS (2000) *The Economic Cost of the War in Sri Lanka*, Institute of Policy Studies (IPS), Research Studies: Macroeconomic Policy and Planning Series, No. 13.

Jayawardena, K. V. (1972) *The Rise of the Labor Movement in Ceylon*, North Carolina: Duke University Press.

Kadian, R. (1990) *India's Sri Lanka Fiasco: Peace Keepers at War*, New Delhi and Bombay: Vision Books.

Lakshman, W. D. (1997) 'Introduction', in Lakshman, W. D. (ed.), *Dilemmas of Development: Fifty Years of Economic Change in Sri Lanka*, Colombo: Sri Lanka Association of Economists.

Muttukumaru, A. (1987) *The Military History of Ceylon: an Outline*', New Delhi: Navrang.

National Peace Council (2001) *The Cost of the War: the Economic, Socio-Political and Human Cost of the War in Sri Lanka*, Colombo: National Peace Council.

Oberst, R. (1986) 'Politics of ethnic preference in Sri Lanka', in Nevitte, N. and C. H. Kennedy (eds.), *Ethnic Preference and Public Policy in Developing States*, Colorado: Lynne Rienner.

Roberts, M. (ed.) (1979) *Collective Identities, Nationalisms and Protest in Modern Sri Lanka*, Colombo: Marga Institute.

Sardeshpande, S. C. (1992) *Assignment Jaffna*, New Delhi: Lancer Publishers.

Senaratne, J. P. (1997) *Political Violence in Sri Lanka, 1977–1990: Riots, Insurrections, Counterinsurgencies, Foreign Intervention*, Amsterdam: VU University Press.

—— (1998a) *The Sri Lanka Air Force: a Historical Retrospect, 1985–1997*, Volume 2, Colombo: Sri Lanka Air Force.

—— (1998b) 'Intra-Tamil violence in Sri Lanka', *Nethra* (International Centre for Ethnic Studies, Colombo), 2 (3) (April–June).

SIPRI (Stockholm International Peace Research Institute) (2001) *SIPRI Yearbook*

2001: Armament, Disarmament and International Security, Oxford: Oxford University Press.

Smith, C. (2001) 'Security-sector reform: development breakthrough or institutional engineering?', *Journal of Conflict, Security and Development*, 1 (1).

Social Scientists' Association (1984) *Ethnicity and Social Change in SriLanka*, Colombo: Social Scientists Association.

Somasundaram, D. (1998) *Scarred Minds: the Psychological Impact of War on Sri Lankan Tamils*, New Delhi, California, London: Sage Publications.

Sri Lanka Army (1979) *Army Magazine: 30th Anniversary*, Department of Government Printing.

Sri Lanka Army (1999) *Sri Lanka Army: 50 Years On, 1949–1999*, the Sri Lanka Army.

UTHR(J) (1995) *Military Operations in Jaffna and the Civilian Exodus*, Special Report No. 6, University Teachers for Human Rights, Jaffna (UTHR(J)).

UTHR(J) (1999) *Gaps in the Krishanthy Kumarasawamy Case: Disappearances and Accountability*', Special Report No. 12, University Teachers for Human Rights, Jaffna (UTHR(J)).

Wilson, A. J. (2000) *Sri Lankan Tamil Nationalism: Its Origins and Development in the 19th and 20th Centuries*, Harmondsworth: Penguin Books.

Notes

1 I wish to record my appreciation of Dr Robin Luckham for his helpful observations and suggestions on earlier drafts of this chapter.

2 In addition there are another dozen or so numerically small ethnic groups (0.8 per cent of the population), mostly descendants of various trading groups who arrived on the island during the colonial period.

3 Department of Census and Statistics 1998: 10. These details were based on the 1981 Census. The census of 1991 was not conducted because of severe internal conflict. The details of the 2001 Census – which excluded significant areas of the North and East – have not as yet been released. These difficulties are indicative of the political and administrative problems of censuses in a multi-ethnic society convulsed by internal conflict.

4 There is a large scholarly literature on ethnic identity and class struggle in Sri Lanka (Jayawardena 1972; Roberts (ed.) 1979; Social Scientists' Association 1984; K. M. de Silva 1986; Oberst 1986; K. M. de Silva 1988; Hoole *et al.* 1990; Wilson 2000).

5 After the island became a Republic in 1972 the nomenclature changed to the Sri Lanka Army, Navy, Air Force and Police. The police department is an unbroken continuation of the institution created under British colonial rule.

6 See Senaratne 1997: 55–61 for an account of the processes through which the secessionist insurrectionary groups emerged.

7 See Senaratne 1998b for an analysis of intra-Tamil violence.

8 The Tamil insurrection worsened diplomatic relations between Sri Lanka and India, precipitated the Indo-Lanka Accord and outlasted India's direct military operational presence in Sri Lanka. It also outlasted the second JVP

insurrection of 1987–9.

9 See Senaratne 1997: 53–102 for an overview.

10 Not long after independence in 1948 the police was placed under the MoD and remained there until the change in 2002.

11 On these and other reform efforts, see Coomaraswamy, forthcoming.

12 The extensive literature on human rights violations in Sri Lanka includes UTHR(J) (1995 and 1999), Amnesty International (1991, 1995, 1999 and 2002), Asia Watch (1992).

13 IPS 1999: 29, calculated at a 5 per cent rate of interest.

14 Direct costs include estimates for (a) direct government military expenditure; (b) LTTE military expenditure; (c) government expenditure on relief services; and (d) cost of lost infrastructure. Indirect costs include estimates for (a) lost income due to foregone public investment; (b) lost income from reduced tourist arrivals; (c) lost earnings due to lost foreign investment; (d) lost income due to displacement; (e) lost income due to lost human capital of dead or injured persons; and (f) output foregone in the Northern province in 1996 (IPS 1999: 29).

15 In 1996 rupees and at a modest 5 per cent rate of interest (IPS 1999: 29).

16 At US$1 = Rs55.27 exchange rate for 1996 (source: Sri Lanka Army 1999: 905).

17 SIPRI 2001: 118.

18 See DFID (2000) and Smith (2001).

19 It should be noted that constitutionally the President remains as the Commander-in-Chief of the armed forces. At present (March 2002) the 'cohabitation' between the new UNP government and President Kumaratunga (from the SLFP) works reasonably well. There is, however, great potential for tension and conflict in this volatile arrangement. Any untoward development will impinge on civil–military relations in Sri Lanka.

9

Security Structures in Bosnia and Herzegovina[1]

MARY KALDOR

A key characteristic of the new conflicts is the disintegration of the monopoly of legitimate organised violence. This involves the fragmentation of organised violence – the privatisation of violence, the emergence of paramilitary groups, warlords, guerrilla groups and so on. But it also involves the breakdown of legitimacy. The public security services are no longer regarded as the legitimate agents of the state, either because the state itself has lost legitimacy or because the security services themselves behave in illegitimate or unacceptable ways – violating human rights, failing to protect citizens, and/or pursuing private interests.

It follows that an important tool of conflict management is restoration of public control over organised violence and this, in turn, depends on the legitimacy of public institutions. Military and police forces have to be brought under public control and private or informal security forces have to be eliminated. Public control means that security forces need to be accountable to democratically elected officials or officials appointed through some process that is considered legitimate, and also that they need to operate according to professional standards within the framework of national and international law. In a recent conceptual paper on conflicts (Kaldor and Luckham 2001),[2] we argue that the restoration of public control over legitimate violence does not necessarily need to be done at the level of the state. Control over organised violence could be the responsibility of local or international political institutions provided that this control is exercised within the norms and practices laid down by international law.

Security and the rule of law do not ultimately depend on physical coercion but on legitimacy. People obey laws because they accept the legitimacy of the law and because the security forces are seen as symbols of legitimate power. Legitimacy is not necessarily the same as democracy. Repressive regimes usually endure because they command a measure of respect and not just because they use physical coercion. The legitimacy of public institutions and their control over violence is a necessary but not sufficient condition for democracy. The control of organised violence helps to create the space in which it is possible, but by no means inevitable, for democratic politics – public debates, civil society, inclusive political ideas – to develop.

In this context, the case of Bosnia and Herzegovina (BiH) represents a unique experiment in international efforts to restore public control of legitimate organised violence. The international effort there is unprecedented. SFOR (the Stabilisation Force under NATO command) costs more per annum than BiH's entire GDP. And as well as SFOR, there is the United Nations IPTF (International Police Task Force) and a myriad of civilian agencies. Moreover, the international effort is being monitored in considerable detail so that an outside observer has ample information on which to assess the effectiveness of these efforts.

The main argument of this chapter is that the international community is beginning to be successful in restoring public control over legitimate organised violence, although there is still a long way to go. The key to its success has been the gradual dismantling of extreme nationalist parallel structures both as a result of forceful international policy and because of the changes in Croatia and Yugoslavia. Security sector reform in the classic sense – restructuring and professionalisation of the army(ies) and police, and the role of international security forces – has been important as one element in a strategy which, above all, has aimed to minimise political control by extremist political parties. Even though these parties have been formally elected, they operate outside the rule of law in various ways. The big weakness, however, has been the weakness of democratic politics, both civil society and moderate non-nationalist political parties. This is the consequence both of the legacies of the conflict and of the perceived dependence of moderate political groups on the international community. In the language of our conceptual paper on democracy (Luckham, Goetz and Kaldor 1999), international efforts to establish democratic institutions have not necessarily contributed to, indeed they may have discouraged, the emergence of democratic politics, which is the key to a lasting solution to the conflict.

The chapter starts with a brief overview of the situation in Bosnia and Herzegovina after the signing of the General Framework Agreement for Peace in Bosnia and Herzegovina (hereafter referred to as the Dayton Agreement) in November 1995, which brought an end to outright hostilities. The second section describes the main security forces operating within Bosnia and Herzegovina in the post-Dayton period. The third section includes two case studies of 'hot spots' – insecure areas – and analyses the security response. The final section summarises the main conclusions of the study and draws implications both for international strategy towards Bosnia and Herzegovina and for other post-conflict situations.

Background

The Dayton Agreement was a contradictory document – a complex and unwieldy compromise between extremist nationalist groups tempered by international mediation. The agreement reflected the situation on the ground at the end of the war, when the three nationalist groups, but especially the Serbs and Croats, had more or less succeeded in carving out ethnically homogeneous territories. Some three-quarters of the pre-war Bosnian population had been displaced. At the same time, the agreement also reflected an aspiration, on the part of the Bosniak (Muslim) and international communities to reverse the facts on the ground – to reintegrate Bosnia and Herzegovina, to restore multi-ethnicity, and to provide the conditions whereby refugees and IDPs (internally displaced persons) could return to their homes.

The Dayton Agreement was, in essence, both a constitution for Bosnia and Herzegovina and a ceasefire agreement. The constitutional elements of the agreement included:

- Common state institutions, which are very weak and have limited competence.
- Two entities – Republika Srpska (RS) and the Federation of Bosnia–Herzegovina – that are essentially mini-states with much more power than the common state institutions.
- The Federation is much more decentralised than RS and further divided into ten cantons, based on the Washington Agreement of 1994, which ended the Croat–Bosniak conflict. The canton system allows for separate Croat and Bosniak control over territory.
- The lowest level of government is the municipalities. Municipalities are stronger in the Federation than in RS.

Defence is the responsibility of the entities. Policing is the responsibility of the entity in the case of RS and of the cantons in the case of the Federation.

This framework expressed the position of the three nationalist parties – the SDA (Bosniak), HDZ (Croat) and SDS and SRS (Serb) – at the end of the war. These parties could be considered an extreme example of a post-Communist phenomenon, whereby parties organised on totalitarian lines are linked to organised crime networks. The parties operate a *nomenklatura* system, controlling key appointments and dismissals. Until recently, they controlled the payments bureaux, which are responsible for gathering and distributing taxes, for a wide range of public sector accounts, and for collecting statistics. They controlled the main public enterprises. They have their own media, intelligence, secret police and associated paramilitary groups. As well as creaming off income from payments bureaux, they have had two other sources of finance. All three parties have been dependent on external sources – the HDZ on Croatia, the Serb nationalist parties on Belgrade, and the Bosniaks on support from the Islamic countries. They have also raised funds through various dubious activities: for example, they have controlled the movement of fuel, alcohol, cigarettes and foodstuffs, and have engaged in the smuggling of arms, drugs and people.

The purest example of this type of party has been the HDZ. The election of Ante Jelavic as leader in May 1998 led to a purge of moderate Croats. Until very recently, HDZ operated parallel Croat institutions in Croat-controlled areas; a parallel government of Herceg–Bosne and a parallel budgetary system, even though these structures were officially banned by the Office of the High Representative (OHR). The Serb nationalist parties have been divided between SDS (the party of Karadzic, dominant during the war), the even more extreme SRS (the party of Seselj) and the SPS (the party of Milošević). Subsequently, both the SDS and the SRS split, and the latter party is now banned. The Bosniak areas have remained much more fragmented, reflecting the collapse of central government during the war and the rise of local power bases. Thus Tuzla is still controlled by a non-nationalist municipality and now by a non-nationalist cantonal government, while parts of Bihac have always operated more or less independently. Moreover, the SDA has always espoused an ideology of multi-ethnicity organised on communal lines, as a way of sustaining the unity of Bosnia–Herzegovina.

The Dayton Agreement also established a complicated set of arrangements for international implementation. IFOR (Implementation Force) and later SFOR were responsible for overall security and, in particular, the military part of the agreement. The United Nations was responsible for the International Police Task Force (IPTF), whose initial role was to monitor and supervise local police forces, a task being taken over by the European Union. The EU and the World Bank are responsible for economic reconstruction, while the United Nations High Commissioner for Refugees (UNHCR) was supposed to be responsible for refugee and IDP return. The Organisation of Security and Cooperation in Europe (OSCE) is responsible for democratisation, human rights and regional stabilisation. The OHR was supposed to coordinate civilian implementation. Initially, this role was very weak but gradually the OHR has assumed more and more powers, supported by the Peace Implementation Council (PIC) – the group of governments responsible for implementation of Dayton – which has strengthened the mandate of the OHR at successive meetings starting in Sintra in June 1997. Thus, for example, the OHR is now responsible for the Return and Reintegration Task Force.

There has always been a tension between military and civilian implementation. The military part of the agreement was aimed at preventing the renewal of hostilities. It involved the separation of forces, the cantonment of weapons and the establishment of demarcation lines; by and large, it has been the most successful part of the agreement. The logic, however, of military implementation is towards separation rather than integration. Military forces are kept apart, preventing renewed hostilities but freezing the *status quo*. Civilian implementation, on the other hand, which includes human rights, democratisation, refugee return and reconstruction, is much more oriented towards integration.

Over time, both the OHR and civilian implementation have become more powerful and SFOR has begun to take on more roles in support of the civilian process. A series of interlocking developments have begun to erode the positions of the nationalist parties. These have included:

- The OHR has succeeded in introducing a number of common institutions – the currency, vehicle licence plates, the flag.

- Indicted war criminals have been hunted down, captured and tried, starting in 1997 and gathering pace since then.

- The dismissal of disruptive politicians and officials and the imposition of moderate coalition groups in positions of power. Thus, in RS, for several years the international community sustained a government led by Milorad Dodik, a social democrat with little popular support, and the current Alliance for Change coalition was similarly engineered. The most high-profile dismissals have been Nicola Poplasen, the elected President of RS, in March 1999 and Ante Jelavic, leader of HDZ and Croat member of the B–H presidency, in March 2001.

- The capture of key assets of the nationalist parties. For example, in 1997, SFOR seized the transmitter of SRT (the Serb radio and television station) which had been broadcasting anti-SFOR propaganda. In April 2001, the OHR and SFOR seized control of the Herzogovacka Banka in Mostar and in other towns, which was the main source of HDZ finances. Also, in 2000, payments bureaux were abolished.

- The introduction of property laws, which resulted in the eviction of illegal occupants of houses and, together with improved security, has resulted in a big increase in minority refugee and IDP returns since 1999.

- The decline in external support for the nationalist parties from Croatia and Yugoslavia. This began even before the changes of government in both countries brought about by the death of Tudjman and other key Croat nationalists, the election of a non-nationalist government, and the fall of Milošević in Yugoslavia, but has greatly accelerated since then.

- Constitutional changes, including the Constitutional Court ruling that the rights of all three constituent nations had to be equally respected in both entities,[3] and changes in the electoral rules, which may have contributed to significant but not overwhelming improvements in the electoral position of moderate political parties, particularly the Social Democrats in Bosniak areas and the PDP in RS.

- Finally, serious efforts are being made to control criminal sources of income, by establishing effective border controls to stop smuggling and illegal trafficking, and by closing the notorious Arizona Market, viewed as the centre for illegal trading in the region.

Despite the improvement of the position of the non-nationalist parties, there was 'real disappointment', in the words of Jacques Klein, the head of the UN Mission to BiH, 'that after five years of intensive international engagement, a sizeable proportion of the population continues to support those who led them into war'.[4] Indeed, the Social Democrats polled less in November 2000 (22 per cent of the vote) than they had in the last elections before the war in 1990 (28 per cent). What has been revealed underneath the rubble of the parallel nationalist structures is a grassroots nationalism that is more powerful than before the war and indeed can be described as the legacy or political outcome of the war.

This is reflected not only in the electoral strength of the nationalist parties but also in continuing political and/or criminal incidents, especially but not only in Serb- or Croat-dominated areas, directed against minority returns or at symbols of multi-ethnicity. Thus, for example, in May 2001 there were violent demonstrations in Trebjinje and Banja Luka, when members of the Islamic community, accompanied by international officials, tried to lay the foundation stones of two famous Ottoman mosques, destroyed during the war. It later emerged that classes had been suspended in six schools to allow children to take part in the demonstrations. (The high school directors were subsequently dismissed, as were the officials in charge of security, and the ceremony took place peacefully a month later.) These events provoked a series of incidents throughout Bosnia, including a bomb attack on an Orthodox church in Sanski Most, damage to the Orthodox cemetery in Tuzla, and the distribution of inflammatory leaflets. Similar incidents have taken place in Western Herzegovina; for example, violent demonstrations by Croat veterans (see below) against the seizure of the Herzogovacka Banka.

There are a number of reasons for this continuing nationalist phenomenon. First, the trauma of the war has left a trail of fear and insecurity, guilt and mistrust – emotions that cannot be easily allayed but which seek reassurance in the apparent certainties of ethnic identification. Second, the economy was destroyed as a consequence of the disintegration of Yugoslavia and the war. During the war, GDP fell to 90 per cent of its pre-war level and unemployment rose to 90 per cent; an illegal informal economy linked to the warring parties was established in this period (see Kaldor 1999; Bougarel 1996). Although the economy has begun a slow recovery, unemployment remains at 40–50 per cent and many people are still dependent on a variety of illegal or informal activities, which, up to now, have received 'protection' from the nationalist parties.

Finally, civil society and non-nationalist political forces were greatly weakened by the war. Bosnia–Herzegovina was always an authoritarian society and during the communist period civil society, in the sense of public debate and criticism, hardly existed. A form of democratic politics was beginning to develop in the period 1990–2, especially in the towns. However, it was the urban, educated, secular people – the bedrock of potential democratic politics – who were often the first to be killed or to leave; Selim Beslagjic, the former Mayor of Tuzla, described the war as 'intellectual cleansing'. Today, those that remain among this group of people seem more disillusioned than ever, despite the progress made by the international community and by the non-nationalist parties. Many hoped that once the nationalist structures were destroyed BiH would return to the kind of multi-ethnic harmony that existed, at least in the towns, before the war. Now, there is a growing realisation that this can never be recreated. Many young people, especially educated people, are queuing to leave and to go as far away as possible.

Security structures

The evolution of security structures has been an important component of these developments. The plethora of security forces of different kinds is one of the most important characteristics of the Bosnian situation and reflects the complexity and contradictory nature of political structures in Bosnia. Expenditure on security services in 1998 (including international contributions) exceeded total Bosnian GDP, amounting to nearly 130 per cent of the latter. Of this, around 20 per cent was domestic security expenditure, and 6 per cent was domestic military expenditure. In what follows, I divide security structures into three groups: military forces, police forces, and private or informal forces. I shall then draw some general conclusions about the evolution of security structures since Dayton.

Military forces

In Bosnia and Herzegovina, there are two types of military forces – the international forces tasked with a robust peace enforcement mandate and the Bosnian armed forces, which have the task of defending the entities. Both in practice have assumed certain police and public safety functions; and at the same time some special units of the police forces, especially in RS, resemble military forces, with heavier weapons and more protection than normal police forces.

IFOR/SFOR

IFOR was established to implement Annex 1A of the Dayton Agreement, which dealt with its military aspects. IFOR consisted of 60,000 troops, with a NATO commander in Sarajevo and three divisions in Banja Luka (RS), Tuzla (Federation) and Mostar (a Federation city divided into Bosniak and Croat parts) under British, American and joint European commands respectively. IFOR was replaced by SFOR I in 1996 and SFOR II (33,200 troops) in 1998, and has no expiry date. There are 17 contributing NATO countries and 14 non-NATO countries.[5]

Initially, IFOR stuck to a rigid interpretation of its role. Its task was to prevent a renewal of hostilities by establishing a zone of separation free of armed groups, controlling and storing heavy weapons, and establishing freedom of movement for international military and civilian agencies. There was considerable reluctance to engage in what were regarded as civilian tasks, such as the capture of war criminals, establishing freedom of movement for Bosnia citizens, or creating a secure environment for refugees and IDPs wanting to return. This was regarded as 'mission creep'. The first High Representative (HR), Carl Bildt, complained that the personal cooks and assistants brought by US officers to Bosnia were more numerous than the entire staff of the OHR. Since the main task was separating the combatants and establishing the Inter-Entity Boundary Line (IEBL), IFOR effectively reinforced the *status quo* that existed at the end of the war, based on the ethnic cleansing of territory.

In 1996/7, SFOR I began to adopt a more activist role and to cooperate more with civilian agencies, although it has to be said that policy tended to veer backwards and forwards, partly a consequence of the short tours of duty of senior officers. It began joint patrols with IPTF to inspect police stations. Large caches of illegal weapons were removed. Following the Sintra meeting of the PIC in June 1997, two war criminals were arrested in the British sector. Since then, many more have been arrested, including Krasjnik, one of the trio leading the Serb nationalists along with Karadzic and Mladic. In order to assist Biljana Plavsic, who was viewed as more moderate and pliable, take power away from Karadzic and shift the seat of government in RS from Pale to Banja Luka, SFOR troops assisted the Banja Luka government in establishing control over the police force and excluding the paramilitary police, as well as seizing the television station.

From 1998, cooperation with civilian agencies improved further and a decision was taken to redeploy SFOR forces to assist in providing a secure environment for the return of refugees and IDPs, while in 2001 SFOR assisted the HR in the takeover of the Herzogovacka Banka. In 1999 an additional specialised unit was included in SFOR, the MSU (Multinational Specialised Unit), which included carabinieri or gendarmerie forces to deal with civil disorder.

To some extent, the changes in policy have been influenced by civil society pressure, particularly by international NGOs and media. Groups like the Helsinki Citizens Assembly (both local and international), the International Crisis Group, the Institute for War and Peace Reporting, or even local groups like the Women of Srebrenica have been able to influence the international climate of opinion.

Bosnian armed forces

In theory, there are two Bosnian armies: the Federation Army (Vojska Federacije – VF) and the Bosnian Serb Army (Vojska Republike Srpske – VRS). In practice, there are three and maybe even more. The Croat Army at the end of the war was the HVO and the Bosnian Army was the ABiH. They were supposed to be integrated and placed under the control of the Federation government according to the Dayton Agreement, but the VF remains in practice divided into a Bosniak and a Croat part. Even the Bosniak part retains its decentralised structure, reflecting the way the ABiH was created during the war out of the remnants of the Territorial Defence units,[6] local police and volunteer units.

Until very recently, the three armies were directly under the control of the ruling nationalist parties, which held power at the level of the entity. This has changed both as a result of the November 2000 elections, which led to a non-nationalist ruling coalition, and as a result of recent developments in Western Herzegovina (see below). There is still very little parliamentary scrutiny, despite the efforts of the OSCE Regional Stabilisation office, which has the task of promoting integration and democratisation. In 1998, however, SFOR gained the right to vet promotions to the rank of general and this has been used to veto those accused of corruption; even so, rumours of corruption involving senior officers persist.

Even modest efforts to integrate the three armies – for example, through the Standing Committee on Military Matters (SCMM) created under Annex 4 of the Dayton Agreement to enable the presidency to coordinate the activities of the armed forces, or through NATO's Partnership for Peace programme – have so far been unsuccessful. One minor achievement has been the effort to create a peacekeeping function. A joint police unit was sent to East Timor, and there are proposals to send troops from all three armies to participate in joint peacekeeping training programmes.

All three armies are dependent on foreign military support (see Table 9.1). During the Dayton talks, the US signed a Memorandum of Understanding with the Bosnian delegation to retrain and re-equip the Bosnian Army; in December 1995, the US Congress agreed to send US troops to Bosnia and to re-equip and retrain the Federation Army. A Pentagon report concluded that, given the weapons ceilings agreed under the Dayton Agreement, the main requirement was training. The Federation Army needed only a small number of tanks, artillery pieces and armoured personnel carriers, anti-armour weapons, etcetera, for which the US and other countries – notably Turkey, Saudi Arabia,

Table 9.1
Foreign assistance as a share of military budgets, 1998–2000

	1998	1999	2000 planned
HVO (Croat) (%)	100	100	100
ABih (Bosniak) (%)	27	14	9
FBiH (Federation: Bosniak plus Croat) (%)	46	45	26
RS (Serb) (%)	28	24	19
Total military spending	650,808,922	599,069,557	495,361,298
Total foreign assistance as a share of total military spending (%)	43	41	25

Kuwait, the United Arab Emirates, Malaysia and Brunei – agreed to provide funding.

Two preconditions were set, neither of which has been implemented fully. One was that the Federation should pass a Defence Law uniting the Muslim and Croat armies; it was passed but not implemented. The other was that the Bosniak part of the army and party sever links with Iran and Muslim volunteers groups. The first shipment of arms was held up because the US demanded that the Federation Defence Minister, Hasan Cengic, should stand down because he was too close to Iran. Eventually both Cengic and his Croat deputy stood down and the equipment was delivered. Nevertheless, there are still Mujahadeen and Muslim intelligence services in Bosnia.

The entire funding for the HVO comes from abroad – 83 per cent from the government of Croatia and the rest from the US-sponsored Train and Equip. Funding from Croatia began to decline even before the death of Tudjman. Since the election of a non-nationalist government in Croatia, it has been cut substantially and paid directly to the Federation Ministry of Defence instead of into non-transparent Croatian bank accounts (where it subsidised politicians, military officers and others). The Train and Equip programme has been renamed Train and Integrate, and was temporarily suspended in 2000 because of slow progress in integrating the Croat and Bosniak components; the funding provided under the programme is also declining.

A recent development, which may ultimately speed up integration, has been the dismantling of Croat parallel structures. After the November 2000 elections, during which the HDZ organised an illegal referendum on Croat self-government, the HDZ called on Croats to withdraw from joint institutions, including the army. However, following the dismissal of Jelavic and other senior officials and the seizure of assets, a moderate negotiating team was appointed and by June some 7,000 Croat soldiers had returned to barracks and signed new contracts with the Federation Ministry of Defence.

VRS was receiving funding from Belgrade. This funding also began to decline even before the overthrow of Milosevic, at least in part for economic reasons. But it seems likely that there were political reasons as well. During the Kosovo conflict, Yugoslavia tried to smuggle weapons into Kosovo and gave orders for a guerrilla war against SFOR. On 1 March 1999, SFOR disbanded the 311th infantry brigade of the VRS after its members were caught smuggling. And the Bosnian Serb chief of staff, Momir Talic, confirmed to the British SFOR deputy commander that he had received orders from Belgrade to launch a guerrilla campaign against SFOR and had refused (Judah 2000). It seems that the conflict in Kosovo led RS leaders to realise that the future was more secure within Bosnia than with Serbia,[7] although Belgrade retains considerable influence over the army.

Altogether in 1998, foreign military support amounted to 43 per cent of total expenditure on defence – 46 per cent in the Federation and 28 per cent in RS. Total military spending was much higher in the Federation than in RS. Since 1998, overall military spending has declined in both entities, but the share of foreign military assistance has declined even faster (see Table 9.1). The VF is now much stronger than the VRS, although still suffering from logistical problems owing to the mix of second-hand equipment received and poor infrastructure. The VRS is said to be hardly operational; it does not even do live-fire exercises.

The main function of the three armies is defence of ethnic nations and territory. According to James Pardew, the US Special Representative for Military Stabilisation, Train and Equip was aimed 'to help the Federation build an independent, unified, and professional military under civilian control, *capable of defending the people and territory of the Federation*' (emphasis added; quoted in Dzanic and Erik 1998: 7). Since the policy of the Bosniak part of the Federation is unification, there is always a risk, were it not for the existence of SFOR, that a strengthened federation army could restart hostilities. There has clearly been a tension between SFOR and Train and Equip. As long as separate armies exist, it is very difficult to envisage the integration of Bosnia-Herzegovina and it is difficult to see how SFOR could exit without renewed hostilities.

Police forces

A major concern after Dayton was the so-called 'public security gap'. IFOR/SFOR was primarily responsible for preventing the renewal of hostilities. The goal of integration required freedom of movement, respect for human rights, and the return of refugees and IDPs. These tasks were left to the local police forces, which remained under the control of the nationalist parties. According to the OSCE, most crimes in Bosnia and Herzegovina since Dayton have been political crimes. The burning of houses, the stoning and harassment of returning refugees and IDPs, even murder and riots have been frequent occurrences in security 'hot spots'. Often, as the OSCE has observed, local police are directly implicated or alternatively they fail to take action.

The United Nations International Police Task Force (IPTF) had no enforcement capacity. The UNMIBH profile states that it was charged with 'monitoring, observing and inspecting ... advising ... training ... facilitating ... assessing ... assisting'. The challenge has thus been how, given this mandate, to carry out normal everyday policing. In other words, the public security gap meant that there were effectively no security forces responsible for controlling crime and everyday insecurity, since the international forces did not have the will or the mandate and the local forces were actually a contributing factor in the continuing insecurity.

IPTF

By March 1999 the IPTF had almost two thousand uniformed personnel, who act as civilian police monitors. They come from 42 different countries, with very different cultures and traditions – hence the quality of policing varies considerably. Since 1998, its main strategy has been the reform of local police, including:

- Restructuring and reducing the size of local police forces, from 40,000 at the end of the war to 18,000 in 2001 (many police at the end of the war had been demobilised soldiers).
- IPTF police monitors are co-located at local police stations; their reports have led to the dismissal of many police officers, including police chiefs in 'hot spots' like Stolac or Drvar.

- The establishment of a Law Enforcement Registry – charged with registering and conducting background checks on all police personnel – is intended to weed out those suspected of war and other crimes. All those positively vetted undergo 'transitional and human dignity' courses as well as other specialised police training courses (by 2001, some 95 per cent of officers in both entities had undergone such courses).
- The IPTF has also made efforts to introduce multi-ethnic policing. Thus Bosniak police officers have been recruited in Bijelina, Serb police officers in Drvar and a multi-ethnic police force established in Brcko.

Local police forces

There are 11 police administrations in Bosnia and Herzegovina. In RS, police are directly accountable to the Minister of the Interior and in the Federation they are accountable to the cantonal Ministers of Interior. In 1998, the OSCE ombudsman 'determined that the police is the greatest violator of human rights. The police not only does not protect the citizen's physical well-being and property but it actively participates in criminal activities' (quoted in Calic 1998: 9). Thus the central task in closing the 'security gap' is reform, depoliticisation and professionalisation of the local police forces.

The degree of professionalisation depends very much on political control and on the extent to which hardliners active in paramilitary groups during the war became police officers. In RS, it was the change of government in 1997 and international support for police reform that created the conditions for professionalisation. In the Federation, the greatest obstacles to professionalisation have been faced in the Croat cantons. Tuzla canton, by contrast, is controlled by the non-nationalist SPD. Its Minister of the Interior, Alija Hasic, claimed in an interview that the training undertaken by local police has transformed ways of working, including conflict resolution skills, community and neighbourhood policing, and greater cooperation with citizens. The international community's pressure in calling for the dismissal of disruptive politicians has contributed towards creating a political climate favourable to the professionalisation of police forces.

State Border Service

This new service, created in 2000, is the only security service directly controlled by the state of Bosnia and Herzegovina and not by the entities or cantons, although funding is provided by the entities and by external sponsors, notably the Netherlands. Eventually, it is planned to have some 2,000 personnel and will control smuggling and human trafficking.

Private or informal forces

During the Bosnian war, a plethora of private military organisations were operating on the ground: paramilitary groups, mercenaries, and criminal organisations taking advantage of the circumstances of war. Some of these were absorbed into the armed forces or police forces. Some still exist and a major security challenge is how to eliminate them.

In Bosnia, the distinction between formal (that is, state-controlled) forces and informal or private forces is not always clear. Many of the paramilitary groups or criminal networks are under the control of the nationalist parties. Funding for these can come directly from sponsors, which may include states, as is the case for the more respectable groups like MPRI, or it can come from a range of criminal activities – arms and drug smuggling, controlling the movement of goods such as cigarettes and alcohol, trafficking in women and illegal immigrants (which has been increasing recently). Alternatively, criminal activities may be carried out on behalf of the nationalist parties as a way of maintaining the flow of funds. Indeed, as external finance for nationalist parties, particularly the Serbs and Croats, starts to dry up, the dependence on paramilitary and criminal groups increases. Thus in West Mostar, the Croat stronghold, organised crime is increasing – stolen cars from Western Europe, cigarette smuggling from the East, arms smuggling to Kosovo. Local commentators suggest 'that, having used these illegal networks for military and economic ends during the war, the HDZ is now hostage to the criminal underworld, both because of threats of violence and the fear that the wartime role played by key HDZ figures will become public' (ESI 1999: 10). The same can probably be said of the Serb nationalist parties. Information about these groups, with the exception of MPRI, is necessarily anecdotal and drawn mainly from the Bosnian press.

Military Professional Resources Inc. (MPRI)

MPRI is a private military organisation which has the US government contract to implement the Train and Integrate programme. It was founded by retired senior US officers in 1987. MPRI's 'business focus includes training; equipment procurement; force design and management; professional development; concepts and doctrine; organisational and operational requirements; simulation and wargaming operations; humanitarian assistance; quick-reaction military contractual support;

and democracy transition assistance programs' (Dzanic and Erik 1998).

MPRI was responsible for training and reorganising the Croatian Army and the final offensive in the last stages of the Bosnian war is often credited to its advice if not its active involvement. It would not consider itself in the same category as, for example, the Mujahadeen or the Serb and Croatian paramilitary groups, since it works under contract to governments. 'However,' as one commentator has put it,

> one question arises and that is about the efficacy of giving such power to an effectively private organisation working for profit. It is clear that MPRI has a significant degree of dependency on the US government, but the trend of using mercenaries throughout the world and the shift in military balance they can achieve is tremendous. (Dzanic and Erik 1998)

Mujahadeen

A brigade of Islamic volunteers was registered as an independent unit within the Third Corps of the AbiH, then based in Zenica, in 1993. Many received BiH passports, including reportedly Osama Bin Laden, who was rumoured even recently to be financing camps in Bosnia for the secret training of Islamic militants. Annex 1-A of the Dayton Agreement states that foreign forces 'shall be withdrawn together with their equipment from the territory of BiH within 30 days'. These include 'individual advisors, freedom fighters, trainers, volunteers, and personnel from neighbouring and other states'. In practice, many who acquired Bosnian passports or married Bosnian wives have remained and were permitted to reside in the Zavidoci-Maglaj region. However, many have been expelled as a consequence of the post-September 11 campaign.

Several Mujahadeen are known to have engaged in various types of criminal activities. Some have been associated with Islamic groups in other countries, particularly the GIA in Algeria. In particular, Khalil Jarray, said to be the chief of GIA and a close associate of Bin Laden, was arrested in 1999 (*Dnevni Avaz*, 9 March 2000). In addition to the foreign Mujahadeen, a local Islamic militant group was founded in 1997 in Bugojno, whose aim was to prevent the return of Croats; they were 'accused of setting up explosives, destroying Croatian houses and murdering a police officer' (*Dani*, 14 May 1999).

Serb and Croat paramilitary groups

Annex 1-A on the withdrawal of foreign forces from BiH also committed all sides to 'disarm and disband all armed civilian groups'. In practice, paramilitary and criminal groups with links to the ruling parties persist in all three zones. Serbian paramilitary groups are known to have participated in the Kosovan war. In 1998, young men were reportedly being offered 200 DM per month to go and fight in Kosovo. Frenki's Boys, one of the most active groups in Kosovo, had also been active during the Bosnian war. The murder of Ljubisa Savic-Mauzer, chief of the notorious Panthers, on 7 June 2000, seems to have been part of a string of murders of paramilitary leaders, including Arkan in Belgrade in December 1999.

The veterans' association HVIDRA acts as the paramilitary arm of the HDZ, although it is increasingly engaged in 'business'. It was founded by the indicted war criminal, now in The Hague, Mladen Naletilic, known as 'Tuta'. Its activities include mobilising crowds 'in protest against minority returns and the implementation of the property laws, and threatening Federation tax inspectors and financial police in HDZ-controlled areas' (ESI 1999: 10). Recently, the demands of HVIDRA have focused on the establishment of a third entity, and it was involved in mobilising protests against the seizure of the Herzogovacka Banka. It is worth noting, however, that the current president, Zoran Prskalo, denies the connection to HDZ and has criticised the criminalisation of Croat politicians (*Slobodna Bosna*, 13 April 2000).

Intelligence services

Each of the ruling parties seems to have its own spying service. Thus the SDA has AID (Agency for Intelligence and Documentation) which spies on Serbian and Croat politicians (*Slobodna Bosna*, 10 September 1998); MOS (Moslem Intelligence Service) which spies on dissident Moslems (*Slobodna Bosna*, 24 July 1999); and Seve, a small terrorist group linked to the Ministry of the Interior, which was founded in the war, but still engages in a range of criminal activities, including money laundering, drug smuggling, contract killing and unauthorised surveillance (*Slobodna Bosna*, 10 September 1998).

There are said to be several Croat secret services operating in Western Herzegovina and employing more than a thousand people (*Slobodna Bosna*, 24 July 1998). These include SIS (Secret Intelligence Service), Mostar-based SNS (Service for National Security) and HIS (Croatian Intelligence Services). In October 1999, SFOR uncovered documents showing that HIS and SNS were involved in spying within Bosnia as well as anti-Dayton and other illegal activities. Operations included snooping on the Hague Tribunal research team based in Livno, collecting personal data on Croats employed by international organisations, and trying to influence such organisations (*Dani*, 24 December 1999).

Table 9.2 Security structures in Bosnia

	Functions	Source of finance	Command structure	Accountability
IFOR/SFOR	Prevention of renewed hostility Support for civilian agencies	Governments	NATO Commander responsible to NATO and contributing governments and increasingly to OHR	PIC and international public opinion
IPTF	Monitoring and supervising local police and, increasingly, police reform	United Nations	UN Ambassador responsible to the UN and to the OHR	UN and international public opinion
Bosnian armies: VF (HVO and ABiH) and VRS	Defence of entities	Entity budgets plus foreign military support from Croatia, US, Middle Eastern countries and Yugoslavia respectively	Entity Ministries of Defence, until recently, responsible to nationalist parties and to external sponsors	Until recently, nationalist parties and external sponsors; increasingly, OSCE and OHR
Local police forces	Local security and/or intimidation of returning refugees and IDPs and political dissidents	Cantonal and entity budgets	Ministries of Interior of cantons and RS, increasingly IPTF and OHR	Local politicians and international agencies

State Border Service	Control of smuggling and trafficking	Entity budgets and Netherlands government	State presidency	Ostensibly B–H State, also UNMIBH and OHR
Local paramilitary and criminal networks	Political intimidation and criminal activities	Political sponsors and organised crime	Individual leaders	None
Mujahadeen	Providing training and haven for Islamic fighters in other countries; political intimidation; criminal activities	Federation government; Islamic sources	Islamic networks	None
Intelligence services	Gathering intelligence on other nationalist parties and inter-national community	Nationalist parties	Nationalist political leaders	Very little
MPRI	Implementing 'Train and Equip' programme for VF	US government	US representative in charge of regional stabilisation	US government and shareholders

Summary

It can be seen from this overview that changes in the roles, functions and organisation of security structures have been an important component of the process of dismantling nationalist structures. The main processes involved have been:

- The shift in the role of SFOR from what can be considered classic military tasks (separation of forces) to support of civilian agencies. The latter role does involve the use of force, but not in what are considered classic policing or military tasks. Instead, it has involved the capture of war criminals, the seizure of illegal assets and the deterrent role of SFOR's presence in tense areas, especially areas of minority return. This could be described as a robust form of peace enforcement or, perhaps more accurately, law enforcement.
- The restructuring, downsizing, and professionalisation of defence and police forces, and, importantly, bringing them under the control of moderate politicians, answerable to the international community.
- The gradual elimination of informal security forces as a consequence of the capture of war criminals and the erosion of sources of finance. This task is not yet completed, especially in the area of intelligence services.

Essentially, the international community is succeeding in bringing security services under public control: but this is international control, not democratic control. Table 9.2 summarises the functions, sources of finance, command structures and forms of accountability of the different security services in Bosnia. Four general conclusions can be drawn.

First of all, what is striking is the dependence of all security services on international sources of finance, whether external sponsors (Croatia, Yugoslavia, Islamic countries), informal sources (international smuggling and trafficking), or official international agencies and donors. The process of bringing security structures under control has involved a (still incomplete) shift from the first two sources to dependence on the latter.

Second, none of the security services, with exception of the newly created State Border Service, are directly accountable to the state. And even in the case of the latter, it is not clear what this accountability means in practice, since funding comes from the entities and external donors. Other security services are accountable to official international bodies (NATO and the UN), entities and cantons, and mysterious individual or external sponsors (in the case of informal security services). As power has shifted from nationalist politicians in the entities and cantons to moderate politicians dependent on the international community, so the official international agencies have gradually taken control of the main security services.

Third, it is clear that what is important is political control. The classic security reform tasks, restructuring and professionalisation are not possible without political control, although it is also the case that security sector reform greatly assists the process of establishing political control.

However, the problem in Bosnia is that unified political control is dependent on the international community. The main sources of insecurity in Bosnia are twofold: the risk of renewed hostility and the lack of public safety. The newly trained and professionalised armed forces represent an ever-present threat of renewed hostility since their roles are to defend the entities, not the state; without international control, there is always a risk that they could be used for a future war. Professionalisation and political control over the police are undoubtedly contributing to public safety, but, as in the case of the armed forces, they could always be used to foment insecurity if extreme nationalists were to regain power at cantonal or entity level. The weakness of moderate politicians and continued nationalist incidents illustrate vividly the importance of establishing legitimate police who gain the respect of all citizens, and this is difficult to achieve without a democratic consensus.

Fourth, political control is not the same as democratic control. Because moderate politicians are dependent on the international community, there is almost no accountability to Bosnian citizens. To some extent, NGOs, particularly international NGOs, have pressured the international community, and this has contributed to changes in policy. But this could not be construed as democratic control.

'Hot spots'

'Hot spots' are areas where the tensions in society are most visible. In a post-conflict context, 'hot spots' represent both the unfinished business of the conflicts and at the same time the potential for renewed conflict. 'Hot spots' are examples, perhaps extreme, of how the security situation is changing on the ground.

I have chosen two 'hot spots' to illustrate the evolution of security in Bosnia and Herzegovina, one in the Croat-controlled area, Drvar, and one in the Serb-controlled area, Srebrenica. In both cases, at the time of writing, the situation has begun to normalise as a consequence of both political pressure and police reform. Information is based on two visits and interviews with IPTF.

Drvar

Before the war, 97 per cent of the inhabitants of this town in the far West of the country were Serb. The total population of the town was 9,000 and of the municipality 17,000. The Serbs fled after the Croat onslaughts in the last stages of the war. Some 6,000 Croatian IDPs were moved into the town and also an HVO unit of 2,500 men with their families. Unlike other places, the damage to houses was not great, so there were many empty habitable houses. The international community took the view that Drvar could be an important starting point for the complex arithmetic of returning refugees and IDPs, since Serbs could move back into empty houses, thus freeing space for Muslims and Croats returning to RS.

In the first post-Dayton elections, refugees and IDPs were encouraged to register and vote, although in general participation turned out to be rather low. In the case of Drvar, however, the energetic IDP leader, Marceta, mobilised the IDP vote and was elected mayor in the 1997 municipal elections. Because of continual obstruction to the work of the new council, the Croat deputy mayor was sacked by the then HR, Carlos Westendorp.

After the elections, the Serb IDPs began to return to Drvar; within a year, some 1,600 were back. During the same period, the HVO unit was restructured and downsized to 500 under the Train and Equip programme. The HVO were moved out of the block of flats they occupied, known as site 153, and returning IDPs were moved in.

During the spring of 1998, tension mounted as IDPs returned home and as the international community tried to reform the local police. On 24 April a crowd gathered around the municipality, broke into it and assaulted the mayor, Marceta, who miraculously escaped. They burned down the international offices, including the IPTF office, ransacked the flats at site 153, stoned SFOR vehicles and fired shots. SFOR did not retaliate, although when one shot was fired by SFOR the crowd cheered.

Both the riots and the murders were clearly politically inspired. Workers from Finnvest, the main source of employment, controlled by HDZ, were given the day off, and the demonstration was preceded by a meeting between the ex-deputy mayor and the ex-police chief. SFOR videoed the riots; the presence of the ex-deputy mayor can clearly be identified. Moreover, the riots were evidently orchestrated; a woman in the crowd was calling out instructions.

The events in Drvar could be said to have been a turning point for the Bosnia strategy. The international community came up against the limits of its power. The public security gap was evident; it was impossible to guarantee the safety of returning IDPs. Some argued that the events demonstrated the case for a 'third force' aimed at riot control; this was the justification for the creation of the MSU. However, the MSU is based in Sarajevo; since the IPTF only knew about what was going to happen half an hour before, there would have been no time to deploy it. Could more robust action by SFOR have made a difference? Although SFOR was present, videoing the entire event, robust action might have been worse, with many people killed – the cheering by the crowd when a shot was fired suggests that they hoped to provoke a clash.

In the aftermath of the Drvar events, the strategy has been greater cooperation between the OHR, the IPTF and SFOR, with the creation of a law-and-order working group to share information, increased political pressure on local officials, including the dismissal of two cantonal interior ministers, greater emphasis on police reform and the recruitment of Serb police officers, and the withdrawal and relocation of all HVO troops from Drvar.

By June 2000, some four and a half thousand Serb IDPs had returned to Drvar, and the number of violent incidents had fallen. This suggests the beginning of normalisation, although the conclusion should be tempered by several factors. First, an important factor seems to have been cooperation between the HDZ and both the SDA and the RS government as a way of consolidating the Croat position in the south of Canton 10. There seems to have been a recognition that, for demographic reasons, it would be difficult to maintain Croat control over Drvar, and hence the HDZ was willing to contemplate what in effect has been a *de facto* shift in the Inter-Entity Boundary Line. Second, hardline Croats remain in the police (although, according to local IPTF officers, over 50 per cent of the police are 'normal') and in the judiciary.

Srebrenica

As a UN safe area Srebrenica was overrun by the Bosnian Serb army in 1995, and a genocide of the (male) Muslim population was carried out, killing almost 8,000 people. The survivors now live in Sarajevo, Tuzla and other places in the Federation. The present population of Srebrenica is Serb, with a majority of IDPs from other Bosnian Federation areas and some refugees from Krajina (Croatia).

The situation in Srebrenica is very grim. Many of the Serb IDPs were forced to come to Srebrenica and were unhappy at having to move into houses left in a hurry with toys on the floors and cooking pots still on the stove. The so-called domestic Serbs, those who lived in Srebrenica before the war, do not get on with the IDPs and miss their old neighbours; sometimes, they arrange secret meetings with them. There has been no reconstruction; there is almost no employment and the population is dependent on humanitarian assistance, controlled by the Serb nationalist parties.

The municipal elections of 1997 were won by the SDA. However, it took several months before the municipal council was inaugurated and, even when it was established, very little was achieved. Its attempts to meet were disrupted both by Serb nationalist councillors and by Serb IDPs. Since all discussions are overshadowed by the events of 1995, it is very difficult to concentrate on the concerns of tomorrow without dealing with the tragedies of the past.

Nevertheless, in line with the general situation in Bosnia there are also signs of normalisation in Srebrenica. This became very visible in July 2000 when several thousand Muslim survivors came to Srebrenica and Potocari (the battery factory where a Dutch UN unit was based and where Muslims sought refuge from the Serbs but were eventually handed over) to commemorate the fifth anniversary of the genocide. For the international community, it was a big surprise that the ceremony took place without any serious incident. This is explained by the cooperation between SFOR, IPTF and the local police, clear political direction from the government in RS, and, above all, by the professionalisation of the local police. During the events, there was a substantial SFOR and MSU presence but, most importantly, some 700 RS policemen were stationed along the road to Srebrenica and in the nearby town of Bratunac. In an interview, the local (Serb) police commander emphasised that he was a professional police officer. He favoured proposals to bring Bosniak police officers to Srebrenica, but emphasised that he would act in a professional way and preserve law and order regardless of ethnicity. A few weeks earlier, the local population in Bratunac had stoned buses with returning Muslims who had planned to visit their properties. He said that, as a professional officer, he felt embarrassed by this incident and wanted to restore police credibility.

If the events in Drvar in April 1998 were a negative turning point in post-Dayton Bosnia, the ceremony in Srebrenica may turn out to be a positive turning point. There was a substantial international presence including the OHR, the US ambassador and others, and the success of the ceremony resulted in a decision by the HR to allow the Muslims to construct a cemetery and a memorial centre to the victims. The

President of the Federation, Alija Izetbegovic also attended – it was the first time he had set foot in RS territory since before the war. And finally, the Prime Minister of Republika Srpska, Milorad Dodik, sent a statement of sympathy with the survivors, marking the first public Serb admission of what happened.

Some limited spontaneous return to Srebrenica and the surrounding region is already taking place. Indeed, some 50,000 IDPs and refugees have formally registered to return to the region in which Srebrenica is situated, virtually all those who were forcibly displaced and are still alive. SFOR has also established a temporary base near Srebrenica in order to provide a better security environment. One year later, the ceremony was repeated peacefully again. The foundation stone of the memorial was laid, but without the names of the missing men. Moreover, the Serbs insisted on their own memorial. Thus security has been established but the tensions remain.

Conclusions

The composition and functions of security structures are intimately connected to the character of the state, the form of political rule. The plethora of security structures in Bosnia–Herzegovina could be said to reflect three competing conceptions of the Bosnian state:

- The division of Bosnia into three ethnic statelets. This is expressed in the existence of three armies under the control of the entities, and eleven police forces under the control of the Serb entity and Bosniak and Croat cantons.
- An international protectorate. This is symbolised by the presence of IFOR/SFOR, SFOR control over deployment and equipment of local armed forces, and IPTF control over local police forces.
- A democratic state of Bosnia–Herzegovina. This would not be a traditional state whose main security function is defence of borders. Rather it would be what might be called multilateralist, a state in which security forces would be integrated into wider regional and European structures. Thus B–H might have a small, unified army whose main task is peacekeeping within an integrated international command system.

I have tried to show that, for the time being, the international community has been relatively successful in ruling out the first option, although it still remains a real possibility, and any withdrawal of the international presence could easily mean the slide back towards ethnic statelets more or less continuously in conflict. At present, Bosnia is moving closer towards the second option, as the international community has begun to act more and more forcefully, as moderate politicians dependent on international support have come to power, and as external sponsors have declined.

The problem remains the weakness of the third option, which cannot be created from the top down but which requires democratic pressures from below. At present, none of the security services are democratically accountable. They can be said to be legitimate in that they exist within the framework of the Dayton Agreement that was signed by legitimate international actors. To the extent that the international community is accountable to the PIC and responsive to civil society pressure, they can also be said to be accountable, although not to Bosnian citizens. To some extent, the new moderate governments can hasten a process of democratisation, through various unifying measures, through regional cooperation and through action in areas like the media and education. But it is likely to be a slow process, with many reversals on the way.

There are two main lessons of the Bosnian experience for other areas. One is that security sector reform – restructuring and professionalisation – cannot be considered in isolation. Two other factors are of crucial importance. One is the function of security forces. Defence of territory and other classic military tasks are nowadays less important than law enforcement, even though law enforcement, whether domestic or international, may require more robust action than normal policing. The other is the crucial importance of political control, both for creating the conditions for security sector reform and for ensuring that security forces use their newly found capacities for public safety and not for conflict.

The other lesson is that public control of organised violence means neither conflict resolution nor democracy. It can provide the necessary conditions for the emergence of democratic politics and it can manage the more extreme manifestations of conflict. But in the end the conflicts have to be resolved through broad-ranging political dialogue.

References

Bougarel, X. (1996) *Bosnie: anatomie d'un conflict*, Paris: La Decouverte.

Calic, M. J. (1998) 'Post-SFOR: towards Europeanisation of the Bosnia peace operation', in Clément, S (ed.), *The Issues Raised by Bosnia, and the Transatlantic Debate*, Chaillot Paper 32, Paris: Institute for Security Studies,

Western Europe Union, May.

Clément, S. (ed.) (1998) *The Issues Raised by Bosnia, and the Transatlantic Debate*, Chaillot Paper 32, Paris: Institute for Security Studies, Western Europe Union, May.

Dzanic, E. and N. Erik (1998) 'Retraining the Federation forces in post-Dayton Bosnia', *Jane's Intelligence Review* (January).

ESI (1999) 'Reshaping international priorities in Bosnia and Herzegovina. Part I: Bosnian power structures', European Stability Initiative, 14 October, http://www.esiweb.org/pdf/ESI_rep_bosnia04.pdf

Gnesotto, N. (1998) 'Prospects for Bosnia after SFOR', in Clément, S. (ed.), *The Issues Raised by Bosnia, and the Transatlantic Debate*, Chaillot Paper 32, Paris: Institute for Security Studies, Western Europe Union, May.

International Crisis Group (1999) *Republika Supska in the Post-Kosovo Era: Collateral Damage and Transformation*, 5 July, www.crisisweb.org

Judah, T. (2000) *Kosovo: War and Revenge*, New Haven: Yale University Press.

Kaldor, M. (1999) *New and Old Wars: Organized Violence in a Global Era*, Cambridge: Polity.

Schindler, J. (2000) 'Bosnia: five years after Dayton', *Jane's Intelligence Review* (May).

Schulte, G. (1998) 'SFOR continued', *NATO Review*, 46 (2) (Summer), pp. 27–33.

Notes

1 I am grateful to Adisa Omeragic for providing me with English language summaries of the Bosnian press and for interviewing the Tuzla Canton Minister of the Interior. I am also grateful to Vesna Bojicic, Robin Luckham and Susan Woodward for comments.

2 Prepared, like this book, for the 1998–2002 DFID-funded research programme on Democratic Governance – Conflict-torn Societies at the Institute of Development Studies, Sussex.

3 The Constitutional Court consists of nine judges: four are selected by the Federation House of Representatives; two by the RS Assembly; and three by the European Court of Human Rights.

4 Briefing, UN Security Council, 12 December 2000.

5 For details, see *Military Balance*, various issues.

6 These were decentralised guerrilla type military units, legacies of World War II, that were placed under the control of republics after 1968.

7 International Crisis Group, *Republika Srpska in the Post-Kosovo Era: Collateral Damage and Transformation*, 5 July 1999, www.crisisweb.org

10

Sierra Leone
The Legacies of Authoritarianism and Political Violence

COMFORT ERO

Civil war broke out in Sierra Leone in 1991 and inflicted heavy losses throughout the country. Nearly every household contains a victim and/or a perpetrator of violence. Civil society distrusts the state, its key institutions (in particular the security forces) and political élites. In turn, political élites distrust civil society, especially that section which supported the main rebel group, the Revolutionary United Front (RUF). For most ordinary people, avoiding the state is a better option than relying on it for protection, Reconciliation is necessary at all levels of society, but the climate of trust in Sierra Leone will be difficult to rebuild.

The role of Sierra Leone's security forces, both during and prior to the civil war, was repressive and brutal. Part of the main challenge for Sierra Leone is to turn the security forces into a 'force for good'. Despite the resumption of war on two occasions (January–June 1999 and from May 2000 onwards), attempts were made from 1998 to rebuild and train the security forces in the principles of democratic governance (accountability, transparency, human rights and civil control).

Britain became involved with this programme from the outset, supporting Sierra Leone's government in restructuring the Ministry of Defence, reforming the police (with the assistance of the Commonwealth Police Development Task Force (CPDTF)), strengthening mechanisms for civil supervision, including Parliament's capacity to scrutinise the security sector, and supporting the establishment of a new national security policy.

However, the history of Sierra Leone's security forces, in particular the Sierra Leone Army (SLA), is one of constant human rights abuses and terror towards the civilian population. Sierra Leone's security forces were (to borrow a phrase used by Said Adejumobi in describing the Nigerian military) 'agents of insecurity' (Adejumobi 2000). Democratic governance of security forces with a history of brutal repression, poor discipline and corruption is a complex process. At best, it involves purging personnel at all levels, embedding structural reforms, re-orientation and re-professionalisation. Yet, such a task cannot take place outside of the society from which the members of the security forces emerge.

Moreover, security forces do not operate in a vacuum. The history of mismanagement and misuse of security forces by political leaders, particularly in weak states, is evident. Indeed, the conventional wisdom is to lay the blame squarely at the door of security forces without understanding the extent to which some political leaders weaken or manipulate the key institutions of the state. This is not to suggest that security forces (in particular the military) are not notorious for subverting or manipulating political space through corruption, greed and violence. Security forces often collude with civilian regimes and both often contribute to the overall security problem. What this means, therefore, is that rebuilding security forces in a post-war climate cannot be considered in isolation from a comprehensive programme of transforming (or in some instances re-configuring) the political and socio-economic foundations governing that society.

To do this, however, requires an understanding of the political, economic and social life of the country concerned. In essence, one needs to know what it is that is being reconfigured: the history, dynamics and characteristics of power, and the social structures that delivered violence throughout society. This chapter is based on the premise that to instil democratic governance within the security forces, one needs what Robin Luckham identifies as 'a realistic diagnosis of the legacies of conflicts',[1] and also an informed understanding of the broader political context in which change is to occur. Democratic governance of the security forces, or security sector reform in a post-war climate, will only succeed if placed within a framework that incorporates an understanding of deep-seated political legacies that generated violence.

International agencies, heavily criticised for providing technical solutions to reconstructing war-torn societies, are increasingly acknowledging the need for 'conflict' analysis as a necessary tool to improve their understanding of the terrain in which they are providing assistance, and to ensure that external assistance is more sensitive to conflict issues. However, despite this, the solutions offered for post-war recovery still appear technical. This problem is not limited to international agencies, however. The government officials at the heart of post-war reform in their countries often look for technocratic solutions to what are essentially political and socio-economic problems. Technical capacity is necessary at all levels of a society recovering from war, especially when key institutions are not functioning. Yet this will make little difference unless the technical issues of post-war recovery are placed within the broader context of understanding and ultimately rethinking the wider problems of the state and democracy in countries emerging from civil war.

In Sierra Leone, security sector reform needs to be placed within a broad framework that analyses the nature of the security forces, the society and the power structures that not only existed prior to the war, but also emerged during and after the war, and the complex intermingling of regional security forces in the country's conflict.

Three legacies are pertinent to Sierra Leone and will impact on the process of security sector reform in the country. Broadly speaking, they are: (1) the authoritarian and predatory politics that eventually laid the basis for political violence; (2) the 'de-institutionalisation' of the security forces over three decades and, as a consequence, the informalisation of violence; and (3) the regionalisation of conflict and security.

These legacies form the basis of the discussion in this chapter. Understanding them becomes useful when rethinking the broader context of restoring legitimacy and democratic political authority and the organisational and military problems of rebuilding security structures. With these legacies in mind, the chapter closes with an assessment of the likelihood of democratic governance not just among security forces, but also within political life in Sierra Leone.

The legacy of authoritarian and predatory politics

The future coherence of Sierra Leone's security forces, as well as the desire to instil principles of transparency and accountability in forces not traditionally designed to serve democratic regimes, will depend on a variety of overlapping factors, including internal and regional stability and the future of power relations. Given the ambitious task of trying to rebuild the security sector within the framework of democratic governance, several factors that may impact on the process need to be discussed and underscored.

Any discussion of security sector reform in Sierra Leone must engage with the fact that the conflict in Sierra Leone was not solely about the army and its history of brutality against the population. Rather it arose out of struggles against a history of personalised and patrimonial political rule, exclusionist politics, accumulation and exploitation of state revenues, the misuse of state security forces, and 'the introduction of thuggery into the political landscape' (Abraham 2000: 14). These factors defined political life in Sierra Leone and contributed to violent protest, social cracks and economic dislocation – all fertile breeding grounds for rebellion. Certainly, the justification given by the RUF when it led the incursion in 1991 made these points clear when its rebel leader, Foday Sankoh, declared that he was waging a 'struggle' against the corrupt and repressive regime of the All People's Congress (APC) party. However, as discussed below, the RUF war was devoid of any ideological undertones. Rather it inflicted blind terror on communities throughout Sierra Leone.

Like many states in the early stages of independence, Sierra Leone experienced upheaval after its independence from Britain in 1961. The country initially progressed under a multi-party political system. Key institutions of state, notably the judiciary and the police, managed to operate with some degree of freedom. The slow move towards the decline and erosion of state institutions started with the first politically motivated coups in 1967–8 and the military rule that followed it. Some of the politicians in the Sierra Leone People's Party (SLPP) had urged the army to stage a coup after the SLPP was defeated by Siaka Stevens of the APC in the 1967 elections. The SLPP had produced the first two heads of state, Sir Milton Margai and his brother Sir Albert Margai, but they gradually lost power to the radical socialist APC, which wanted to modernise the political system and remove the vestiges of the colonial legacy.

Stevens did not take office until after a counter-coup in 1968. His fear of further disloyalty in the army led him to create a loyal paramilitary force, the Internal Security Unit (ISU) within the Sierra Leone Police (SLP), and an ISU offshoot, the Special Security Division (SSD), in 1972. Both units acted as private armies for the APC. The ISU and the SSD readily used violence against APC opponents and citizens, especially students involved in protests or demonstrations. The political use of violence thus became institutionalised, and this laid the basis for general instability across the country.

Stevens quickly tore at the heart of the state. His 'speciality' was to deliberately weaken the state's capacity to function. The importance of bodies tasked with guaranteeing democratic control – Parliament, the judiciary, the civil service and the press – gradually declined. Stevens also abolished elected local government officials, replacing them with management committees composed of party loyalists, and undermined traditional authorities in the countryside by supplanting paramount chiefs with loyal APC followers. As a result, democratic accountability was undermined at all levels of state. The move to a one-party state system under the APC in 1971 (later endorsed in a referendum in 1978) marked the beginning of oppressive and predatory rule, an increasingly centralised system of government, and the concentration of power in the capital (Bangura 1997: 135).

In the end, Stevens ran the country on the basis of patronage. Political authority was based on personal networks and loyalty. His style of leadership represented what Patrick Chabal and Jean-Pascal Daloz describe as 'controlled disorder'. This means that there are no formal rules, institutional principles or structures, but rather an intentional weakening of the state's ability to perform. The exercise of political authority often rests on controlling and exploiting state revenues and manipulating access to economic opportunities. At the centre of this disorder is the controlling hand of the patrimonial leader who has access to resources and opportunities. Disorder, as Chabal and Daloz note, becomes a useful political instrument with which to undermine institutions, and ensure that people depend on the leader who controls access to state revenues (Chabal and Daloz 1999: xviii–xx, 13–16 and Chapter 10).

Stevens weakened the capacity of the state to collect revenue from state enterprises such as fisheries, gold and diamonds, while creating and controlling unofficial avenues from which to transfer revenue. Political and business élites competed for access to informal markets. Many, including the young, did not benefit from state resources; rather they were excluded from economic opportunities and social welfare provisions. The nature of governance in Sierra Leone led William Reno to coin the phrase the 'shadow' state, to describe how Stevens ran the country and skewed the distribution of wealth and power into the hands of the favoured few (Reno 1995: 3).

Sierra Leone was marked by the contradictions inherent in state decline. Those young urban and rural dwellers marginalised from the formal economy sought gains in the violent diamond mining regions in the east of the country where they could act as armed gangs offering private protection to political and business élites. Thus there developed under Stevens a violent and clandestine economy, backed by extra-legal and parallel informal militaries and armed groups operating under the politics of controlled disorder.

Stevens's legacy was to crush his successor, Joseph Momoh, when he took power in 1985 because he was never part of this controlled disorder. Rather, Momoh remained outside. His attempts to crack down on corruption and recapture the diamond districts failed. The informalised economy was too vast to dismantle; armed gangs in the business of selling protection to diamond mines challenged Momoh's political rule. Indeed, he found himself at the mercy of 'strongmen' – a combination of Afro-Lebanese traders, businessmen and Freetown cronies within Stevens's circle – who controlled commercial activities.

The period of APC rule (which lasted for 24 years until it was overthrown in a coup by junior officers in 1992) laid the foundations for state collapse and, eventually, rebellion. While Momoh wrestled to regain control of state resources, the state's ability to function continued to crumble. Grievances, built up over several decades, intensified as ordinary people continued to be marginalised.

The RUF rebellion began in 1991 and was founded on the claim that it was going to fight the cause of those aggrieved by years of nepotism, violence and exclusionary politics under the APC regime. Its pamphlet, *Footpaths to Democracy*, spoke about the problems of social fragmentation, the exclusion of youth and the exploitation of diamonds.[2] Sierra Leoneans writing on the personalities within the RUF often define the movement as being made up of *lumpens* who were mainly 'unemployed and unemployable youths, mostly male, who live by their wits or who have one foot in ... the informal or underground economy' (Abdullah 1997). Those who joined or supported the RUF included many of these *lumpen* males who had been bypassed by the APC regime. The movement also included farmers, labourers, intellectuals, and a mixture of Liberian–Sierra Leonean descendants and criminal gangs who saw the war as an opportunity for looting.

However, the RUF was no different from those it wished to topple. It continued the acts of plunder, thuggery and systematic violence pursued by the APC, thus leaving many in doubt as to its true identity.[3] The RUF committed terrible atrocities against the very people on whose behalf it claimed to be fighting. Like the APC, the RUF thrived on disorder and fear; this was the only way to ensure support. Its worst excesses – decapitation, cutting off the hands of civilians and burning villages – followed its rejection of the 1996 elections, which saw the return of the SLPP under Ahmed Tejan Kabbah. The RUF collaborated with disaffected soldiers calling themselves the Armed Forces Revolutionary Council (AFRC). This collaboration resulted in President Kabbah being overthrown on 25 May 1997. The destruction of Freetown in 1997–8 and again in January 1999 followed. The theft, looting and brutal nature of the RUF war made Sierra Leone ungovernable. The damage to institutions that began with the APC was completed by the RUF with assistance from renegade soldiers. In the end, the RUF became a reflection of the regime it had fought against, with the rebel forces mimicking the undemocratic practices of the APC regime.

The de-institutionalisation of the security forces and the informalisation of violence

The process of security sector reform has been under way for some time in Sierra Leone. Those assisting in the programme, particularly from the outside, are acutely aware of the deeply entrenched problems of transforming the forces of repression into bastions of democracy. It would, therefore, be naïve to think that they are unaware of the history of Sierra Leone's security forces. The aim of this section is to isolate some of the crucial factors that need to be properly addressed if the efforts currently under way are not to be wasted.

At the heart of Sierra Leone's security sector is a history of deliberate break-up of and political interference in the running of the security sector. The SLA and the SLP became increasingly politicised as Stevens sought to ensure that appointments to both were based on ethnicity or political allegiance to the APC. The SLP was undermined by political interference in the recruitment and promotion of officers. Between 1968 and 1985, the SLP became, in essence, a private wing of the APC.

The worst excesses of Stevens's fracturing of the state's security apparatus came with his management of the military. He pursued a policy of restricting the size of the country's armed forces to some 2,000 (predominantly loyal) personnel. This was to have a significant impact on how these forces responded to the rebel insurgency in 1991. Under Stevens, and later under Momoh, the army became ill-equipped and poorly trained to the extent that it was too small and was unable to respond to the rebel incursion. Instead its defensive weaknesses led to the further deterioration of the state.

There were two attempts to increase the size of the SLA. In 1992, under Momoh, the SLA increased to 6,150 in a poorly devised strategy that eradicated the few remaining elements of cohesion in the military. In the words of Momoh's foreign minister, Abdul Karim Koroma, recruits were 'mostly drifters, rural and urban unemployed, a fair number of hooligans, drug addicts and thieves' (quoted in Gberie 1997: 155). Similarly, following the 1992 coup by junior officers, the military junta under Captain Valentine Strasser also pursued a poorly conceived policy to increase the size of the SLA to about 14,000 over four years, using young criminals, school drop-outs and semi-illiterate youths. As a consequence, the army became further fragmented, leading to the complete breakdown of command and control during the war, and again following the AFRC coup in 1997.

This led to a terrible period of collusion between the RUF and elements of the army. Junior officers abdicated their functions of defending the country and joined the RUF in looting and diamond mining. The war was an opportunity to exact revenge against the old order, to loot and to chase the resources unobtainable during Stevens's reign. In addition, the military was also affected by economic decline, with many soldiers being paid low wages (if any at all). On several occasions during the war the dissident forces and the military changed the course of events and inflicted widespread suffering on Sierra Leonean citizens, earning them the *sobriquet* 'sobels' – soldiers by day, rebels by night. The term was coined by Sierra Leonean citizens to signify that violence and looting was not only the domain of the RUF, but was also conducted by sections of the army that were collaborating with the insurgents in waging war against the people (Ero 2000a: 18).

The emergence of renegade militaries needs to be linked to the policies that critically deepened social insecurity within the army and in turn spurred some elements to pursue private agendas. Aggrieved by poor service conditions, a shortage of equipment and low wages, several officers and members of the lower ranks played the role of predatory gangs, extracting resources from civilians, regardless of where their sympathies lay in the conflict. This predatory character is not specific to Sierra Leone. It is a feature of societies where the regime in power employs a deliberate policy of breaking the army (the Zaïrian army under Joseph Mobutu is an example) or where cuts in military expenditure or shortage in equipment and inadequate training force soldiers to engage in criminal behaviour (as in Angola and Tajikistan) (see Kaldor 1999: 92–3).

As a consequence of the breakdown of the SLA, civil or self defence forces (CDFs) rose to become 'counter-insurgency forces' in the war (Muana 1997: 78). The CDFs included several hundred Gbethi, Tamaboro, Kapara and several thousand Kamajors. According to Alfred Zack-Williams these CDFs were an 'adjunct of civil society' (Zack-Williams 1999: 150) although they often challenged the comfortable notion that civil society is in fact civil. The involvement of CDFs also led to the informalisation of violence. Mistrust between the military and the civilian population contributed significantly to the spread of militia groups.

The emergence of CDFs is linked to the security vacuum that resulted from the failure of successive regimes and the army to guarantee the safety of the population against rebel attack. Traditional chiefs recruited internally displaced civilians to act as armed self-defence groups to protect villages from RUF attacks. These groups drew on a heritage of traditional hunter guilds and secret societies in Sierra Leone. These militia were structured around ethnic or communal identities similar to those of the hunter groups of the pre-colonial and colonial era. In Sierra Leone, the CDFs swear allegiance to their paramount chiefs, communal or tribal leaders or civilian patrons.

Of all the militia groups in the country, the Kamajors registered the most consistent successes throughout the conflict. They were used to protect the government from three attempted coups between 1996 and 1997, before the government fell to the RUF/AFRC rebel group in the coup of May 1997. Two notable battles against the RUF took place in March 1998 when the Kamajors joined forces with the Nigerian-led ECOWAS Monitoring Group (ECOMOG) to restore the government of President Kabbah following the coup. The second was their defence of Freetown against the RUF in May 2000 after the collapse of the 1999 Lomé peace agreement. The success of the Kamajors at critical moments in the conflict has given them a prominent, but also a dangerous status. This is primarily because their role in the conflict has tended to be ambiguous. They are seen as 'saviours' in Freetown and in the south and eastern provinces. Like other CDFs, they exist to defend their communities and this cannot be overlooked. However, deeper analysis has revealed a host of anomalies that are briefly examined here.

On one hand, the Kamajors are generally perceived to be loyal to the SLPP, making them a party-political militia. Moreover, the Kamajors and the core leadership of the SLPP, with the exception of Kabbah, are Mende and, as such, reflect the concerns of their ethnic group. The Kamajors are not a homogeneous entity but are loyal to various individuals within the SLPP. In effect, they have continued the pattern (established by the SSD and the ISU under Stevens) of being inextricably linked to the governing regime. The link with their patron, Chief Hinga Norman, is often mentioned. Along with this link, for example, the Moyamba Kamajors are generally loyal to Vice-President Demby.

On the other hand, the Kamajors have become a quasi-military force. While their original involvement in the war was to defend their communities, 'one of the most bitter observations is that they were successfully mobilised to use extreme coercion to fight against rebel forces, and those suspected of supporting the rebels' (Ero 2000b: 28). The Kamajors continued to use force to determine the future of security in the territories they control. Consequently, the Kamajor system of managing law and order may undermine internal security.

Despite their close links with individual members of the SLPP, the Kamajors operate with near-autonomy. There is no central authority to control their activities and the group continues to break up into smaller gangs. The government is unable to respond, demonstrating that the Kamajors have become a law unto themselves. Human rights monitoring groups based in Sierra Leone have reported a catalogue of atrocity against civilians in Kamajor-controlled regions since January 2000. Similarly, the United Nations noted incidents of abuses among civilians when it reported major concerns over the Gbethis and CDFs in the southern and eastern regions, the home of the Kamajors. According to the UN, civilians allege CDF involvement in 'harassment, including summary executions, arbitrary detentions and extortion of money and property at checkpoints' (United Nations 2000b: 5).

Opinions vary on the role of the Kamajors. Some Sierra Leoneans view them as 'gradually turning into demagogues' while others reject the 'Kamajor bashing'. The difficulty with criticising them is that they were prominent defenders of their communities during the war. They may also be a necessary breeding ground for the creation of a new political space and ensuring that grassroots initiatives guide the future of post-war recovery, in particular as regards moves towards democratic governance. However, the prospects for the success of security sector reform in Sierra Leone may be limited by the fact that several militia groups began building parallel security structures, developing their own penal codes and systems of taxation, all of which are aimed at undermining the military and the police. Furthermore, their role in determining security could also lead to widespread disorder, where the militia groups are not accountable to anyone and political life is militarised and determined by the power of the gun. This, in effect, will reduce Sierra Leone to a militia state – a reflection of its former self.

The various links and activities associated with the Kamajors raises several questions as to their future role in the security apparatus of post-war Sierra Leone. As part of the military assistance programme, British military officials and the Sierra Leone government have devised a plan to turn the CDFs into territorial defence forces similar to the British Territorial Army structure. This would allow them to operate within their localities in defence of the country in times of crisis and would ensure a more disciplined and coordinated force. However, the expanded influence of the Kamajors during the war and the extent to which violence was informalised has made the task of rebuilding security structures within a democratic framework more difficult. The prominence of the Kamajors and other CDFs is a clear demonstration of the breakdown of the monopoly of organised violence in which the national army had virtually lost all means to control the use of force, and where various conflict actors – private, state and non-state armed groups – emerged to decide the fate of Sierra Leone. Greater emphasis must be placed on understanding the links and associations between conflict actors and military groups such as the Kamajors. Their role in the war added to the diversity of internal and external actors that shaped the war and will impact directly on the future of governance in Sierra Leone.

The regionalisation of conflict and security

A key feature of Sierra Leone's civil war has been the number of external actors that became entangled. In the years of fighting, Sierra Leone found itself in a position where the only forces the country could depend on were external forces. This raises questions about the future ability of the internal security forces to manage and contain violence without the overt reliance on external forces to bolster or protect regimes. Other fundamental questions relate to the accountability and transparency of external forces, especially when used to bolster the mixed fortunes of weak, ineffective regimes that lack legitimacy in the eyes of ordinary people. The implications are that the positions and interests of external forces could subvert a democratic transition and the development of real political authority in Sierra Leone.

The driving force behind the external interventions was closely associated with the pool of resources, mainly gold and diamonds. Foreign private military forces, ECOMOG forces, various militia groups and young criminal gangs soon found themselves confronted by other armed opposition groups, foreign businessmen and a conglomeration of Lebanese, Israeli and Asian traders vying to smuggle gold and diamonds onto the world market. The use of private military forces by successive regimes, including President Kabbah, to manage violence marked the beginning of a dangerous phase in which African leaders were increasingly prepared to employ private security forces to secure peace and to exert control rather than seek political solutions to internal violence (Ero 2000c: 108).

The most worrying external actors in Sierra Leone were the neighbouring states of Liberia and Nigeria, although for different reasons. Liberia's role under its former rebel leader, Charles Taylor, was that of a predatory state. Most analysts conclude that Taylor was instrumental in sustaining the RUF war by providing it with substantial military capacity. Taylor's role came under intense international scrutiny following the resumption of war in Sierra Leone in May 2000. There were a number of commentaries on and belated UN-sanctioned inquiries into Taylor's links with the RUF between May and December 2000.[4] A UN Security Council mission to Sierra Leone reported that Taylor 'exercised strong influence, even direct control, over the RUF' (UN 2000a: 5). Following UN Security Council Resolution 1343 of 7 March 2001, sanctions were imposed on Liberia on 7 May 2001.

Taylor's pivotal role in the RUF leadership was evident from the start of the conflict. In part, his involvement was in retaliation for Joseph Momoh's decision to send peacekeepers to support ECOMOG in Liberia, a decision that Taylor maintained had prevented him from taking the Liberian presidency earlier. Sankoh and Taylor were, however, inextricably linked through the diamond fields that the RUF controlled in the eastern district of Kono and which Taylor used to sustain his international and regional business connections. Taylor not only sustained warfare in the country, but shaped Sierra Leone's rebel forces and by implication, the internal violence that plagued the country. Moreover, Taylor exported the internal security dilemmas confronting his leadership in Liberia to Sierra Leone and also to Guinea.

Between October 2000 and March 2001, the extent of Taylor's regional meddling was exposed when the three countries that make up the Mano River Union – Guinea, Liberia and Sierra Leone – engaged in cross-border fighting. After a decade of accusations and counter-accusations of support for dissident activities on their common border, the possibility of combined intra- and inter-state conflict in the Mano River region became a reality as Guinean forces joined Kamajor militia in Sierra Leone in pushing RUF forces back from the Guinean borders.

The situation in the Mano River region not only demonstrated the widespread security dilemma confronting the region, but provided a clear indication that security sector reform has regional implications, especially when internal forces are used as destabilising forces in neighbouring states. Many dissidents and armed groups forged their careers by ensuring permanent instability in the region and undermining neighbouring states. As a consequence, the future of political life and the prospects of democratic governance in Sierra Leone became inextricably linked with the private interests of Taylor and the regional security of Guinea which (like Sierra Leone) has long and porous borders that attract insurgent movements.

Nigeria's role in Sierra Leone, while different, has thrown further light on the regional dimensions of security sector reform. The criticisms against Nigeria are vastly different from those against Liberia and focus on the way in which military officials conducted peacekeeping operations under the auspices of ECOMOG. Unfortunately for Nigeria, its attempts to portray its actions in Sierra Leone as a 'force for good' were heavily tainted by the aggressive stance of the country's military leadership under General Abacha. Use of force by Nigeria in Sierra Leone did not come with constitutional checks and balances. Nigeria's military regime at the time continually bypassed institutions such as the country's National Assembly or sought *post facto* approval from ECOWAS in deciding on security matters or obtaining support for dubious interventions.

Nigeria's role in preventing the RUF and its AFRC collaborators from taking control of Sierra Leone cannot be overlooked. During their time in Sierra Leone some 700 Nigerian troops were killed. Nigerian and Kamajor forces were also instrumental in reinstalling the democratically elected President Kabbah nine months after he was toppled in 1997. Similarly, Nigerian forces led the offensive to repel the RUF/AFRC forces in the aftermath of the rebel attack on Freetown on 6 January 1999.

However, the complexities and entrenched political events surrounding Nigeria's involvement in Sierra Leone were exposed in a damning memorandum written by the former commander of the UN Mission in Sierra Leone (UNAMSIL), General Vijay Kumar Jetley, several months before the Indian contingent withdrew from their peacekeeping duties in Sierra Leone. Jetley made several allegations about the collaboration between some Nigerian troops and RUF rebels in the diamond-mining regions. Although there is no concrete evidence to confirm such accusations, the memorandum added to persistent rumours of poor discipline and looting and has further damaged Nigeria's claim that it is able to manage regional security. The memorandum also drew attention to efforts by Nigerian officials to ensure complete control over military and political decisions in Sierra Leone.

The transition to democratic rule in Nigeria saw a reversal in the use of military force by that country. President Olusegun Obasanjo's decision to streamline Nigeria's engagement in the region by beginning a phased withdrawal of Nigerian troops in August 1999 and placing elements within UNAMSIL can be viewed as an attempt to limit Nigeria's power projection in the region. It can also be viewed as an endeavour by Obasanjo to develop stronger mechanisms for the sharing of resources among other West African countries without undermining Nigeria's strategic interests in the region. Nigeria's prominent role in Sierra Leone's post-war recovery, notably the provision of security alongside

British and UN forces, is an indication that it will continue to maintain its influence on the future geopolitical shape of the West African region.

Prospects for democratic governance of the security forces

On the basis of the legacies outlined in this chapter, the prospects for democratic governance of security are daunting. Two enduring legacies are the use of violence to gain economic benefit and the militarisation of society. Both will have corrosive effects on political, social and security institutions at all levels. The prospect for democratic governance of the security forces is also dependent of several factors, including:

- economic reconstruction;
- demobilisation and reintegration of all armed forces;
- public safety and security in preventing the renewal of hostilities;
- restoration of the rule of law, including human rights provisions;
- confidence-building programmes between the security forces and civil society;
- a vibrant and educated civil society that understands security issues and concentrates attention on reform at all levels; and
- a conducive political landscape (including strong leadership, political parties and a system of parliamentary supervision).

This last point is critical in shaping the future political order and ensuring democratic governance of the security structures in Sierra Leone. As delegates to a forum on governance of the security forces recognised, 'the prospects of democratic control improve dramatically when there is an obvious shift of political power'.[5] However, a major problem for Sierra Leone is that numerous politicians and strongmen from the pre-war order reappeared on the political scene and continued to promote the style of politics that had led Sierra Leone to war. The war did not dismantle the politics of exclusion or corruption. It lingered under the SLPP administration that returned to power after 29 years.

To adopt a phrase coined by Chabal and Daloz, 'recycled élites', claiming to bear the symbols of democratic principles, emerged to lead the country after the 1996 elections, but their presence resembled that of the former regime (Chabal and Daloz 1999: Chapter 3). Officials within the government were self-seeking and continued the practice of diamond smuggling. Many, according to Zack-Williams, were in fact remnants of the discredited SLPP regime of the 1960s. President Kabbah was seen as the best of a group of politicians 'contaminated by the politics of kleptocracy' (Zack-Williams 1999: 153). Sierra Leoneans perceived Kabbah to be 'paying lip service to the welfare of the people; phlegmatic to the security and financial irregularities in Government' (Zack-Williams 1999: 153). The SLPP government proved to be ineffective during periods when strong leadership was required to avoid the resumption of war, first in January 1999 and later in May 2000.

But the Kabbah administration was also dealt an unfortunate hand when it inherited a country that had all but collapsed. Indeed, Sierra Leone is so weak that officials have minimal room in which to develop the capacity needed to sustain peace-building processes. Moreover, the country lacks the necessary internal mechanisms of democratic accountability and control needed to keep the security forces in check once they have been rebuilt. Finally, Sierra Leone lacks the necessary resources to embed security sector reform or to ensure good governance at all levels of society.

This is partly the reason why the role of the international community is critical to the rebuilding process. However, the international community did not make a serious commitment to helping Sierra Leone in the ten years of fighting that preceded the fragile peace, signed in late 1999 but crumbling by May 2000. Instead, quick-fix solutions were applied to complex and deeply entrenched problems.

Sierra Leone will be dependent on the international community for some time, however, as post-war reconstruction is a long-term endeavour that requires high levels of engagement throughout society. The answer, however, is not for external actors to take complete control of the country. Sierra Leoneans need to own the process of state reconstruction to ensure their commitment to democratic governance. However, they do need the international community to engage financially and politically in the gradual process of building institutions with strong foundations, which will result in the slow change of culture, attitudes, procedures and the practice of governing the country.

Despite the resumption of war in May 2000, Britain made considerable progress in assisting Sierra Leone with rebuilding key security-sector institutions between 1998 and 2001. The British Labour government said that it would commit its military personnel to Sierra Leone for some time. However, this needs to be treated with caution. Britain virtually has *carte blanche* to decide the fate of Sierra Leone's depleted security sector, and the implications of this need to be carefully considered.

Three issues are pertinent. The first is the need to limit external involvement. The rebuilding of institutions in Sierra Leone should be regarded as part of a long-term rehabilitation programme that will need to bridge different generations. The older generation will have little impact on the future shape of Sierra Leone. The younger generation is the vehicle for development in the country. This generation need to gain skills and experience and to be coached towards a more just and transparent society without losing ownership of the process of forging the future of their country. The likelihood of creating democratic and professional security forces that adhere to the principles of impartiality, accountability and transparency appears remote when judged against the historical behaviour of the SLA. One is left wondering how a largely fragmented and demoralised military can be rebuilt into a credible force that is loyal and able to protect its citizens.

Such a programme involves a lengthy commitment, something not lost on Britain. However, donor initiatives are largely not long-term, intimate projects. Moreover, before entering a country, donors predetermine the time and money that they are prepared to invest in a project, thus raising questions about the viability of and commitment to their programmes. Clearly the British Labour government has assured the people of Sierra Leone of its commitment to assisting in rebuilding the security sector, including wider development initiatives. Considerable progress has been made since the programme began in 1998. There is a limit, however, to what external actors can do. External advisers can set in train values and principles, but much is dependent on the willingness and capacity of recipients to ensure that these take hold. Moreover, security sector reform is unlikely to succeed without a strong domestic constituency committed to reform.

This relates directly to the core issue of local ownership and avoiding donor dependence. Since the start of security sector reform in Sierra Leone, British officials have stressed that their assistance is largely at the request of the Sierra Leone government. Nevertheless, there is a sense that the political impetus for reform is coming from Britain, with Sierra Leone's strategic vision appearing to be heavily directed by Britain. This is not necessarily a bad thing. Sometimes external actors can serve as positive catalysts in moving peace processes along for improving security – for example in Bosnia and Herzegovina, where external forces provided the necessary space to promote the democratisation of the security forces, although with mixed results (Kaldor, in this volume).

However, the main problem identified in Bosnia, and pertinent to Sierra Leone, is that government officials and policy makers are often unwilling to restore democratic control. The incentives for and benefits of continuing past practices are far greater. The question of who gains and who loses is paramount in security sector reform. The process is dependent on a few receptive people and/or a ripe domestic constituency that believes in democratic governance sufficiently to continue with it once external interest has been exhausted. If the process of security sector reform is going to succeed, then the solutions need to be locally owned and negotiated.

In fairness to Sierra Leone, dependency on external aid is unavoidable, especially in the immediate post-war recovery phase. As noted above, Sierra Leone lacks the financial capacity to stand on its own. Moreover, Sierra Leone has limited manpower to fill the necessary spaces in key institutions. Between 2000 and 2001, British personnel featured heavily in institutions of state. It is openly acknowledged that they are driving the formation of and strategic outlook for a number of institutions, including the police and the Ministry of Defence.

Despite reservations about the role of external actors in rebuilding Sierra Leone's security sector, some progress has been made. Take, for example, the attempts to embed democratic principles in the SLP. The police were unable to protect citizens during the war. Members of the SLP suffered brutal attacks, including the burning of their homes and offices by the RUF because of their links with the previous APC regime. In addition, the police 'had been responsible, during the 1998 treason trials [of those involved in the May 1997 coup], for prosecuting members of the RUF/AFRC junta' (Charley 2000: 75). Since 1998, the restructuring of the police has made significant progress partly because of the need to stabilise internal security, but also because they were less fragmented and politicised than the army.

The rehabilitation of the police started virtually from scratch. A British police officer was made Inspector General and tasked with restructuring policing in the country. Police advisers from various Commonwealth countries were the main providers of technical and strategic assistance, helping the government to formulate the mission, force level, functions and structure of policing. On 14 August 1998 President Kabbah set out his vision for the SLP in 'The Policing Charter'. He stated that the service would work with the community to ensure stability in the country under the principle of 'local needs policing' (community policing) (Ero 2000a: 51). The aim is to restore confidence in the police within their communities and to establish stronger links with regional and local government structures, and in particular with the paramount chiefs. Pilot programmes under the umbrella of community policing were set up in Freetown (at the Congo Cross and Kissy police stations) and at the Waterloo and Bo police stations. The aim is to establish similar programmes throughout Sierra Leone, but a lack of resources remains a stumbling block to substantive development (Charley 2000: 75). The concept of community policing may loosen the grip the regime has on the police and decentralise power to allow decision making by regional commissioners and local administrations.

The progress made between 1998 and 2000 suggests that Sierra Leone has made some progress in reforming and governing security institutions. An important issue in the post-war context is the question of how to handle the problem of impunity for past and present abuses, both by the military and the dissident and rebel forces seeking integration into a new Sierra Leone army. Many Sierra Leoneans were outraged when the Lomé peace agreement of July 1999 awarded amnesty to rebel forces for crimes committed during the war. However, the question of justice remains a contentious issue, especially in a situation where it is difficult to differentiate between perpetrators and victims. The creation of the Sierra Leone Special Court 'to try those who bear the greatest responsibility' as stipulated under UN Security Council Resolution 1315 in August 2000, has limited the possible range of addressing impunity. Only those who master-minded the war will be prosecuted, where there is sufficient evidence. But in discussions with Seirra Leoneans, victims of the war have often stated that some of the perpetrators were fighting their own personal war often removed from the RUF and dissident army war. More importantly, the army, dissident and rebel forces, politicians and civil society all blame one another for the war, thus making it difficult to create a sense of justice and reconciliation – a critical tool for the future of democratisation.

Postscript: Sierra Leone after elections

After eleven years of fighting and with war declared officially over on 18 January 2002, elections were held in Sierra Leone on 14 may 2002 with the SLPP winning a resounding victory. President Kabbah won 70 per cent of the votes. The elections were a demonstration of a willingness by Sierra Leoneans to start the necessary but arduous task of transition and reform. By the time of the elections, the RUF appeared to be a broken force, unable to regain their former strength. Their command and control structure crumble significantly following the capture and imprisonment of their leader Foday Sankoh in May 2000. Many RUF fighters who chose not to disarm fled to Liberia to support President Taylor in his war against the Liberians United for Reconciliation and Democracy (LURD) rebel group.

Others have opted to enter the integration programme in the newly created Republic of Sierra Leone Armed Forces along with former combatants drawn from the AFRC and DCFs. The new army has been well trained under the British-led International Military Assistance Training Team (IMATT) programme, which is ongoing. The army appears more professional, disciplined and robust. All of this suggests that notions of civil control have taken a foothold in the new army.

But the harsh realities of Sierra Leone's 11-year war which diminished already weak institutions of state, and the legacy of violence that accompanied it, will greatly complicate the transition to democratic governance. More importantly, years of fighting have not removed many of the fault-lines in the country, thus making it difficult to assess how these may be overcome. Many of the conditions that led the country to war have not disappeared. These include the pervasive presence of corruption, one-party rule, and regional insecurity (International Crisis Group 2002: 15).

For the foreseeable future, the country will face both internal and external threats to peace, suggesting that nothing less than a comprehensive reform programme is needed to strengthen both the military and the police, and the civil capacity needed to manage these institutions. The key challenge is how to take the necessary steps to sustain the initial progress made within policing, thus addressing the immediate problem of internal security and post-war stability.

Furthermore, there is recognition that a focus on the security sector alone (in particular the army) is unlikely to address the long-term and complex changes needed. Reform must incorporate broader public sector reform and a change in the system of political rule. Much is dependent on how receptive political leaders are to changing past practices and on the ability of civil society to mobilise action and force change. Democratic governance will also depend on ensuring that the rule of law takes precedence in all the institutions of state and governs all aspects of socio-economic and political life.

Chronology

23 March 1991: Around 100 Revolutionary United Front (RUF) fighters launch an attack on the government of the All Peoples' Congress (APC) party.

29 April 1992: Junior officers carry out a coup and establish the National Provisional Ruling Council (NPRC) with Captain Valentine Strasser as chairman.

Late 1992/early 1993: A newly recruited army (mainly urban unemployed) launches attacks against the RUF.

February 1995: Pro-government forces including the Kamajor civil defence force and 2,000 Nigerian soldiers stop an RUF advance on Freetown.

16 January 1996: Brigadier-General Julius Maada Bio replaces Strasser as the NPRC chairman in an internal coup. Under international pressure, Bio calls elections for the following month, won by Ahmad Tejan Kabbah.

30 November 1996: President Kabbah and the RUF leader, Foday Sankoh, sign the Abidjan peace agreement.

25 May 1997: Military coup by the Armed Forces Revolutionary Council (AFRC), chaired by Major Johnny Paul Koroma. President Kabbah flees to Guinea.

15 January 1998: ECOMOG forces, including Nigerian troops and the Kamajors, attack Freetown.

15 February 1998: AFRC/RUF forces leave Freetown.

10 March 1998: Tejan Kabbah is reinstated as President of Sierra Leone.

6 January 1999: AFRC/RUF forces re-enter Freetown by force, inflicting heavy casualties on the civilian population.

7 July 1999: The Lomé peace agreement is signed by President Kabbah and Foday Sankoh.

22 October 1999: UN Security Council Resolution 1270 establishes a UN peacekeeping mission in Sierra Leone (UNAMSIL).

Late April–6 May 2000: After several incidents of non-compliance with the terms of the peace agreement, the RUF takes 500 UN peacekeepers hostage.

6 May–17 May 2000: The Kamajors, elements of the AFRC and British Special Air Service protect Freetown from RUF attacks. RUF leader Foday Sankoh is captured and faces war crimes charges.

25 August–10 September 2000: The West Side Boys, a splinter group from the AFRC, hold 11 British Royal Irish Regiment troops hostage. Five are initially released before British forces intervene (Operation Barras) to release the rest of the hostages.

Mid-August–November 2000: Regional clashes lead to refugee crisis between Guinea, Liberia and Sierra Leone.

10 November 2000: A 30-day ceasefire agreement between government

and RUF is signed in Abuja, Nigeria.

19 December 2000: United Nations panel of experts issues a report on diamond smuggling and illegal arms sales in Sierra Leone.

4 January 2001: The United States circulates a draft resolution at the United Nations Security Council seeking to impose an arms embargo on Liberia following allegations that President Taylor of Liberia has been arming Sierra Leone's RUF rebels.

12 January 2001: Government of Liberia announces 'a new policy of disengagement' toward the RUF.

January–March 2001: Continued regional clashes lead to further refugee crisis at Parrots Beak on the borders of Guinea, Liberia and Sierra Leone.

7 March 2001: UN Security Council passes resolution to impose a variety of sanctions on Liberia. The resolution is delayed for two months.

2 May 2001: The RUF meets with the UN and the government of Sierra Leone in Abuja, Nigeria, for a review of the ceasefire agreement signed on 10 November 2000.

7 May 2001: Sanctions, including travel ban, imposed on government of Liberia.

18 May 2001: Disarmament programme restarts.

13–15 November 2001: National Consultative Conference held to discuss Sierra Leone's road to democracy and schedule for elections.

17 January 2002: Disarmament declared complete.

18 January 2002: War declared over by President Ahmed Tejan Kabbah.

References

Abraham, A. (2000) 'The quest for peace in Sierra Leone', in Centre for Democracy and Development, *Engaging Sierra Leone*, CDD Strategy Planning Series, No. 4, p. 14.

Adejumobi, S. (2000) 'Demilitarisation and democratic reorientation in Nigeria: issues, problems and prospects', unpublished manuscript presented at the round-table forum on 'Democratic Control of Military and Security Establishments in Nigeria and South Africa', Johannesburg, South Africa, 20–23 September 2000.

Bangura, Y. (1997) 'Understanding the political and cultural dynamics of the Sierra Leone war: a critique of Paul Richard's *Fighting for the Rain Forest*', *Africa Development*, 22 (3/4).

Chabal, P. and J. Daloz (1999) *Africa Works: Disorder as Political Instrument*, Oxford: James Currey.

Chris Charley, J. P. (2000) 'Arms regulation: a challenging issue for the police force in post-war law and order enforcement', in Ayissi, A. and R. Poulton (eds.), *Bound to Cooperate: Conflict, Peace and People in Sierra Leone*, Geneva: UNIDIR.

Ero, C. (2000a) *Sierra Leone's Security Complex*, Working Paper No. 3, London: The Conflict, Security and Development Group, Centre for Defence Studies, King's College.

Ero, C. (2000b) 'Vigilantes, civil defence forces and militia groups: the other side of the privatisation of security in Africa', *Conflict Trends* (June).

Ero, C. (2000c) 'ECOMOG: a model for Africa?', in Cilliers, J. and A. Hilding-Norberg (eds.), *Building Stability in Africa: Challenges for the New Millennium*, No. 46, South Africa: Institute for Security Studies Monograph Series, February.

Gberie, L. (1997) 'The May 25 coup d'état in Sierra Leone: a militariat revolt?', *Africa Development*, 22 (3/4).

International Crisis Group (2002) 'Sierra Leone After Elections: Politics as Usual?' *Africa Report*, No. 49, 12 July 2002.

Kaldor, M. (1999) *New and Old Wars: Organised Violence in a Global Era*, Cambridge: Polity Press.

Muana, P. (1997) 'The Kamajoi militia: civil war, internal displacement and the politics of counter-insurgency', *Africa Development*, 22 (3/4).

Reno, W. (1995) *Corruption and State Politics in Sierra Leone*, Cambridge: Cambridge University Press.

United Nations (2000a) *Security Council Mission to Sierra Leone*, UN Document, S/2000/992, 16 October 2000.

United Nations (2000b) *Seventh Report of the Secretary-General on the United Nations Mission in Sierra Leone*, Security Council, UN Document S/2000/1055, 31 October 2000.

Zack-Williams, A. B. (1999) 'Sierra Leone: the political economy of civil war, 1991–98', *Third World Quarterly*, 20 (1).

Notes

1 Personal communication.

2 *Footpaths to Democracy: Towards a New Sierra Leone*, 1995, www.sierra-Leone.org/footpaths.html

3 For an excellent review of the RUF – its background, values and strategies – read the collection of essays in the special issue of *Africa Development*, 22 (3/4) (1997), especially I. Abdullah, 'Bush path to destruction: the origin and character of the Revolutionary United Front (RUF/SL)', pp. 45–76.

4 See, for example, Report of the Panel of Experts Appointed Pursuant to UN Security Council Resolution 1306 (2000) in relation to Sierra Leone, December 2000.

5 'Summary Report', round-table forum on 'Democratic Control of Military and Security Establishments in Nigeria and South Africa', Johannesburg, South Africa, 20–23 September 2000. The report noted, however, that 'paradoxically ... political change could elicit a backlash if not properly managed', p. 4.

11

A Failing State
The Democratic Republic of Congo

ROGER KIBASOMBA

The security problems in the Great Lakes region of Africa are very complex.[1] The region has a post-Cold War record of systematic genocides, massacres of defenceless civilians and other war-related calamities. Efforts to end intra-Congolese[2] conflict will only succeed if the Congolese become more concerned about their national security and their national interests rather than sectional interests. Without such a national consciousness, the Congolese people will continue to be vulnerable to foreign attacks and manipulation. External forces take advantage of internal weaknesses.

Congo gained independence from Belgium in June 1960. During its 80-year colonial rule, Belgium did not prepare the Congolese people for self-rule. As a result, a lack of political and administrative experience became evident during the first five years of sovereignty. Indigenous skill and experience in managing cultural diversity, nation-building, civil–military relations, development administration and international relations were almost non-existent. This political deficit facilitated the coup led by Mobuto Seseseko in November 1965. Mobutu's 32 years of rule were marked by the absence of democracy and a lack of socio-economic development.

In 1996–7, with the military support of Rwanda and Uganda, Laurent Désiré Kabila's Alliance of Democratic Forces for the Liberation of Congo–Zaïre (ADFL) took only six months to remove Mobutu from power. Kabila's rule was recognised internally, regionally and internationally. However, his regime was immediately confronted with the need for rapid democratisation, the legitimisation of its power, and the integration of members of the former Zaïrian armed forces. Rwanda and Uganda also did not have a clear termination strategy for their support. Internal divisions weakened the ADFL. There was no national consensus on issues related to the Rwandan and Ugandan military mandate, threats of United Nations (UN) sanctions in response to massacres of Rwandan Hutu refugees, and the controversial issue of the nationality of Congolese Tutsis (Banyamulenge), common border security, and so on. The collapse of the ADFL led Rwanda and Uganda to forge new alliances and coalitions with those opposing Kabila. The second Rwandan and Ugandan invasion of Congo, in 1998, attracted Kabila dissidents and led to the launch of new rebel movements. Kabila himself was assassinated on 16 January 2001, and his son Joseph became President.

Rwandan, Ugandan and rebel forces now occupy half of Congo's territory, specifically the northern and eastern provinces. The occupation is very unpopular and has given rise to a vast, charismatic militia resistance movement known as the Mai-Mai. High levels of insecurity and limited freedom of movement lead one to conclude that eastern and northern Congo are not really controlled by anyone. Government forces supported by Angola and Zimbabwe control the capital city Kinshasa and the western, southern and central areas of the country.

This chapter examines Congo's vulnerability to internal and external threats or attacks. It is evident that the country has lost the capacity to defend its people, its borders and its resources. Congo is the site of one of the world's most complicated wars, with about three million war-related deaths between 1998 and 2001. Seven governments have been involved, either supporting or opposing the present regime. About twenty-two known internal and external rebel forces are fighting in eastern and northern Congo. Congolese rebels compete against each other, against governmental forces, and against the local population. Non-Congolese rebels use Congolese territory as rear bases for carrying out so-called liberation wars against their respective governments in Angola, Burundi, Rwanda and Uganda. As Seybolt has noted: 'The intertwined involvement of governments, insurgents and refugees from countries in the African Great Lakes region and to the rest of the west and south also makes the war in the Congo one of the world's most troubling' (Seybolt 2000: 59).

Background: the security dynamic in the Congo

The Congo's security problems have a long history dating back to the Berlin Conference (1884–5) that recognised King Leopold II of Belgium as the uncontested ruler of the Congo Basin. He immediately organised a military apparatus called the Force Publique to exploit his estate. The colonial army was formally established on 5 August 1888. By 1948, it had become an ethnically heterogeneous and well-integrated body that had a sense of national mission because of its role in the nation-building process. Its outstanding performance in the Second World War showed the level of discipline, professionalism and cohesion it had achieved (Emizet 2000: 206–7). However, the Force Publique defended the colonial authority only and not Congolese society. It assisted in suppressing indigenous political dissidence and mass revolt. Nevertheless, the majority of Congolese later came to realise that the Force Publique was disciplined and efficient relative to the post-independence military and police forces.

The image of the military as a civilised and organised body, a symbol of state authority, disappeared a few hours after the Declaration of Independence in June 1960. The Congolese army of 25,000 men, which had never had an African officer corps, rose up and demanded the ousting of its Belgian officers and pay increases for the enlisted men. Many disappointed civilians who had expected to inherit all the Belgian possessions in the country joined in the mutiny. The mutiny also divided the old generation of soldiers from the new. The old generation still displayed the professional and apolitical characteristics inherited from Western military culture. The new generation considered independence an opportunity to be promoted and to gain political power, both of which depended on affiliation to one or another political party. Since party organisation was based on geopolitical considerations, soldiers mutinied for political reasons, including secession. The Cold War rivalry between the major powers – especially France, the Soviet Union and the US – also influenced internal politics. With the support of the US Kennedy administration, UN peacekeeping forces intervened to stop secessionist movements. The UN mission, Organisation des Nations Unies au Congo (ONUC), was the bloodiest UN peacekeeping operation ever undertaken. The UN was dragged into a multifaceted civil conflict that claimed the lives of nearly 200 peacekeepers in hostile action, while the UN Secretary-General, Dag Hammarskjöld, died in a plane crash.

As chief of staff, Colonel Mobutu seized the opportunity to take power. He first attacked the existing political and social institutions. The Prime Minister, Patrice Lumumba, was assassinated in January 1961 and the President, Joseph Kasa-Vubu, was removed from power in November 1965. Mobutu's junta was quickly transformed into absolute personal rule. His power was such that 'he could do anything his heart desired':

> He seized expatriate-owned small and medium enterprises and disbursed them to members of the Congolese élite in 1973; and he encouraged the latter to plunder the public treasury and state enterprises, which made them into the most voracious 'kleptocracy' on the African continent. He used his ill-gotten wealth and his powers of patronage to outfox potential opponents and to keep wavering officials in line. (Nzongola and Green: 1993: 1002)

Mobutu made his coup and ruled until 1990 with full political, military and financial support from Western powers. During the Cold War period, Northern Americans and Western Europeans used Mobutu to fight communism and Soviet expansionism in Africa. He also facilitated their campaigns against the Islamisation of Uganda and Southern Sudan. These political and ideological motives were accompanied by economic objectives, mainly exploitation of raw materials. When the Cold War ended Mobutu's security services for Western interests became obsolete, and the US finally cut off military assistance to the Mobutu regime in 1991. The Congolese opposition and civil society organisations took advantage of the weakening power of Mobutu to launch the Sovereign National Conference (La Conférence Nationale Souveraine – CNS) in 1991. This initiated the first post-indepedence democratisation process, a process that was interrupted by Laurent Kabila's military intervention.

Kabila's seizure of power in May 1997 is generally regarded as a revolution. An internal, regional and international consensus against Mobutu's regime blessed the movement and credited it with some kind of legitimacy even though it undermined the ongoing democratisation process initiated by the National Conference. At its onset, Kabila's presidency was popularly accepted and recognised by the majority of the Congolese, including the military. Elements of the Zaïrian armed forces – Forces Armées Zaïroïses (FAZ) and Mobutu's Division Spéciale Presidentiale (Presidential Special Division (DSP)) joined the masses in welcoming Kabila and the ADFL when they entered Kinshasa.

However, the change of regime threatened the jobs of about 50,000 soldiers. Disarmament, demobilisation and demilitarisation required substantial resources and appropriate strategies, which were not forthcoming. The situation required integration and unification of the three internal armies – the FAZ, the DSP and the ADFL – into the newly formed Forces Armées Congolaises (Congolese Armed Forces (FAC)). Compensation for Rwandan and Ugandan military services also needed to be treated as a national problem, not as a concern for the ADFL alone. An attractive retirement package could have been used for a smooth process of downsizing the armed forces while favourable inducements could have led to the formation of a national army of dedicated professionals or volunteers. Many FAZ soldiers expected adequate retirement compensation after many years of unpaid service. The DSP soldiers were disoriented by the unexpected disruption of their command and leadership structure and were more open to retirement than to integration into an ADFL-dominated army. Most ADFL soldiers were under 18 years of age and were nicknamed *kadogo*, Swahili for 'little kids'. The majority of the *kadogo* soldiers were rural youth who joined the army in search of salaried employment. The Banyamulenge (Congolese Tutsi) branch of the ADFL was predominantly made up of young peasants commanded by Rwandan and Ugandan officers. The situation was complex. However, it would have been manageable had it been well planned and effectively sponsored.

The ADFL regime of Laurent Kabila was beset with tensions, however, especially over the role of Uganda and Rwanda. The ADFL soldiers and leaders disagreed on modalities of compensation and the termination of the deployment of Rwandan and Ugandan troops in Congo. Rwanda and Uganda reportedly expected long-term involvement and substantial rewards. Former FAZ and DSP soldiers resented the Rwandan and Ugandan presence in the Congo. They feared being discarded by the new government without compensation.

Tensions also emerged over the desire of the UN to investigate the massacres of Hutu refugees and other human rights violations allegedly committed by the ADFL Tutsi soldiers and the Rwandan forces on their way to Kinshasa. The government opposed the UN investigation in order to protect ADFL and Rwandan suspects. Thereafter, the UN and the international community suspended their cooperation with and support for the ADFL government. Proposed reconstruction programmes collapsed owing to a lack of funds.

Congolese opposition parties took advantage of the ADFL crisis. They attempted to mobilise the local population and former FAZ and DSP soldiers against the ADFL and its foreign sponsors. The government responded by banning political parties. In the absence of political parties, geopolitical solidarity emerged. Katanganese leaders and youth mobilised political support for Kabila, expecting senior positions in government as rewards. The mobilisation also succeeded because of the linguistic divide between Lingala speakers (western Congo) and Swahili speakers (eastern Congo), and because of a coalition of easterners established to shift power from the west (which had been Mobutu's power base) to the east (Kabila's power base). Geo-linguistic divisions also affected the military and politicians. Prior to Kabila, Lingala was the language of the army and the government, the symbol of power, and the main instrument of political, military and strategic communication. Geo-linguistic tensions retarded the formation of the national army and the police, both of which Congo needed urgently to combat aggression, to control insurgencies and to reduce long-term dependence on military assistance from Rwanda, Uganda and the Southern African Development Community (SADC).

These crises transformed the Congo into a centre for acute division, intrigue and exploitation (Masire 2000). The crisis was marked by widespread and systematic human rights violations, including mass killings, rape and the destruction of property (Friman 2000). All foreign forces contend that they are present for border security and/or humanitarian reasons. This was probably the case when Angola, Chad, Namibia and Zimbabwe first sent troops to help the Congolese government protect its sovereignty and the liberties and rights of its defenceless peoples. Rwanda, Burundi and Uganda had some security concerns related to Congo's lack of capability to neutralise dissidents or rebels. But later, the need to finance these military and political activities added economic interests that were incompatible with the military and political objectives of the 1996–7 campaign against Mobutu's dictatorship. In this sense, the Lusaka Peace Accord (LPA) constitutes a corrective attempt to bring about sustainable democracy, peace and development in Congo.

Although its members had unanimously supported Laurent Kabila's armed rebellion against Mobutu's government in 1996–7, by 1998 SADC was divided. Angola, Namibia and Zimbabwe opted to continue supporting Kabila's government both politically and militarily, while South Africa and others did not. The supportive states seem to have been motivated by two factors. First, they feared that the events in Congo would create a poor precedent for the defence of their own sovereignty and regimes. Second, their participation in the 1996–7 operations against Mobutu gave them the advantage of knowing that the 1998 crisis was one between Kabila, Kagame (of Rwanda) and Museveni (of Uganda), rather than a genocidal campaign against Tutsi minorities, as portrayed by the Western media.

The Lusaka Peace Accord

This human tragedy and security impasse obliged the international community to initiate the Lusaka Peace Accord (LPA), signed by the

Congolese government, the two main rebel movements operating at that time, and the governments of Uganda, Rwanda, Zimbabwe, Angola and Namibia on 10 July 1999. The signing was mediated by Zambia's president, Frederick Chiluba, and was witnessed by the UN, the Organisation of African Unity and SADC. The LPA gave rise to the Mission de l'Organisation des Nations Unies au Congo (MONUC), a UN Security Council-mandated peacekeeping operation aimed at implementing the LPA.

The peace accord aimed to sensitise all the parties involved in the conflict to the need for an immediate ceasefire, dialogue, reconciliation, the restoration of the rule of law and common security. Its four main points are as follows:

The sovereignty and territorial integrity of the Congo and of all the surrounding states. The LPA does not condemn the Rwandan and Ugandan intervention but it does discourage future aggression and recognises the authority of the central government in Kinshasa.

The imperative of attaining peace through credible political negotiations that lead to a new political dispensation and a true national reconciliation. The peace process will derive its credibility from an inter-Congolese dialogue to be organised under the aegis of a neutral (external) facilitator acceptable to all parties. Foreign political assistance is necessary.

As Wolpe rightly contends:

> There is little institutional capacity, little sense of a coherent national political community, little uniting infrastructure, and no individual or movement with a national political constituency ... [there is] fragmentation, decay, economic collapse, the institutionalisation of corruption, and the erosion of bonds of trust among Congolese and between the Congolese and their government. (Wolpe 2000: 29)

Without the establishment of inclusive, competent, accountable and credible transitional institutions, current peace initiatives may not be sufficient to prevent future insecurities and vulnerabilities in a region where coups and wars have been wielded as a means of accessing state power and resources.

The LPA initially focused on securing a ceasefire and on power sharing between the government and the rebel leaders. The focus later shifted from power sharing to the search for appropriate governance principles and structures. The participation of civil society and non-armed opposition organisations was accepted.

Affirmation of the need to deal with common security concerns by halting any assistance to and collaboration with negative forces by controlling the cross-border illicit trafficking of arms and infiltration of armed groups. Interpretation of the concept 'negative forces', as articulated in the LPA, has evolved. Initially, Rwandan *genocidaires* and any armed groups opposing or fighting Burundian, Rwandan and Ugandan forces in Congo were called negative forces. Congolese rebels fighting Kabila's forces were implicitly considered positive forces. Currently, the term 'negative forces' refers to any group involved in any human rights violations, mass killings and crimes against humanity. All armed groups are urged to respect the Convention on the Prevention and Punishment of the Crime of Genocide (1948 and 1951) and the Geneva Convention IV relative to the Protection of Civilian Persons in Time of War (1950). All governments are requested to recognise and communicate with rebels and opposition parties in their countries.

The need for disarmament of all armed groups and the formation of a national army. A Joint Military Commission (JMC) was formed and tasked to facilitate the attainment of this objective with the assistance of the UN/OAU. The initial intention of the LPA was only to disarm forces other than FAC, the Rassemblement Congolais pour la Democratie (RCD, Congolese Rally for Democracy) and the Mouvement de Libération du Congo (MLC), all of whom are signatories to the peace accord. Non-signatory armed groups were considered negative forces. It appears that the expression was used to confer a legitimacy on the RCD and the MLC and to institute a *de facto* partition of the Congo into three probable independent states. Most Congolese refer to this scenario as 'the international conspiracy for *de facto* partition of the Congo'. This conspiracy is explained as originating from rivalry between France, the USA and China. While the USA and its ally Britain back Rwanda and Uganda, who created the RCD and the MLC to fight Laurent Kabila's regime, France and China have been supporting Kabila. In the last instance, many Congolese believe that the economies of all the permanent members of the UN Security Council benefit from the Congo war. The Congo is transformed into a market for arms and a source of materials such as minerals and timber that primarily benefit the peoples and economies of industrialised countries. This situation has prevented the international community from dealing with the humanitarian crisis from which the Congolese people, especially women and children in rural areas, have unjustly suffered following the Rwandan and Ugandan invasion (which has never been condemned by the international community).

This scenario constitutes the single major factor that helped Laurent Kabila's government to mobilise national and African opinion against a possible strategic outcome of the LPA whereby the southern, western and central provinces would be administered by the government of the DRC and the FAC with the military and strategic support of the Angolan and Zimbabwean armed forces; the northern provinces would be administered by the MLC with Ugandan support; and the eastern provinces would fall under the RCD, with support from the Rwandan and Burundian armed forces.

The security complex in the Congo and especially in the northern and eastern provinces was further complicated by a rapid growth of the Mai-Mai resistance, ideological crises in the RCD and MLC leadership, hostilities between Ugandan and Rwandan forces, and the systematic plunder of Congolese natural resources. Currently, an estimated 85 per cent of the rural northern and eastern territories are occupied by 22 active rebel organisations (Potgieter 2001). Elements of these armed groups are also active in major towns.

Since early 2000, there have been fewer military confrontations. War continues in the form of psychological warfare and human suffering continues owing to deprivation of basic commodities, utilities and liberties. The Joint Military Commission created by the LPA has been operational since 1999. Its headquarters moved from Lusaka, Zambia, to Kinshasa in January 2002. The JMC has supervised the progressive withdrawal of Namibian, Ugandan, Rwandan and Zimbabwean troops from key strategic towns in the central, northern and eastern provinces, creating space for the deployment of MONUC peacekeepers. Sir Sekumire Masire, the UN facilitator of the Inter-Congolese Dialogue, and former president of Botswana, facilitated several preparatory meetings, which established a comprehensive agenda for the actual dialogue which began in South Africa in February 2002. The agenda centred on four major issues: the composition of the transitional government, the problem of nationality, the composition of the army, and the electoral process. Interestingly, all these achievements occurred under Joseph Kabila, who took power after the assassination of his father Laurent Kabila on 16 January 2001.

Despite the relative progress in implementing the LPA, social and human conditions have deteriorated rapidly. Life expectancy at birth has been reduced to 52 years. The impact of war on the environment and the people has been disastrous. Minerals and timber are savagely exploited, game has fled, and landmines are a threat to humans and animals. About 200,000 landmines have been placed in the central and eastern Congo and are likely to hinder any post-war reconstruction initiatives. The destruction of habitat and the violation of human rights have been extreme. The International Rescue Committee (IRC), led by US epidemiologist Dr Lees Roberts, reported to the US government that

Table 11.1 Implementation of the Lusaka Peace Accord (as at January 2002)

	Measures	Level of achievement
1	Cessation of hostilities	Satisfactory
2	Disengagement	Satisfactory
3	Release of hostages and exchange of prisoners of war	Satisfactory
4	Orderly withdrawal of all foreign forces	Satisfactory
5	National dialogue and reconciliation	Satisfactory
6	Reestablishment of state administration over the territory of Congo	Subject to 5
7	Constitution of the Joint Military Commission	Satisfactory
8	Deployment of the UN peacekeeping mandate	Satisfactory
9	Disarmament of armed groups	Subject to 4, 5, 7 and 8
10	Formation of a national army	Subject to 9
11	Redeployment of the forces of the parties to defensive positions in conflict zones	Satisfactory
12	Normalisation of the security situation along the common borders between Congo and its neighbours	Subject to 10

the results of a mortality survey showed that there were 1.7 million deaths in Kivu province (eastern Congo) between August 1998 (when Rwanda and Uganda invaded the country) and May 2000. This equates to 77,000 deaths per month. About 34 per cent of these were of children younger than five years of age. Of the violent deaths reported, 47 per cent were those of women and children.

War has displaced about six million inhabitants of the Great Lakes region. There are 700,000 Ugandans in internment camps for the internally displaced inside Uganda; 400,000 Rwandans in internment camps inside Rwanda; 500,000 Burundians in camps in Burundi; and two to three million displaced eastern Congolese. About 1.5 million Congolese, Burundian and Rwandan refugees are in Tanzania. Only state and interstate interventions can deal effectively with such a severe security crisis and a human disaster of these proportions.

It is for these reasons that one of the LPA's priorities is the rehabilitation of state capacity, including the creation of a professional army, the organisation and training of a professional police service, the institutionalisation of the rule of law, the reestablishment of state administration throughout the national territory, the creation of a sound macro-economic environment and a transparent and accountable bureaucracy.

Withdrawal of foreign forces and disarmament of armed groups

The withdrawal of foreign forces from the Congo also includes the Angolan, Namibian and Zimbabwean armies. Namibian forces have completely withdrawn. Rwandan, Ugandan and Zimbabwean forces have pulled back.

However, the northern and eastern Congolese provinces are still a refuge for the Rwandan, Burundian and Ugandan rebels who are fighting to return to their countries and take power by force. The dilemma, however, is that it is difficult to rebuke Burundian, Rwandan and Ugandan rebels without rebuking Congolese rebels who are fighting to seize power in the Congo with official military and political assistance from Burundi, Rwanda and Uganda. Keen argues that the apparent chaos of civil war can be used to further local, short-term interests. War in the Great Lakes region has increasingly become the continuation of economics by other means, a way of creating an alternative system of profit, power and protection (Keen 1998: 11).

The military–security situation is currently characterised not only by the dynamics of government, rebel, commercial and foreign forces but also by a complex civil resistance (militia) movement called the Mai-Mai, which constitutes a major security concern – that of civilian armed combatants. The Mai-Mai claim supernatural protection against bullets, a simple marketing artifice often used for motivating new recruits and to provide combat charisma. Prah (1999: 47) ranks the Mai-Mai in the category of 'types of social expression which were manifested as cults, secret societies, millenarian and messianic movements ... sometimes combined with military activity'. The Mai-Mai resistance is growing quickly in eastern and northern Congo, and distances itself from all other belligerents including government forces, although it remains essentially an anti-Rwanda movement.

Even assuming all foreign forces withdraw, the task of disarming and demobilising the plethora of armed groups operating in Congo, and engaged in a variety of struggles within Congolese territory and in neighbouring countries, will be immense.

Potgieter has identified at least 22 armed parties currently influencing the security situation in the eastern and northern Congo and the Great Lakes region (Potgieter 2001). The main groups are:

The *Armée Nationale Congolaise (ANC)* is the military wing of RCD–Goma. It has about 17,000 to 20,000 armed men made up of dissident ADFL Rwandans and FAC units which were stationed in the eastern Congo in 1998. They are the principal allies of Rwanda, but are reputed to be highly undisciplined and unreliable in combat.

The *Armée de Libération Congolaise (ALC)* is the military wing of the MLC. The force is composed of about 9,000 soldiers including former FAZ and DSP soldiers and defectors from the armed forces of Congo–Brazzaville. The ALC mainly recruits from the northwestern provinces and relies on Mobutu's former armies and intelligence circles, with substantial military and political assistance from Uganda.

The *Congolese People's Army* is the military wing of the RCD–Kisangani. The group first seceded from the RCD–Goma. It was absorbed by the MLC and later seceded from it. The group strives to build alliances with the Congolese government, the Mai-Mai and Uganda against the Rwanda-sponsored RCD–Goma. Similar attempts occasioned military confrontations between Rwandan and Ugandan forces in Kisangani in April 2000.

The *Mai-Mai* fighters are difficult to number because they are often disguised and use guerrilla tactics. The Mai-Mai resistance has been so effective in eastern and northern Congo that all the groups want to incorporate them into their military formations.

The *Front de Libération Nationale du Katanga/Congo (FLNK/C)* is a group of about 5,000 former Katangese *gendarmes* who exiled themselves in Angola following the defeat of the Katanga provincial government's secession bid in 1960–2. As part of the Angolan army, they joined the ADFL in 1997 and played a critical role in defeating Mobutu in Kinshasa. They demand independence or greater autonomy for the Katanga province and control over its mining industry. After 1998, some FLNK/C leaders and soldiers joined the rebellion against President Kabila and became close allies of Rwanda.

The *Union pour la République* (*UPR*) – Union for the Republic – is a movement of neo-Mobutuists mainly composed of a few former FAZ soldiers from the Equateur Province. They claim to have a military wing but remain inactive on the ground.

The *Union des Nationalistes Républicains pour la Libération (UNAREL)* is sponsored by rich former generals from Mobutu's regime who are in exile abroad. UNAREL leaders continue campaigning against Kabila's regime abroad, especially in Europe and Canada.

The *Front de Libération Contre l'Occupation du Territoire (FLOT)* is a political and military movement that has been fighting the Tutsi presence in South Kivu since 1977. FLOT is currently consolidating its military capabilities.

Alliance pour la Résistance Démocratique (ARD) is a political movement grouping Congolese, Rwandan, Burundian and Ugandan rebel forces opposing Tutsi hegemony in the Congo and in the region.

The *Forces Républiques et Fédéralistes (FRF)* are mainly composed of dissident Banyamulenge (Congolese Tutsis). They seceded from the RCD–Goma, which is dominated by Rwandan Tutsis who, apparently, do not represent their interests.

The *Interahamwe* consists of about 12,000 to 15,000 mainly extremist armed Hutu militia, who are presumed responsible for the Rwandan genocide and who support their operations through mining gold which they sell through Congolese middlemen. They sometimes combine their operations with the former members of the FAR (see below). They are poorly equipped and lack regular supplies.

The *False Interahamwe* are Hutu groups commanded by Tutsi leaders targeting local communities and health facilities in order to create instability around Rwandan military posts.

The *former Forces Armées Rwandaises (FAR)* are former members of the Rwandan army, estimated to be 15,000 to 20,000 strong. They are mainly Hutu and were defeated by the Front Patriotique Rwanda (RPF, Rwandan Patriotic Front) in 1994. Together with the Interahamwe, they form the *Armée du Libération du Rwanda*. They are well trained and organised and are known for carrying out *ad hoc* cross-border operations into Rwanda.

The *Allied Democratic Front (ADF)* has about 600 to 1,000 men, was established by the Tabliq Moslem sect, and is commanded by Taban Amin, a son of the former Uganda dictator Idi Amin Dada. The ADF operates in the Ruwenzori Mountains area in Congo and in Kampala and southwestern Uganda.

The *National Army for the Liberation of Uganda (NALU)* mainly operates from eastern Congo into western Uganda.

The *Front Rebel de Libération Nationale (FLN)* is a military branch of the Partie pour la Libération des Peuples Hutu. Its 7,000 to 10,000 (mainly Hutu) soldiers operate in Burundi using hit-and-run guerrilla tactics. The FLN has considerable popular support in western and northern Burundi and among the Burundian refugees in camps in eastern Congo and western Tanzania.

The *Forces pour la Défence de la Démocratie (FDD)* is a military wing of the Conseil National pour la Défense de la Démocratie. The FDD has about 30,000 combatants in the field who use guerrilla attacks on strategic targets such as electricity installations, ambushes on communications routes and military targets to destabilise the Tutsi-dominated government in Burundi. The FDD is active in southwestern Burundi.

The *Forças Armadas de Liberação de Angola (FALA)* is the military branch of the Angolan rebel movement UNITA. The number of FALA soldiers based in Congo is unknown. The FALA works closely with Ugandan and Rwandan soldiers and with Bamboo's Movement for the Liberation of the Congo in the eastern, northern and southern provinces.

The *Frente de Liberação do Enclave de Cabinda (FLEC)* has a military wing called the Armed Forces of Cabinda with a capacity of about 600 men. The FLEC has been trying to secede from Angola since the 1960s. Securing Cabinda appears to be one of the strategic reasons for the Angolan government's support to the post-Mobutu Congolese government.

With the exception of the Mai-Mai, all these groups are characterised by three major tendencies:

- to restructure and transform themselves into political–military organisations;
- to expand on the basis of ethnic affinity and/or affiliation;
- to establish alliances with larger groups that have strong political, military or economic connections with foreign countries.

Most of these groupings lack sustainability, legitimacy and credibility. They constitute short-term responses to the LPA, and a temporary way through which their leaders can gain potential access to central government offices and powers. In the long run, most of the Congolese groups are likely to disappear as the implementation of the LPA creates space for the integration of armed and unarmed opposition and civil society into government. Political employment constitutes the one single objective of all these groupings: the Mobutu experience has persuaded Congolese that political employment pays better than any other jobs in the market.

A failed state

The withdrawal of all foreign armies is likely to exacerbate the security situation in the Congo if alternative military assistance is not provided immediately. Congo needs both time and external assistance before it will be able to rebuild and equip its self-defence and peacekeeping capacity.

Failing states are security-deficient states. Congo is today a vulnerable country. The defence and security sector is disorganised and disempowered. As previously discussed, until 2000, about ten thousand Zimbabwean and Angolan soldiers were protecting the southern, western and central territories. The same foreign forces protect the central government and Kinshasa. In the northern and eastern territories Rwandan and Ugandan efforts to create dissident states and install parallel governments have failed. The Congo is thus facing what Hendrickson (1999: 29) refers to as 'a dysfunctional security situation' characterised by a political and administrative vacuum created by a significant deterioration in the state's capacity to deliver services.

In fact, in the Congo the state started collapsing in the 1970s. Most provinces and rural areas were operated under Mobutu's tax collectors and commission agents. Their main task was not to administer these regions, but rather to mobilise monies, diamonds and gold and transfer them to the president through a chain of intermediaries who were often rewarded with spoils or with government posts. State institutions were systematically and deliberately destroyed to allow for this kleptocratic accumulation. For instance, the national system of posts, telecommunications and air transport was neutralised because of the extremely lucrative commissions and shares offered to private cellular telephone and airline companies. The privatisation of the information, communication and transportation sector served to cover up continued kleptocratic transfers. In addition, 'privatised'[3] soldiers reporting directly to Mobutu's personal commissioners often protected these ill-gotten gains. Military officers and soldiers who were not members of the Mobutu mafia were disarmed, demilitarised and marginalised. A Civil Guard division was formed in 1993 to institutionalise the mafia.

Underlying much of the current collapse in the Congo are two parallel developments. First, a decline in the economic sector (much of it attributable to ineffective state institutions); and, second, a lack of confidence in the political institutions that were inherited from the colonial powers and never reformed beyond the relatively superficial act of deracialisation. Hyden (2000: 11–12) views state collapse as occurring when:

- people have lost confidence in the public realm, which becomes a very insecure place;
- rules have become more and more arbitrary and participation in public affairs is often associated with personal risk and loss;

- the state no longer fulfils the role of protector of life; and
- local vigilante groups emerge to carry out the tasks that (in a functioning state) belong to the police and other security organs.

Congo remains vulnerable to any threat or attack, be it military, political or economic. The sole hope is that the country can utilise its substantial natural resources and economic opportunities in a way that will speed up recovery. The Congo is bankrupt but not insolvent.[4] It will be able to pay its debts if peace is restored, if the country is better organised, if patriotism increases, and if democratic institutions are established to enhance the rule of law. In fact, the Congo has many commercial and diplomatic relations that can be translated into critical political and economic resources. Before mineral exports started falling in 1986, the copper, cobalt, zinc and diamond exports of state-run firms generated $1.15 billion in the formal economy that year. Coffee provided an additional $80 million. The profits from underground businesses – money laundering, cross-border trafficking, etcetera – are often not counted, although they net some two to three times more than official (declared) figures. MacGaffey (1991) calls it the 'real economy' of the Congo. He contends that the actual size of Congo's economy may be as much as three times that of its current official gross domestic product (GDP). Cilliers and Dietrich associate lower popular pressure for democratic change in countries like Congo with the culture of chronic political disengagement occasioned by this extensive informal, and often illegal (dis)economy. They argue that the latter 'keeps the disastrous national economy going, contrary to mainstream thinking that sees the informal sector economy as an adjunct to the formal sector' (Cilliers and Dietrich 2000: 11).

Congo's total external debt is currently estimated at $15 billion, equivalent to about 255 per cent of its GNP. Since the civil disturbances of 1991, private investment has all but ceased. The outbreak of civil war has caused a continued rise in inflation. The need to finance the war effort has also prompted the government to stop repaying its debt arrears to the International Monetary Fund. Insufficient revenues and its inability to borrow internationally have forced the government to mortgage the country's future heavily in exchange for military as well as monetary support. Leases of strategic mineral and oil reserves are likely to continue being distributed to foreigners who support the country's war effort.

This manner of financing conflict does not bring about peace and it does not promote the national economy. The strategy also fails to improve the morale and conditions of service of Congolese soldiers. Consequently, the combat performance of government soldiers is inefficient and they suffer from low morale. On the other side, the rebel groups have so far failed to form any kind of cohesive and professional army. Rebel soldiers are unpaid and earn money by extorting from local populations and by providing security services to foreign mining and timber companies. These groups strive to forge political and military alliances in support of or in opposition to the foreign armies fighting against government forces. However, most of the alliances and coalitions do not last long as they lack both legitimacy and local support.

Border security, common security

The partition of Congo into small states or the wider geopolitical reconfiguration of the territorial boundaries of the Central African states is not necessarily conducive to achieving sustainable peace and security.

State collapse in Africa results from the inability to build and consolidate nation states as structured by the Berlin Conference of 1884–5. Dismantling the existing territorial configurations is, however, not the solution since people have *learned* since then to be Burundians, Congolese, Rwandans, Tanzanians, Ugandans, South Africans, etcetera. Africa does not need to dismantle its borders. The cases of Rwanda and Burundi clearly demonstrate that a small territory and cultural homogeneity are not necessarily the key factors in preventing conflict. In reality, Congo, like many other African countries, suffers from undemocratic leadership, the inefficient management of people and their fundamental needs and liberties. Nation building can promote effective leadership and the management of peoples and resources if the process involves mechanisms that integrate change, innovation, adaptation, and so on. Nation-state formation in Africa did not fail because of territorial divisions. Rather, a lack of intra- and inter-state change management strategies seems to explain why African states are so vulnerable to all manner of external and internal threats and attacks.

Unlike Breytenbach, I tend to disagree with the view that 'had the boundaries of the eastern Belgian Congo and western Rwanda and Burundi been drawn differently during the colonial carve-up, the present instability might have been avoided' (Breytenbach 1999: 99). Kemmichi Ohmae's idea of a 'borderless world' (1990) is also inappropriate, as Nossal (1998: 248) points out:

> Such a characterisation might be appropriate to describe (and understand) how some factors of production move across borders in a 'border-

less' way in the contemporary economy, but it bears little relationship to the world of borders encountered by at least one factor of production – people.

It is my view that territorial borders will continue to determine the political and economic reality of modern states. Short-term violations (such as raids and snatches) or long-term violations (such as seizures and invasions) of territorial integrity offend not only states but also ultimately, the people who occupy those states.

Militarist opposition

Sustainable peace and security demands the promotion of democratic practices and values. Opposition in the Congo tends to be undemocratic and militarist. Many opposition parties in Congo believe that their purpose is to destabilise and weaken the government. Yet the aim of good politics should be to improve or perfect government, not destroy it. Opposition and civil society should exist and operate for better government, for better public choice and service delivery. Thus undemocratic violent opposition and an opportunistic civil society are also responsible for the political impasse in Congo.

In fact, the Congo has a significant number of active political parties and many civil society organisations. Both groups played a vital role in the democratisation process which was disrupted in 1996 and 1998. Government, political parties, churches and other influential civil society and business organisations were all involved. Unfortunately, the process had already been hijacked by opportunistic opposition groups and non-governmental organisations whose main objective was to remove Mobutu from power but maintain his kleptocratic system.

The current war is characterised by the same power struggle. Military organisations or armed groups have been created to seize and retain power. Defending the nation, maintaining law and order, securing people and their property do not seem to be a priority. Those who already have power organise private or tribal armies to maintain control of the government and those who are outside the government system organise private armies to seize control. We are currently witnessing an unprecedented abuse of military organisations. The Congo needs to urgently review or redefine the role, functions and responsibilities of national defence and the security sector. National security thinking is presently dictated by the logic of military threats and vulnerabilities occasioned by heavily armed neighbours with a history of aggression. The Congo needs a professional national army to act as a deterrent, one that is disciplined, well trained and well equipped for self-defence and peacekeeping.

It is my firm belief that sustainable peace also requires the existence of responsible and mature opposition political groups. Currently opposition parties in the Congo have demonstrated an insufficient degree of political maturity and responsibility, and can thus be better understood in the context of lobbying interest groups. Four critical lobbying groups feature on the current political landscape:

- The Afrocentric Lumumbist lobby, which is highly respected by the majority but is dominated by academics.
- The 'change for change' lobby, based on the idea of power rotation and strongly influenced by ethnicity and geopolitical ideology.
- The Mobutist barons, who constitute over 90 per cent of the Congolese high-income class. This class reportedly holds capital outside the country valued at double the country's annual GDP, excluding Mobutu's personal wealth. Most of them identify with Jean Pierre Bemba's rebellion movement.
- The 'Euro-sympathisers' lobby, a group of people nostalgic for pre-independence economic conditions and Western models. Semi-literate youth, professionals, the aged and peasants dominate this lobby.

In brief, governance, opposition groupings, economy, defence and security have all broken down in the Congo, which is currently vulnerable to any kind of threat or attack. The solution is to enhance internal capacity to manage people and respond to their demands for change and innovation. As Godsell (1997: 32–3) argues, value is added and wealth is created not by cabinets and ministers and not by national leaders and national plans, but by a myriad of individual actions performed by a myriad of individual entrepreneurs. Parliament can make laws and the courts can enforce them. Politicians can make proposals, but, in the end, it is the people on the street who dispose of or reinforce laws by their actions and attitudes. Unfortunately, this category of people is often excluded from conventional peace-making processes. The Lusaka Peace Agreement is no exception.

Conclusion

This chapter has shown how vulnerable the Congo is, its vulnerability exacerbated by greed and a kleptocratic culture. As Bronowski argues:

> War, organised war, is not a human instinct. It is a highly planned and cooperative form of theft. And that form of theft began ten thousand years ago when the harvesters of wheat accumulated a surplus, and the nomads rose out of the desert to rob them of what they themselves could not provide. (In Leeds 1987: 81)

What is happening in the Great Lakes region is organised theft and, unfortunately, the Congolese and other Africans are the main culprits.

I have also tried to dismiss the argument that blames the enormous size of the Congo for the current crisis. Of greater importance is the internal capacity to manage, optimise and protect internal assets. Instead of striving to divide the Congo into several small territories, the focus should rather be on building the capacity of the Congolese people and their leaders to manage, develop and defend their country and its resources. Nations will always seek independent states or geopolitical entities with distinctive sovereignty and boundaries. Boundaries serve not only to safeguard independence and sovereignty but also to protect resources and the wealth generated by the exercise of that independence and sovereignty.

The current insecurity in Congo is related to both state and market failures. Peace making and peace building cannot be achieved without both the state and the market. The survivalist economies (where most people took refuge) are becoming responsible for the insecurity and disorganisation that currently devastate the country. Survivalists, warlords and illicit arms suppliers share underground networks and markets that fuel war, violence and instability. Peace-building measures should aim at rehabilitating and consolidating development institutions in the public and private sectors. The formation of a professional national army is of paramount importance.

Africa and the world need a stronger, peaceful and more productive Congo. A failing Congo is a threat to regional and global security. However, this trend is unlikely to reverse unless the Congolese élite and its people decide to learn from this experience and choose to become the masters and leaders of their own destiny, development and security. They possess all the natural resources and economic opportunities to achieve this goal. State failure in this case may be a question of human failure.

References

Breytenbach, W. (1999) 'The history and destiny of national minorities in the African Renaissance: the case for better boundaries', in Makgoba, M. W. (ed.), *African Renaissance. The New Struggle*, Cape Town: Mafube–Tafelberg.

Cilliers, J. and C. Dietrich (eds.) (2000) *Angola's War Economy: the Role of Oil and Diamonds*, Pretoria: Institute for Security Studies.

Emizet, K. N. F. (2000) 'Explaining the rise and fall of military regimes: civil–military relations in the Congo', *Armed Forces and Society* (Winter).

Friman, H. (2001) 'The Democratic Republic of Congo: justice in the aftermath of peace', *African Security Review*, 10 (3).

Godsell, B. (1997) 'Six strategies for African development', in Rimmer, D. (ed.), *Action in Africa. The Experience of People Involved in Government, Business and Aid*, London: Royal African Society, James Currey and Heinemann.

Hendrickson, D. (1999) *A Review of Security-Sector Reform*, London: Centre for Defence Studies Working Papers.

Hyden, G. (2000). 'The governance challenge in Africa', in Hyden, G. *et al.* (eds.), *African Perspectives on Governance*, New Jersey: African World Press.

Keen, D. (1998) 'The economic functions of violence in civil wars', Adelphi Paper 320, International Institute for Strategic Studies.

Leeds, C. (1987) *Peace and War*, England: Stanley Thomas.

MacGaffey, J. (1991) *The Real Economy of Zaïre*, London: James Currey.

Masire, K. (2001) 'The Lusaka Agreement. Prospects for peace in the DRC', *African Security Review*, 10 (1).

Nossal, K. R. (1998) *The Patterns of World Politics*, Ontario: Prentice-Hall.

Nzongolo-Ntalaja G. and D. A. Green (1993) 'Ex-Zaïre', in Krieger *et al.* (eds.), *The Oxford Companion to Politics of the World*, New York: Oxford University Press.

Potgieter, J. (2001) *Armed Groups Affecting Peace Process in Congo*, Pretoria: Safer Africa Archives.

Prah, K. K. (1999) 'African Renaissance or wardlordism', in Makgoba, M. W. (ed.), *African Renaissance. The New Struggle*, Cape Town: Mafube–Talelberg.

Seybolt, T. B. (2000) 'The war in the Democratic Republic of Congo', in Stockholm International Peace Research Institute (SIPRI) Yearbook, *Armaments, Disarmament and International Security*, Oxford: Oxford University Press.

Smith, C. (1988) *The Law of Insolvency*, Durban: Butterworths.

UN Expert Commission on the Congo Plunder, *Report S2001*, 357, April 2001.

Wolpe, H. (2000). 'The Great Lakes crisis: an American view', *South African Journal of International Affairs*, 7 (1) (Summer).

Zartman, I. W. (ed.) (1995) *Collapsed States: the Disintegration and Restoration of Legitimate Authority*, Boulder, Colorado: Lynne Rienner.

Notes

1 The Great Lakes region refers essentially to the countries that form the Economic Community of the Great Lakes Countries (CEPGL): Burundi,

Rwanda and the Democratic Republic of Congo (the former Zaïre). But the term has generally been extended to include the Republic of the Congo (Congo–Brazzaville), Tanzania and Uganda.

2 Throughout this article the terms 'Congolese' and 'the Congo' refer to the Democratic Republic of Congo and not to the Republic of the Congo (Congo–Brazzaville).

3 The term 'privatised soldiers' refers to the use of regular soldiers or security forces for private activities.

4 Insolvency does not imply an inability to pay debts but rather a situation in which one's liabilities exceed one's assets (Smith 1988).

12

In Whose Interest Is Security Sector Reform? *Lessons from the Balkans*

SUSAN L. WOODWARD

The end of the Cold War ordering of international politics and security created a global opportunity to shift resources from national defence to economic development and social welfare. But in some parts of the world this shift entailed far more than levels and sectoral targets of public expenditure. In south-eastern Europe, not only security structures but entire systems of government, economy and society had been structured around particular strategies of national defence for conditions that ceased to exist. International and regional security regimes and allies, socialist economies and one-party rule had to be transformed all at once. This was particularly the case of Albania and the former Yugoslavia, which had devised foreign relations, economic policies, political structures, and social relations to support a policy of military self-reliance outside the two Cold War military blocs. But it was also the case of Romania, which had tended more toward such independence after 1958 than not, with corresponding foreign and domestic policies, and of Bulgaria and Moldova, which had domestic systems completely defined by incorporation into a larger security environment (the Warsaw Pact or the Soviet Union) that had disappeared overnight.

This chapter examines the consequences when the conditions of both external and internal security differ from those on which donor-driven programmes of security sector reform and democratic accountability are based.

Preconditions of security sector reform

The experience of south-eastern Europe in the first post-Cold War decade suggests there are two elements necessary to security sector reform, neither of which has been present in the region thus far. The first is the lesson of South Africa: the vital spark of fundamental internal political change to generate domestic interest in transforming the security sector and demilitarising state, economy and society. In no cases in south-eastern Europe had that special set of political conditions emerged by the end of 2001. While democratic accountability of security structures is not conceivable without democratisation, this pre-condition is not sufficient to generate domestic demands for reform. In fact, the process of democratisation can generate greater insecurity and a larger role for security forces of all kinds (Snyder 2000).

The second element is an external environment of relative security that makes both democracy and security sector reform possible. For many countries, including all of those in south-eastern Europe, the end of the Cold War created greater insecurity because its structure of international security collapsed and was not replaced by anything new. The result, at one extreme, was the violent break-up of the former Socialist Federal Republic of Yugoslavia, beginning in 1991 but not complete a decade later, and the regional instability and disruption that its wars and international response to those wars created. That regional instability then prevented what should have been a normal process, necessary to democratic consolidation, of establishing new trade and security relations for Romania, Bulgaria and Albania. Even if they had been able to distance themselves from the disputes over borders and new states, and they could not, the weakness of governments under these uncertain conditions made them vulnerable to the kind of violent involution that occurred in Albania in 1997, when the collapse of pyramid schemes provoked widespread revolt and looting of military arsenals, the total disintegration of discipline in the security forces (military and police), and a flood of arms and ammunition throughout the country. The violence between Transnistria and its parent republic, Moldova, was minor compared to the Yugoslav wars, but it stalled the creation of a new Moldovan state and the exit of foreign (Russian) military units from its soil. Nor did the end of the Cold War reduce the periodic threats of war between Greece and Turkey, facilitate a solution to the Cyprus conflict, or improve the ability of these two countries to follow through on repeated agreements to engage in reciprocal cuts in military budgets and armaments.

The difficulty facing projects for security sector reform in the Balkans and the analysis of trends in that direction is that these two preconditions or their absence – fundamental domestic change and external security – interact. This interaction creates an analytical difficulty, crucial to effective policy, in disentangling cause and effect, and it produces a series of vicious circles that make any actual progress difficult to achieve. To get domestic demand for democratic accountability and reform of security structures, one needs a minimum of external security. Instead, the prevailing external insecurity, as a result of nationalist challenges to existing state borders and an absence of secure alliances and a regional or sub-regional security framework that would either prevent these challenges or provide mechanisms for managing them politically, confronts governments with very real needs that make it difficult to argue for cuts in defence.

Under conditions of new democracies, moreover, such insecurity advantages politicians who choose to gain popularity, win votes and remain in power by generating and exploiting fear and insecurity and by offering protection against dangerous others, both at home and across the border. Even for those who avoid militaristic appeals, the high levels of inchoate or explicit threats to the state and the new regime make control over the security forces – military and police – a critical domestic resource. The emergence of democratic competition for power will include partisan competition over the loyalty of and control over the armed forces and internal security forces, and whatever rhetoric such competition provokes.

For individual citizens, moreover, according to public opinion polls in the region, the role of the armed forces is far less important than a new form of insecurity unknown for nearly fifty years, the meteoric rise in their own physical and economic insecurity. The economic and political transformations have generated high unemployment, rising prices for necessities, a dramatic end to generous systems of social welfare, and weak states that appear incapable of providing minimal public protection and public goods. At the same time, these consequences of the transition are exacerbated by external insecurity and regional instability because of the continuing requirements for defence spending, the obstacles to intra- and cross-regional trade, criminalised economies, low tax yields and fiscal capacity, and the deterrents to foreign investment.

To the extent there are any limits on this complex insecurity and its vicious circles, the 'controls' do not yet come from democratic government, but from temporary policies of foreign actors – for example, the presence of NATO troops in two international protectorates (Bosnia–Herzegovina and Kosovo), in Macedonia to assist implementation of an internationally mediated constitutional revision, and in Albania, Croatia and Hungary for the logistical needs of these three deployments. The demand for security sector reform within countries is also coming from outsiders, either as part of conditions for further economic assistance (such as cuts in public budgets) or through myriad programmes of military and police assistance aimed at creating peace and stability in the region. Yet all of these external actions are governed by a policy of *containment* – by the European Union, NATO, the OSCE, the United States, among others – aimed at protecting their prosperous democracies against the effects of the region's instability: refugees and internally displaced persons; organised crime and trafficking in drugs, persons and arms; and threats of further war to the neighbourhood. The result, according to Bulgarian sociologist Ivan Krastev, is a situation of 'controlled insecurity' promoted by the international community, from which an exit is difficult to imagine (Krastev 2000: 8).

Background to current instability

Between June 1991 and June 1999, the region saw four wars – in Slovenia, in Croatia, in Bosnia–Herzegovina (though one might identify here at least two wars, between Bosnian Croats and Bosnian Muslims, and between Bosnian Serbs and Bosnian Muslims, later a Croat–Muslim alliance), and in Yugoslavia (Serbia and its province of Kosovo). Deadly violence also accompanied the effort by Transnistria to set up an independent state rather than remain in Moldova, and the collapse of the pyramid schemes in Albania in 1997. A fifth war, by Albanian nationalists from Kosovo and Macedonia against the Macedonian state, began in February 2001, but appears to have been cut short by EU and NATO intervention. Borders throughout the region remain unsettled and challenged by one or more groups. Millions of persons remain refugees or internally displaced, unable to go home.

At the same time, all governments in the region are now elected in competitive, multi-party elections. Each has had at least one turnover in power. Since 2000, with the first turnover after 1990 in Croatia, Serbia, and Bosnia–Herzegovina, all parliaments are active places of contestation and law making. Constitutionally, all security forces are responsible to civilian authorities, and the process of economic reform and transformation generates additional reasons for transparency and accountability in military, police, and intelligence matters. Nowhere can one say, however, that democratic governance has been consolidated (with the possible exception of Bulgaria) or that the prevailing insecurity in the region might not yet win out against consolidation. Pockets of frozen instability and stalemate, as is suggested by the circumstances in Moldova and Bosnia–Herzegovina, could generalise to the region as well. Attempting to pursue security sector reform in such conditions of fundamental systemic transformation and profound human and state insecurity requires a conceptual framework quite distinct from that normally underlying the sectoral aid policies of development donors.

Such a framework would have to take into account that it was precisely these three current processes – democratisation, economic reform, and constitutional change, including the role of the armed forces – that caused the break-up of the Socialist Federal Republic of Yugoslavia. What will make the difference in this second effort? Many other countries in the world, including a large number of those that appear in this volume, confront the same set of interacting processes in conflict-torn environments. Understanding the tensions that must be managed as a result of the interaction of democratisation, economic liberalisation, and changes in the constitutional role of the security forces is a necessary first step to a conceptual framework that could apply far beyond the Balkans.

(1) The tension between liberalising economic reform under an IMF-led debt repayment programme and democratising political reform

This tension drove the political dynamic in Yugoslavia in the 1980s that led to the end of socialism and the country's dissolution in 1990–1. In contrast to the policy of the United States and the international financial institutions, which view economic reform and democratisation as complementary, these two processes tend far more often to be in conflict. These tensions are both institutional and distributive.

The primary institutional tension is between centralisation and decentralisation. First, the goal of IMF economic reform packages in exchange for loans – an open, globally participant economy – requires certain conditions and institutional capacity for effective macroeconomic policy, such as a national market, central powers over monetary and foreign exchange policies including an independent central bank, uniform policies on laws affecting economic transactions (property rights, tax legislation, etcetera), and fiscal discipline that limits government expenditures and regulatory powers. Yet such liberalisation tends to weaken governmental capacity in general, especially in poorer countries, at the very moment when a transition from war or authoritarian rule requires the opposite, to build up an effective and legitimate state. Liberalisation reduces the powers and resources available for effective development policy and the public investments necessary to capital goods and infrastructural reconstruction. It hits hard at prevailing rules of the political game in many poorer countries by squeezing resources that can be used to co-opt potential rivals or opponents of economic reforms, including regional politicians with autonomist demands. And it eliminates the fiscal resources for public services and social welfare that might prevent serious social unrest and build legitimacy for the new regime. At the same time, standard IMF programmes and the economists who design them insist that the best method for reducing such public expenditures and fiscal deficits is not temporary cuts but fiscal and administrative decentralisation. This not only reduces further the powers of the central government to manage transition but it also generates and exacerbates resource conflicts between central and regional governments at a time when the simultaneous shift to export-oriented economic policy increases regional inequalities and accompanying regional grievances with the centre.

The distributive conflicts, for their part, are particularly severe in the early stages of these reforms when new democracies are unusually fragile and opponents of reform particularly strong. The first stages of macroeconomic stabilisation and structural adjustment policies introduce serious austerity, rising unemployment often accompanied by inflation, the increases in regional inequality mentioned above, and the obvious political consequences of these economic hardships. These conditions are particularly fertile for politicians who want to gain popular support through populist appeals to ethnic, religious, or sectarian differences and antagonisms that have a territorial base, because the distributive consequences intensify not only vertical but horizontal inequalities. In the early stages of democratisation, the political loyalties, identities, and organisations suited to electoral competition will be weakly institutionalised, giving advantage to those who can call on communal symbols and bonds in mobilising substantial popular discontent.

Discontent over economic austerity and distributional inequalities exacerbates the institutional tension between the simultaneous pressures for greater central powers over the economy and greater local autonomy to adapt to new economic conditions. Thus, the politics of economic reform and the politics of democratisation interact to the advantage of politicians choosing communal legitimation in elections or in the centre–regional contest and a dynamic tending toward autonomist and even secessionist demands, even if only intended initially as a bargaining tactic. In the Yugoslav case, the break-up began with such threats from the Slovene government (the wealthiest of the six republics) in a contest over terms of the IMF policy (especially Slovene opposition to devaluation, wage freezes, and recentralisation of monetary policy) and over federal expenditures and transfers.

Despite this disintegrative dynamic, few countries have a choice to refuse the conditions of assistance from the IMF and the World Bank, given the current international monetary and trading regimes, the foreign debt of conflict-torn and transitional societies which must be addressed before any other aid is forthcoming, and the initial dependence on foreign capital for economic reconstruction. Nor is there much support for the choice made by the newly industrialising countries of East Asia, to abandon democratic reforms when the two processes conflict.

(2) The effect of constitutional reform in countries that are multi-ethnic, multi-religious, multilingual, and federal

Both economic reform and democratisation occur through constitutional change and legal reform of a fundamental character (such as the nature of property rights). The former Yugoslavia is far more typical, in its heterogeneous character, of most countries undergoing economic reform and democratisation than are those often cited as successful cases of transformation, such as Hungary or Poland. In Yugoslavia, the federal question – that is, the rights of the republics (federal units) versus those of the central government, particularly over economic assets (tax policy, federal expenditures, property rights, foreign exchange policy, and so on) – was the driving focus of all constitutional change. When constitutional change included early stages of democratisation, it compounded the federal question by adding the issue of balance in the central government between parliamentary and executive power. Politicians from republics that favoured less central power and greater states' rights demanded parliamentary supremacy, while those who preferred greater central power or depended on a continuation of fiscal redistribution tended to favour the executive branch. But democratisation also meant that politicians began to seek popular support for their positions and thus to debate the constitutional issues publicly. Operating in a vacuum of democratic institutions and institutional interests, politicians exploited rhetoric that asserted patterns of association between certain institutional and constitutional arrangements and perceived ethnic and religious discrimination in the past.

Even in South Africa, constitutional reform could have had the effect we saw in Yugoslavia had the disputes between the new African National Congress (ANC) government and Inkatha in KwaZulu–Natal, including the role of President Buthelezi, not been resolved in the way they were. The collapse of Yugoslavia was not inevitable; political choices could have been made, as in South Africa, to escape the spiral of dissolution. But other transitional democracies that are multi-ethnic, multi-religious, multilingual, and divided into administrative regions (whether technically federal or not), such as Nigeria, Russia and Indonesia, are still navigating these dangerous waters.

(3) The role of the army and its evolution under democratisation and economic transformation

A crucial element of democratisation is the evolution of the armed forces as an institution whose constitutional responsibility had been to secure not only the country's territorial integrity but also a particular political regime. In the case of Yugoslavia, the Jugoslovenska Narodna Armija (the federal Yugoslav Peoples' Army, or JNA) had an external role that was tied to the Cold War order, to defend the country against attack from both the Warsaw Pact forces and NATO forces, and also an internal role, to defend its socialist regime and the legacy of its anti-fascist liberation in the Second World War. This internal role included organisational representation equivalent to that of a state in the federation in both the federal presidency (a collective body of nine – eight territorial regions and the armed forces) and the collective presidency of the party (League of Communists). To implement successively harsher IMF loan programmes during the 1980s, federal budget cuts required ever steeper cuts in the military budget. Arguments from the general staff that to reduce military expenditures, modernisation had to occur that was initially *more* expensive did not fall on receptive ears in the wealthier republics that paid higher (in absolute terms) federal tax. At the same time, the autonomist, secessionist and nationalist rhetoric surrounding the constitutional reform battle challenged the army's constitutional obligations – to defend the multinational and anti-nationalist values of the country and the country's territorial integrity. As political parties began to organise in the late 1980s on anti-communist (and in some cases neo-fascist) grounds, the very origins of the army itself came under attack. In many ways, the armed forces itself became a core issue in the politics of economic reform.

On one hand, the politics of economic reform and rebellion against the federal system, particularly by the Slovenes, focused on the federal army. Although the issues of economic interest to the republican government were more about monetary and labour policy, the size of the military budget, the language rights of conscripts in the army, and the policy of arms exports were easier political targets to mobilise popular support for republican rights and, eventually, independence. By 1989–90, in the neighbouring Croatian republic, nationalists viewed the very disintegration of the federal army as the necessary critical step on their road to independence.

On the other hand, military officials also had to adjust, simultaneously, to budget cuts, fundamental changes in both external and internal threats to the state, and democracy, in the sense that persons previously considered enemies of the state were now being elected in the republics. Moreover, the concept of civilian control under these new conditions meant a surfeit of competing civilian demands without clear constitutional guidelines. The federal army's effort to protect the constitutional order and the country's borders, under contradictory political direction, was confused, messy, and in the end subject to a condemnation wide enough to include the creation of an international criminal tribunal in The Hague.

The result, as Croatian nationalists had planned, was the army's disintegration into national units, its transformation into instruments of civilian nationalists and their independence goals or subordination to armed units of the internal security police (favoured by new leaders over the army, which retained some professional integrity), and a proliferation of paramilitaries and arms dealers from within and outside the area.

The democratic era

With few exceptions (Slovenia, no longer even considered a part of the region, and probably Bulgaria), the first decade of democratic government in south-eastern Europe, 1990–2000, was actually an era of state formation. The contest to build new, post-communist states was largely a contest within élite factions over *who* would shape that state and become the new political class. As nominally democratic states, the primary resource was popular legitimacy, and the critical contest was over definitions of the political community each claimed to represent. Who belonged and who did not, and what was the political identity and focus of political loyalty of that community?

This process of new state formation has included massive expulsions of populations on the basis of (imputed) ethnic loyalties and presumed disloyalty, and the violent prevention of their return home through murder, arson, organised mobs, and the destruction of new homes by grenades or bombs. Even in Romania, Bulgaria, and Albania, where expulsions were not a contest over new state borders as in the former Yugoslav cases, threats of expulsion and actual violence accompanied debates about whom the post-socialist *nation* included and did not. Nor was this process complete by 2002.

A critical element of state formation was a struggle for control over state security forces and the creation of paramilitary organisations attached to political parties. An integral part of political competition was arrests of political enemies, of ruling personalities, assassinations of journalists, rivals and critics, hyperactivity in domestic surveillance by intelligence services, and the generalised threat to civilian security posed by the presence of special forces in major capitals (such as Belgrade). Presidents Tudjman in Croatia, Berisha in Albania, Milošević in Serbia, all three nationalist leaderships in Bosnia–Herzegovina, and even, latterly, Djukanović in Montenegro, all supplemented their electoral victories with special police units, particularly militarised units of the internal security police (in Serbia, for example, the numbers in 2000 were 140,000, or three and a half times their size in the socialist period), special guards (such as Tudjman's *Gardijske Brigade*), three separate intelligence services allied with nationalist political parties in Bosnia–Herzegovina, and, it appears, a revived Communist-era secret police in Romania and Albania.

The process of state formation was also intimately intertwined throughout the region with organised crime and its associated elements of gang warfare, violent settling of accounts, and attacks on political figures (Strazzari: 2001). The line between party competition, protection rackets, and police-organised pogroms was often thin indeed. These conditions, and a lawlessness more characteristic of frontier conditions than democratising states, were exacerbated by the Yugoslav wars and international response. The economic sanctions imposed on the Federal Republic of Yugoslavia (Serbia and Montenegro) in May 1992, the two economic embargoes imposed on Macedonia by Greece, the influx of international military forces, and the open violation of the UN arms embargo by the USA and others to assist those fighting against Serbs in Croatia, Bosnia–Herzegovina and Kosovo created ideal conditions for smugglers and trafficking in cigarettes, fuel, persons (enslaved children, female prostitutes, Asian and Middle Eastern migrants seeking asylum or work in western Europe), drugs, weapons, and ammunition. Even nationalist contests contained a strong dose of competition over smuggling routes and the revenues such control entailed.

The consequence of an environment with extremely high unemployment, widespread availability of small arms, and thousands engaged in some small part in the trafficking networks is that the daily incidence of ordinary robbery, theft, and violent crime is unusually high. Even the former president of Macedonia, Kiro Gligorov, nearly lost his life in an attempted assassination that most consider the result of competition between criminal gangs in Macedonia and Bulgaria and efforts by the Macedonian government to crack down.

Whereas the economic activities and causes of this criminality and political corruption gain most attention, Bulgarian sociologist Ivan Krastev's research suggests that the primary cause is the failure of the state to provide basic security: there is a search by individuals, families, and businesses for private solutions, and bribes turn out to be primarily to private security services, protection rackets and other means of safety (Krastev: personal communication). In fact, most *governments* in the region are buying protection from external actors – from NATO, the UN, EU police assistance, and private security companies such as the US-based Military Professional Resources, Inc. (MPRI).

The lesson of the first decade of democratisation in south-eastern Europe is that eventual consolidation of democracy, improved civilian control over security, and increasing security overall are not guaranteed. Particularly if democratisation is an instrument of new state formation, the opposite trend is more likely. At best, the trend has not been one of linear progress. Competitive elections became instruments in some places such as Croatia and Serbia to legitimise arbitrary power, creating 'democratically legitimated dictatorship' as Croatian sociologist Vesna Pusić characterised the regime of President Franjo Tudjman and his party, the Croatian Democratic Community (HDZ) (Pusić 1994). Nationalist projects were used to justify *de facto* emergency rule in some cases, and even countries on an upward track for much of the decade, such as Albania and Macedonia, saw serious reversals after 1996–7.

For example, democratic elections and national independence in Croatia ushered in a decade of autocratic rule by President Tudjman and his family circle, with effective governance in the hands of an extra-parliamentary (and extra-constitutional) organ, the National Security Council chaired by Tudjman's son. Tudjman's government ignored international commitments made, such as the ceasefire signed through UN mediation in November 1991 and January 1992, and launched a military onslaught against UN peacekeeping troops and Serb inhabitants in three UN-protected areas in May and August 1995. The Croatian government, in fact, used the signing of the ceasefire to build up, train and equip its military forces, to assist Bosnian Croat forces, and to aid others in the wider region who might open new fronts against Serbs. Public expenditures on defence remained inordinately high at 60 per cent of the central budget (itself consuming 55 per cent or higher of GDP), and much more 'off-budget', and the army, police and paramilitary forces were actively engaged in domestic politics.

In Serbia, despite regular elections and, until the late 1990s, relative freedom of speech, association and employment, the government became increasingly autocratic, engaging in selective police terror and state-directed assassinations of independent voices. In this case, the cause was primarily international isolation and sanctions, which made economic activity so risky that it was increasingly overtaken by those who would bear the risks – smugglers and their complex of illegal operations, including kickbacks to politicians and protection from the police – and eventually led to criminalisation of the state and revenue sources as well. Most important in terms of security sector reform was the effect of the NATO bombing campaign, Operation Allied Force, against Serbia in March–June 1999, because it ended the decade-long effort by the army to adjust to democratic principles while retaining professional integrity, against persistent government demands to act domestically. The NATO campaign gave Milošević the excuse to replace the army chief of staff with a more compliant chief and made the army's responsibility for defending the country's borders an internal fight, in Kosovo.

The lack of linear progress is even clearer in Macedonia. Independence began with a successful negotiation between the chief of the federal Yugoslav army and the President of Macedonia to allow peaceful withdrawal of the remaining federal troops, with their equipment, in early 1992. The government committed itself to building a small defence force appropriate to post-Cold War conditions. But its southern neighbour, Greece, refused to recognise that independence and held up European Union and American recognition until the end of 1995. Turkey countered with recognition and a pact for military assistance, and President Gligorov persuaded the UN Security Council, in December 1992, to deploy a preventive force of UN peacekeeping troops along its northern and western borders as an implicit security guarantee. Although this signal of commitment to Macedonian independence enabled the government to focus on economic reform and democratisation, it could not protect Macedonia from the devastating economic effects of the sanctions on Serbia, its primary trading partner (two-thirds of its economy was tied to Serbia in 1991), including increasing criminalisation, corruption of border guards and police, the violence that accompanies competition over smuggling routes, and the shift southward, through Macedonia, of the Balkan route for drug and other illegal trafficking by organised crime from Asia to Western Europe. Nor could the UN border monitors protect Macedonia against the activities of militant Albanian nationalists who, while focusing on Kosovo, also chose assassination targets in Macedonia, ran cross-border illegal activities in arms, drugs and guerrillas, and led to a new front in Macedonia itself in early 2001. Indeed, the NATO military preparations for action against Serbia, beginning in the autumn of 1998 and culminating in the air campaign, led to the removal of the UN force, leaving Macedonia vulnerable to new uncertainties about its border and external security and a temporary influx of Kosovo refugees that burst the fragile internal bargaining over intercommunal relations and its constitutional order. NATO took control of strategic communications in Macedonia and its border, and in the course of 2001 deployed its own force in Macedonia to oversee the terms of an EU/US-negotiated constitutional reform to satisfy the Albanian minority and disarm a portion of the Albanian militants. The Albanian insurgency of 2001 raised serious questions about the extent of democratic consolidation in Macedonia, while its security sector reform never took off because of the massive external, and eventually internal, threats that arose.

These vacillations, reversals, and deterioration in the countries emerging from the former Yugoslavia can be understood in the light of the break-up of a state, but Albania also illustrates the non-linear path of democratisation in the Balkans. Despite enthusiastic Western reception for the first democratically elected government of President Sali Berisha, his regime had by 1996 become increasingly buttressed by the former secret police and by money laundering through pyramid schemes. His nationalist support for the Kosovo Liberation Army (KLA) in northern Albania included weapons trafficking and training camps. When the pyramid schemes collapsed in 1997, the lack of discipline by the country's security forces forced Western countries to deploy a temporary security force (Operation Alba led by Italy under an OSCE mandate). Forced by the intervention into extraordinary elections, President Berisha chose to increase insecurity as a campaign tactic, including local shoot-outs and looting of army arsenals. Despite this dramatic collapse of internal security and democratisation and a continuing fragility worsened by organised crime networks throughout the country, the country has apparently returned to its prior path of peaceful democratisation, economic reform and European integration.

In addition to the insecurities unleashed by state formation in an uncertain, undefined external environment and the violence, arbitrary rule, and deterioration of security that has characterised democratisation (in contrast to the socialist era) in the Balkans, a third characteristic of this first decade is a region dotted by pockets of frozen instability that are strikingly similar to the negative African scenarios described by participants in this project. Moldova, Kosovo, Albania, Macedonia, and even Serbia–Montenegro are all trapped in a half-way house of insecurity that one might call a negative equilibrium. That is, external policies toward these entities favour containment while ruling élites benefit economically from the rents, kickbacks, and smuggling profits that such unstable, unregulated environments encourage. Crisis management by relevant European and international actors and personal interest in the agendas that produce such crises among political leaders can perpetuate such a situation for a long time. And the more interventions lead to fragile political compromises or the creation of temporary sub-state 'entities' that do not have sovereign rights or responsibilities, the more democratisation is delayed and regional instability continues.

Security sector reform

This picture of insecurity in south-eastern Europe has a lot in common with West Africa, particularly as described by Comfort Ero in her contribution on Sierra Leone. There is one major difference – the overriding international presence and role in the Balkans. This international role has two motivations. The first is regional peace and security in Europe, and the second is the economic transformation of the region from socialist regimes to liberal market economies. The first motivation has generated a host of engagements and policies throughout the decade aimed at crisis management, war termination, the provision of a 'secure environment' for two United Nations-mandated international administrations (in Bosnia–Herzegovina and in Kosovo) to build peace and local self-governance, and campaigns against corruption, organised crime, illegal migration and trafficking in drugs and persons so as to interrupt the flows into Western Europe. The second motivation comes from creditors and donors who have programmes of economic reform and transformation, developmental assistance and post-conflict reconstruction premised on the belief in liberalisation and privatisation as prime motors of economic growth. In policies to reduce public expenditures and the public sector, the defence sector is a prime early target. The result of both motivations is an extensive array of efforts aimed at reforming security apparatuses, from militaries to police and border regimes, and at generating democratic accountability. Only examples can illustrate such a vast array.

The first explicit effort at security sector reform (1994–5) was the retraining and equipping for 'democratic reform' of the Croatian army by MPRI, a private American security firm on contract to the US Department of State. The programme was designed to transform what it called a 'Soviet-style' army into a Western (American-type) professional force subordinated to civilian control. The result was two massive military offensives by the Croatian army against three UN-protected areas and their Serb inhabitants in 1995. The role of MPRI – first in Croatia, then in administering the Train and Equip programme for the Federation army in Bosnia–Herzegovina, next in training and equipping the KLA (although not the only actor so engaged) and finally, when an offshoot of the KLA began an insurgency in Macedonia, in working with the Macedonian military – did not help to win friends or erase suspicions about Western interest in military reform.

The relation between democratisation and security sector reform, moreover, is indirect. In Croatia, the MPRI programme for democratic accountability of the army meant little during the Tudjman era, despite periodic elections. When the opposition parties won, after Tudjman's death in December 1999, one of their first acts in power was to announce plans for serious cuts in the military budget. But the cause was an economic crisis due to the corruption and flawed economic reforms of the Tudjman regime and the deep cuts in public expenditures required by new World Bank and IMF loan programmes. Even then, the agonizingly slow progress of restructuring and reform of the armed forces in the following two years suggest that the real aim was the symbolic signalling of a new foreign policy. Under international scrutiny, to prove more cooperative than Tudjman had been in his commitments to the Dayton Agreement, the government cut subsidies to the Bosnian Croat army such as the funding of military officers' salaries. The crisis this provoked in the Bosnian federation (over these funds, a new defence law, and Bosnian Croat militancy), moreover, demonstrates that reform of the external security sector by definition will always have external effects. In Croatia two years later, little if any downsizing or cuts in military expenditures have occurred, although some transparency and a reduction in off-budget expenditures can be claimed. Moreover, the decision of the new government to purchase F-16 airplanes from the United States after the new President and Prime Minister visited Washington in the summer of 2000 occurred without public debate or discussion about an appropriate national security strategy for the future, including what possible use Croatia would have for F-16s.

Public debate on military matters occurred instead in reaction to the government's efforts to cooperate with the International Criminal Tribunal on Former Yugoslavia (ICTY) in The Hague in providing evidence and extraditing Croatian military officers indicted for war crimes in the wars in Croatia and in Bosnia–Herzegovina. Despite high-profile cooperation by the Croatian president, Stipe Mesić, and a judge in Rijeka, the Prime Minister and his cabinet back-pedalled in response to massive demonstrations by nationalist right-wing parties and veterans' groups, with the blessing of Catholic Church bishops. Growing pressure from the prosecutor in The Hague to extradite officers provoked three ministers from the second-largest party in the coalition, the centre-right Social Liberals, to resign their posts in protest, and the party's leader, a leading contender for President, to step down. Even revelations of massive corruption in the military could not overcome the public turmoil surrounding ICTY demands to mobilize popular demand for reform. For Croatian nationalists, the army created in the 'National Homeland War' was beyond reproach, inseparable from the Croatian nation itself and the formation of its independent state.

The most extensive efforts at security sector reform have occurred in the two territories that are currently international protectorates, Bosnia–Herzegovina[1] and Kosovo. In fact, national security in both instances is provided by foreign troops – the NATO-led military operations, IFOR/SFOR and KFOR respectively. Negotiations over and terms of implementation of agreements on arms control and limitations for Bosnian armed forces (and those of neighbouring Croatia and Yugoslavia as co-signators) were mandated by the peace accord and conducted in Vienna under the OSCE, while downsizing (discharging 200,000 soldiers) and reintegration (funded by the World Bank) were conducted by IFOR. Similarly, in Kosovo, KFOR supervised the transformation of the KLA into a Kosovo Protection Corps responsible, ostensibly, for civilian protection in areas of disaster preparedness along the lines of the French Securité Civil. In both areas, the private security firm MPRI trained and equipped the two anti-Serb armies, the KLA and the Bosnian Federation army, while NATO officials worked (unsuccessfully by 2002) to integrate the two Bosnian armies into one.

Equipment came to Bosnia from the United States and Islamic states. International officials charged with implementing the peace agreement required the creation of a central government Standing Committee on Military Matters as the first step toward a single national security policy (the Dayton Agreement gave jurisdiction over defence to the two entities, the Federation and the Serb Republic, not to their common state). Numerous bilateral (British in particular) and multilateral (NATO) programmes have sought to persuade and educate Bosnians to design national defence and security plans. Professionalisation, reform and democratic supervision (by parliament and non-governmental organizations) of the militaries have been the subject of frequent training seminars under the Office for Regional Stabilisation of the OSCE that has responsibility for implementing Annex 1B of the Dayton Agreement. By July 1999, members of the triune presidency of Bosnia–Herzegovina were pressured by international officials to agree to cut the military budget by 15 per cent and to make a symbolic display of unity on defence by announcing the decision at the inaugural summit of the Stability Pact for South-eastern Europe in Sarajevo. At 41 per cent of domestically financed public revenue in the Bosnian Federation and 20 per cent in Republika Srpska, in neither case counting external assistance (substantial in the case of the Federation), defence expenditures were judged the main obstacle to domestic generation of economic growth.

In both Bosnia and Kosovo, police training and reform are also extensive, down to the creation of police academies, the vetting of all persons who apply for employment in the police forces, the obligation of 'multi-ethnic' composition, and the provision of new uniforms (and their design), all managed by United Nations civilian police units (the International Police Task Force (IPTF) in Bosnia and UNCIVPOL in Kosovo).[2] UN police also monitor local police and provide domestic security. Rules on the legal possession of firearms are enforced by IFOR and KFOR, amounting to daily seizures (and occasional raids) in the case of Kosovo. Judiciaries are being massively reformed and restructured by international direction in both cases, although progress is far too slow for the tasks they must handle. In both cases, the indictment, arrest and trial of persons accused of war crimes and investigation of mass graves and alleged massacres is a major international preoccupation, with daily media attention led by the ICTY in The Hague. In addition, international donors to Slovenia, Bosnia and Kosovo design and fund de-mining programmes (including a United Nations Mine Action Centre in both areas). There is generous EU assistance throughout the region to border police for training, cross-border cooperation and communication, and equipment.

Three other international interventions to end civil violence in the region also imposed temporary security by foreign troops and focused efforts to create or reform modern police units. The United Nations Transitional Administration in Eastern Slavonia, Croatia (UNTAES) implemented a peace accord (the Erdut Agreement) from 1995 to 1997, providing border monitoring, demobilisation and the creation of multiethnic police units. When political authority over eastern Slavonia returned to Croatia and UNTAES departed, a police monitoring mandate (given to a United Nations Police Support Group) was considered necessary for a nine-month transition period. In October 1998, an OSCE mission and an office of the UN High Commissioner for Human Rights were established to continue monitoring Croatian activity toward the Serb minority. In Albania, a coalition of European states deployed Operation Alba in summer 1997 as a security presence in the lead-up to elections after the anarchy provoked by the collapse of pyramid schemes. Some units remain. The West European Union (WEU) then deployed police units to instigate police training under a programme still in place called MAPE. NATO had a heavy presence in Albania and Macedonia during the preparation for and running of Operation Allied Force against Yugoslavia (24 March–10 June 1999), and many NATO units remain as part of the logistical tail for KFOR in both countries. In the summer of 2001, NATO deployed 4,500 soldiers under British command to Macedonia in Operation Essential Harvest to collect weapons (more than 3,300) from National Liberation Army guerrillas, and it followed this operation with a Macedonian Security Force of 1,000 under German command to be a security presence during implementation of the August 2001 Ohrid Framework Agreement between the Macedonian government and Albanian political parties which the Macedonian parliament adopted in November.

In Montenegro, although it was nominally part of a single state with Serbia (the Federal Republic of Yugoslavia), NATO countries proposed and enabled the creation of a separate police force through training, equipping and finance as a deterrent counterweight to Yugoslav army units deployed in the republic. Its goal was to send a signal to the Milošević government that the West would support Montenegrin independence against any moves by the Yugoslav army, should it be necessary. This example demonstrates that some security sector reform programmes have actually been used as vehicles of political revolution, with negative effects for their popular credibility.

Beyond these temporary engagements to stabilise the Balkans, the European Union has increasingly focused assistance and policies, particularly through its office of Justice and Home Affairs, on the perceived threat to Western European security of the trafficking routes for drugs, the sex trade, illegal migrants and asylum seekers that traverse the Balkans. This longer-term attention is on police, customs, judicial and governance reforms. The EU has also designed association agreements for countries in south-eastern Europe called Stabilisation and Association Agreements (SAAs) that contain additional requirements and preconditions addressed to stability-related political criteria as well as conformity with standard membership requirements. In addition, all countries in the region aspire to NATO membership, beginning with Partnership for Peace (PfP) and NATO's Membership Accession Plan (MAP).

In June 1999, recognition that peace required a regional strategy and cooperation between and among states in south-eastern Europe even led the EU and other interested states (the US, Russia, Canada, Norway and others) and organisations (such as the OSCE, World Bank and UN) to create a new facility called the Stability Pact for South-eastern Europe. Its role was to facilitate the financing of specific projects and multiple forums for regular communication on issues of the Pact's focus as a parallel, complementary process to that of European integration. One of the three working tables of the Stability Pact, Working Table III, specialises in security, with two sub-tables: justice and home affairs, and defence and security.[3] Its projects include arms control, non-proliferation and military contacts; defence reform and economics, including budgetary transparency and base closings and conversions; humanitarian de-mining; small arms and light weapons; disaster preparedness and prevention; two institutionalised regional initiatives, one to fight corruption and the other to fight organised crime; asylum and migration; trafficking in human beings; and reforms of judiciary, civilian police and border police. At the fourth meeting of Working Table III in June 2001, the sub-table on defence and security chose to focus future efforts on 'security sector reform'. Even World Bank programmes for economic development in countries of the region, such as for Kosovo, Bosnia and Yugoslavia, give priority in their design to stability and security (Gligorov 2000).

Thus, Romania, Bulgaria and Macedonia are all engaged in reforming their militaries as a result of membership in NATO's PfP and under the rules of MAP. NATO and the EU have encouraged them to create regional security forums, such as the South-east Europe Initiative, the Consultative Forum, and the South-east Europe Security Cooperation Steering Group (SEEGROUP). Unfortunately, the Albanian insurgency in Macedonia, beginning in February 2001, escalated just as the government signed an SAA with the EU. Security sector reform and trade opportunities were interrupted by military and police counterinsurgency operations and skyrocketing military expenditures, while public antagonism towards NATO, high as a result of the campaign against Yugoslavia in 1999, worsened dramatically. And to forestall an economic crisis, the government chose to impose a special tax for military operations.

Finally, even in Moldova, the primary security threat – the possibility that fighting might again erupt between Chisinau and its separatist region of Transnistria – is managed by outsiders. According to a ceasefire agreement of June 1992, the internal border between Moldova and Transnistria is controlled and supervised by Russian troops and

Ukrainian monitors (as the two Guarantors of the ceasefire), together with some Moldovan and Transnistrian units. Relations between the two capitals occur through the mediation of a resident mission of the OSCE, and Moldova is attempting to balance the Russian troop presence and the failure of Russia to dismantle its remaining (Soviet-era) bases and armaments with negotiations to join NATO, beginning with Partnership for Peace. In mid-2001, it was accepted into the Stability Pact for South-eastern Europe.

These examples of externally provided security and pressure for restructuring of the security sector in the region only scratch the surface of the myriad projects and activities of bilateral and multilateral, country-specific and pan-regional programmes. An American initiative under Austrian leadership, the South-east European Cooperation Initiative (SECI), for example, has done much on border management – creating and training border police and customs officials and facilitating cross-border cooperation. INTERPOL and EUROPOL are active in the region. In addition to the UN police reform programmes and the EU's MAPE in Albania, more than twenty separate bilateral programmes are running on police and border management, including those of the US's ICITAP, the International Law Enforcement Academy (ILEA) in Budapest, the Association of European Police Colleges (AEPC) and a regional civilian police training institute sponsored and funded by Norway. The South-east European Common Assessment Paper on Regional Security Challenges (SEECAP), a joint initiative of NATO's South-east Europe Initiative (SEEI) and the Stability Pact's Working Table III under the umbrella of SEEGROUP, began in early 2001 to bring together ministers of defence and interior in the region on a regular basis to assess threat perceptions. A Regional Arms Control Verification and Implementation Assistance Centre (RACVIAC) in Croatia is funded by the German government, while the UK financed a new centre on transparency in military budgeting and planning in Sofia, Bulgaria. The US and Norway finance missions to assess small arms stocks and flows in countries willing to request the service, while the US and Germany finance the destruction of weapons, as in Albania. Even the United Nations Development Programme initiated and funded research on human security in south-eastern Europe by local scholars for its 1999 Human Development Report (Centre for Liberal Strategies 1999). The one aspect to which little attention appears to be given by monitoring authorities, with the partial exception of the international mission in Bosnia–Herzegovina, is the intelligence services.

Are there lessons to be learnt from the Balkans?

There appear to be two basic assumptions behind the extraordinary resources and efforts being invested in security issues, structures and reform in south-eastern Europe. The first is that the democratic peace hypothesis – that democracies do not go to war against each other – should guide post-conflict reconstruction in the war-torn and war-vulnerable area. Democratic governance, it is assumed, will end the proclivity to war and make peace sustainable. The second is that civilian and democratic control over the security apparatus will make it serve the interests of citizens – not of states, as under authoritarian regimes. If the demand for security and the allocation of citizens' taxes more generally across various items of public expenditure and investment reflect citizens' preferences and listing of priorities, then people's universal desire for improved standards of living – 'butter over guns' – will also reduce the incidence of war, the size of military budgets and the abuse of human rights.

In the case of south-eastern Europe, however, the first assumption, that external security will be produced by internal reforms, was turned on its head in the 1980s and 1990s. The severe conflicts of interest over internal reforms led, in a context of external insecurity and change that gave opportunity to some and increased perceptions of threat to national security and survival for others, to secession, war and new state formation legitimised as national defence. Moreover, international response to the resulting violence was to help build up some old and create some new armies, to negotiate with those who had chosen violence and controlled arms, and not to assist in resolving border disputes by negotiation but either to declare such disputes illegitimate or to use military means itself to support some and oppose others who sought changes through war. To reverse this dynamic in post-war conditions requires addressing the symbolic importance of armies, as national heroes, and the perception of external threat as a key element of the new national ideologies. Without addressing the external environment in which the countries of the region undertake reforms, those reforms and public debate about them will remain hostage to a domestic political dynamic in which views about a strong military and military responses to internal conflicts become signifiers of national loyalty or treason.

No external programme of assistance, or demand for reform as a condition of assistance or membership in broader security organisations, thus far addresses this need. All focus on internal reforms and bilateral relations, treating each country separately without considering its regional context of insecurity and assuming that the weakening of the Cold War's justification for militarised security in the West applied to the Balkans automatically. There is one exception. The concept of the Stability Pact, and related efforts such as SECI and SEEGROUP, focus on cooperation across borders in the region on the assumption that such cooperation will reduce mutual hostilities. But this approach makes a similar mistake, assuming that the interstate relations in Western Europe after the Second World War apply to the Balkans now. This is to ignore the very real threats that remain, including some created by outsiders (as in the effect of Western policy toward Kosovo on its neighbours, starting with Macedonia, or continuing Greek hostility towards Macedonian statehood). It also ignores the fact that each country perceives such demands for cooperation with neighbours as a profound threat because such cooperation appears to be made as a *precondition* of membership of the EU and NATO. The one goal on which every reform government is basing its entire strategy for domestic change, eventual acceptance by Brussels, becomes dependent on a condition over which they have only partial control – their own willingness to cooperate but not that of their neighbours.[4] As for internal reforms that provoke further threats of secession and border change, like those that began in Macedonia and Yugoslavia in 2001 (or those not yet definitively settled in Romania, Moldova and Bosnia–Herzegovina), they can only be undertaken in a context of external guarantees of territorial and state integrity that have not been forthcoming. In other words, the 'democratic peace' thesis has unspoken preconditions.

The second assumption of democratic governance, moreover, is not being allowed to operate in much of south-eastern Europe. The demand, financing and mechanisms of accountability for security sector reform are all coming from outside the countries and the region. Instead of turning authoritarian regimes, in which security is for the state and the regime, into democratic regimes in which security is the right of the citizens, the myriad reforms and programmes in south-eastern Europe are aimed at providing security for Western European states and citizens in defence *against* south-eastern Europe. The *interest* in security sector reform is, first, that of Euro-Atlantic structures (NATO, OSCE, the EU) and international organisations and norms (UN peacekeeping, the international human rights regime in the case of ICTY, the World Bank) in their process of adapting to the new international conditions since the end of the Cold War – a process of *their* reform played out in the context of south-eastern Europe – and, second, that of Western European populations angered at illegal migration, asylum seekers, and traffickers in heroin, women, and children threatening *their* standards of living. The anti-terrorist campaign after 11 September 2001 intensified this focus on the Balkans. The disembodied character of these many programmes, a result of their foreign provenance, is exacerbated, moreover, by their sectoral focus and design. Can such an approach reduce the causes of war and the externalities (in organised crime, refugees, or trafficking in illicit goods and in persons) of regional instability? The lessons of the Yugoslav wars suggest the opposite.

Returning to the three tensions that led to the break-up of Yugoslavia, it becomes clear that it is not military expenditures or armies that cause wars, or even huge stockpiles of armaments and military equipment, but fundamental disagreements over issues of state, constitution and property that make people willing to fight, and the absence of procedures (internationally as well as domestically) and/or freedom to manage these divisive issues democratically. The profound differences in former Yugoslavia were caused by externally imposed conditions regarding economic and political reform in exchange for assistance and the conditions of national survival. The same conditions and reforms are now being required of the new states and regimes in the area, and in far more difficult circumstances. There is no more freedom to debate public policies on such conditions than before, despite democratic governance. All the burden lies, therefore, on the mechanisms and procedures available for accepting and managing the conflicts these conditions produce. Only a socially inclusive, public dialogue about strategic choices and priorities for the whole country at a time of difficult transformation can hope to staunch the destructive potential. The issues to be debated are economic liberalisation and its costs; constitutional reform and the balance between strong executive central power and simultaneous decentralisation to heed demands for autonomy or federalisation; and the costs and consequences of NATO membership if pursued as a substitute for debate about the role of the army and the kind of security policy appropriate to new conditions.

An additional consequence of foreign-driven demand, however, is the increasing sense of helplessness and impotence among citizens throughout the region. This is most palpable where external actors are most present, as in Bosnia–Herzegovina, Kosovo and recently Macedonia, but it is also revealed in the reactive posture of most political activity around such issues. It is here that the lesson of South Africa is vital. The posited benefits of democratic governance in regard to security questions do not come from any democratisation process but from special conditions. In south-eastern Europe, the case of Serbia since the democratic elections of September and December 2000 that replaced Slobodan Milošević and his ruling coalition may be generating the germ of those special conditions.

Western policy toward Serbia from the very beginning of the Yugoslav collapse in the spring of 1991 was extremely influential, not because it supported reform but because it hounded the regime, its policies and security forces. Milošević's creation of a fortress state – one that wore increasingly away at the professional qualities of the Yugoslav army inherited from the communist period, that more than tripled the communist-era size of the internal security police (MUP) to 140,000, that indulged an explosion of armed paramilitaries (estimated at 8,000 still active in early 2001) tied to political parties and organised criminal gangs, and that, like Tudjman's Croatia, increasingly turned élite units of the security forces[5] into internal occupying armies – was made possible by and in many ways motivated by Western policies of isolation, punishment and rising threats of military action.

Perhaps because of Western policies, including a NATO war against the country, the new government in Belgrade seemed in its first six months to be asserting far greater independence than seen anywhere else in the region in defining its own policies, goals and interests, and in encouraging its citizens to debate public priorities and war guilt, while participating in designing social programmes for a democratic future. Quite early, officials began discussions about membership in NATO's Partnership for Peace, to the astonishment of many and amidst expectation that both the army and large segments of the public would adamantly oppose this initiative. Simultaneously, though, non-governmental and semi-governmental institutes and organisations also began to debate future security policy and to initiate programmes of security sector reform independently. Pressure from non-governmental organisations to shorten mandatory military service to six months was sufficient by January 2001 to force the army general staff to agree and to begin work on a better system of conscription. As in South Africa, a sharp reversal in external conditions, an opposition movement that had to act in largely hostile external conditions and thus to define its own path to power (including an ability to take advantage when events moved in its favour), an electoral change in government that reflected a virtual social revolution (extending to elements of the security apparatus), and people in the new government who had themselves come out of an armed movement (South Africa) or the army and police (Serbia), seemed in the first year to be generating a domestically driven process of reform.

The causal arrow between foreign and domestic action was also reversed in Yugoslav foreign policy. The political change was having a strikingly rapid effect on relations with neighbours – replacing hostile confrontation with agreements on recognition and cooperation almost immediately, and changing fundamentally the behaviour of the army when it had to respond to a military threat to Serbian territory (from Albanian nationalist guerrillas in southern Serbia) between the autumn of 2000 and the following spring. Far, however, from illustrating the rationale of security sector reform – that making armies accountable to democratic, civilian authority will make them behave professionally – the new Yugoslav and Serbian governments used the threat in southern Serbia to create the nucleus of an entirely new army and to harmonise military action with other elements of national policy. The deployment in southern Serbia combined professional infantry, mass media, political negotiations, anti-terrorist units and police operations, all under a civilian government minister, Nebojša Čović, working closely with the commanding army general, General Krstić.[6]

Nonetheless, the unresolved issue over the political status of Kosovo and the growing threat from Albanian guerrillas in Serbia itself could also prevent the more sweeping kind of change in priorities and efforts at demilitarising state, economy and society that occurred in South Africa. Popular anger over the Kosovo issue and the abused rights of Serbs in Kosovo was revived after it seemed clean off the public agenda. Then, demands from ICTY for the extradition of Slobodan Milošević to The Hague and for the transfer of other indicted war criminals created an even greater governmental crisis than in Croatia, leading to the collapse of the federal government (when the Montenegrin half withdrew in protest) and an end to the agreement to keep the anti-Milošević ruling coalition together and personal rivalries at bay for the first two years.

Finally, the dominance of Western interests over local interests in shaping the demand for security sector reform in south-eastern Europe goes so far as to deny the declared interests of the region's citizens. If public opinion polls are to be trusted, it is not externally directed threats or unreformed militaries and police but weak states unable to provide internal security and some protection against the profound insecurities of economic transformation and collapse (such as high unemployment, inflation and capsized welfare systems) that most concern citizens in south-eastern Europe. Indeed, the 'social question', meaning the consequences of the jettisoned welfare systems of socialism and the external requirements for downsizing public bureaucracies and enterprises, defines most people's concept of security. It is the primary cause of organised crime and the insecurities it generates. The welfare question has transformed militaries increasingly into political pressure groups aiming like unions to protect soldiers from unemployment, as mentioned above. Democratic governments must be responsive to such discontent.

The result thus far in conditions of achingly high unemployment and widespread poverty is to defeat the purpose of security sector reforms where demobilisation and downsizing only divert former soldiers into other forms of public employment for which they are not trained or could possibly be dangerous, such as new border services or community police forces. Moreover, this is only the beginning. According to recent estimates, in the former Yugoslavia alone, two million persons out of a labour force of seven million were employed in defence sector activities (reportedly at least 200,000 in Serbia in 2001; in Bosnia–Herzegovina before the war, 40,000 were directly employed in military industries, and 40–55 per cent of the Bosnian economy was engaged in some way in the defence sector). The conversion of such industries requires massive new capital that shows little sign of materialising in the next ten years. As long as citizens seek other avenues of safety and survival than political action or even 'non-governmental' activity, the vicious circle with which this article began is reinforced.

References

AIM Belgrade (2001) 'Yugoslavia's army: the challenges of transition' (22 January).

Centre for Liberal Strategies (1999) *Human Security in South-East Europe*, study written by a regional team of scholars (and the Centre for Liberal Strategies in Sofia) under the leadership of Ivan Krastev, Skopje: August.

Gligorov, V. (2000) *The West and Economic Stabilisation of Western Balkans*, study prepared for the Militarwissenschaftliches Buro des Bundesministerium for Landesvertridingung, Vienna, 6 May.

Hansen, A. S. (2001) 'Exploring mechanisms to strengthen the indigenous civil-police capacity and the rule of law in the Balkans: prospects and problems', paper prepared for the IPA–DFAIT Workshop on Managing Security Challenges in Post-Conflict Peacebuilding, Ottawa, 22–23 June.

Krastev, I. (2000) 'De-balkanizing the Balkans: the state of the debate', in *Foreseeing the Future of SEE One Year after the Stability Pact: a Policy Outlook from the Region*, position papers presented at the First Annual South-east European Policy Institute Network Meeting, Ohrid, 24–25 June.

Pusić, V. (1994) 'Dictatorships with democratic legitimacy', *East European Politics and Societies*, 8 (3) (Autumn): 383–401.

Snyder, J. (2000) *From Voting to Violence: Democratization and Nationalist Conflict*, New York and London: W.W. Norton.

Strazzari, F. (2001) 'Between ethnic collision and mafia collusion: the "Balkan route" to state making', unpublished manuscript.

Woodward, S. L. (2001) 'The way ahead for Working Table III (Security) of the Stability Pact for South-east Europe', discussion paper prepared for the fourth meeting of the Working Table (III) (Security), Zagreb, Croatia, 11–13 May.

Notes

1 See the chapter in this volume by Mary Kaldor for more detailed discussion.

2 See the excellent survey in Hansen 2001.

3 Information on the activities, meetings and projects of Working Table III is available on the Stability Pact website: www.stabilitypact.org. A discussion of the status of Working Table III in June 2001 can be found in Woodward 2001.

4 In 2000 the Bulgarian parliament demanded the government pull out of the Stability Pact for this reason. The government refused, but risked a crisis in doing so.

5 In the case of Croatia, the *Gardijske Brigade* under Tudjman's personal control.

6 I am grateful to Dušan Janjić for this information. Although this experiment could be the germ of an entirely new army, an analysis in January 2001 by journalists of the Alternative Information Network argued that 'civilian control of defence matters and joining the system of collective security could show that the crisis in the security zone towards Kosovo and Metohija is the smallest problem the Yugoslav army will have to put up with in the near future' (AIM Belgrade: 2001).

Conclusion

13

Democratic Control and the Security Sector

The Scope for Transformation and its Limits

GAVIN CAWTHRA AND ROBIN LUCKHAM

This book has examined the governance of security – or in most cases insecurity – in developing and former communist countries that are riding, or at least being buffeted by, the jagged 'third wave' of global democratisation (Huntington 1993; Luckham and White 1996). One of its central concerns has been how to assure democratic control of military and security institutions.

Yet control is not a simple concept (Chuter 2000: 27). Arguments over the appropriate degree of civilian control of defence and security functions themselves can be sterile and somewhat miss the point: to ensure that the military (which cannot be a democratic institution) is governed in a democratic manner. This requires both that democratic institutions be in place and a basic acceptance of democratic politics by the political leadership, civil servants and security personnel. State control or civilian control of military and security structures is not necessarily equivalent to democratic control. As our case studies have confirmed, it is perfectly possible to have civilian control of the military that is non-democratic, anti-democratic or even militaristic.

But even democratic institutions do not necessarily deliver democratic governance, least of all in the security sector. Democratisation is a very long-term process; it does not end with formal transition to an elected government, and may be derailed or reversed, especially in conditions of national and international insecurity.

Democratic control of military and security institutions is strategic to democratisation for two main reasons. First, because these institutions have a peculiarly intimate relationship to political power. Second, because their security functions, including the management of insecurities that may be generated by democratisation, are essential for the survival of any democratic state.

In examining our broad range of case studies, some common strands have emerged in the approach taken to democratic governance and the management of insecurity. Context is critical, and differences are as important as commonalities. Yet there appear to be lessons that have some general applicability, providing account is taken of the type of democratic transition (or lack of it) that is under way. Below we examine the governance and policy implications emerging from this study, and make some recommendations as to an emerging best practice.

There is a growing literature and practice around 'security sector reform' that includes base-line 'good governance' norms in relation to security management (Hendrickson 1999), but this is only part of the story. There is also a large body of international research and analysis on conflict prevention, conflict resolution, peace making and peace building. The latter incorporates both medium-term objectives such as demobilisation, disarmament, repatriation and reintegration into society of former combatants (DDRR), as well as longer-term objectives such as establishing democratic governance and rebuilding sustainable national economies (Boutros-Ghali 1992; Haugerudbraaten 1998). This latter transformatory agenda overlaps with, and has profoundly impacted on, traditional development agendas (Duffield 2001).

In this book the contributors have interacted with some of this literature, although we have not sought to test its applicability in a case study context. Instead, we have aimed to draw upon specific country experiences in an empirical way, hoping to develop indigenous perspectives from the South and the former communist countries. One finding that emerges strongly is that there can be no 'one size fits all' solution to governing security in transitions, and that careful attention has to be paid to national variations. More specifically, it is evident that there is not a linear road to democracy from authoritarianism. There is broader agreement about the end point than there is about the ways and means of getting there.

The categorisation of countries that have been caught up in the 'third wave' as being necessarily engaged in democratisation is probably simplistic. The Introduction has put forward a typology that highlights important differences between states and the historical trajectories they have followed in the post-Cold War period. Some countries are genuinely consolidating democratic governance, or are in varying states of transition towards it. Others, however, may be seen as 'contested' or 'stalled' democratic experiments. In others authoritarianism and military dominance persists. In several states conflict is or has been endemic. Many of these are 'failed' or collapsed' states (although, as discussed in the

Introduction, both terms have their difficulties). But some states have survived conflicts, even when they have been extremely violent; and in other 'post-conflict' countries, states are under reconstruction.

Arguably, the literature on security sector reform – and the donor assumptions relating to it – apply largely to transitional and consolidating democracies, although the wider literature on conflict resolution and peace building takes into account the other categories. But quite different strategies are applicable in relation to security sector reform in each historical situation. What works in a country in democratic transition may be irrelevant or counter-productive in a lapsing democracy or a country emerging from protracted armed conflict.

In other words, the 'standard' policy and governance recommendations falling under the security sector reform rubric arguably only stand a chance of success where the state has remained reasonably functional during the transition, and its security institutions have remained largely intact, even if degraded by authoritarian imperatives or complex transitions. In this book, the case studies meeting these conditions appear in Part II, and include South Africa, Chile, Ghana and Nigeria, together with some of the countries examined by Kees Koonings in his comparative survey of Latin America (Chapter 6). In all these cases, security sector reform is possible, and in some a deeper process of reform, sometimes called transformation, has taken place.

In the countries featured in Part III of this book, however, one or more of the following have happened: violent conflict has remained endemic; the democratic transition has failed or even been reversed; the security structures have fractured or disintegrated and been replaced by informal militias or external forces; or the state has collapsed. Under these conditions, the security sector reform agenda is usually by itself insufficient or can at best be very partially implemented. National reconstruction of the whole framework of public authority, not just reform of state security institutions, is needed, although it may be possible to carry out some reforms as part of the reconstruction process. In essence, the policy challenges in these contexts are more closely related to those that appear in the literature and practice of peace making and peace building.

This book has also highlighted the regional dimensions of security governance in the chapters on the Balkans and Latin America, as well as in some national cases, notably Bosnia–Herzegovina, Sierra Leone and the DRC. In many cases the political and security predicaments of the countries studied are related to wider challenges within what might be termed 'regional security complexes' (Buzan 1991): often this is a relationship both of cause and effect as insecurity in one country feeds into that of another. Furthermore, it is difficult if not impossible for a country to carry out profound security reforms if its external security environment is unstable or threatening. The international dimensions, too, are important in all the cases studied. The stance taken by international actors has often been critical to the success or failure of democratic transitions: unfortunately sometimes to failure.

One of the first – and most successful – examples of security sector reform in the post-Cold War period was in *South Africa*, a clear case of a careful and successfully managed transition to democracy from authoritarianism. The process of reforming the security sector began before the term was in common usage, and South Africans sometimes developed their own eccentric solutions, but it is nevertheless emblematic of the process as it is now understood. It is also a reasonably successful example of conflict resolution, including the disarmament, demobilisation, repatriation and reintegration of combatants (although many would argue the process was somewhat one-sided), and of post-conflict peace building through the construction of democratic institutions and democratic politics and a human rights regime.

Importantly, South Africans focused as much on process as on content. Approaches, ideas and goals were systematically 'workshopped' amongst key role players, and in most cases it was only after broad agreement on the overall aims, objectives and methods had been achieved – after what became known as 'sufficient consensus' had been reached – that reforms were implemented. The sequence of security reforms was also carefully targeted: first, the lifting of repressive security legislation; then, the reform of the police service to ensure that the political process could be freed up; and finally, but only once a decision had been taken on interim multi-party rule, the reform of the defence force. After the successful transition to democracy, a more formalised approach to reform could be pursued through government institutions, but even here great care was taken to build consensus around key principles through public consultations.

Although by no means peaceful (at least 15,000 South Africans were killed in political violence during the transition), the South African process was very effective in securing democratic political control and supervision of the security structures. It also led to the demilitarisation of politics, although localised residues of political violence remain.

The process is described by South Africans as 'transformation', implying deep, systematic and radical reform, but it is less clear that the institutional cultures and pathologies generated by authoritarianism and violent struggles have been entirely eradicated. Some political violence persists, militaristic approaches to social conflicts still occur, and within the Southern African region as a whole, states and other political actors continue to resort to violence and militarism to deal with political challenges. South Africa, in effect, has been unable to export its model to neighbouring African countries, with the possible exception of Mozambique.

Key to the success of the South African transition was 'élite pacting' where the rules of the game were agreed between the outgoing and incoming élites. But this is not to say that the process itself was only élite-driven. The transition was marked by a very high degree of popular consultation by the ANC, and by mass popular protests. Civil society organisations played a critical role, and the international community intervened successfully. Key to this was the construction of a national consensus on the process and the end state. Academics also played a role, particularly by popularising a new security paradigm to replace that of the militaristic 'Total Strategy' of the apartheid period. This drew heavily on the emergence of human security concepts in the post-Cold War period.

In *Nigeria*, the transition to democracy since President Obasanjo came to power in 1999 has been less certain, and is less well advanced. The pathologies of militarised politics stemming from decades of corrupt military rule are extremely hard to root out. Unlike in South Africa, there was no need to integrate liberation forces with regime forces or bring an end to conflict through demobilisation. However, the challenges of security sector reform in the transition from authoritarianism are very similar to those in South Africa, and now correspond to orthodoxy. It is useful to summarise this now 'classic' agenda. According to Kayode Fayemi what is required is:

- Depoliticisation and subordination of the military to civilian authority, including the establishment of an effective Defence Ministry and the empowerment of parliament.

- Reorienting and reprofessionalising the military, including redefining its missions and roles.

- Demilitarisation of public order policing and police reform, including reorientation of the police towards civil crime-fighting.

- Balancing the demands of national defence with those of development.

- Engaging the international community in the security sector reform programme.

To these one may add a further goal implicit in Fayemi's analysis, namely:

- Ensuring that the military, police and security agencies operate under the constitution and within the rule of law; and are held accountable for human rights violations.

In this task, Fayemi argues that agency is as important as structure, psychology as important as politics, and informal mechanisms as important as the formal ones. Furthermore, security reform can only take place as a subset of wider political reform, and requires a new conceptual understanding of security based on human security imperatives rather than the security of the rule of a regime, cabal or individual. In other words, although the policy objectives are clear (essentially those of effective public management, or 'good governance') getting there requires a complex process in which subjective factors such as the quality of leadership, ideological orientations and psychological predispositions are equally as important as structural and formal political factors. The international community has an important role to play in all this, but here Fayemi finds it somewhat wanting, as formulaic prescriptions that pay little attention to these subjective conditions have been all too prevalent.

Similar policy challenges exist as *Ghana's* transition to democracy unfolds. Ghana came dangerously close to the second category of countries in our study, but as Eboe Hutchful argued, it 'pulled back from the brink' and it is now possible to pursue a security sector reform agenda. The militarisation of politics and the politicisation of the military had degrading effects on both military and political institutions. But especially during the 1990s the Rawlings regime adopted more pragmatic policies and was able to meet the challenges of democratisation and transform itself into an elected government. As in South Africa, and to a lesser extent Nigeria, civil society – although different in nature and composition in each case – proved critical in the process. Reform, however, has been partial and uneven, and civil supervision has been hard to achieve. Again, Hutchful holds that security sector reform has to be part of a broader political process and be situated in the context of development imperatives, and that success or failure will depend to a large degree on the quality of political leadership.

Chile, like South Africa, is often regarded as among the more successful examples of a managed or 'pacted' transition to democracy. There is little doubt that democracy is being consolidated, more perhaps than in most Latin American countries. Yet reform of the security sector has lagged far behind political reforms. This is due largely to a Faustian bargain, under which the military tolerated a return to democracy on condition that many of its own prerogatives and privileges were left intact. Successive democratic governments adopted various strategies to deal with the legacies of authoritarianism. Some of these were later to be drawn upon by South Africa and other transitional democracies: an apparent case of reform through institutional learning. They included mobilising civil society behind the transition; instituting a truth commission to deal with past human rights abuses; and engaging the military in policy development, but only after initially expending much energy in struggling over the principle, rather than the practice, of civil supremacy. That these strategies have been less successful in curbing the military than in some of the other countries considered owes much to the institutional arrangements of the Chilean state, the culture and institutional autonomy of the military and the sharp political polarisation within Chile over the authoritarian record.

Chile had, and possibly still has, a 'political army', which Koonings (Chapter 13) argues typified the military in *Latin America* (although political armies are by no means confined to that continent). Military institutions in most Latin American countries tried to maintain the political and institutional prerogatives they had arrogated during lengthy periods of military rule. At the same time great difficulty was experienced in finding appropriate roles, missions and doctrines for the armed forces which would free them from the non-military, internal security tasks they had assumed, and in dealing with the legacy of human rights abuses by the security forces. Even more striking was the emergence in parallel with formal democratic institutions of new, more covert or extra-legal forms of violence, sometimes perpetrated by state security agencies, and sometimes by non-state paramilitaries, militias, guerrillas and criminal mafias. These reflected both deep-rooted patterns of socio-economic and political exclusion throughout Latin America, and a growing regional and world-wide trend toward the privatisation of violence.

These problems have only been partly addressed, Koonings argues. Only in some cases, like Brazil, are political armies withering away. In others, like Guatemala, they maintain their institutional prerogatives and tutelary powers within the shell of formal democracy, preserving spaces for extra-legal violence. In some, there has been deliberate regime-induced perversion of the political process, as in Peru, where the elected populist government of President Fujimori veered toward authoritarianism, creating a climate of both state and non-state violence. In others again, like Colombia, a widening gap has opened up between the formal (and in many respects genuinely democratic) polity and a realm of armed conflict, criminal violence and fear. These Latin American countries highlight the threats to democracy – and democratic governance of the security sector – of a variety of extra-legal forms of violence. These are by no means confined to conflict-torn states, although they have been more severe in the latter.

While these country studies demonstrate the importance of context in democratic transitions, and any policy proposals arising from them are thus likely to be strongly context-specific, a number of conclusions can be drawn and recommendations made for practitioners involved in post-authoritarian transitions.

A necessary first step before or in tandem with security sector reform is a process of confidence building to overcome legacies of authoritarianism and violence. A key issue has been how to deal with the past, in particular with human rights abuses carried out by security establishments previously acting with impunity. Many options are available – 'forget if not forgive', accept there is 'nothing that can be done', 'forgiveness through confession' through to 'punish and restitute'.

It is clear that balancing justice against political expediency and stability requires a judgement by those involved in driving the transition, which will be determined in large part by the context, the balance of political power and the nature of the transition process. Often outgoing security establishments are at pains to make sure, as in Chile and Ghana, that they will not be prosecuted. It may be expedient for incoming democrats to 'leave the back door open' so the beast can slip out rather than be drawn into a battle, the outcome of which may be uncertain. In most of the cases studied, however, at least a minimal process has been necessary to allow people to come to terms with the past and the worst excesses of despotism to be exorcised.

Security sector reform cannot take place on its own, as all our case studies confirm. It has to be part of a wider reform of politics, governance and the public sector. It is also preferable to harmonise economic and political reforms, as some aspects of economic liberalisation can work against political liberalisation. For example, neoliberal economic policies prescribing draconian structural adjustment may undermine human security at the same time that state security is being placed under stress through political transition.

Domestic agreement on the process, phasing and political objectives contributes greatly to success. In some cases, agreeing on a national vision, or an appropriate conceptual framework (such as human security) has assisted in the process of reform by facilitating the construction of policy hierarchies in which defence and policing policy can find their appropriate places. It is critical that civilians drive this meta-policy process, and for legitimacy it should involve popular consultation.

Hence the role of civil society is a key issue in transitions. How this term is understood, and the appropriate role for civil society organisations in security governance, varies considerably. Certain kinds of civil society organisation may play a baleful role though the politics of communalism, as shown in our case studies of Nigeria, Bosnia or the Congo. Yet at their best, civil society organisations can form a useful counterweight to security establishments and can constructively assist in security sector reform. During transitions, they tend to be especially prominent, either because of their ability to control or mobilise masses of people, or because they are able to fill policy voids through expertise; although their influence tends to wane once a legitimate democratic regime has been established.

To establish the principle of democratic control, 'turf wars' between civilians and the military may sometimes be unavoidable. Yet democratic control may more easily be achieved by the expedience of civilians 'getting their hands dirty' and actually addressing security policy issues, rather than arguing over principles of control. What is really required for effective policy making is partnership between those in uniform and those out of it, based on a common understanding of democratic institutions and politics. Achieving this is not easy, of course, and the day-to-day interactions needed for successful policy making are probably a better way of making this partnership work than adhering rigidly to abstract principles.

The role of the legislature is naturally a critical success factor in democratic control and reform of the security sector, although often this is possible only after democratic reform itself has taken place. As noted above, this has been most successfully achieved where national assemblies and their committees responsible for security affairs have adopted an appropriate hands-on role in policy formulation and security supervision. Expertise, or at least a broad understanding of the issues, is key to establishing credibility. But even without this, the national assembly can assert its authority over security issues by establishing national policy and budgetary frameworks that include security functions.

Budgetary control is critical: in many authoritarian systems the security organisations were able to avoid civil control by the expedient of off-budget funding or by raising their own funds through business or criminal activities (Hendrickson and Ball 2002). Our case studies show it is vital to eliminate off-budget funding (although ironically in some cases this might require increased security budgets), and to subject the security budget to the same scrutiny and democratic political processes as other government budgets. Similarly, there is little reason why security agencies should not be subjected to the same controls as other government departments with regard to accountability through auditors-general and other officials, although special systems might have to be set up for intelligence agencies given the requirement of secrecy.

Civil supervision in the consolidation phase is also exerted through the executive and the civil service. In some cases, incoming democratic regimes have found it necessary or desirable to establish 'civilian secretariats' or similar bodies within defence establishments, to support the (civilian) minister and (usually civilian) head of department. In some cases this principle has been extended to the police service. Whether it is desirable in the long term has much to do with organisational and political culture, but again, as democracies mature a partnership or an integrated planning function between uniformed and non-uniformed personnel is probably optimal.

In the process of establishing democratic governance of security, defining appropriate roles, missions and doctrines for the various security agencies becomes crucial. This is particularly so when police forces have become militarised and taken on political roles; or when conversely defence forces have become politicised, taken on policing tasks or developed praetorian tendencies. The obvious resort is to the concepts of classical realism: the defence force is responsible for defence of the sovereign integrity of the state against external aggression, and the police service for fighting crime and internal security. This formulation has the advantage of taking both the defence and police forces out of internal politics whilst still giving them something to do. But it begs the question of whether the conventional defence function is actually needed, or can be afforded, given that in most developing countries internal not external security threats are paramount. It also dodges the issue of whether the defence force has a role in the human security project.

The issue of roles and functions is compounded by changing security environments in democratic transitions, or at least in successful ones. Typically in these cases political violence (and often external threat as well) diminishes. But criminal and perhaps some types of political violence may increase (at least for a time), as the authoritarian controls and support systems collapse, and countries are opened to the outside world. Reorienting and equipping police and security forces to deal with these new conditions takes time. Police reform is arguably even more difficult than defence reform, partly due to the apparent tenacity of 'cop culture' and the fact that police are constantly operational (and exposed on a daily basis to criminals), whereas military forces can be taken out of potentially corrupting operations for re-training. The obvious temptation is to use the military in crime-combating tasks: here similar arguments and counter-arguments with regard to developmental roles apply.

While such a security sector reform agenda makes sense in public management terms for reasonably intact states, it does not necessarily speak to the political processes needed to put them into effect. Our case studies suggest that a number of factors are relevant:

- Leadership and policies have made a difference in each of the cases of 'successful' reform we have considered. One can identify critical historical moments when *different* political and policy decisions could easily have snuffed out democratisation or escalated political violence.
- In each national context a different balance has been struck between transformation and Faustian bargains with the old order, often including elements of the military and security establishments. This has set limits to what could realistically be achieved, and is one reason some of our authors prefer to talk of incremental security sector reform, rather than security sector transformation.
- The mobilisation of strong domestic reform constituencies has usually made changes easier. In South Africa the ANC, the mass movements and civil society generated sustained pressures for transformation. In Chile and Ghana, active civil societies and political parties helped consolidate democracy, although it took longer to initiate meaningful military and security sector reform. In Nigeria, by contrast, the pace of reform has been slowed by a weak and fractious political party system and by the marginalisation of previously active civil society groups.
- A well-articulated democratic strategy toward the military and the security sector has helped, based on an adequate understanding of its specific problems and needs, as well as on building national consensus on political and military reform, as in South Africa.
- Proper attention to the sequencing of security reforms, as well as to their relationships with economic and political reforms, has been

important. Both Chile and Ghana, for example, benefited from painful economic reforms being pushed through by authoritarian governments in advance of democratisation and security sector reform, making life somewhat easier for their elected successors.

- Changes have been less destabilising when coordinated with measures tackling underlying political and socio-economic exclusions, including those resulting from market-oriented economic reforms. Leaving these exclusions to fester feeds into insecurity and conflict, as illustrated by our case studies of Sri Lanka and Algeria.
- Appropriate international support has facilitated reform, especially when based upon partnerships rather than externally imposed reform models (the inability of the US-based military services provider, MPRI, to build a working relationship with the Nigerian armed forces, described by Fayemi, provides a salutary example of what can go wrong).
- In sum, the *process* of reform has often been as important to success as its substance. It has been easier when the main stakeholders have been brought on board, including military and security decision makers themselves, but also national legislatures, the media and informed groups in civil and political society.

The 'classic' security sector reform agenda outlined above would seem to be less appropriate and feasible, however, in cases of protracted political violence and civil war. Two main situations can be distinguished (see Chapter 1): first, where the state, whilst confronted by armed opposition, has remained more or less intact; second, where all or most of the superstructure of public authority and public coercion has broken down. This is what is often termed state collapse.

Two of our case studies, those of Algeria and Sri Lanka, address the first of these situations, where conflict-torn societies are still presided over by a still more or less intact state. In *Algeria*, the government and the armed forces orchestrated a reversal of the democratisation process, following bungled efforts at economic reform and the victory in national elections of the Islamic opposition, which had committed itself to the creation of an Islamic state. The resulting perversion of the democratisation process was even greater than in Peru. Re-transition to authoritarianism also triggered a transition to extreme political violence. Elements of the Islamic opposition went underground to wage war on the state, themselves splintered into warring factions, and provoked counter-violence and a dirty war by the state and its military and security agencies. During the ensuing security and political crises, the armed forces were further politicised and entrenched in political control.

Frederic Volpi argues that the military has co-opted subsequent political reform initiatives, and now manipulates the nominal institutions and processes of democracy to maintain itself in power. Security sector reform is not yet on the political agenda, although it would clearly be highly necessary for democratisation to succeed. But security sector reform will not be possible without fundamental reform of the state itself (including grasping the nettle of military political power) and without resolving the country's conflicts and addressing their terrible legacies.

Sri Lanka is a rather different case. Not only the state, but also a relatively vibrant multi-party democracy, has survived a protracted armed conflict. In contrast to Algeria, there has been no military rule, and the civilian executive has maintained firm control of the armed forces. Yet, as in Colombia, a sphere of apparently normal democratic governance and market-oriented development has coexisted with major political violence and civil war between the state and the LTTE guerrilla forces.

Jagath Senaratne argues that the conflict arose from failures in the democratic process itself, which reinforced the political, economic and social marginalisation of the Tamil minority.[1] The government's heavy-handed military response to the conflict in its turn deepened the fissure between the country's majority Sinhala and minority Tamil communities. There have been massive human rights violations by both sides, and the security forces have had effective impunity from investigation and prosecution. In spite of firm civilian control of the armed forces and police, there has been little democratic accountability.

Security sector reform, peace building and political reform are thus mutually interdependent. The prospective negotiated end to the conflict may make it easier to curb the behind-the-scenes influence of the military and security establishments, to tackle their human rights abuses and to assure democratic accountability. But a durable peace is unlikely without fundamental political reform, both in democratic institutions and in the form of the state itself. The Tamil community's political alienation, and the LTTE's military and political control of much of the North and East, will permit nothing less.

Bosnia and Herzegovina is another country that has been pulled asunder by identity-based political violence and armed conflict, partly as a result of botched processes of political and economic liberalisation. It differs from Sri Lanka in that neither democracy nor the state survived the onset of hostilities. However, as Mary Kaldor describes, the international community – mainly NATO – negotiated a truce between the warring parties under the Dayton Agreement, which also functioned as an externally imposed constitution, opening political spaces in which longer-term peace building could start.

Hence security sector reforms have been almost entirely externally driven, in the context of a major international peacekeeping operation. Some (limited) progress has been made in reprofessionalising the armed forces and police and reducing the influence over them of extremist nationalist parties and criminal mafias. However, the international community has established not democratic control but a measure of international control. None of the forces (except a recently created State Border Service) are accountable to the Federal state, let alone to a democratic polity, and they are all highly dependent on external finances. Bosnia–Herzegovina remains essentially an international protectorate, containing three ethnically defined statelets, each with its own army and police force.

Mary Kaldor points out that security sector reform will achieve little without a broader process of political transformation. This would need to encompass the reconstitution of legitimate public authority, diminishing the influence of extremist nationalist parties and severing their military and criminal links. Moreover, a democratic state of Bosnia–Herzegovina, if it finally emerges, would not be a traditional state whose main security function is the defence of borders. Rather it would be a new kind of state, whose security forces would be integrated within wider multilateral regional and European structures.

Even this might not be enough in Bosnia-Herzegovina and the other states spawned by the fall of Yugoslavia, argues Susan Woodward. Democratisation is a necessary but not a sufficient condition for security sector reform, which she argues will only succeed if it is domestically driven, in particular through a social revolution such as occurred in Serbia when the Milošević regime was overthrown. She also argues that domestic security reforms require a stable external security environment: the Balkan states were victims of external pressure for economic and political reforms in a context of regional instability, which led to a breakdown of domestic security, including political and human security.

Sierra Leone too is to all intents and purposes a collapsed state, as Comfort Ero argues. As in Bosnia, a security reform agenda has been pushed by external actors – in this case the British, who have been engaged since 1998 in an effort to reconstruct the Sierra Leone armed forces and police service. While they have made some progress with the police service, it is extremely difficult to rebuild and legitimise a defence force without embedding this process in a wider one of reestablishing legitimate public authority, of rebuilding democratic institutions and politics, and of effective public sector reform.

Furthermore, Sierra Leone's security imbroglio has a strong regional dimension, and the reconstruction of a functioning state and security sector is much harder without regional stability. The Economic Community of West African States (ECOWAS) has a potentially important role to play, but its track record in restraining the use of cross-border force is patchy at best and the organisation's contribution to defending democracy in Sierra Leone and Liberia was compromised by the fact that the ECOWAS hegemon and major interlocutor in the linked crises of the two countries, Nigeria, was itself a military dictatorship at the time of key interventions. However, despite the almost accidental way in which ECOWAS's peacekeeping arm, ECOMOG, was created, and its flawed interventions in Liberia and Sierra Leone, it has provided the impetus for some potentially important institution building. This includes the creation of a new regional mechanism for the prevention, management and resolution of conflicts. Whether the mechanism will function as it should, will depend in part on whether West African governments can exert effective peer pressures upon recalcitrant member states to abide by standards of democratic governance and non-interference in their neighbours' conflicts.

Security sector reform has barely started in the *Democratic Republic of Congo*, like Sierra Leone and Liberia a country where the national armed forces and other security agencies were utterly degraded through personal rule and the politics of controlled 'disorganisation' (Chabal and Daloz 1999). In this failed state, there is little hope of any substantial progress until the provisions of the Lusaka Peace Accord are put in place, foreign military forces withdrawn, an international peacekeeping operation involving DDRR made effective and the Inter-Congolese Dialogue successfully completed to lay the basis for a democratic order. Even then, the security sector will need to be reconstructed in the context of an entire state reconstruction process. Again, the security dynamics are embedded in a regional context. Reform in the Congo will require similar processes in neighbouring Burundi and Rwanda, and possibly in other countries drawn into the conflict, to succeed.

As stated earlier, it is evident that security sector reform is most likely to work when the institutions of the state have remained relatively intact, and where it is possible to construct democratic institutions and democratic politics. But in situations of ongoing conflict or state collapse, peace first has to be secured through conflict resolution, national negotiations, DDRR and so on. This does not mean that no attempt should be made to carry out reforms, as some of these can take place alongside and reinforce peace making.

Indeed, conflict and state disintegration can sometimes open spaces for reform, by clearing away the clutter of vested state and military interests, such as those impeding changes in Chile, Nigeria or (to a lesser extent) South Africa. On the other hand, they may also bring into being new and sometimes more noxious interests, including the various privatised armed bodies and international interests that tend to move into the vacuum left behind by the state.

Our case studies reinforce our contention that programmes and policies to transform the security sector should pay due regard to the differences among conflicts and their varying historical trajectories in each national and regional context. Nevertheless, one may extrapolate some general principles. These do not necessarily differ from those appropriate in 'normal' democratic transitions. But they demand a more fundamental reconceptualisation, not just of military and security structures, but also of the entire framework of public authority and of the state. A more holistic approach is needed since:

- Conflicts highlight, more even than authoritarianism, the deep contradictions between state or national security and human security.
- They also raise especially deep questions about the nature of state legitimacy and public authority, including public control of the means of coercion.
- They pose equally fundamental questions about what military and security forces are for, and whether they could be dispensed with or replaced by a different kind of public security force, designed mainly for policing and public order functions.
- Since most 'civil wars' or 'internal conflicts' are not in reality confined within national boundaries, they pose a range of questions about how states and their security structures are embedded in wider regional and international security complexes.

Although our case studies do not lend themselves to ready-made policy prescriptions, because of the complexity and diversity of their problems, they have much to teach about the choices and dilemmas violent conflicts pose for policy makers. A democratic strategy toward the state and its military and security apparatuses is even more necessary than during peacetime transitions to democracy, and would need to deal with a number of issues, some of which we raise in the remaining pages of this book.

Building state (and military) security on the foundations of human security

The human costs – the casualties, the refugees driven from their homes, the poverty and disease, the personal insecurity, the massive violations of human rights – have been immense in all the conflicts we have studied. One clear policy conclusion follows for post-conflict reconstruction: that human security should be the bedrock of state security. State security – and rebuilt military, police and security apparatuses to provide it – can only be justified if they are compatible with and create the conditions for human security. Of course in the short run bringing wars to an end and reestablishing peace may involve casualties and other human costs – this is the classic dilemma faced by all statesmen and indeed all peacekeepers. But in the final analysis the security of states, and the rebuilding of state military and security agencies, can only be justified if they deliver greater security to citizens, including those most at risk from poverty, discrimination and conflict.

Building peace to create the political space for reform

Our case studies generally endorse Mary Kaldor's assertion, in her chapter on Bosnia-Herzegovina, that the negotiation of a peace and the ending of hostilities helps to create a breathing space in which political authority can be reconstituted and reforms can take place. There is, of course, no simple formula for conflict resolution, and it is not the central concern of this book. It may take place in tandem with reforms, as well as before them. As our case studies also illustrate, the formal signature of a peace agreement seldom definitively 'ends' a conflict. Peace agreements themselves, like the Dayton Agreement in Bosnia-Herzegovina, may 'freeze' conflicts and place obstacles in the way of longer-term peace building and security sector transformation – the Dayton Agreement, among other questionable provisions, ratified the continued existence of a number of separate, ethnically based military and police forces.

Reconstituting legitimate public authority and democracy

A major legacy of violent conflict (and of authoritarianism) is that citizens and civil society fear and mistrust the state and its agents (above all the military, police and security agencies). States not only have to be reconstituted. They must also be vested with legitimacy and made more inclusive. Peace building thus cannot be separated from democratisation, not just because donors tend to insist on the latter, but also because they are or should be mutually reinforcing.[2] Our case studies of the Congo and Sierra Leone provide salutary warnings of the enormous perils of conflict resolution and state building without tackling the sources of state illegitimacy.

Reconverting agents of insecurity into agents of development and security

In her case study of Sierra Leone, Comfort Ero describes how military, police and state security agencies were de-institutionalised and became 'agents of insecurity'. A similar dismal picture of the supposed protectors of the public turning into predators – abusive governments, corrupt and divided military commands or undisciplined soldiers – can be drawn in almost every other case we have looked at.

The reconstruction of military and security institutions – from scratch, by integrating state and non-state forces, or by reforming state forces alone – provides an opportunity for fundamental review of their functions, and even whether they might be disbanded (a possibility that was seriously considered in Sierra Leone).[3] In none of the countries studied, however, have democratic policy makers decided that there is no role for the military at all.

But in most cases new roles and functions have been explored. In some countries, it has been decided that the military should be given a developmental role more consistent with human security imperatives. But in other cases policy makers have feared that such a mandate might lead to repoliticisation of the military and remilitarisation of politics, and have sought to define the military role as narrowly as possible (as conventional defence). Some countries have found that focusing on different missions entirely – United Nations peacekeeping, for example – has been a useful way of reprofessionalising the defence force and keeping soldiers busy (not to mention re-equipping and funding them).

Ensuring democratic and not just civilian control

In the final analysis the most assured way of preventing military and security structures from regressing into agents of insecurity is to build strong mechanisms for democratic accountability and control. As we have already argued, this in turn depends on the rebuilding of democratic institutions and politics. But it should not be delayed until the latter are already fully in place, as in Sierra Leone and Bosnia, where military and security forces are being rebuilt and reprofessionalised without, so far, an adequate framework for democratic accountability and control. The principle of democratic accountability must be asserted, and mechanisms to assure it should be established in parallel with the reconstruction of democratic institutions; if not, the latter are far less likely to survive.

Filling the public security gap

In conflict-torn states yawning public security gaps tend to open up, in which law and order scarcely exists, insecurity is widespread, the law of the gun prevails, and military, police and security agencies are either ineffective or part of the problem. Our case studies confirm the existence of such a gap, not only during and after conflict, but sometimes also before it. In the Congo, the state had 'disappeared', giving up on its public security functions, many years before the final overthrow of the Mobutu regime. Nigeria still faces formidable public order problems under its new democratic government.

How to fill this gap is one of the most difficult problems of post-conflict reconstruction. Policing, court systems and other public order institutions are a vital part of security sector transformation; so too are the public order capabilities of the armed forces. Another linked issue is that of groups that have emerged, so to speak, from civil society to fill the public security gap, like the Kamajors in Sierra Leone or the Bakassi Boys in Nigeria. They can sometimes deliver a measure of security and have some popular legitimacy; but they may well be captured by special interests, violate human rights and weaken the rule of law.

Demobilisation, disarmament, repatriation and reintegration – and the restoration of the state's monopoly of legitimate force

The fragmentation of military establishments into competing fractions and the proliferation of irregular or privatised forces have been referred to by many of our authors. As we have already argued, DDRR is an essential aspect of post-conflict security transformation, and is heavily prioritised by donors and IFIs (Colletta *et al.* 1996).

However, DDRR should not be seen as a purely technical task. It has political dimensions, which may indeed abort reforms if ignored or mis-handled – as in the Congo following the collapse of the Mobutu regime. It works best where coordinated with the political as well as military demobilisation of armed oppositions, or their inclusion in the democratic process. In Mozambique, RENAMO was allowed not only to integrate its fighters into the armed forces, but also to convert itself into a legitimate political party. But if there is no serious political accommodation and no democracy, rebuilt military and security establishments could easily perpetuate the corrupt, divisive and repressive military politics of previous regimes.

Balancing the national composition of military, police and security structures

Our case studies illustrate how conflicts both arise from the politicisation of ethnic, religious and other identities and create further political, economic and social exclusions. Ensuring that democratic institutions are more inclusive contributes to peace building – both in failed states, like Bosnia and the Congo, and in those where, despite conflict, the centre has held, as in Sri Lanka.[4] Constitutional reform needs to be carefully coordinated with military and security sector reform to ensure that the state's security arrangements are perceived as inclusive. This would usually require a clear political commitment to balanced recruitment, especially where the official armed forces and police have been dominated by a single ethnic or racial group, as in Sri Lanka and apartheid-era South Africa. Bosnia–Herzegovina, where these forces are divided on ethnic lines and linked to extreme nationalist parties in a context of deep ethnic polarisation, presents especially tricky political problems – and is prompting some rethinking of traditional models of the nation state and integrated national armies.

Balancing state and military reconstruction and national development

Transformation does not come cheap, and is especially burdensome where national economies and tax revenues have been degraded by conflict. In Bosnia–Herzegovina and probably also Sierra Leone, the combined costs of military and security services (including international contributions) are well in excess of total national budgets and indeed GDP. This must raise serious questions concerning the sustainability and affordability of national military and security structures once they have been rebuilt, and concerning their compatibility with development, especially in a world in which donor economic stabilisation and adjustment policies impose tight restrictions on national budgets and military spending.

Containing and controlling the privatisation of violence

The economic incentive systems which often propel conflicts are well illustrated in the chapters on Bosnia, Sierra Leone and the Congo. Security sector reform in such countries is simply wishful thinking, if it is not backed by effective measures to contain criminal mafias, reduce smuggling, control small arms, and in Sierra Leone's case stem the flow of conflict diamonds. None of these are easy, and still harder as these extra-legal activities are often tangled up with the vested political interests of nationalist parties or corrupt governments. Moreover, they are usually entangled also with wider regional and international networks: the regimes and armies of neighbouring states, where these have developed cross-border economic interests; diaspora networks; commercial and mafia networks; arms supply networks, etcetera. The waters have also been muddied by the fact that governments themselves have turned to mercenaries and military companies for military support, advice and training. Added to this has been the widespread growth of private security companies to fill the public security gap vacated by governments: often poorly regulated, or not regulated at all, they are themselves sometimes a source of insecurity.

Building regional and international collective security mechanisms

Peace building and security sector transformation should not, indeed cannot, halt at national boundaries. For none of the conflicts we consider – not even that in Sri Lanka, arguably the most self-contained – can be understood in isolation from their regional and international contexts. In each, all or most of these have happened: violence has spilled across national boundaries; it has been financed or supported by external interests; neighbouring governments and/or foreign powers have intervened militarily; and a great variety of international bodies have intervened to provide humanitarian assistance, send in peacekeepers or promote peace negotiations. That is, both the problems and the solutions are already thoroughly regionalised and also globalised.

Hence a stable external security environment is a necessary condition for effective domestic reform in many situations. Regional security organisations or multi-functional organisations can play an important role in this. Moreover, if reforms can be harmonised across countries constituting a 'security complex', this can be an important confidence- and security-building measure. One may draw some encouragement from the fact that conflicts themselves have sometimes catalysed regional organisations into action.

In some cases state collapse and the international supervision of state reconstruction have come dangerously close to being mutually reinforcing. States like Bosnia–Herzegovina, Sierra Leone and the DRC are in many respects *de facto* multilateralist states, which have come to rely on the international community for the majority of the state's security functions and many of its other functions as well. Regional security arrangements are one way of reducing this dependence, but suffer from being unresponsive to democratic pressures from below. Neither international control of military and security structures, nor control by regional organisations can substitute for democratic control.

Thus while regional and international organisations can and should support security sector transformation, it is important that the latter be domestically driven and owned. External interventions should not be prescriptive, but should aim to find solutions compatible with domestic, cultural, political and social conditions and history.

Our studies, to conclude, have shown that most democratic transitions are fragile and non-linear. Even in cases such as South Africa where the outcome now appears to be so naturally teleological, it was not. Bad decisions, even small ones made at key junctures, and adverse domestic, regional or international inputs can have multiplier effects and cause a democratic transition to stall or even be reversed. In this regard, we re-emphasise that time frames and timing are important during transitions and after conflicts. While it is vital to have an integrated approach to the reform of all security institutions, it might not be necessary or advisable to attempt to reform them all at the same time. However, windows of opportunity need to be exploited by democrats, when security establishments are wrong-footed or discredited and political space is briefly opened up for reform, as it is never clear for how long democratic opportunities will persist. As noted earlier, it is not merely that democratic transitions are non-linear, but they are of different types, and some become frozen or reversed. Nevertheless, our country and regional studies show that, although progress has been uneven, in many countries democratic institutions and democratic politics have been brought to bear on security structures, often in situations where this would have been unthinkable a decade or so ago. These structures are thus more likely to be agents of security for the people of their country, instead of agents of insecurity as was often the case in the past.

References

Boutros-Ghali, B. (1992) *An Agenda for Peace*, New York: United Nations.

Buzan, B. (1991) *People, States and Fear: an Agenda for International Security Studies in the Post-Cold War Era*, Hemel Hempstead: Harvester Wheatsheaf.

Chabal, P. and J. P. Daloz (1999) *Africa Works: Disorder as Political Instrument*, Oxford: James Currey.

Chuter, D. (2000) *Defence Transformation: a Short Guide to the Issues*, Pretoria: Institute for Security Studies.

Colletta, N. J., M. Kostner and I. Wiederhofer (1996) *The Transition from War to Peace in Sub-Saharan Africa*, Washington, DC: World Bank, Directions in Development.

Duffield, M. (2001) *Global Governance and the New Wars*, London and New York: Zed Books.

Haugerudbraaten, H. (1998) 'Peacebuilding: six Dimensions and two concepts', *African Security Review*, 7 (6): 17–26.

Hendrickson, D. (1999) *Security Sector Reform*, London: Centre for Defence Studies Conflict, Security and Development Group Working Paper No. 1.

Hendrickson, D. and N. Ball (2002) *Off-Budget Military Expenditure and Revenue: Issues and Policy Perspectives for Donors*, CDSG Occasional Papers No. 1, London: Conflict, Security and Development Group, King's College, London.

Huntington, S. P. (1993) *The Third Wave: Democratization in the Late Twentieth Century*, Norman (Oklahoma) and London: University of Oklahoma Press.

Notes

1 As well as the marginalisation of youths, which unleashed separate, class-based conflict, mainly affecting the majority Sinhala community.

2 As argued in our companion volume, Bastian and Luckham (forthcoming).

3 There was much Sierra Leonean interest in the examples of Costa Rica, Panama and Mauritius.

4 Again, see Bastian and Luckham (forthcoming).

Index